SAVONAROLA
and FLORENCE

SAVONAROLA
and FLORENCE

*Prophecy and Patriotism in
the Renaissance*

by DONALD
WEINSTEIN

PRINCETON, NEW JERSEY
PRINCETON UNIVERSITY PRESS

1970

To Anne

PROVERBS 31:10

Preface

MY theme is the Prophet and the City. Savonarola the Dominican from Ferrara was a preacher of repentance, a prophet of doom. Savonarola the Prior of San Marco in Florence became a preacher of civic freedom and empire, the prophet of the millennium. How and why this transformation came about, the affinities between the Prophet and the City, their effect upon one another, their brief sharing of a dream of apotheosis—these are my principal subjects. More years ago than I care to recall I first put forward my conviction that Savonarola's prophecy was transformed in the milieu of Florence and particularly under the impact of the crucial events of 1494. This was in a doctoral dissertation at the University of Iowa, begun under George L. Mosse and completed under Giles Constable. Since then my thinking and my research on Savonarola and Florence have changed considerably and this is a very different work (and twice as long); but I still maintain that early conviction.

To Dr. Hans Baron who, when we discussed my interest in the relations between secular culture and religion in the Renaissance, suggested Savonarola to me as a subject for study, I owe a great debt. He has maintained his interest and, I think, his faith in my work, and I can only express the hope that he will not consider them to have been misplaced. To Professors Eugenio Garin and the late, sadly missed, Delio Cantimori I am grateful for warm receptions in Florence and generous sharing of learning and wisdom. Marvin B. Becker's love of history and his exciting historical imagination have stimulated me throughout the years of our friendship. Herbert H. Rowen, my teacher, colleague, and friend, has been a constant but sympathetic goad and source of good advice. My wife, Anne K. Weinstein, has at various times served as a reader and bibliographical assistant and at all times as a wellspring of moral support. To her I dedicate this book in gratitude and love.

Others to whom I wish to express special thanks are: Roberto

Abbondanza, Ivaldo Baglioni, the late Gertrude Bing, Morton Bloomfield, the late Federico Chabod, Felix Gilbert, E. H. Gombrich, Paul O. Kristeller, the late Nicky Mariano, Anna Omodeo, Guido Pampaloni, Marjorie E. Reeves, Roberto Ridolfi, Nicolai Rubinstein, Maria Sampoli Simonelli, Giampaolo Tognetti, Roberto Vivarelli, Richard Webster, and Olga Zorzi.

In the course of my work I have been materially assisted by a Fulbright Student Fellowship (1953-55), an American Council of Learned Societies Fellowship in the Institute for Research in the Humanities of the University of Wisconsin (1959-60), a Fellowship in the Harvard University Center for Italian Renaissance Culture, Villa I Tatti (1962-63), and grants from the American Philosophical Society and the Rutgers University Research Council.

To Professors Marshall Clagett, then Director of the Institute for Research in the Humanities, and Kenneth L. Murdock, then Director of I Tatti, I wish to acknowledge my appreciation for hospitality and friendship. Finally, a word of appreciation to the directors and staffs of the Biblioteca Nazionale, Biblioteca Mediceo-Laurenziana, Biblioteca Riccardiana and Archivio di Stato, all in Florence, and the Newberry Library, Chicago.

Contents

Abbreviations

ASF	Archivio di Stato, Florence
BLF	Biblioteca Mediceo-Laurenziana, Florence
BNF	Biblioteca Nazionale, Florence
BRF	Biblioteca Riccardiana, Florence
BNP	Bibliothèque Nationale, Paris
Copinger	W. A. Copinger, *Supplement to Hain's Repertorium bibliographicum*, 2 vols. in 3 (London, 1895-1902)
GW	*Gesamtkatalog der Wiegendrucke*, vols. I-VII[a] (Leipzig, 1925-38)
Hain	Ludwig F. T. Hain, *Repertorium bibliographicum*, 2 vols. in 4 (Stuttgart, 1826-38)
Magl.	Magliabechi Collection, BNF
Reichling	Dietrich Reichling, *Appendices ad Hainii-Copingeri Repertorium bibliographicum Additiones et Emendationes*, 6 fascicles (Munich, 1905-1908)

All dates are new style.

SAVONAROLA
and FLORENCE

Introduction

TEACHERS AND PROPHETS HAVE STRANGE AFTER-HISTORIES.
—Lytton Strachey, *Eminent Victorians*

MODERN Savonarola scholarship began a little more than a hundred years ago with the revival of the Savonarola cult.[1] By the middle of the nineteenth century the Dominican Convent of San Marco in Florence had become the meeting place for a group of devotees called the New Piagnoni, after the friar's original followers.[2] For the New Piagnoni Savonarola was a saint and a prophet, his example and his teaching as valid for the nineteenth century as for the fifteenth. The Risorgimento they envisioned for Italy would be more than a political unification: it would be a great spiritual and moral regeneration of the Italian people, just such a regeneration as Savonarola had attempted to lead in his own time. The leader of the New Piagnoni, Vincenzo Marchese, like Savonarola a friar of San Marco, suffered, if not martyrdom, at least exile for the cause. But unlike the earlier Savonarola cultists, Marchese was also a scholar determined to establish the facts of his hero's life on a solid historical basis. Together with other enthusiasts, most notably Luigi Passerini, Isidoro Del Lungo, Cesare Guasti, and Guasti's pupil, Alessandro Gherardi, Marchese began collecting and editing the relevant sources which included Savonarola's sermons, letters and treatises, and a great quantity of documents, for an eventual historical reconstruction of Savonarola's life and times. No one in the group of New Piagnoni actually wrote a biography of the friar who died on the

---

[1] For what follows on the New Piagnoni, see Giovanni Gentile, *Gino Capponi e la cultura toscana nel secolo decimonono*, 2nd edn. (Florence, 1926). For surveys of Savonarola literature, see below, note 37.

[2] "Piagnone" was at first the abusive term used to describe a follower of Savonarola, but it has come to be the most widely used name for the friar's devotees, without pejorative intent.

twenty-third of May, 1498, in Florence, but it was their collective accomplishment to have made available some of the most important source materials as well as to have inspired others who came later with their zeal for the unfinished task and with their high standards.

The reconstruction toward which the New Piagnoni were working came sooner than anyone had reason to expect. Pasquale Villari, a Neapolitan professor who fled to Florence from Bourbon persecution after the riots of 1848, undertook to discover "the true historical figure" of Savonarola, to learn "his most intimate thoughts," and to establish the true relation between the man and his times. Villari's expressed admiration for Padre Marchese, whom he compared to Savonarola for "purity of mind, ardent zeal for religion and holy love of sober liberty," indicates the extent to which he shared the New Piagnoni ideals and objectives, although his own enthusiasm for Savonarola stemmed perhaps more from his own Neo-Guelf nationalism than from San Marco cultism. His biography, *La storia di Girolamo Savonarola e de' suoi tempi*, appeared in two volumes, the first in 1859, the second in 1861. It was a remarkable achievement, readable, intelligent, scholarly, with a bold, unified historical vision. Villari used not only the materials made available by the San Marco group but also many new sources which he himself had uncovered. His appendices, thick with selections from these materials, guarantee the book's continuing importance to scholars, since in many cases these are still the only published versions we possess.

The central drama of Villari's biography is his retelling of the story of Savonarola's appearance at the deathbed of Lorenzo de' Medici in 1492. Tradition had it that when Lorenzo called the friar to him to hear his confession Savonarola imposed three conditions on the dying man. The first two—that Lorenzo acknowledge his faith in God's compassion and that he promise to restore everything he had unjustly seized from others—Lorenzo granted; but when he heard the third demand—that he restore the liberty of Florence—Lorenzo turned his face to the wall and died without Savonarola's absolution. In insisting upon the validity of this legend Villari was not up to his own critical standards; the story rested upon very shaky foundations. However—and this is no doubt why Villari insisted upon it—the story expressed the very essence of Villari's conception of Savonarola and his times: Savonarola as the champion of Florentine liberty against Medicean tyranny. Moreover, for Villari this scene was more than a struggle between two Florentine political figures; it was the confrontation between what was eternally valid and splendid in the history of Italy and what was corrupt and transitory. Villari's Savonarola was a Janus-figure looking both backwards into the Middle Ages and forward to the modern era. But the Middle Ages to which Savonarola looked back were the era of communal liberty, of public virtue founded upon private morality, of creative faith. Villari's Savonarola thus fulfilled the valid mission of prophets, to recall a people to its own true self. In opposing Lorenzo Savonarola was opposing the evil features of the Renaissance, its unbridled egotism, its moral corruption in both the private and the public worlds, the very features which rendered ineffective its essential achievement—the awakening of an independent spirit. For Villari, Savonarola was as much the representative of the true Renaissance as Columbus; both were restless seekers of unknown worlds; both "demolished the shadows, opened the way to a new path, more by force of will and faith than by force of reason"; both had "the mind of prophets, the heart of heroes, and the destiny of martyrs."[8] In Villari's judgment Savonarola's special mission was to harmonize reason and faith, religion and liberty. His work was connected with the best efforts of the past, the Council of Constance, Dante, and Arnold of Brescia; in short, with those efforts of Christian and Catholic reform which, according to Villari, had been the constant desire of those great Italians who are also among the great thinkers of civilization.

That the aspirations of these great Italian champions of civilization had not yet been fulfilled was just the point that Villari was making; he believed that they could be fulfilled in his own time, and with the New Piagnoni he believed that Savonarola's formula of religion and liberty was the correct one for the Risorgimento. This remained Villari's faith throughout his lifetime. Almost forty years after the publication of his biography of Savonarola, in an address

[8] Pasquale Villari, *La storia di Girolamo Savonarola e de' suoi tempi*, 2 vols. (Florence, 1859-61). Throughout, however, I cite the second edition, reprinted in 1926; here vol. I, p. 258.

for the fourth centenary of the friar's death, he spoke of Savonarola's religion as the true religion of Christ, the expression of what is divine in man and in the world, a religion which through morality sanctified both liberty and *patria* and favored all civil progress.

Villari's conception of the Italian Renaissance had much in common with that set forth by Jacob Burckhardt in his masterpiece, *The Civilization of the Renaissance in Italy*, which appeared in the year between the publication of Villari's first and second volumes on Savonarola. Burckhardt pictured the Renaissance as an age that prefigured the modern era in its discovery of the world and of man. He also stressed the uncertain morality of that era of which individualism was both glory and curse. The ambivalence of his own attitude toward his historical creation is strikingly similar to Villari's, yet Burckhardt's treatment of Savonarola is very different. Where the Italian saw a prophet who had a profound insight into his own times, the Swiss saw a self-deluded, if morally superior, fantast who at the end seemed to have recognized the vanity of his own visions and prophecies. Where Villari held Savonarola to be the apostle of moral renewal and the civil life, Burckhardt regarded him as "the most unsuitable man who could be found for such a work."[4] Most important, where Villari believed that Savonarola's profundity was demonstrated in his joining the Renaissance spirit of innovation with the Christian vision of moral renewal, Burckhardt concluded that Savonarola adopted "a childish method of reasoning," a monkish separation of culture from the contamination of the new ideas: "The simple reflection that the new-born antiquity and the boundless enlargement of human thought and knowledge which was due to it might give splendid confirmation to a religion able to adapt itself thereto seems never to have occurred to the good man."[5] Thus Burckhardt denied the basic assumptions of Villari's vision of Savonarola as a modern prophet who tried to reconcile Christianity and modern civilization.

While Villari's biography has had a lasting fame, it is not his judgment of Savonarola that has prevailed but Burckhardt's. Therefore

[4] Jacob Burckhardt, *The Civilization of the Renaissance in Italy*, trans. S.G.C. Middlemore, 2 vols. (New York: Harper Torchbooks, 1958), vol. II, p. 460.

[5] *Ibid.*, vol. II, p. 461.

there has been a curious ambiguity in the literature concerned with the historical figure of Savonarola. Pick up almost any general work on the Renaissance and you will see Burckhardt's characterization of the friar, not Villari's, even while Villari will be cited in the footnotes or bibliography as the authority.[6] To all but a handful of specialists Savonarola has been fixed in our minds as a man at odds with his time, a voice from an increasingly irrelevant medieval past. No doubt Burckhardt's characterization is more compelling, more consonant with that general notion of a clear-cut demarcation between the Middle Ages and Renaissance which his own book, somewhat unwittingly, helped to propagate. Perhaps Burckhardt's skepticism with respect to the ability of spokesmen for the old religion to adapt themselves and it to the "boundless enlargement of human thought" is also more akin to the modern temper than is Villari's Neo-Guelf faith.

At the same time, the general acceptance of Burckhardt's judgment did not extend to the handful of devotees who had special reasons for refighting the battles of the past, the cultists who until quite recently have dominated Savonarola research. An exception was Leopold von Ranke who in the 1870's returned to his youthful interest in Savonarola and showed what might be done by an historian of broad views and masterly scholarship. Free of both New Piagnoni hero-worship and Burckhardtian skepticism, Ranke was able to see Savonarola in relation to Florentine and European political and religious forces. Moreover, he pointed out the importance of certain neglected sources, notably the chronicle of Piero Parenti, and he dispassionately returned to the question of the value of certain others, particularly the biography by Gianfrancesco Pico della Mirandola and the life of Savonarola falsely attributed to Fra Pacifico Burlamacchi, which were the mainstays of the old miracle-working Piagnone tradition.[7] However, Ranke never set himself the task of writ-

---

[6] Burckhardt himself cites Villari and Perrens, *Jérôme Savonarole* (*ibid.*, vol. II, p. 456, n. 6). The observation therein that Villari's view differed from Burckhardt's own must have been added by an editor. It is not in the German text published by Werner Kaegi which is based on Burckhardt's final corrected manuscript. See Burckhardt's *Gesamtausgabe*, vol. 5 (Berlin, 1930), pp. 344, n. 44; and 409.

[7] Leopold von Ranke, "Savonarola und die florentinische Republik gegen

ing a full-scale study of the friar and his times. He was chiefly interested in Savonarola as a figure in the prehistory of the Reformation, a line of approach that is ultimately as anachronistic as the New Piagnoni's.

If for Ranke Savonarola was an occasional interest, for Joseph Schnitzer he was a ruling passion. A Catholic priest who later became a professor of theology at Munich, Schnitzer entered the lists in 1898. At that time a controversy was raging between Lorenzo Luotto and Ludwig von Pastor, the great historian of the popes, over the issue of Savonarola's disobedience to Pope Alexander VI. Schnitzer took Luotto's side against Pastor, arguing that in terms of the specific circumstances as well as in terms of the authoritative teaching on canon law at the time Savonarola could not fairly be convicted of disobedience. The controversy serves to demonstrate that for Catholic scholars Savonarola's standing in the Church has been more than a matter of historical interest. It has been, in fact, a living issue in two respects: one, because of the continuing efforts of cultists not only to clear the friar's name but also ultimately to win his canonization; the other, because it touches on the question of papal authority and therefore on the question of the nature of the Church itself. On both these issues, Schnitzer, as we shall see, was deeply committed, but it is to his credit as a scholar that he saw his main task was to put the religious personality of Savonarola back into historical perspective. In the years of preparing the biography which ultimately appeared in 1924 he never lost sight of that goal. His mastery of the sources made him the worthy successor of Villari, whose work he corrected at many points, and he also published many new materials, such as the pertinent sections of the chronicles of Piero Parenti, Tommaso Ginori, Bartolomeo Redditi, and Bartolomeo Cerretani. The biography itself, which he subtitled *Ein Kulturbild aus der Zeit der Renaissance*, remains the most detailed examination we have of Savonarola's life and thought and the human environment in which he acted.

True to his original purpose, Schnitzer focused on Savonarola's

---

Ende des fünfzehnten Jahrhunderts," *Historisch-biographische Studien*, in *Sämmtliche Werke*, 2nd edn., vol. 40-41 (Leipzig, 1878), pp. 181-357.

religious personality. For him Savonarola's self-conceived mission was to reform the Church and with it society, and from this all else flowed. This, according to Schnitzer, was the central inspiration that explained the friar's prophetism, his political activities, his dealings with his order and with the papacy, and his relations with the intellectual leaders of Florence. Schnitzer was more deeply versed than Villari in Savonarola's religious writings as well as the writings of the friar's contemporaries, and much more sensitive to the religious tone and aspirations of the age. Villari's abstractions about the Renaissance ideals of liberty and virtue Schnitzer replaced with concrete information about personalities, issues, and events. As a result he presents a much more convincing portrayal of Savonarola and a much more realistic account of his relation to his times than Villari, although his book is much denser, much less easily absorbed than Villari's.

In the preface to the Italian translation of his work, which is really a new edition, Schnitzer writes, "I have always been profoundly convinced that the dominating tendency of his [Savonarola's] life was . . . the reform of the Church and society, the reform of hearts and habits which he willed to have begun first in himself, then extended in ever wider circles to the convent of San Marco, to the city of Florence, to Italy, and to all of Christendom. All of Savonarola, the man of religion who meditates, the friar who preaches, the statesman who counsels, the seer who foretells the coming tempest, has no other end than that of reform. . . . Frate Girolamo does not think up new doctrines, he does not speak of indulgences plenary or partial, he does not praise pilgrimages, nor relics nor miraculous prayers. . . . But he preaches peace, union, charity, alms for the poor, frequent use of the sacraments, probity, inner piety, a Christianity active, practised, sincere, profound. . . .

"If Rome had fulfilled what he proposed, the fervent desire of Christianity would have been satisfied. Luther, Calvin and all the reformers could have come but they would have found no echo. With Savonarola sounded the last hour for the legitimate reform of the Church. His reform would not have divided the nations, would have generated no heresies nor schisms. This was the providential mission of the Friar! Seeing him condemned by Rome and burned on the pyre, the people lost all trust in the good will and the good faith of the ecclesiastical leaders and willingly listened to new apostles and new doctrines. This, it seems to me, is the deep meaning of the history of Girolamo Savonarola. It is a Savonarola different from that of Villari; a new book was necessary to demonstrate it."[8]

In this passionate evocation of the historical figure of Savonarola as a religious reformer, Schnitzer reveals the fundamental continuity between his own earliest efforts as the friar's defender against the charges of disobedience to the Pope and the results of his mature scholarship some thirty years later when he presented Savonarola as the last and best hope of the pre-Reformation Church. It is no mere coincidence that Joseph Schnitzer himself was one of the leaders of the movement of Catholic Modernism in Germany, that he was excommunicated for his opposition to the papal encyclical *Pascendi* in February 1908 and suspended from his professorial chair in the same year, nor that in 1912 he published *Die katholische Modernismus*. Schnitzer's Savonarola, while more convincing than Villari's, is deeply colored by an awareness of this other struggle for renewal and liberty, by his concern with Catholic Modernism rather than with the Italian Risorgimento. It is indispensable for Schnitzer that Savonarola be saintly in life, orthodox in belief, and perfectly attuned to a public equally orthodox and spiritually motivated. It is a consequence of Schnitzer's own position vis-à-vis the Church that Savonarola's personal tragedy becomes the tragedy of Christendom, that his life and death become an object lesson to those who would ignore the warnings of their prophets and so fail in their duty to themselves and to the future. But, in the last analysis, the flaw in Schnitzer's treatment of Savonarola is his ascription to the friar of a single-mindedness, an unvarying inspiration that is not only unhistorical but superhuman as well. Despite the many realistic tones of his portrait, his sensitivity to Savonarola's religiosity and humanity, what emerges is not a man but an inspiration, not a history but an elaboration of a prophetic illumination. By the time we come to the end of his long book we are not surprised that it closes with these words: "He was a man dreadfully sinned against in his lifetime and after

---

[8] I cite the revised Italian edition: Joseph Schnitzer, *Savonarola*, trans. Ernesto Rutili, 2 vols. (Milan, 1931), vol. I, pp. v-vi.

his death. He has not yet been canonized or beatified, but his time will come, as did Joan of Arc's. The time will come when Christianity will attain to moral heights where, far from regarding as a hateful rebellion his heroic resistance to an infamous Pope in exceptional times when the Church was at its lowest ebb, men will recognize and celebrate it for what it really was, as his greatest merit, and his most shining glory. It will not be that the altars will reflect glory on him, but he will shed glory on them."[9] Even though Schnitzer's biography is the worthy product of a lifetime of research, it is still a Piagnone biography.

The third major biography of Savonarola, the life by Roberto Ridolfi,[10] is also Piagnone. Ridolfi devoted many years to investigating the life and work of the friar. Even more than Villari, he has been deeply influenced by the Florentine milieu in which he lived and worked, a milieu that he understands as only a Florentine whose ancestors took a direct part in the conflicts of the Savonarola years can. Yet the Florentine Ridolfi is a proclaimed disciple of the German Schnitzer, conceiving of his own biography as correcting and adding to the information provided by the older man, but in no way recasting it to fit a new or different conception. In fact Ridolfi explicitly renounces the task of interpreting Savonarola's thought, claiming to write "simply a biography" in order not to duplicate the work that has already been done by Schnitzer. And he finds no better way to end his own book than with a eulogy of Schnitzer and with Schnitzer's eulogy of Savonarola just quoted.

Given the limited objectives Ridolfi set for himself, it is difficult to conceive how it might have been done better or that it might some day have to be done again. Ridolfi is a superb scholar and every problem he touches bears the proof of his mastery. He has given definitive answers to such questions as those Ranke raised about the early biographies of Gianfrancesco Pico and pseudo-Burlamacchi, as well as those about the so-called Savonarola Bible,

[9] *Ibid.*, vol. II, p. 603. Quoted in Roberto Ridolfi, *The Life of Girolamo Savonarola*, trans. Cecil Grayson (New York, 1959), p. 317. I have altered the word order of one phrase of the translation.

[10] Roberto Ridolfi, *Vita di Girolamo Savonarola*, 2 vols. (Rome, 1952). The translation, cited in note 9 above, lacks the notes; therefore, where the notes are pertinent, I shall cite the original (*Vita*), otherwise, the translation (*Life*).

the relations between the surviving texts of Savonarola's sermons and the originals, the dependability of the various diplomatic reports which issued from Florence during the Savonarola years, the authenticity of Savonarola's confessions during his imprisonment, and many more. He has made innumerable corrections in and additions to our knowledge of Savonarola's life. Moreover, Ridolfi has done more than any other scholar to put the study of the friar on a solid textual basis by publishing an excellent edition of Savonarola's letters and directing the national edition of his sermons and writings, a project which has already run to a dozen impeccable volumes. In short, while professing himself satisfied with Schnitzer's view of Savonarola, Ridolfi has provided others with new materials with which to revise that view.

Even while Ridolfi was preparing his study other scholars had already begun to examine the assumptions and the abstractions upon which the older interpretations were based. Thus Delio Cantimori, in a review of the Italian edition of Schnitzer's biography, criticized the German's monolithic portrait of the prophet and taxed him particularly with having isolated Savonarola from the currents of late medieval piety.[11] Cantimori himself was a fine historian of Italian religious radicalism with a deep knowledge of pre-Reformation piety; moreover he was a subtle historical thinker who, while accepting the concept of the Renaissance, believed it should be treated as a working hypothesis rather than as an objective historical fact. Hence he was critical of the persistent tendency to treat Savonarola and his movement as an external force thrusting itself into the heart of secular Renaissance culture and society.

Another critic of both Burckhardtian and cultist tendencies is Giorgio Spini. Spini has attacked the unhistorical, a priori character of interpretations which set up a dialectical opposition between medieval and modern, orthodox and protestant, conservative and liberal, etc. With Savonarola in mind, he has written, "Only in the realm of fantasy can men be located outside their own time or accidentally lost in a time other than their own."[12] If, says Spini, Savona-

---

[11] Delio Cantimori, "Giuseppe Schnitzer: Savonarola," *Annali della R. Scuola Normale Superiore di Pisa. Lettere, Storia e Filosofia*, II (1932), 90-104.
[12] Giorgio Spini, "Introduzione al Savonarola," *Belfagor*, III (1948), 416.

rola was a man of the Middle Ages, these were not the Middle Ages of Augustinianism and Benedictinism with their symbolism of the two cities, nor the Middle Ages of the burgeoning city and puissant papacy. These were rather the Middle Ages of an uneasy and tragic autumn, the crumbling of imperial universalism, the crisis of the Western monarchies in the terrible Hundred Years War and War of the Roses, the menace of the Turks, and the internecine struggles of the Italian states. It was an age in which traditional certainties were being brought into question in all spheres, in which exasperation alternated with deepening belief, in which refinement and cruelty, sophistication and superstition, realism and apocalyptic millenarianism lived not merely side by side but flowed into each other. At the same time, Spini maintains, it was an age in which new institutions, such as the emerging states, and humanistic culture were making their appearance, although they were as yet unable to exorcise the frightening ghosts of the dying past. This, he tells us, is really what the age of Savonarola was like. It is obvious that Spini's model of the period is that of Johan Huizinga rather than Jacob Burckhardt, although for Spini, Italy as well as France and Burgundy were tinged with Huizinga's autumnal colors. In assaying the content of Savonarola's thought he takes his lead from Cantimori rather than Villari or Schnitzer. It is precisely the "eschatological, palingenetical elements of a Joachimite flavor" which form the base of Savonarolan preaching, elements to which Schnitzer had attached slight importance and which the excessive attention to the development of humanism on the one hand and the repressions of the Counter-Reformation on the other had obscured. Indeed, as Spini points out, Konrad Burdach had already suggested a more positive relation between Joachite and humanistic aspirations.

Spini also had some pertinent observations to make on the old quarrel about Savonarola's orthodoxy. To call Savonarola a Protestant, a precursor of Martin Luther, he argues, is unhistorical and absurd. If we find in him certain theological positions which bear a resemblance to Luther's, such as predestinarianism, Scripturalism, and the repudiation of certain dogmas, like the Immaculate Conception, this does not make Savonarola a Lutheran *ante* Luther but a Dominican *post* Aquinas, fully at home in the theological quarrels that animated the rivalry between his order and the Franciscans. On the other hand, Spini points out, the attempt of New Piagnoni historians to uphold Savonarola's orthodoxy and Catholicity is equally unhistorical, since they exaggerate the continuity between the Catholicism of the late fifteenth century and Catholicism after Trent and underestimate the unorthodox aspects of Savonarola's Joachite eschatology. After all, his Thomism, while correct enough in itself, did not save him from the pyre.

In accounting for the failure that brought Savonarola to that pyre, Spini carries still further his insistence that the friar's mentality was the mentality of his time and place. Neither Savonarola nor Florentine society generally were inclined to pursue the consequences of their positions to a logical conclusion. Savonarola called for a council to reform the Church, as Luther did later, but he never went on to ask by what right the Pope held his authority or how far that authority ran. Savonarola formulated a foreign policy calculated to bring about a *renovatio* in Italy (through the instrumentality of the French monarchy) and a domestic policy of upholding a popular regime in Florence, but he never saw, as Calvin would later see with regard to Geneva, that the success of his policies depended upon his ability to build a political base in the Florentine republic that would continue to give him the majorities he needed to resist the opposition of the oligarchic and pro-Medicean forces. Nor, maintains Spini, was the failure merely a personal one. For the success of his program Savonarola needed the help of the humanists and the political leaders of the republic, the former to use their critical equipment on the problem of creating a new theological structure, the latter to establish a popular political base for the new republic. Neither of these things happened. Thus, Spini views the Savonarola movement as an experiment in revolution that failed because neither Savonarola nor the leaders of Florentine society had enough understanding or enough courage to bring it off.

Spini has more in common with the New Piagnoni and Neo-Guelf Savonarolans than he leads us to expect at the outset. There is in his work the same tragic sense of opportunities missed, of groping for a shore too dimly seen. Together with Schnitzer he feels that the moment was ripe for Italy to reassert its religious leadership; with Villari he agrees that it was ripe for a new birth of social justice and liberty. But while Spini is not altogether free of a present-ist orientation, he sees much more clearly than Villari or Schnitzer the historical fallacy of making Savonarola a hero of either the Risor-gimento or Catholic Modernism. His Savonarola is neither Schnitz-er's saintly prophet nor Villari's political hero; he is just such a com-bination of popular zealot, conservative theologian, and radical mil-lenarian as could have existed only in the milieu of Italy before the Reformation and the conquest of Hapsburg Spain.

Neither Cantimori nor Spini followed up his own suggestions for a new synthesis; nor has anyone else. Still, the past few decades have been full of work on Florentine history at the turn of the sixteenth century and much of it has implications for a new view of Savona-rola and his times. In intellectual history the writings of Eugenio Garin have been a major stimulus to the rethinking of the relations between Savonarola and the first city of Renaissance culture. Garin's *Italian Humanism* brilliantly describes the intellectual interests and the mood of Florentine thinkers at the end of the Quattrocento and makes highly plausible the enthusiastic reception of Savonarola by the humanists and the philosophers of the Ficinian circle.[13] In an essay published in 1954 Garin addressed himself to the issues of Savonarola research.[14] After pointing out the lasting effect of nine-teenth-century polemical and apologetical considerations on the his-torians' treatment of Savonarola, Garin sums up the problem in this pithy sentence: "Heretic or saint, precursor or survivor, but always divorced from his age, Savonarola, in sum, seems to have remained irreconcilable with a culture that yet was fascinated with him and with a world which fought him but afterward listened to him devotedly as the sincere expression of its own deep needs." The fact of the matter, continued Garin, is that "Florence at the end of the Quattrocento, even its most sophisticated part, did not feel that unbridgeable gulf between itself and the Frate that the historians of the nineteenth century assumed." He points out that Savonarola

---

[13] Eugenio Garin, *L'umanesimo italiano* (Bari, 1952), especially pp. 37-39, 142-45. English trans. Peter Munz, *Italian Humanism* (Oxford, 1965).

[14] "Girolamo Savonarola," *Il Quattrocento* (Florence, 1954), pp. 3-22. Re-printed in Eugenio Garin, *La cultura filosofica del Rinascimento italiano* (Florence, 1961), pp. 183-200.

had much in common with the Florentine intelligentsia. As a champion of the popular republic against tyranny the friar allied himself with the Florentine tradition of *vita civile*, a concept in which the Neoplatonists, as well as the humanists of the city had long since united *buoni costumi* and religion with *libertà*. As a Dominican who involved himself in the life of the republic, he had forerunners in Giovanni Dominici and Saint Antoninus. As a prophet of the divine scourge and reform, he reflected the widespread eschatological beliefs of his time: those of fellow Dominicans like Giovanni da Viterbo as well as those of the astrologers who predicted great changes in realms, empires, and religion, and the philosophers, like Marsilio Ficino and Egidio da Viterbo, who believed in the coming golden age. In short, for Garin, Savonarola summed up the widespread aspirations of his time and place for an "ideal reconciliation of all the great spirits of Florence at the end of the Quattrocento, reunited, despite all differences, in a common work of human reconstruction."[15]

Such statements indicate that Garin has not, any more than did Spini, entirely discarded the point of view of the earlier biographers for whom Savonarola symbolized Renaissance Italy at the crossroads and embodied the best hopes for a future that never came. This does not mean, however, that Garin and Spini share in Savonarola cultism; rather they share in a common historical sensibility that can be traced back as far as Machiavelli and helps explain certain strengths and weaknesses in the Italian historical tradition. The sense of tragic loss, the search for explanation as well as inspiration in the national past, have endowed Italian historians with qualities of humanity and relevance which, when joined with the analytical ability of a Cantimori, the insight of a Spini, the learned originality of a Garin, make for very good historical writing indeed. But the obverse of these qualities is a tendency to use the past for political purposes, to convert it into an ideal construct and its key figures into rhetorical abstractions. Thus, to suggest that Savonarola and Marsilio Ficino were related by a common dream of human reconstruction is nearer the truth than to describe Savonarola in Florence at the end of the

---

[15] *La cultura filosofica*, p. 200.

fifteenth century as *vox clamantis in deserto*, as Giovanni Gentile once did,[16] but the suggestion is historically questionable nonetheless. Between Ficino's and Savonarola's dreams of reconstruction there were differences which were fundamental and irreconcilable, and if some of their mutual admirers tried to minimize this, neither Savonarola nor Ficino did.

Garin and others have rightly challenged the anachronisms of both the New Piagnoni and Burckhardt, arguing that Savonarola was neither the unworldly, self-contained visionary portrayed by the former nor the monkish, medieval fanatic depicted by the latter, that he was a man in touch with the aspirations and the needs of his time, very much a part of the contemporary culture. But of which culture? Cantimori and Spini have suggested that he was eminently a product of latter-day Joachite chiliastic tendencies. Garin, on the other hand, emphasizes Savonarola's deep affinities with the esoteric visionaries of the Ficinian Neoplatonic circle. Suggestive as they are, these views are largely impressionistic; they are not based upon systematic analyses of Savonarola's thought;[17] moreover, they point in quite different directions. This is not to say that they are mutually exclusive but that the problem of understanding Savonarola's relation to the culture of his time is a complex one because the culture itself was complex and because Savonarola related to it in a complicated and not necessarily consistent way. It is necessary to evaluate the relative importance of various influences upon his thought and activity, not just those tendencies put forward by the three historians here discussed, important as these were. Moreover, it is necessary to consider how Savonarola made such influences peculiarly his own, to rediscover the individuality of the man as well as to calculate his debt to the various trends of his time. Savonarola's vision transformed the preoccupations and aspirations of the historical moment

---

[16] Giovanni Gentile, *Il pensiero italiano del Rinascimento* (Florence, 1940), p. 35. Savonarola referred to himself as *vox clamantis in deserto* (Isaiah 40:3, Matthew 3:3, et al.) in his sermons on the Apocalypse in 1490. MS BNF Magl. XXXV, 110, fol. 126 verso.

[17] An exception to this statement is Eugenio Garin's important study, "Ricerche sugli scritti filosofici di Girolamo Savonarola. Opere inedite e smarrite," *Bibliothèque d'Humanisme et Renaissance*, XXI (1959), 291-300. Reprinted in his *La cultura filosofica*, pp. 201-12.

in Florence and Italy into a program, one which offered more than consolation or hope, a program to be realized on the level of political and social action. This was his special genius and the key to his impact upon Florence, if not, as he hoped, upon Italy and all Christendom.

Here, too, one of Cantimori's observations is of the utmost value. In his review of Schnitzer's biography Cantimori wrote, "Schnitzer thinks that Savonarola must be taken all of a piece, that he was always at one with himself (*uguale a sè stesso*),[18] that, therefore, there is no development or qualitative change in his spirit; thus he [Schnitzer] uses expressions employed much later by the Friar (in his sermons, especially those from 1494 on!) to explain the ideas of his novitiate (1476). . . ."[19] We might well extend Cantimori's observation to cover Savonarola studies generally, particularly the writers of the New Piagnone tradition, who have dominated the field. The central methodological problem has been the tendency to treat Savonarola monolithically, either as a man without a history or as one whose history serves to illustrate a solid, unchanging core of personality, rather than, as with ordinary men, to provide the experience that shaped his personality. Roberto Ridolfi, the most important recent biographer and heir of the New Piagnoni, makes it perfectly clear that this tendency is based on conscious conviction rather than some unconscious error of method: "Rarely if ever," writes Ridolfi, "does one find in the adolescence of a great man, not merely the germs of his future actions and life, but also their whole and perfect image; but we do so in Girolamo Savonarola."[20] Such a conviction has apologetical rather than historical roots; faith in Savonarola as a prophet and the aim of bringing about his canonization make it almost impossible for these writers to treat him as anything but a monolith. To be sure, such apologetics can be traced back to the ancestors of the New Piagnoni, to the controversies that sprang up during the friar's own lifetime over the source of his

[18] The phrase was used by Villari in a slightly different sense, to indicate the perfect consistency between Savonarola's private thoughts and public statements. Villari, *Savonarola*, Preface to 1st edn., vol. I, p. xxv.

[19] Cantimori, "Giuseppe Schnitzer," p. 91.

[20] Ridolfi, *Life*, p. 5.

prophecies, and to the Piagnoni biographies of the sixteenth century. On the other hand, those who have been unsympathetic to Savonarola have adopted a polemical approach which is almost equally inflexible and unhistorical, if less conscious. For example, reading Gennaro Sasso's account of Machiavelli's rejection of Savonarola as a liar whose "extraordinary incoherence" and inconsistencies stemmed from a lust for power, it is difficult to tell where Machiavelli's judgment leaves off and Sasso's begins, while Warman Welliver's depiction of the friar's evil demagoguery would seem to have had its ultimate source in the attack upon Savonarola as Antichrist by the disillusioned Marsilio Ficino.[21]

The present study is an effort to free Savonarola scholarship from apologetics and polemics. Unlike Villari, who baldly stated that he had undertaken and conducted his study entirely free of any preconceptions, I am quite ready to recognize my own. One is that any life, even one as extraordinary as Savonarola's surely was, must be explained in human, historical terms as the product of the interaction between personality—itself the product of human factors—and experience. A corollary assumption is that any success Savonarola may have had in predicting the future course of events was the result of his shrewd observation as to the direction events were taking. Whether critics may regard this as a rationalistic bias just as incapable of proof as the faith of the New Piagnoni is of no concern to me. What is of concern is that the state of Savonarola scholarship is such as to make it still necessary, in this day and age, to deal with these issues. I hope I do not have to add that my determination to treat Savonarola in rational-historical terms stems from no desire to debunk. I am quite willing to take Savonarola on his own terms as a believer in his own prophetic inspiration and his divinely impelled mission, in fact I think it is necessary to do so in order to understand him. Almost all the evidence suggests that the friar was supremely dedicated to the high tasks for which he believed God had chosen him. Besides, given the limits of our knowledge of such

---

[21] Its immediate inspiration was, as the author indicates, the American demagogue of the 1950's, Senator Joseph McCarthy. Warman Welliver, "La demagogia del Savonarola," *Il Ponte*, XII (1956), 1197, 1201.

psychological problems as belief and motivation, the question of sincerity, except in the most flagrant pathological cases, is misleading and fruitless.

NEXT TO SAVONAROLA's historical role as a prophet and religious reformer no question has interested scholars more than that of his career as a political reformer, and it seems necessary, therefore, to devote a few lines to the three main problems involved. The first is that of determining the extent to which Savonarola was the architect of the new republic which, after a brief interval, followed the expulsion of the Medici in November 1494. The second is the problem of determining Savonarola's political role in the new government until his downfall in April 1498. Finally, there is the problem of Savonarola's political thought—his sources, his originality, his influence upon subsequent political thinking in Florence. All three questions are closely related to each other, so much so that they have been insufficiently distinguished, and this has led to considerable confusion.

The three major biographers discussed in these pages, Villari, Schnitzer, and Ridolfi, are all emphatic in crediting Savonarola with the primary, if not the sole responsibility for having introduced the *governo libero* in Florence. Villari, whose interest in Savonarola was concentrated particularly upon the friar's political career, insisted that Savonarola's greatness consisted precisely in having proposed institutions so wonderfully adapted to the needs of the Florentine people, not radically new ones, but just those which their traditions and their character as a people demanded. For this "he must be placed among the greatest founders of republics."[22] Schnitzer, for whom Savonarola's role as political reformer was subordinate to his mission as a prophet of spiritual regeneration, was of a more balanced opinion. He too insisted that Savonarola's part in securing the adoption of the new constitution was decisive— everything proceeded "under the fascination of his preaching," and he was invited to be present at the hearing when the final choice of reform measures was made. However, Schnitzer declared that Savonarola was far from being master of the city, and he pointed

---

[22] Villari, *Savonarola*, vol. I, p. 319.

out that not all of the friar's central proposals were adopted.[23] Ridolfi sheds no new light upon these problems. He describes Savonarola's intervention in the mounting political crisis of December 1494 in dramatic terms and dismisses the question of whether he was the initiator of the new proposals as nonsense: to Savonarola must go the credit for the new government because it was due to him that the reform plan was selected and adopted by the city.[24] Thus, by shifting the emphasis from the question of who originally conceived of the attempt to balk the oligarchs by initiating proposals for further constitutional reforms to the question of the process by which support for the reforms was aroused, all three biographers are able to concentrate on just that aspect of Savonarola's political role that is least in doubt, for his popular influence from the pulpit is certain. But this begs just those questions which are most at issue: was the idea of a popular republic an integral part of Savonarola's reforming inspiration? If not, how and why did he adopt it? Was Savonarola the spokesman for Paolantonio Soderini who, perhaps together with other Florentine *primati*, may have decided to push for further constitutional revisions and enlisted the friar's support?

Equally unsatisfactory is the treatment of the question of Savonarola's political power in the new government. All three biographers deal with the day-to-day activities of the friar in great detail, yet it is impossible to discover from their accounts what part he played in the actual conduct of political affairs. The same idealizing motives which led them to put such positive emphasis upon Savonarola's role as lawgiver and statesman seem to have led them to minimize his role as politician. Having never been able to transcend the polemics which confused the whole question from the start, they have not been able to deal with the problem of how the friar conducted himself politically. They reject indignantly the allegation of some modern historians that Savonarola was dictator of the city, just as the early Piagnoni bridled at the scornful allegation that Florence had become "a government of frati." They accept at face value Savonarola's denial that he interfered in politics, suffering with him as he underwent the tortures of interrogators bent on proving that he had

[23] Schnitzer, *Savonarola*, vol. I, pp. 233-35.
[24] Ridolfi, *Life*, p. 93.

engaged in factional plotting condemned by Florentine law. And yet, by protecting their hero from any taint of political dealing, they only succeed in making him less believeable, giving substance to Machiavelli's sneer about unarmed prophets, to Giorgio Spini's judgment that Savonarola's failure to develop a realistic politics was the cause of the "fatal political inconsequence of the Florentine Piagnoni," and so, ultimately, to Burckhardt's less-than-inspiring characterization of Savonarola as a vain fantast. This does not mean that we need accept the modern revival of the old view that Savonarola was the political master of Florence in order to arrive at a more realistic assessment of his political activities.[25] We can follow the lead of Nicolai Rubinstein, who offers a much more knowledgeable and better balanced analysis of both the problem of Savonarola's part in introducing the new government and the question of his continuing political influence in it. With respect to the first of these questions, Rubinstein, using both documentary and chronicle sources and drawing upon his own unequalled knowledge of how the Florentine government worked, makes a strong case for the view that Savonarola's part in the introduction of the new government was secondary to that of certain members of the ruling circle.[26] On the other hand, Rubinstein, with no particular ideological axe to grind, is quite ready to acknowledge that Savonarola made a difference in the politics of the new government, that within the city he had enormous influence which he was not above using, sometimes with

[25] Cantimori, "Giuseppe Schnitzer," p. 93. Cantimori argues that while Savonarola was juridically not the Signore of Florence any more than were the Medici before him, he nevertheless dominated the city by *modi civili* as they had done, i.e. by manipulating the governmental machinery. This remains to be proven. It is not apparent to me that Savonarola exercised anything like the control over, say, the selection of office holders that Lorenzo de' Medici did. Moreover, the chief instrument of Lorenzo's control after 1480, the Council of Seventy, was abolished in the anti-Medicean reaction. Nevertheless, Gennaro Sasso accepts Cantimori's argument; see his *Niccolò Machiavelli storia del suo pensiero politico* (Naples, 1958), pp. 9-10, n. 3. For an earlier characterization of Savonarola as master of Florence, see Francesco Ercole, "La dittatura di Gerolamo Savonarola," *Civiltà Moderna*, II (1930), 197-223. For my own views, see below, pp. 247-88.

[26] Nicolai Rubinstein, "Politics and Constitution in Florence at the End of the Fifteenth Century," *Italian Renaissance Studies*, ed. E. F. Jacob (London, 1960), especially pp. 154-62.

decisive effects. He points out that Savonarola's own political party, the Frateschi, was the largest, the most cohesive, and the best led in Florence. As to its weaknesses, Rubinstein is able to point to specific factors, such as the limits deriving from Savonarola's position as Prior of San Marco as well as his own conception of his mission. Granting Savonarola's importance in such matters as the city's adoption of and adherence to a pro-French foreign policy, Rubinstein also reminds us that there were other strong arguments in favor of such a policy besides the religious ones of the friar, and he concludes with the judgment that "Florentine history of the end of the fifteenth century has too often been written in terms of 'Savonarola and his time.' "[27]

Savonarola specialists have tended to find the friar's political genius best exemplified in his practical works rather than in his formal theorizing. However, the question of his impact on the great Florentine political discussions of the sixteenth century merits some consideration, and historians of political thought, Machiavelli scholars, and others with related interests have not entirely neglected it. Some believe this impact was minimal or nonexistent. Thus Francesco Ercole dismissed Savonarola the political thinker as an exponent of medieval theocracy who had no conception of an independent state at all,[28] while the distinguished Machiavelli scholar Federico Chabod contrasted Savonarola, "whose principal theme is one of revolt against the times and the historical situation," with Machiavelli, who based his political analysis upon a realistic acceptance of the historical situation.[29] Carlo Curcio appears to agree with this estimate but invests it with a different dimension. For Curcio, Savonarola was a revolutionary idealist whose principal target was

---

[27] *Ibid.*, p. 183. To this should be added the judgment of Felix Gilbert: "From 1494 to 1498 Savonarola was the central figure in Florentine politics. Savonarola was never the ruler of Florence, and his adherents were in the majority in the Signoria only intermittently and for short periods. Nevertheless, Savonarola's sermons with their moral exhortations and political counsels dominated Florentine life." *Machiavelli and Guicciardini* (Princeton, 1965), p. 55.

[28] Francesco Ercole, *Da Carlo VIII a Carlo V* (Florence, 1932), p. 58.

[29] Federico Chabod, *Machiavelli and the Renaissance*, trans. David Moore (London, 1958), p. 17.

the bourgeoisie.[30] On the other extreme, Ireneo Farneti calls Savonarola the apostle of liberal republicanism and the first person in the Renaissance to conceive of man in his role of citizen.[31]

Fortunately some scholars have kept their heads and their contact with the sources. Joseph Schnitzer's analysis of Savonarola's political thought makes it very clear that Savonarola did indeed have a distinct conception of the state and its importance in human society; in this he was merely following the teachings of his principal masters, Aristotle and Aquinas. Quite recently Rodolfo De Mattei has reaffirmed the Thomistic basis and the ethico-religious inspiration of Savonarola's political thought. De Mattei sets up the antithesis between Savonarola and Machiavelli which so many historians have found irresistible; but he is nonetheless aware that in some respects, as for example in the conviction that forms of government ought to be adapted to local conditions, the Dominican preacher and the chancery secretary were in agreement.[32] Approaching the question of religion and politics from another angle, that of the common fund of political assumptions in Florence at the turn of the sixteenth century, Felix Gilbert shows that the inclination to refer political decisions to God's will and the ascription of a divine origin to Florentine governmental institutions were not exclusively Savonarolan impulses but were traditional patterns of Florentine political thinking.[33]

While Professor Gilbert recognizes the important formative influence of the Savonarolan period upon Machiavelli and Guicciardini, he does not notice any direct impact of Savonarola's political ideas on the two great Florentines.[34] In this he stands in contrast to two other recent students of these problems, J. H. Whitfield and Rudolf

[30] Carlo Curcio, *La politica italiana del '400* (Florence, 1932), pp. 201-204.

[31] Ireneo Farneti, *Genesi e formazione del pensiero politico di Girolamo Savonarola* (Ferrara, 1950), p. 27 et passim.

[32] Rodolfo De Mattei, "Istanze politiche e sociali nel Savonarola," *Studi in onore di Gaetano Zingali*, Università di Catania Pubblicazioni della Facoltà di Giurisprudenza, vol. 53, 3 vols. (Milan, 1965), vol. III, pp. 287-316.

[33] Felix Gilbert, "Florentine Political Assumptions in the Period of Savonarola and Soderini," *Journal of the Warburg and Courtauld Institutes*, XII (1957), 187-214.

[34] See his *Machiavelli and Guicciardini*, especially pp. 153-200 and 271-301.

von Albertini. Whitfield argues that the break toward an empirical, relativistic approach to political institutions began with Savonarola "who first denies the legitimacy of rule and a preconceived pattern for institutions to adhere to" and who, in his opposition to tyranny and in his advocacy of a *governo civile* for Florence, was the teacher of Machiavelli.[35] Von Albertini goes even further, placing Savonarola "am Anfang der kommenden, grossen Diskussion über den besten Staat und seine Möglichkeit in Florenz," and crediting the friar with having given the free republic and its future partisans an essential part of their political ideology.[36] Villari and the Risorgimento Savonarolans could scarcely have claimed more! I myself believe that it is too much, since the literature at least as far back as Aquinas is replete with both the anti-tyranny theme and the empirical relativism which Whitfield and von Albertini seem to believe originated with Savonarola. I have presented my own analysis and evaluation of Savonarola's political thought in Chapter IX below.

IN THE FOREGOING introduction I did not intend to review all the modern literature on Savonarola, which is far more extensive than I have indicated here,[37] but to discuss the major trends of the past century and to identify the general questions which underlie my own study. These questions, it seems to me, are not best dealt with by adding another conventional biography, nor have I undertaken one. Thanks to the work of Villari, Schnitzer, and Ridolfi, we already know a great deal about Savonarola's life, while in those

[35] J. H. Whitfield, "Savonarola and the Purpose of 'The Prince,'" *Modern Language Review*, XLIV (1949), 49.

[36] Rudolf von Albertini, *Das florentinische Staatsbewusstsein im Übergang von der Republik zum Prinzipat* (Berne, 1955), p. 26.

[37] The most thorough survey of the writings on Savonarola is that of Joseph Schnitzer in his *Savonarola*, chapters XXXVIII-XL. Mario Ferrara provides an excellent annotated bibliography of books and articles from 1801-1952 arranged in chronological order in his *Savonarola*, 2 vols., 2nd edn. (Florence, 1952), vol. II, pp. 73-234; revised as *Bibliografia savonaroliana* (Florence, 1958). See also Urban Bergkamp, "Savonarola in the Light of Modern Research," *Catholic Historical Review*, II (1925), pp. 369-409; Antonio Panella, "Alla ricerca del vero Savonarola," *Pegaso*, III (1931), pp. 655-67; Claudio Varese, "Problemi savonaroliani," *Rassegna della letteratura italiana*, 7th ser., LVII (1953), 319-23.

areas where we know too little—for example, Savonarola's early education and his activities in the period between his first and second residence in Florence—we may be forced to remain in the dark, since major new finds have been few.[38] What I have done is to study Savonarola's prophetic and political ideas, how they developed and how they were received; that is to say, I have tried to understand Savonarola in the context of his time and place without, I hope, undervaluing his individuality and his originality. In pursuing my principal theme of the relation between the prophet and the city, I have broadened my focus by including a discussion of prophecy and apocalyptic ideas in Florence, both before and after Savonarola, and narrowed it by excluding a discussion of pious and devotional themes as such in Savonarola's spirituality. The quality of Savonarola's piety very much needs discussing, and now that his devotional writings are becoming available in excellent modern editions is the time to do it.[39] But this would require a separate book and one very different from mine.

While my book is not a biography it does follow a biographical approach in those sections where I deal with the development of Savonarola's career as a reformer and prophet. Elsewhere I abandon the biographical approach to give my attention to related currents in Florence. Consequently, some of my chapters may be read almost as separate essays, but they are related, in my own thinking at any rate, by the underlying theme of the persistence of a Florentine mythology of a special civic destiny.

[38] For some new finds in other areas of Savonarola scholarship, see Romeo De Maio, *Savonarola e la curia romana* (Rome, 1969).

[39] Some information can be found in Schnitzer, *Savonarola*, especially Chapter XXIX. See also Robert Klein, "La dernière méditation de Savonarole," *Bibliothèque d'Humanisme et Renaissance*, XXIII (1961), 441-48; and M. Goukowski, "Réponse à M. Robert Klein," together with Klein's reply, *ibid.*, XXV (1963), 222-27. Marcel Bataillon has done very important work on Savonarolan influence upon Iberian piety: "Sur la diffusion des oeuvres de Savonarole en Espagne et en Portugal (1500-1600)," *Mélanges de philologie, d'histoire et de littérature offert à M. Joseph Vianey* (Paris, 1934), pp. 93-103; "Une source de Gil Vicente et de Montemor: La méditation de Savonarole sur le 'Miserere,' " *Bulletin des études portugaises*, III (1936), 1-16; "De Savonarole à Louis de Grenade," *Revue de Littérature Comparée*, XVI (1936), 29-39.

I

*The Myth of Florence**

IN DECEMBER 1494 the newly restored Florentine republic faced a menacing future. Having overthrown the Medici regime and weathered a brief occupation by King Charles VIII and his army, the Florentines found their troubles just beginning. Piero de' Medici had ceded to the French king the strategic fortress towns of Pietrasanta and Sarzana on the northern Tuscan border. Worse still, he had also turned over the citadels of Livorno and Pisa, Florence's lifelines to the sea, and on November 9, the same day on which the enraged Florentines had expelled Piero and his brothers, the Pisans, taking advantage of the French presence, had reclaimed their own liberty. Montepulciano and Arezzo followed suit. The Tuscan state which had taken the Florentines over a century of labor to put together had come undone in a matter of days, and this just when Florence found herself dangerously isolated from powerful neighbors on the north, east, and south who were furious with her for allying with the French invader.

The political situation within the city presented an even more immediate danger. The patricians who had led the uprising against the Medici and intended to remain in control of the new government found themselves the objects of mounting hostility from vari-

---

* This chapter is a somewhat altered version of my essay of the same title in *Florentine Studies: Politics and Society in Renaissance Florence,* ed. Nicolai Rubinstein, published in 1968 by Faber and Faber Ltd. in Great Britain and by Northwestern University Press in the United States. I wish to thank the publishers for permission to include it here.

ous quarters. Having raised the cry "popolo e libertà!" against the Medici, they now found it being turned against themselves. The "good citizens" felt deceived; they had taken up arms for liberty only to find that they had fought merely to perpetuate the same men in power.[1] Returning exiles, suspicious of anyone who had stayed and prospered under Medici rule, added another divisive element. The *principali cittadini*, afraid they would not be able to maintain their hold, began to think about granting some concessions, but they were divided among themselves as to what they should do.[2] Deteriorating economic conditions heightened the tension. The revolt and the French invasion had disrupted the countryside; the land was not being worked; many *botteghe* in the city were closed; many workers were without jobs or bread. All this encouraged the partisans of the Medici to expect that they would soon be able to restore the old regime. The Florentine chronicler Parenti commented that it was "truly the very worst situation for a city, from which one could expect ruin and death or at least a great spilling of blood and civil war."[3]

But the republic survived this crisis without bloodbath or civil war, and for this it owed a large debt of gratitude to the Prior of the Dominican Convent of San Marco, Fra Girolamo Savonarola. Since November 1, Fra Girolamo had been preaching the Advent sermons in Florence's Cathedral of Santa Maria del Fiore to throngs of citizens who hung upon his every word as coming from God. Four years ago, he reminded them, he had begun preaching to the Florentines, exhorting them to prepare themselves spiritually for the

---

[1] Piero Parenti, *Storia fiorentina*, part of which was edited by Joseph Schnitzer, *Quellen und Forschungen zur Geschichte Savonarolas*, vol. IV, *Savonarola nach der Aufzeichnungen des Florentiners Piero Parenti* (Leipzig, 1910), p. 21. Except as otherwise indicated reference to Parenti's important history will henceforth be to Schnitzer's partial edition. For a fuller account and analysis of the constitutional crisis of December 1494, see Nicolai Rubinstein, "Politics and Constitution in Florence at the End of the Fifteenth Century," *Italian Renaissance Studies*, ed. E. F. Jacob (London, 1960); and Felix Gilbert, *Machiavelli and Guicciardini* (Princeton, 1965), as well as Chapter IV below.

[2] Parenti, *Storia fiorentina*, ed. Schnitzer, p. 22.

[3] *Loc. cit.*

flagellum Dei which was soon to be visited upon all Italy for her sins;[4] then he had begun to warn them of the New Cyrus who would come to Italy to wield the sword of God's wrath; more recently he had urged them to build an Ark of the spirit in which they might take refuge from the Flood which was about to engulf the peninsula. The Flood—in the form of Charles VIII and his fearsome army—had come and rolled on, and the Ark had held. To many, Savonarola, who had twice interrupted his Advent preaching to go on embassies to the King on behalf of the city and twice more interceded with him during the tense days of the French occupation, seemed indeed to be the prophet of God, sent to save this particular city from the cataclysm. Savonarola himself described his mission in that way and explained the marvelous rescue from the Flood as the result of God's special election of the Florentine people. The world, he said, would soon enter the Fifth Age, when Antichrist would appear, but a renewed Christianity would vanquish Antichrist and cross over to the East. The "Turks and Pagans" would be baptized and there would be a single sheepfold under one shepherd. In all this Florence would have a crucial role: she would be a new Zion, the center of the reform that would spread to all of Italy, to all Christendom, and ultimately to all the peoples of the earth. But first the Florentines must prepare themselves for the task that lay ahead with a *renovatio* both spiritual and temporal. Having thrown out the tyrant they must now establish a government that would promote the common good and stand as a model for others. Everyone, he said, has heard the saying that states are not governed with paternosters,[5] but the very opposite is true: the more spiritual a government the more stable and powerful it is, the greater its riches. The light of human reason is insufficient for governing a city; God's grace is necessary to augment human reason and to overcome the self-love that interferes with the attainment of the com-

---

[4] The account of Savonarola's Advent preaching is a summary based upon the latest text now published in Girolamo Savonarola, *Prediche sopra Aggeo*, ed. Luigi Firpo (Rome, 1965). For a fuller account and analysis, see below, Chapters III-IV.

[5] A saying commonly attributed to Cosimo de' Medici (d. 1464).

mon good. The Florentines have already made a start in building the Ark of the spirit. Let them now continue by making a general peace among all the citizens, forgetting and cancelling the hatreds of the past. Let them make laws to regulate the moral and religious life of the citizenry and to help convert them to the life of the spirit. These are the first, indispensable steps for the city which will be a *Ierusalem superna*. Let them adopt new laws to prevent one-man rule so there will never be a recurrence of tyranny. Finally, let them prepare plans for a new government; let it be based, so far as is suitable, on the model of Venice; devise it so as to protect the interests of all citizens and distribute more equitably the offices of state. All this (and much more which he cannot yet reveal) the Prophet has through God's illumination. If Florence will heed she will be a new city, the city of God, and richer, more powerful, more glorious than she has ever been.

The Florentines heeded sufficiently to adopt, in the succeeding weeks, a plan for constitutional reform embodying as its central feature a broadly based council which sat to elect the holders of certain offices and the occupants of the magistracies of the Florentine state. This was the Great Council (*Consiglio maggiore*) and it became the hallmark of the new, free republic (*governo civile*). Florence continued to face serious problems; the reform of the constitution did not automatically produce the domestic peace so ardently preached by Fra Girolamo; still there is no doubt that his intervention on the side of reform was decisive in averting the disaster of civil strife that threatened in December. Nor is there any doubt that his apocalyptic preaching had a powerful impact upon the city. Florentines of every class and occupation—former friends of Lorenzo and Piero de' Medici, disciples of Ficino and of Giovanni Pico, artists as well as artisans, patricians as well as *popolani*—were among those who ardently believed that Savonarola spoke with divine authority and that his prophecy of world renewal radiating from Florence was soon to be fulfilled, indeed within the lifetime of many who heard him.

Girolamo Benivieni, one of the Magnificent Lorenzo's *brigata* of favorite poets and a close friend of Giovanni Pico della Mirandola (up to Pico's untimely death on November 17), addressed Florence in this way:[6]

> Arise, O New Jerusalem and see
> your Queen and her beloved son.
> In you, City of God, who now sit and weep
>
> Such joy and splendor will yet be born
> as to decorate both you and all the world.
> In those days of bliss
>
> You will see all the world come to you,
> devoted and faithful
> folk, drawn by the odor of your holy lily.

All peoples and all nations, wrote Benivieni, would conform to the one true religion of Florence, and the world would be united in one sheepfold under a single shepherd. In the new age Florence would extend her hegemony in a benevolent *imperio* because she was the city of the elect and of the true religion. All those who returned voluntarily to rest between the paws of the lion would be blessed with temporal and spiritual rewards, while any who disdained her future glory would be accursed.[7] In 1497 another Savonarolan enthusiast from the same circle as Benivieni, Giovanni Nesi, published his *Oraculum de novo saeculo*, a dream-vision compounded of Christian millenarianism and Hermetic and Neopythagorean occultism.[8] To Nesi, Savonarola was both the prophet of the Christian millennium and the oracular fount of esoteric knowledge; he was the "Socrates of Ferrara," possessed of the wisdom of Plato, Plotinus, and the Kabbalah as well as the Holy Scriptures, who dispensed the divine illumination by which men would be able to reconstruct Florence in liberty, spirituality, and truth, according to the models of both the celestial Jerusalem and the Pla-

[6] Girolamo Benivieni, *Commento sopra a piu sue canzoni et sonetti dello amore e della belleza divina* (Florence, 1500); Hain no. 2788, fol. cxiii verso (incorrectly numbered cxii). On Benivieni, see below pp. 205-208, 216-20, 372-73.

[7] *Ibid.*, fols. cxii recto–cxiii recto.

[8] *Iohannis Nesii Florentini Oraculum de novo saeculo* (Florence, 1497). On Nesi, see Eugenio Garin, *Medioevo e Rinascimento* (Bari, 1954), pp. 277-78, and below pp. 192-205.

tonic Republic. On the basis of Savonarola's teaching, Florence would augment her *imperium* and create the new era (*novum illud saeculum*). In Florence Christ reigned and the golden age had begun.[9]

Such were the dreams dreamed in Florence, city of hard-headed businessmen, practical politicians, and sophisticated artists and thinkers in the time of Savonarola. How shall we understand this? The old explanations that focus upon the compelling power of Savonarola's prophetic personality are inadequate and simplistic. They attribute too much to the man and too little to the city. The Florentines, a people of strong wills and deeply rooted traditions, were hardly likely to have let themselves be led so abruptly into unfamiliar paths of thinking and acting, particularly by a mendicant friar who, however popular and well-established in the city, was, after all, a "foreigner" from Ferrara. Postponing to a later chapter an examination of the political aspects of this problem—how Savonarola came to intervene in the domestic crisis with a plan for popular reform and what sort of government the Florentines established[10]—we shall concentrate here on the Friar's millenarian message and its widespread reception in Florence. Interestingly enough, it is only recently that Savonarola's prophecy has come to be described as millenarian or chiliastic, in part, no doubt, because his biographers have been concerned with minimizing the heterodox aspects of his thought,[11] and in part because the phenomenon of millenarianism has only recently become the object of intensive study by historians,

[9] *Oraculum*, sig. c, fol. 7 recto–sig. d, fol. 2 verso.

[10] See below, Chapters IV-V.

[11] Thus Joseph Schnitzer discusses the various aspects of Savonarola's prophecy, including certain standard elements of late medieval millenarianism like the Angelic Pastor, and even quotes the discussion of the coming millennial reign by Giorgio Benigno, one of Savonarola's early supporters, without acknowledging Savonarola's own millenarianism as such. Schnitzer, *Savonarola*, trans. Ernesto Rutili, 2 vols. (Milan, 1931), Chapter XXX: "Il Profeta." André Chastel, in his important article, "L'Antéchrist à la Renaissance," *L'umanesimo e il demoniaco nell'arte, Atti del Congresso Internazionale di Studi Umanistici*, ed. Enrico Castelli (Rome, 1952), pp. 177-86, together with Cantimori and Spini in the articles already mentioned in my introduction, were the first, so far as I know, to deal with the Savonarola movement as belonging to the millenarian type. See also my article, "Savonarola, Florence, and the Millenarian Tradition," *Church History*, XXVII (1958), 3-17.

anthropologists, and social scientists.[12] All the characteristics of the
millenarian pattern as it has been delineated by scholars were present in Savonarolan Florence: social crisis, a charismatic leader, a
view of the world as a battleground between good and evil forces,
a chosen people, a vision of the ultimate redemption in an earthly
paradise.[13] The formula is useful, not only to establish the typicality
of the Savonarola movement as a much needed corrective to the
more usual stress on its uniqueness, but also to help in identifying
some of its components more precisely.

A further insight can be gained by borrowing a conceptual framework from the history of political thought. From this point of view
we can say that under the stress of revolution, war, and domestic
crisis the Florentines had become susceptible to and, in part at least,
adopted a mode of legitimation for their new republic which was
an alternative to their more usual ones. Having experienced the collapse of the order which had been established in sixty years of
Medici pseudo-republicanism and finding it impossible to resume
the pre-Medicean order of oligarchic republicanism, they embraced
the model of the Elect Nation. The choice was not fortuitous;
Savonarola "was explaining Florence to itself by locating it in sacred
history, the proper locus—according to contemporary ideas—for the
unique and astonishing contemporary event."[14] This framework has

[12] That is, millenarianism as a social rather than an exclusively theological
phenomenon. See the collection of studies, which includes one of my own on
the Savonarola movement, in *Millennial Dreams in Action*, ed. Sylvia Thrupp,
Comparative Studies in Society and History, Supplement II (The Hague,
1962).
[13] See Norman Cohn's *The Pursuit of the Millennium*, 2nd edn. (New
York: Harper Torchbooks, 1961). Cohn does not discuss the Savonarola
movement.
[14] J.G.A. Pocock, " 'The Onely Politician': Machiavelli, Harrington and
Felix Raab" (review article), *Historical Studies: Australia and New Zealand*
(April, 1966), pp. 275-76. I should point out that, as he indicates, this part of
Professor Pocock's analysis of modes of legitimation is based on my article,
"Millenarianism in a Civic Setting: The Savonarola Movement in Florence"
in *Millennial Dreams in Action*, pp. 187-203. The conceptual framework is his.
See also William Haller, *The Elect Nation* (New York, 1963); and Joseph R.
Strayer, "France: The Holy Land, the Chosen People, and the Most Christian
King," *Action and Conviction in Early Modern Europe: Essays in Honor of
E. H. Harbison*, ed. Theodore K. Rabb and Jerrold E. Siegel (Princeton, 1969),
pp. 3-16.

the merit of offering an explanation which relates the Florentine turn to millenarianism under Savonarola's banner to the Christian apocalyptic consciousness of the late Quattrocento. It provides a link between Savonarola's own prophetic mode of thought and that of the Florentines, for whom apocalyptic prophetism was an available model, and one they would be likely to turn to in such a time of anguish.

These explanations of Florence's resort to Savonarolan millenarianism, however, are incomplete without still another perspective—that of Florentine history. The Florentine apocalyptic vision was more than a typical contemporary response to crisis and a charismatic preacher. It was prepared for by long-standing civic tradition, by the way that Florentines habitually regarded their city and themselves in relation to her. To the citizens of Florence their city was a living creature with a destiny shaped by God. Divine Providence had attended her birth and continued to guide her throughout her history. She was a favorite of the Lord,[15] and as such her statesmen had the responsibility of considering the moral and religious implications of their deliberations. Unusual occurrences in the city were interpreted with the aid of astrologers and prophets as signs of this hidden design. The successes and failures of the city's undertakings were seen as rewards and punishments for the virtues and vices of her citizens. To be sure, at the end of the fourteenth century Florentine humanists had begun to expound a new public ethos which emphasized the active virtues of the citizen in guiding the destinies of a state whose purpose was the enhancement of freedom and the development of the individual.[16] In order to fulfill their task they had begun to reexamine and reevaluate many of the traditions and assumptions by which Florentines lived. But the humanists did not

[15] Felix Gilbert, "Florentine Political Assumptions in the Period of Savonarola and Soderini," *Journal of the Warburg and Courtauld Institutes*, XII (1957), 211.

[16] Fully developed by Leonardo Bruni in the first quarter of the fifteenth century, after the successful stand against the Visconti threat, according to Hans Baron, *The Crisis of the Early Italian Renaissance*, 2nd edn. (Princeton, 1966). See also Eugenio Garin, "I cancellieri umanisti della repubblica fiorentina da Coluccio Salutati a Bartolomeo Scala," *La cultura filosofica del Rinascimento italiano* (Florence, 1961), pp. 3-37.

make a clean break with the values and traditions of the past. If they developed a new view of the founding of the city, they retained the notion that Florence, as the daughter of Rome, had a special heritage; and if they no longer saw Florence as the dutiful servant of Papalist Guelfism, they incorporated into their new view of the city as the champion of republican liberty certain features of the old Guelf ideology—its moralism and its sense of special civic destiny. As much as civic humanism may have reshaped and intensified the historical consciousness of the Florentines, it did not terminate their disposition to look at themselves in the light of prophecy. Florentine civic humanism developed on an established base of popular and patriotic traditions, and humanist classicism and the older *volgare* culture grew not merely side by side, but in a mutually influential relationship.[17] Similarly, in the Laurentian era of the 1470's and 1480's, the poets, artists, and Neoplatonist thinkers who cultivated the notion of Florence's intellectual and artistic greatness leaned upon popular civic traditions.[18]

Apocalyptic prophetism, however, was but one aspect of the cult of Florentine greatness. In both popular and sophisticated expression we find not one but two central themes of civic destiny—the idea of Florence as the daughter of Rome and the idea of Florence as the center of rebirth and Christian renewal.[19] These themes

[17] Baron, *Crisis*, especially part IV.

[18] André Chastel, *Art et humanisme à Florence au temps de Laurent le Magnifique* (Paris, 1961), p. 4; Warman Welliver, *L'impero fiorentino* (Florence, 1957), especially chap. I.

[19] Nothing said here is meant to imply that either the daughter of Rome or the sacred city themes were exclusively Florentine. One thinks immediately of Albertino Mussato's idea that Padua was worthy of being called a second Rome, for which see J. K. Hyde, *Padua in the Age of Dante* (Manchester, 1966), p. 298. More generally, see F. von Bezold, "Republik und Monarchie in der italienischen Literatur des 15. Jahrhunderts," *Historische Zeitschrift*, 81 (1898), 433-68; William Hammer, "The New or Second Rome in the Middle Ages," *Speculum*, XIX (1944), 50-62; Nicolai Rubinstein, "Some Ideas on Municipal Progress and Decline in the Italy of the Communes," *Fritz Saxl Memorial Essays*, ed. D. J. Gordon (London, 1957), pp. 165-83; J. K. Hyde, "Medieval Descriptions of Cities," *Bulletin of the John Rylands Library Manchester*, 48 (1966), 308-40; and Robert Konrad, "Das himmlische und das irdische Jerusalem im mittelalterlichen Denken. Mystische Vorstellung und geschichtliche Wirkung," *Speculum Historiale*, ed. C. Bauer, L. Boehm, M.

appear in the earliest historical literature of the city, in the thirteenth century, and significantly, they persist until the end of the Republic in the sixteenth century. The theme of Florence as the daughter of Rome located the city in secular history, the theme of rebirth and renewal, in sacred history. Sometimes they appear separately; more often in mutual dependence. The story of this dynamic interplay makes up the special quality of what might be called the myth of Florence, an expression of belief in the Republic's destiny of leadership for high political, moral, and religious purposes. Rarely were those who reflected most soberly upon Florentine history and politics completely immune to its appeal. Rarely, on the other hand, was the myth pure fantasy, completely divorced from the realities of the historical situation. Rather, it was a mode of thinking about the city which the Florentines drew upon, sometimes consciously, sometimes implicitly, to support themselves in their civic enterprises and to comfort themselves in their collective fears, a mode of legitimation that seldom appears entirely separated from other modes, such as those of Guelfism or civic humanism. When we look at Savonarolan Florence from this perspective the city's self-glorification as the Elect Nation that will be "more glorious, richer, more powerful than ever" appears neither unique, nor foreign, nor as a regression to "medieval" ways of thinking, but as another instance of her resort to the old myth and another stage in the protean relationship of the two themes of which it was composed. In order to gain access to this perspective, therefore, we shall first survey the history of the Florentine myth of a special destiny.

THE FIRST HISTORY of Florence, the thirteenth-century *Chronica de origine civitatis*, traced her origins to Roman colonization in the time of Julius Caesar. According to the *Chronica*, Florence was

---

Müller (Munich, 1965), pp. 523-40. Fundamental is Ernst H. Kantorowicz, *The King's Two Bodies* (Princeton, 1957). See especially his discussion of the transfer of *corpus mysticum* from the Church to political entities, pp. 193-272. For a wide-ranging and suggestive treatment of forms of "religious ethnocentrism," see Werner Stark, *The Sociology of Religion*, 3 vols. (New York, 1966-67), especially vol. I. Another aspect of the exaltation of the city has been studied by Hans Conrad Peyer, *Stadt und Stadtpatron im mittelalterlichen Italien* (Zurich, 1955).

founded *ex flore hominum Romanorum*, from the flower of Roman manhood, and she was *parva Roma*, a little Rome.[20] Thus she was marked out for a special destiny from her very beginnings, and in the earliest Florentine chronicle, prophecy and history were intertwined. The *Chronica* also introduced the theme of Florence's rebirth after a divine scourge: five hundred years after her founding she was destroyed by Totila, *flagellum Dei*; when the Romans rebuilt the city they founded churches, each of which corresponded to a church in Rome.[21]

It has been suggested that the origin of the theme of Florence's special destiny as a child of Rome was related to the first Florentine military incursions into the Tuscan *contado* in the twelfth century.[22] After 1250, when the Ghibelline government was overthrown by a popular revolution, the Florentines embarked on a new phase of expansion under the aegis of Guelfism. They also elaborated on the myth of the city's destined greatness. One version was inscribed on the walls of the Palazzo del Popolo about this time: Florence is full of riches; her rule brings happiness to Tuscany; she will be eternally triumphant over her enemies; she reigns over the world.[23] But the great defeat of the Florentine Guelfs by the Ghibelline exiles and the forces of Manfred of Hohenstaufen in the Battle of Montaperti in 1260 checked the city's territorial drive and put an end to the government of the *Primo Popolo*. When the Guelfs were restored in 1266 with the support of the Papacy and its Angevin ally, popular government and kinship with France as well as alliance with the Papacy became integral parts of the Florentine Guelf ethos.[24] There-

---

[20] Nicolai Rubinstein, "The Beginnings of Political Thought in Florence, A Study in Mediaeval Historiography," *Journal of the Warburg and Courtauld Institutes*, V (1942), 198-227. Professor Rubinstein describes it as a work compiled of popular legends, mythological traditions, and historical facts derived from ancient and medieval authors (p. 199). Thus popular belief and more sophisticated history blended from an early date.

[21] *Ibid.*, pp. 201-203.

[22] *Ibid.*, p. 212, n. 1, citing B. Schmeidler, *Italienische Geschichtschreiber des 12. und 13. Jahrhunderts* (Leipzig, 1909), pp. 44-5.

[23] See the text of the inscription in Rubinstein, "Beginnings," p. 213. For the idea of *renovatio Romae* in the Baptistery of Florence, see Mario Salmi, "La Renovatio Romae e Firenze," *Rinascimento*, I (1950), 3-24.

[24] Nicola Ottokar points out, however, that the restoration of the Guelf

after Guelfism itself came to be regarded as part of the Florentine destiny, as we can see from the fourteenth-century legend of the prophecy of "the White Cardinal": "The conquered shall conquer victoriously, and they shall not be defeated unto eternity." This, according to Giovanni Villani, meant that the Guelfs who had been defeated and driven from Florence would return victoriously to power (*in istato*), and that they would never again lose their ascendancy in Florence (*loro stato e signoria di Firenze*).[25]

About the same time a new legend took root, replacing the earlier belief that Florence had been reconstructed by the Romans after Totila's devastation. In this newer, fourteenth-century account the time of Totila's destruction remains the same, but the Romans are replaced as restorers of the city by the Emperor Charlemagne. Apparently this linking of Florentine destiny with the great Emperor Charles had to do with the rise of Angevin power in Italy in the thirteenth century and with the consequent diffusion of the prophecy of the Second Charlemagne. The Second Charlemagne prophecy, itself a compound of older legends with the prophecies of Joachim of Flora and his imitators,[26] foretold that the Empire would come

---

regime was not a return to the government of the *Primo Popolo* as the fourteenth-century chroniclers represented it to be, but rather it resulted in the establishment of the *Parte Guelfa* as the predominant power in the city. *Studi comunali e fiorentini* (Florence, 1948), p. 81.

[25] *Cronica di Giovanni Villani*, ed. F. G. Dragomanni, 4 vols. (Florence, 1844-45), vol. I, p. 304. The story is also found in Lapo da Castiglionchio, *Epistola o sia ragionamento*, ed. L. Mehus (Bologna, 1753), p. 115. Master John of Toledo, named to the Cardinalate in 1343, was known as the White Cardinal because of his Cistercian habit. According to contemporaries he was a prophet and necromancer who employed his gifts in the anti-imperial cause, predicting the coming of a new King who would make peace in the world after wiping out the Sicilians and the race of Frederick [of Hohenstaufen]. He was confused with the author of the "Toledo Letter," a prophecy which originated in the twelfth century and versions of which continued to circulate long afterward. For all this see Herman Grauert, "Meister Johann von Toledo," *Sitzungsberichte der philos-philol. und der histor. Classe der kgl. bayer. Akademie der Wissenschaften*, II (1901), pp. 111-325.

[26] For the sources and scholarly literature, see Morton Bloomfield, "Joachim of Flora: A Critical Survey of His Canon, Teachings, Sources, Biography, and Influence," *Traditio*, XIII (1957), 249-311. The important work on Joachim and his influence, by Marjorie Reeves, *The Influence of Prophecy in the Later Middle Ages: A Study in Joachimism* (Oxford, 1969), reached me too late for me to make extensive use of it here.

under the leadership of a French king, a new Charles, who would cleanse the Church, cross the seas to the East and, conquering the Infidel, unite the world in one flock under a single shepherd, whereupon he would lay down his crown upon the Mount of Olives.[27] Both the legend of the Carolingian restoration and the prophecy of the Second Charlemagne are found repeatedly in fourteenth-century Florentine sources, although only towards the end of the century, as we shall see, were they linked in such a way as to give Florence a share in the ultimate triumph of the Carolingian line. The legend of the city's restoration by Charlemagne appeared in Florence for the first time in the chronicle which Giovanni Villani began to write in the early fourteenth century. Villani emphasized the religious aspects of the restoration, which he said took place on "the Easter day of the Resurrection," and included the founding of the Church of the Holy Apostle "to the honor of God and the holy apostles." He also stressed Florence's continuity with the Roman past and her special place in Christian eschatology, for, he said, while Totila had destroyed the city, her cathedral (*il duomo di santo Giovanni*),[28] which had originally been a temple of Mars, had remained standing and would remain standing until the Day of Judgment.[29]

But what was the mission and the destiny of this city which Providence had caused to be founded under the auspices of eternal Rome and reborn under the auspices of Charlemagne, the emperor of Rome

---

[27] Text in Oswald Holder-Egger ed., "Italienische Prophetien des 13. Jahrhunderts," *Neues Archiv der Gesellschaft für ältere deutsche Geschichtskunde*, II (1904), 383-84; see also Franz Kampers, *Kaiserprophetien und Kaisersagen im Mittelalter* (Munich, 1895), pp. 145-53. The source of the image of *unum ovile et unus pastor* is John 10:16. For the older background of some of these prophecies and a discussion of methodology in their use by the historian, see Paul J. Alexander, "Medieval Apocalypses as Historical Sources," *American Historical Review*, LXXIII (1968), 997-1018.

[28] This is the present-day Baptistery of Saint John the Baptist, which served as the cathedral until the early twelfth century.

[29] *Cronica*, vol. I, p. 89: "e infra la città presso alla porta *casa, sive domo*, interpretiamo il duomo di santo Giovanni, chiamato prima casa di Marti. E di vero mai non fue disfatto, nè disfarà in eterno, se non al *die judicio*; e così si truova scritto nello smalto del detto duomo." The same story is in Castiglionchio, *Epistola*, p. 67. Compare the Roman proverb: "Quamdiu stat Colysaeus stat et Roma; quando cadet Colysaeus cadet et Roma; quando cadet Roma cadet et mundus," quoted in Charles T. Davis, *Dante and the Idea of Rome* (Oxford, 1957), p. 3.

reborn? Villani noted that when Charlemagne refounded the city he also granted her communal privileges: "and he made the commune and citizens of Florence and for three miles around independent and free." After this a government on the Roman model was established, with a council of one hundred senators and two consuls.[30] Thus, free republican government was a fundamental part of the Carolingian-Roman heritage. Villani also thought of Florence's Roman heritage in terms of "greatness" and the doing of great deeds, as we see in the famous passage in the eighth book of his chronicle where he explains how he came to write the history of his city. In 1300, he tells us, he went to Rome to participate in the Jubilee indulgence of Pope Boniface VIII. He saw the wonderful sights of the ancient city, he read the story of Rome's great deeds in her ancient authors, and then and there he decided to write the history of his own city, for, just as Rome was in decline, "Florence, the daughter and creature of Rome," was in the ascendant and on the verge of accomplishing great things.[31] And yet, for Villani Florence's Roman inheritance had little or nothing to do with Rome's imperial mission. With Florentine territorial expansion he had little sympathy. Villani castigated those of his fellow citizens who offended God by their dissatisfaction with the benefits He had bestowed upon the city and who aspired to go beyond their proper boundaries in aggression against their neighbors.[32] For him Florentine greatness was a composite of her wealth, her republican institutions, her culture, and her

[30] *Cronica*, vol. I, p. 129. Professor Rubinstein suggests there may have been a forged charter of franchise, since Villani's account is so detailed. Rubinstein, "Beginnings," p. 215, n. 3. Villani took the trouble to deny other stories of the rebuilding of Florence which described it as having taken place under pagan auspices.

[31] *Cronica*, vol. I, p. 39.

[32] Villani recounts how, after the Florentines had been defeated by the Pisans (in 1341), he told a Florentine *cavaliere* why God had permitted this defeat: "la vera carità è fallita in noi; prima verso Iddio, di non essere a lui grati e conoscenti di tanti beneficii fatti e in tanto podere avere posta la nostra città, e per la nostra presunzione non stare contenti a' nostri termini ma volere occupare non solamente Lucca, ma l'altre città e terre vicine indebitamente." *Cronica*, vol. III, p. 370. Similarly, in 1342 Villani suggested that the loss of Lucca was the judgment of God, "per abbassare la superbia e avara ingratitudine de' Fiorentini e de' loro rettori," and he recalled the prophecy of his friend Maestro Dionigio dal Borgo a San Sepolcro in 1328, that Florence would

charitable and pious citizenry. Moreover, Villani's view seems to have been characteristic of his time. Expansionist ambitions there were, but the Florentines of the first half of the fourteenth century do not seem to have reformulated their old territorial ambitions into an ideology of imperialism.[33] Military activity beyond the city walls was generally justified as a defence of Guelfism—that is, of domestic republicanism, civic virtue, and service to the cause of the Church.[34]

In the years following mid-century it became increasingly difficult to hold to this position, as we can see in the writings of Giovanni Villani's brother, Matteo. In taking up his pen to continue Giovanni's chronicle after he died of the Black Death in 1348, Matteo had to come to terms with that disaster. For him the Black Death was a second Flood, a divine judgment upon men's sins even more severe in its toll of human lives; but like the first Flood it was the beginning of a great renewal.[35] Consequently he felt that his task was to interpret Florentine events in the light of God's judgment so that his readers would understand them and learn that the remedy for adversity was to conform to the Divine Will.[36] In politics as in other activities his countrymen should conform to the canons of virtue. Matteo condemned the use of deception (*inganno*) by the civic leaders in their attempt to take over the city of Pistoia,[37] as he condemned generally the tyrannical rapacity with which city attacked city, "departing from the straight road of true justice."[38] On the other hand he justified Florence's occupation of the neighboring towns of Colle and

---

have the lordship of Lucca, but only at great expense and for a short time. *Ibid.*, vol. III, p. 380; see also vol. III, p. 376.

[33] See also *La Cronica di Dino Compagni*, ed. Isidoro Del Lungo, *Rerum Italicarum Scriptores, Raccolta degli storici italiani*, vol. IX (Città di Castello, 1916), part II, p. 3.

[34] For example, see Giovanni Morelli, *Ricordi*, ed. Vittore Branca (Florence, 1956), p. 127.

[35] ". . . propuosi nell'animo mio fare alla nostra varia e calamitosa materia cominciamento a questo tempo, come a uno rinnovellamento di tempo e secolo, comprendendo annualmente le novità che appariranno di memoria degne, giusta la possa del debole ingegno, come più certa fede per li tempi avvenire ne potremo avere." *Cronica di Matteo Villani*, ed. F. G. Dragomanni, 2 vols. (Florence, 1846), vol. I, p. 9. See also Millard Meiss, *Painting in Florence and Siena after the Black Death* (New York, 1951), pp. 65-66.

[36] *Cronica: di Matteo Villani*, vol. I, pp. 7-9.

[37] *Ibid.*, vol. I, p. 114.   [38] *Ibid.*, vol. II, p. 119.

Prato as well as Pistoia when it seemed that they might otherwise submit to the tyranny of Milan and thus increase the threat to Florentine security.[39] Matteo thought of Guelfism as the party of piety, of liberty, and of Latinity, the bulwark against the tide of German barbarism which was threatening to engulf the free cities of Italy.[40] Ghibellinism, the party of imperialism, was tyrannical; therefore, he reasoned, an Italian who became a tyrant would find it necessary to become a Ghibelline also.[41] Matteo's Guelfism was an ideal that regarded the good of the whole in terms of the civic liberties of each of its parts. Individual cities were to subordinate their ambitions to the common good of Italian civilization; no one state must seek supremacy over any other, for the ultimate value to be defended was the freedom of the Christian commune, with equal emphasis on both "Christian" and "commune."

Even as Matteo Villani wrote, however, the fibre of his Guelfism was undergoing heavy strain. In Florence he saw the *Parte Guelfa* being used as an instrument of private ambitions and oppression,[42] while in the neighboring Papal States he saw a challenge to Florentine liberty in Cardinal Albornoz' extension of papal power. Matteo had very sharp words for those governors of the Church who used their positions to gain power for themselves. He charged that, unmindful of how Florence had aided the Roman Church to enlarge its temporal state on many past occasions, these tyrants were both secretly and openly trying to impose their lordship upon Florence and to undermine her liberties. This put the Florentines in the false position of having to act against the Church of Rome, which was

[39] *Ibid.*: on Colle and Prato, vol. I, pp. 51-52; on Pistoia, *ibid.*, pp. 113-14.

[40] "Appresso è da considerare, che la lingua latina, e' costumi e' movimenti della lingua tedesca sono come barbari, e divisati e strani agl' Italiani, la cui lingua e la cui leggi e' costumi, e' gravi e moderati movimenti diedono ammaestramento a tutto l'universo, e a loro la monarchia del mondo." *Ibid.*, vol. I, p. 381.

[41] "E di vero la parte guelfa è fondamento e rocca ferma e stabile della libertà d'Italia, e contraria a tutte le tirannie, per modo che se alcuno guelfo divien tiranno, convien per forza ch' e' diventi ghibellino. . . ." *Ibid.*, vol. I, p. 109.

[42] For Matteo, Guelfism as an ideology and the interests of the *Parte Guelfa* were not identical. As an ideological Guelf he did not feel bound to an unquestioning support of the Party.

tantamount to acting against their very selves, although Villani maintained it was not against the Church but against its evil and worldly pastors that the Florentines were resisting.[43]

While developments both inside and outside Florence in the middle of the fourteenth century were working to undermine the traditional Guelf ideology of republican pluralism and papal leadership, it was not until 1375, when Florence went to war with Pope Gregory XI, that this ideology received its death blow.[44] Even before that, however, a new view was forming, one in which Florence no longer defined her Roman inheritance in terms of papal leadership but claimed leadership for herself.

In the growth of this new view radical Christian apocalyptic ideas played a part. One source of these ideas was a radical offshoot of the Spiritual Franciscans, the movement of the Fraticelli, who were very active in fourteenth-century Florence.[45] Through such men as Frate Salvestro da Monte Bonello and Frate Simone Fidati da Cascia we can trace some strands of Fraticelli influence among laymen. Frate Salvestro, an uneducated wool carder, joined the Frati dal Castagno, a Fraticelli group in the Florentine *contado* connected with a confraternity of artisans and merchants called the Ciccialardoni. Frate Salvestro was active both in the Camaldulensian Convent of Santa Maria degli Angeli in Florence and in a circle of devotees which used to meet at the villa of Tommaso Corsini, a prominent Florentine lawyer and member of a patrician Guelf family. He preached poverty and isolation from the world and was believed to have the gift of prophecy.[46] His close friend and disciple, Frate Simone Fidati da Cascia, also preached the doctrine of apostolic poverty and was

---

[43] *Ibid.*, vol. II, pp. 178-80.

[44] "In Florence it [the War of the Eight Saints] destroyed a major political tradition." Gene A. Brucker, *Florentine Politics and Society 1343-78* (Princeton, N.J., 1962), pp. 265, 266-96. For a good account of Florence's relations with the Papal Legate, see pp. 177-83.

[45] On the Fraticelli, see Felice Tocco, "I Fraticelli," *Archivio storico italiano*, 5th ser., XXXV (1905), 331-68; Decima Douie, *The Nature and Effect of the Heresy of the Fraticelli* (Manchester, 1932).

[46] *Vita del Beato Salvestro in Distici per Don Zenobi Tantini in Leggende di alcuni santi e beati venerati in S. Maria degli Angeli di Firenze*, ed. Casimiro Stolfi (Bologna, 1864), vol. II, pp. 137-69, also 19-81; on the Ciccialardoni, see p. 139, n. 1. On Tommaso Corsini, see Brucker, *Florentine Politics*, pp. 30 et

protected against papal repression by the Florentine city fathers, who may have found it useful to encourage anti-papal feelings while Roman-Florentine relations were worsening.[47] That the Fraticelli were well-organized in Florence and influential enough to be considered a serious problem we know from several sources but especially from the writings of Giovanni dalle Celle.[48] This Vallombrosan hermit, revered as a saint and looked to as a religious adviser by a number of laymen, began to attack the local Fraticelli when one of his own lay devotees, a carpenter named Tommaso, decided to join their sect.[49] Giovanni attacked them as schismatics who were said to have their own secret church with bishops and pope, and he noted that despite continual preaching against the Fraticelli "many lambs continue to run after the wolf."[50] He also attacked them for teaching heretical ideas, the coming of the Angelic Pastor, and the millennium. "They say that the world is about to be renewed, and I say it is about to be ruined. They cite their predictions and false prophets,

---

passim; and on the Corsini family, Luigi Passerini, *Genealogia a storia della famiglia Corsini* (Florence, 1858).

[47] On Simone Fidati da Cascia, see Mary Germaine McNeil, *Simone Fidati and his De Gestis Domini Salvatoris* (Washington, 1950); and Douie, *Fraticelli*, pp. 65, 362. For his letter on the death of Angelo Clareno, one of the most important Fraticelli sectarians of the early fourteenth century, see Nicola Mattioli, *Il beato Simone Fidati da Cascia dell'Ordine Romitano di S. Agostino e i suoi scritti editi ed inediti* (Rome, 1898), pp. 337-39. On the Florentine Signoria's protection of Simone against the Inquisitor, see Felice Tocco, "La eresia dei Fraticelli e una lettera del Beato Giovanni dalle Celle," *Rendiconti dell'Accademia dei Lincei, Cl. di Scienze Morali*, 5th ser., XV (1906), 161-62; Marvin Becker, "Florentine Politics and the Diffusion of Heresy in the Trecento: A Socio-Economic Inquiry," *Speculum*, XXXIV (1959), 60-75. See also, R. Trexler, *Economic, Political and Religious Effects of the Papal Interdict on Florence, 1376-78* (Frankfurt-on-Main, 1964), pp. 132-40 and 160. Trexler denies that the Florentine government generally failed to cooperate with the Inquisition in this period, arguing that it only opposed "illegal use of the tribunal" (p. 133, n. 76).

[48] P. Cividali, "Il beato Giovanni dalle Celle," *Atti dell'Accademia dei Lincei, Cl. di Scienze Morali*, 5th ser., XII (1907), 353-477. Trexler sees a decided upsurge during the war, *Effects of the Papal Interdict*, p. 133.

[49] Stolfi believes this Tommaso to be the same Maso or Tommaso *romito* who drew many people to the Fraticelli of Castagno. *Leggende*, vol. II, p. 25, n. 1.

[50] Letter to the Fraticelli in Cividali, "Il beato Giovanni dalle Celle," pp. 453-54.

and I cite Christ in the Gospel, who says that false prophets will arise and work miracles and there will be more tribulations than there have ever been."[51]

Giovanni acknowledged the truth of one aspect of the Fraticelli teaching, that is, the corruption of the Church: he realized that the pastors of Florence were negligent and allowed their flock to be devoured by wolves, and that this turned them to heresy and schism. Such clerics, he wrote, should be put to death.[52] A few years later, although still violently opposed to "those members of Antichrist, that is, these heretical Fraticelli, who have already deceived so many people and continue to deceive them every day," Giovanni dalle Celle had moved even closer to them in his thinking about the Church. Citing *Il papale*, a book of prophecies about the popes, which was then believed to be the work of Joachim of Flora,[53] Giovanni wrote that the then reigning pope, Gregory XI, was to be the last pope before the coming of Antichrist. The Church was darkened; the first tribulations were coming and after them the second, those of Antichrist, which would bring the last torments. The evil would come from the north, in the direction of Fiesole, and it would come in the lifetime of men then living. Giovanni's discussion of the end of the Roman Church and of the Last Judgment took place during the final breakdown of Florence's relations with Pope Gregory XI which culminated in war with the Church in 1375. At that time he was writing to Guido Del Palagio, a lay patrician admirer who had asked him to discuss his ideas about the end of the world.[54] Torn between

[51] Letter to Tommaso in Giovanni da Prato, *Il Paradiso degli Alberti*, ed. A. Wesselofsky (Bologna, 1867), vol. I, p. 351.

[52] Letter to Guido Del Palagio in *Lettere del Beato don Giovanni dalle Celle* (n.p., 1844), p. 15.

[53] On the revision of *Il papale* in Florence at this time see Herbert Grundmann, "Die Papstprophetien des Mittelalters," *Archiv für Kulturgeschichte*, XIX (1928), 77-139. Giovanni indicated that he had a shorter version which lacked one pope, from which he concluded that either his copy was corrupt or that someone had added to the original text.

[54] Letter to Guido in *Volgarizzamento inedito di alcuni scritti di Cicerone e di Seneca*, ed. Giuseppi Oliveri (Genoa, 1825), pp. 111-12. See also, on his ideas on the imminent end of the world, his letters to Giorgio Gucci and to Francesco Datini in *Lettere del Beato*, pp. 42, 45. The distinguished Augustinian monk, Luigi Marsili, gave similar advice, for which see Becker, "Florentine Politics," p. 72.

his loyalty to the city and his loyalty to the Church, Guido also asked the monk whether he, Guido, could in good conscience serve in a civic office when his city was under interdict and at war with the Pope. Giovanni's reply shows how the issue was being drawn between papal leadership and communal self-assertion: he assured Guido that the excommunication of the Florentines by the Pope was invalid and that he need not hesitate to support the Republic in the war. Guido should first have regard for the honor of God (which Giovanni obviously no longer equated with the papal position), then for the good of his city. It was lawful for Guido to defend his city and to help preserve it.

The Fraticelli, then, were not the only ones undermining the traditional Florentine Guelf ideology. Giovanni dalle Celle rejected Fraticelli millenarianism and schism, but he accepted the pseudo-Joachite *Il papale*, which was probably of Fraticelli origin, in formulating his own eschatology of the approaching Day of Judgment and the destruction of the Church of Rome. Perhaps because he was so pessimistic about the future, he did not pursue the implications of his advice to Guido Del Palagio on the moral independence of the Florentine Republic. Some shared his pessimism, for example the poet Franco Sacchetti;[55] but others began to dream of a great role for their city in a splendid future. The exiled poet, Fazio degli Uberti, was one of these. Throughout most of his life Fazio had been a Ghibelline, true to the aristocratic tradition of his family,[56] but with the repeated failures of the German emperors in Italy he turned his thoughts to Rome herself and to the possibiliy of an independent Italian revival. In 1355 he wrote:

[55] In a letter of 1392 to Pietro Gambacorti, Signore of Pisa, Sacchetti wrote: "e' mi pare comprendere il mondo essere venuto presso all'ultimo fine." To Giacomo de Conte he wrote to the effect that unless God in his compassion provided otherwise, it seemed that the Last Judgment was at hand. *I Sermoni Evangelici, le lettere ed altri scritti inediti o rari*, ed. O. Gigli (Florence, 1857), pp. 206, 220. For some insights into the background of Sacchetti's pessimism, see Marvin B. Becker, *Florence in Transition*, 2 vols. (Baltimore, 1968), vol. II, pp. 14-15, 38, 44-47, 77-82.

[56] On Fazio degli Uberti, see Natalino Sapegno, *Il Trecento* (Milan, 1934), pp. 479-84; Guglielmo Volpi, *Il Trecento* (Milan, 1907), pp. 268-72.

My song, search the garden of Italy,
Closed by mountains and by its own sea,
And do not travel forth again.[57]

In his two poems "Florence" and "Fiesole" he returned to the old theme of Florence the daughter of Rome. In the first poem he stressed the Roman origins of the *donna*, Florence, who had the characteristics (*tutte impronte*) of that "valorous and weighty people" from whom she had sprung.[58] In "Fiesole" he has that town tell of the birth of Florence from her own descendant, Rome, and of Florence's inheritance of the Roman mission:

Rome acted as long as she was strong;
And in that happy and not-far-off time,
Gave birth to a young maiden such
As to be considered her equal.
She was called "Flower," which was truly her name,
And I shall tell of her deeds.

· · · · ·

Of her who descended from my descendant,
Florence, flower of every good root,
To make herself empress
As her mother had been in past ages.

· · · · ·

What more perfect and true work
Can one tell of this high lady
Than that she is the pillar
Of Holy Church, and of temporal goods,
Prudent, just, and enemy of wickedness?[59]

---

[57] Quoted in Volpi, *Trecento*, p. 271.

[58] "Firenze," *Poesie minori del secolo XIV*, ed. E. Sarteschi, *Scelta di curiosità inedite o rare*, vol. 77 (Bologna, 1867), pp. 6-11.

[59]   Roma pur operò finchè fu sana;
       E in quel tempo felice e non lontana,
       Da se creò una donzella tale;
       A dir a chi fu eguale
       Fior si chiamò, chè ben fu ver suo nome:
       E l' opere dirò, e'l che, e'l come.

· · · · ·

       Di che discese de la mia nipote
       Firenze, fiore d'ogni ben, radice,

So far, Fazio seems to share the idea of Florence as the pillar of the Holy Church with the Guelf loyalties of the Villani brothers; but unlike them he combines this idea with the notion of a Florence destined for leadership:

> Since Fortune smiles at you
>> To you, Florence, clear light, I speak;
>> Follow signs that lead you;
>> Strong Mars, with Jove's will
>> Honors your heirs, to whom he brings
>> Vitality, and in you produces
>> Beauty, in you all crowned anew.
>> And that Lord of Heaven who makes all things
>> Seeing so much virtue reigns in you,
>> Will want your well being
>> To increase, to triumph so fully
>> That it makes one rejoice merely to imagine it.[60]

Moreover, Fazio had a definite idea of what Florence had been chosen to do: to "bring down tyrannies and those of evil life."

> Per farsi imperadrice,
> Come sua madre fu del secol tutto.
>> • • • • •
> Qual più perfetto a verace costrutto
> Dir si potrebbe di quest' alta donna,
> Se non ch' ell' é colonna
> Di santa chiesa e de' ben temporali
> Prudente, giusta e nimica de' mali?

"Fiesole," *ibid.*, pp. 11-13. The poems are not dated, but since Fazio was an ardent Ghibelline throughout most of his life these would seem to be from a late period. I should like to thank Professor Richard A. Webster for his help in translating some of the difficult passages of these poems.

> [60] Poichè fortuna nel viso ti ride
> A te dico, Firenze, chiara luce,
> Segui chi ti conduce;
> Il forte Marte, col voler di Giove,
> Onora le tue rede, in cui conduce
> Vivezza, e in te produce
> Bellezza, in te d'ogni corone nove.
> E quel signor del ciel che tutto move
> Veggendo in te regnar tanta virtute,
> Vorrà che tua salute
> Sormonti, trïonfando per tal modo
> Che pur nel 'maginar tutto ne godo.

Finally, he turns to the citizens themselves, whose duty it is to support their city in her mission:

> O citizen of her whose honor
> You ought to defend more than life itself,
> I pray that you will take delight
> From your duty to the lily's well being
> If only you cause her to reign in safety.

Similar ideas were expressed in a poem by Braccio Bracci, a Tuscan in the employ of Bernabò Visconti of Milan.[61] The year was 1375. Florence and Milan had just made an alliance against the Papacy, and Braccio was obviously using rhetoric that the Florentines liked to hear:

To Florence

> Florence, now rejoice and show courage
>> Because God has given you such a noble state
>> That each of your children resembles Cato
>> In reviving the liberty that once was dead;
>
> This great fame has smashed walls and gates
>> And throughout Italy has raised such a cry
>> That the sleeping slave has woken,
>> And follows the step of your safe guidance.
>
> Rome never did what you are doing,
>> But held her provinces subject,
>> While you raise them from their servitude.
>
> This is why your aims are bound
>> With those of the Visconti, and never
>> Does God want them to be drawn apart.[62]

---

[61] On Bracci, see Volpi, *Trecento*, pp. 278-79.

[62] A FIRENZE
(1375)

> Firenze or ti rallegra or ti conforta
>> Che Dio t'ha dato si nobile stato,
>> Ch' e nati tuoi ciascun somiglia Cato
>> In suscitar libertà ch' era morta;
>
> Questa gran fama ha rotto muri e porta
>> E per Italia un tal strido elevato,
>> Che 'l servo, che dormia, è risvegliato,

In the poetry of Uberti and Bracci the model for the civic ethos was republican Rome; but in certain other quarters there was another model, the New Jerusalem. In 1378, shortly after the war with the Church, there erupted in Florence the Ciompi Rebellion.[63] With the upheaval came a renewed interest in and, apparently, a dissemination of apocalyptic prophecy in which the influence of the Fraticelli is often explicit. Typically, the prophecies were expositions of a biblical book—Daniel was a favorite—and they seem to have been reworkings of older Joachite-type texts in the light of recent events in Florence. One, for example, purported to be an exposition of Daniel written in 1368 by a Minorite friar. It "predicted" the uprising of 1378, when the *popolani* and *gente minuta* would kill all tyrants and traitors and despoil them, as well as many princes and powerful lords, of their estates.[64] The common people would join with a reformed clergy stripped of all its temporal possessions, and after the appearance of Antichrist, a false restorer, and a heretic emperor, a holy pope (*papa santo*), would appear. Together with the poor Fraticelli led by a mystical Elias of the Franciscan order, this new pope would drive all the luxury-loving and avaricious priests from the Church. The King of France would be elected Emperor of the Romans and would become lord of the whole world, healing the breach between Guelfs and Ghibellines and conquering

---

E segue l'orme di tua salva scorta.

Roma non fece mai quel che tu fai,
Ma tenne le provincie soggiogate,
E tu da servitu tutte le trai:

Quest' è perchè tue voglie son legate
Con quella del Visconte, sì che mai
Non voglia Iddio che stien più separate.

Sarteschi, *Poesie minori*, p. 41

[63] On the Ciompi, see now the excellent critical essay, which also contains the relevant bibliography, by Gene A. Brucker, "The Ciompi Revolution," *Florentine Studies*, ed. Nicolai Rubinstein (London, 1968), pp. 314-56.

[64] Described in *Diario d'anonimo fiorentino dell'anno 1358 al 1389*, ed. A. Gherardi, in *Cronache dei secoli XIII e XIV*, Documenti di Storia Italiana pubblicati a cura della R. Deputazione sugli Studi di Storia Patria per le Provincie di Toscana, dell'Umbria e delle Marche, vol. VI (Florence, 1876), pp. 389-90. The chronicler inserted his description of the prophecy after an entry for December 1378.

Jerusalem. In another Daniel prophecy, this one described as an exposition of certain "masters of Toledo and of England" and copied in Paris in 1365, a similar string of uprisings and devastations was to culminate in a great revolution (*grande novità*) in the year 1380.[65] The holy government of the great city having been divided into many parties, the daughter of Rome would suffer many tribulations from bloody internal conflicts, wars, and a revolution; and her condition would seem hopeless until one of her humble citizens (*un suo picciolo cittadino*) would be made governor. He would rule a long time, purge the city of her evils, bring repose to all her citizens, enlarge her territory, and magnify her name. Three neighboring cities would be brought under her rule with the good will of their own citizens. Afterwards this popular leader would render his soul to God amidst great mourning, having left the city in liberty with a government *comune e pacifico*.

In both these prophecies the cause of the common people is identified with a Christian millenarianism emphasizing world renewal, a spiritual Church, and the leadership of a French king. In the second Florence was singled out as the daughter of Rome, destined to be a beacon of liberty and a leader in Tuscany. The Guelf tradition is still evident in the moral, religious, and French context in which the renewal is conceived. But it is Guelfism with a difference, or rather with two differences: first, the satisfaction of lower-class aspirations for justice and equality; second, the displacement of the Roman Church as the Guelf leader and the corresponding rise of Florence. It seems that the assertion of Florence's independence from ecclesiastical Guelfism was accompanied by a growing tendency to look to the Florentine state itself as the arbiter and protector of social justice.

The Ciompi Rebellion did not consolidate itself. The revolutionary government lasted but six short weeks, and by 1382 a *Parte Guelfa* oligarchy was firmly in control. Since the earlier policy of protecting the Fraticelli had proved to be a two-edged sword, the

---

[65] "Qui son venute lettere de Maestri di Tolletta e da quelli d'inghilterra. . . ." MS BNF Magl. XXXV, 173, fol. 1. The letter was supposed to have been sent originally to Cardinal Anibaldo degli Orsini in Paris. I can find no trace of a cardinal of this name.

new government took steps to repress heretical preaching, and sent one radical, a Minorite named Fra Michele, to the stake in 1389.[66] Meanwhile, the looming threat of Milanese expansion gave the Florentines a strong motive for seeking internal harmony. In poetry and in the prophecies we hear appeals for internal reconciliation. In one poem, addressed to the beautiful lady with golden hair, the poet, probably Bruscaccio da Rovezzano,[67] recalls the example of "lofty Rome" which suffered decline because of false counsel, envy, greed, and pride.

> O my beautiful lady! O beautiful country!
> O you who have her tresses in your hand!
> O kind populace

[66] On suppression of the Fraticelli, see Becker, "Florentine Politics," p. 73; Trexler, Effects of the Papal Interdict, pp. 133-34. On the execution of Fra Michele, see Storia di Fra Michele Minorita come fu arso in Firenze nel 1389 (Bologna, 1864).

[67] The poem is attributed to Guido Del Palagio (on whom see above, pp. 45-46) by G. Carducci, Rime di M. Cino da Pistoia e d'altri del secolo XIV (Florence, 1862), pp. 597-600; by G. Volpi, Trecento, p. 284; and by N. Sapegno, Trecento, p. 490. Antonio Medin included it in his "Le rime di Bruscaccio da Rovezzano," Giornale storico della letteratura italiana, XXV (1895), 222-24, under the title, "Cançon del detto Bruscaccio quando messer Donato Acciaiuoli fu confinato a Barletta." This would date the poem 1396, the year of Donato Acciaiuoli's exile, or soon thereafter. While a definitive attribution would have to be based upon a study of the manuscripts, I would argue for Bruscaccio's authorship on the following grounds: Guido was not otherwise known to have composed verse; Andrea Stefani included the poem in a collection of Bruscaccio's poetry in the early fifteenth century (Medin, p. 185); moreover the poem is similar to several other political poems by Bruscaccio; finally there are some stylistic similarities with other of Bruscaccio's poems.

BRUSCACCIO:
> Ché piú non posso far brieve latino:
> Sia qual si vuole, o guelfo, o ghibellino,
>
> (Medin, "Le rime," p. 217)

BRUSCACCIO OR GUIDO:
> Gentile o ppopolano,
> Sia qual si vuole, ascolti il mio latino.
>
> (Medin, "Le rime," p. 222)

On the other hand, there seems little in the poem to warrant connecting it with Donato Acciaiuoli's exile as Medin does. The poet seems to be talking about a general reconciliation between citizens.

Whoever you may be, listen to my discourse.
Forget the offences of the past.

· · · · ·

Do not rend the golden tresses,
  Do not wound her golden limbs with slander,
  So that the sword of justice and the pillar
  Are not ripped apart by you.[68]

The poet ends with the statement of his faith that God will help the city of flowers ever to flourish anew.

In another poem, written after the victory over Milan at Governale in 1397, Bruscaccio urged the Florentines to grasp the opportunity God and Fortune had given them, and he drew the parallel with the position of Rome during the wars with Carthage:

You are Rome, and the Duke is Hannibal.
If you will, transmit
To the people the light of freedom in their state.
This rejected dog
Ought to be destroyed; it will please God.
And peace for all Italy will follow.

· · · · ·

But above all, Florence is such
That in her power
I have my hope, as in a mighty tower. . . .[69]

[68] O bella donna mia, o bel paese,
    O voi c' avete le sue trecce in mano,
    Gentile o ppopolano,
    Sia qual si vuole, ascolti il mio latino
    Non ricercate le passate offese;

· · · · ·

No lle scenpiate la dorata chioma,
    Non vulnerate i dilicati membri,
    Sicché non si dismembri
    Da voi la giusta spada e lla colonna.

Medin, "Le rime," pp. 222-23

[69] Voi siete Roma, e Anibàle è il Duca.
    Se volete riluca
    Liberamente il popol loro stato,
    Questo can rinneghato
    Convien che ssie disfatto, ch'a dDio piace,
    E seguiranne a tutta Ytalia pace.

· · · · ·

Ma sopra tutto la tal mia Fiorença

Similarly, the anonymous author of a dialogue between Florence and the neighboring town of Colle has Florence draw this parallel between Rome and herself:

> Rome did not reign without great suffering
> by her citizens, who staked their possessions and their lives
> in order to gain possession of the world.
>
> Her example and my own good leads me
> to defend myself to the utmost, and indeed removes
> all fear. Ah, be united with me!
>
> and you will see me over all
> our defeated and weary enemies, garbed
> with garlands of olives in white robes.[70]

Such appeals for unity in the interest of Florentine power and glory did not succeed in stifling the voices of social protest; but even the prophecies show a new concern for reconciliation and a broader, civic point of view. In one which styled itself "Some little flowers drawn from the Apocalypse" the conflicts in the city were blamed upon the attempts of certain persons to make the burden of the laws fall upon the weak rather than the strong.[71] But the humble people

---

> Che nella sua potença
> Ò mia sperança come 'n salda torre; . . .

"Cançon del detto Bruscaccio quando fu rotto il duca di Melano a Mantova," *ibid.*, pp. 224-26. Cf. the remark made by Leonardo Bruni in 1415 in his *History of the Florentine People*, that " 'in our time' Florence had reached the point where Rome stood after her victory over Carthage." Baron, *Crisis*, p. 370.

[70]
> Roma non imperò senza gran doglie
> de' suoi, che poser l'avere et la vita
> per por del mondo in lei tutte le spoglie.
>
> Il suo exemplo et lo mio ben m'invita
> ad farne ogni difesa, et sì me toglie
> ogni timore. Deh sia pur meco unita!
>
> et vedra' mi vestita
> sopra i nostri nimici vinti et stanchi
> con ghirlanda d'ulivo in panni bianchi.

Orazio Bacci ed., "Due sonetti politici in figura di Colle e Firenze," *Miscellanea storica della Valdelsa*, II (1894), 6. The dating is uncertain. Bacci thinks they were written between 1399-1402, but other possibilities are 1429, 1447, and 1452.

[71] "Qui si cominciano alquanti fioretti tratti del' Apocalisa," MS BNF, Magl.

were also to blame, for they had abandoned "the straight way" and therefore had been led into deception. As a consequence, the "city of the flowers," ordinarily such a good example to others, had fallen ill, and her internal weakness made it difficult for her to maintain her position abroad. She was at the mercy of the great rich foreigner who, raised from lowly origins to royal dignity, was taking castles and cities by deception, including "the city of P" (Pisa) and "the city of L" (Lucca). Nevertheless, Florence would ultimately come into her own. She was called "the lion" because of her nobility;[72] she was also the queen and princess of other cities. After the death of one who represented the apostolic way, Judas and his followers would be discovered, the traitors to God and the commune would be finished, and the city of flowers would become a new center of lordship, liberty, and grace. Florence, the daughter of Rome, would recover from her sickness with the aid of the French, who would help her put down the German Eagle, the Ghibellines, and their followers, including the Pisans, and the lion would be lord and master of the other cities around her. Prayers would be sung and good works performed, for the just would be separated from the sinners. A new pastor would arise, one who would be solicitous for his flock and for the freedom of the friends of Peter's See, and Holy Church would nourish the children of the daughter of Rome and of the Gauls and create them anew.

This prophecy carried on the Ciompi tradition of popular aspirations for social justice; all those who favored a government of force and exploited the people would be driven out and their palaces ruined. But the point of view has changed from that of the earlier prophecies of the Ciompi era. Here the prophet involves the *popolo* in the responsibility for civic strife and shows his concern for the effect of internal dissension on Florence's position abroad. He vents his hatred not only upon the oppressors of the poor but also upon the "great foreigner" who is destroying the liberty of the Italians by means of his deceit—an obvious reference to Gian Galeazzo Visconti of Milan, who died in 1402. As a Florentine of Guelf sympathies,

---

XXXV, 173, fols. 1 verso–6 recto. The prophecy purports to be based upon a nonexistent 35th chapter of Revelation.

[72] The lion (*marzocco*) was, of course, a common symbol for Florence.

the author of the prophecy attacks not only the Ghibellines but also all those who favor a government of oppression rather than liberty and all those who forget that the chief responsibility of citizenship is the civic good, and on this ground he criticizes the lowly as well as the great. Referring to the example of Rome he points out how the tiny house of Romulus had become the bastion and ruler of the world and prevailed as long as it loved the common good and served "the commune" in unity and liberty.

So it was that under the double pressure of civic discord and foreign aggression the mythic Florence of the Guelfs and the prophetic Florence of the Fraticelli and Ciompi tended to coalesce. Good government and piety, social justice and power, temporal and religious leadership—Rome and Jerusalem—were blended in a single vision which seems to have functioned both as a model of a civic ethos and as a promise of ultimate rewards.[73] From its inception in the early fifteenth century this vision continued to serve as an inspiration to the city's prophets, orators, and poets. In the rhyming prophecy "Awake o proud lion to my loud cry," one of the many prophecies ascribed to St. Bridget of Sweden but clearly of fifteenth-century Florentine origin,[74] we see Florence arising from her struggle with

[73] For a different view, that the Ciompi rising "had left no traces that might have shaped the outlook and culture of the citizenry about 1400," see Baron, *Crisis*, p. 8.

[74] I am speaking here of the versions found in Florence; it is highly likely that other versions originated elsewhere since these prophecies conform to a few basic types. On political prophecies generally, see Rupert Taylor, *The Political Prophecy in England* (New York, 1911), which, notwithstanding its title, contains some information on continental sources; Reeves, *The Influence of Prophecy in the Later Middle Ages*; and, for the continued use of political prophecy long after our period, see Harry Rusche, "Prophecies and Propaganda, 1641 to 1651," *English Historical Review*, LXXXIV (1969), 752-70. On St. Bridget, see Johannes Jørgensen, *Saint Bridget of Sweden*, trans. Ingeborg Lund (London, 1954). The ms used here is BNF Magl. VII, 1081, fols. 12-15, 56-57, entitled "Prophetia di Sancta Brigida [del judicio che debbe venire sopra Toscana]." Another copy, in ms BNF II. IX. 125, ends, "Finita la profetia di sancta Brigida la quale tratta di quella a' da venire dal 1460 infino al 1470, ridotta in volgare in versi da Iacopo da Montepulciano mentre era nelle carcere del Comune di Firenze." This is attributed to Iacopo by Angelo Messini, "Profetismo e profezie ritmiche italiane d'ispirazione gioachimito-francescane nei sec. XIV e XV," *Miscellanea francescana*, XXXVIII (1937), 50. On Iacopo da

Milan. Milan the serpent would be in great trouble; the See of Peter would lose the keys; but Florence, lying pregnant in a feverish sleep, would give birth, whereupon every hatred and bitter pain would disappear. In the new age she would shed her old skin and have a joyous peace.

"The Bridget prophecy" expressed the more independent Florentine spirit that had been developing since the war with the Pope in 1375 and particularly since the city's successful resistance against Milan; but it did not voice an unrestrained imperialism. While the prophet took a more positive view of Florence's right to hegemony over her neighbors than the Guelfs of the previous century, he nevertheless shared the older view that justice and moderation were more important than unlimited power, and he advised Florence to limit her territorial ambitions.[75] In most instances, however, moderation gave way to enthusiasm for the unlimited possibilities of Florence's destiny. The death-bed dictum ascribed to Cosimo de' Medici in 1464, that kings and other peoples would turn to Florence for counsel on how to govern, until all Italy was under her dominion, was merely a restatement of what the prophecies had by then been saying for decades.[76] In the vision of Fra Antonio da Rieti, a prophecy that survives in many fifteenth-century manuscripts, the Florentine Lily is seen putting out ever more beautiful branches, flowers, and leaves until it has covered all of Italy,[77] an image that the Savona-

---

Montepulciano, see Guido Laccagnini, *Giornale storico della letteratura italiana*, LXXXVI (1925), 225-88.

[75] Ma ben convien che torni a suoi confini
  Et viva in più letitia
  In soda e gran giustitia
  Insieme tengha.

"Prophetia di Sancta Brigida," MS BNF Magl. VII, 1081, fol. 14 recto.

[76] Warman Welliver, *L'impero fiorentino* (Florence, 1957), pp. 42-43. While I am not convinced by Welliver's characterization of a "Florentine theology" and his ascription to Lorenzo de' Medici of a conscious design for a Florentine "empire" and a Florentine church, I think he has done more than anyone to show the importance of the mythical Florence in the culture of the Laurentian period. See also Chastel, *Art et humanisme*, p. 4.

[77] *Copia d'una rivelazione che ebbe frate Antonio da Rieti dell'ordine di Sancto Francescho de Frati Observanti* (Florence, n.d.). For a description see *British Museum Catalogue of Books Printed in the Fifteenth Century*, vol. VI,

rolans would later employ repeatedly. In another prophecy that begins, "The bear arises from tribulation," Florence the daughter of Rome is envisioned as the "mistress and capital" of all those around her,[78] while one of the prophecies attributed to Merlin predicts that she will become head (*capo*) of all Italy. In all three, Florentine leadership is associated with a coming age of spiritual perfection and peace, although each has a somewhat different idea of what the new age will be like. Fra Antonio prophesied that the Pope would fly to the protection of the Lily, that is, of Florence. Italy would have peace for five hundred years; the Cross would extend its arms from West to East; Antichrist would appear and be vanquished; all human labor would cease. In "The bear of tribulation" the emphasis was on the Church's renunciation of all its claims to temporal power and on Florence's rise from her bed of pain to become the Nest of Christ the eagle[79]—another image later used by certain Piagnoni. While the Merlin prophecy was unusual in predicting the ultimate triumph of the German emperor over the Church and "the Gauls," the first two persisted in the traditional Florentine Gallophilism, each envisioning some form of a joint Franco-Florentine hegemony.

Similar themes appear in the rhetoric of some of the Republic's paid orators and poets of the period. Thus, Stefano Porcari, a humanist civil servant who was Florentine *capitano del popolo* in 1427,[80] in a public oration urged the Florentines to fulfill their destiny: "And acting in this way [i.e. for the common good] you will see this your most fortunate rule (*imperio*) continually flourish: you will see this broad leadership (*amplissimo principato*) ever enlarge itself: you will see the triumphant name of Florence grow in the world in ever more honored fame, and earn the veneration of all

---

p. 631. The following MS texts date the vision 1422: MS BNF Magl. XXV, 344, fol. 33 recto; and VII, 1081, fol. 29 recto.

[78] "Lievassi l'orsa della tribolatione dove ella sia stata," MS BNF Magl. XXV, 344, fols. 31-2 recto; and VII, 1081, fol. 28.

[79] MS BNF Magl. XXV, 344, fol. 24 recto.

[80] See Baron, *Crisis*, pp. 434-35. The orations have been attributed to Buonaccorso da Montemagno (on whom see *Crisis*, p. 557), by G.B.C. Giuliari ed., *Prose del giovane Buonaccorso da Montemagno* (Bologna, 1874), pp. xvi-xviii; but this is not generally accepted and is, in fact, refutable by internal evidence, e.g., the sixth oration, where the speaker refers to himself as "Stefano vostro," *Prose*, p. 68.

peoples."[81] And in another public address: "Uniting so many hearts in one heart, so many wills in a single will, so many powers in one power, from which are formed a richness, a power, a fame universal . . . this most beautiful Republic is formed, which we possess by the grace of God."[82] Similarly, in 1434 Antonio di Meglio, the herald of the Republic, addressed "the Florentine people so glorious" who could observe their own ascendancy, their "great power dominating others";[83] while in 1442, at the time of another crisis with Milan, Anselmo di Gioacchino Calderoni rallied Florence as "the queen and lady of liberty to whom Italy bears reverence" and pictured the branches of the Florentine Lily flowering over every other palm and green olive:

> This lady whom you now must lead
> Wishes to show you her government
> which has taken its happy and holy birth
> from that eternal choir.[84]

Thus the myth of Florence's great destiny had, by the mid-fifteenth century, at the latest, become a conscious tool of official civic rhetoric; but it was an official rhetoric that seems to have corresponded to a felt need and a real faith among the Florentines, judging from its agreement with the more spontaneous and popularly oriented prophecies. These, neither abandoning their aspirations for social justice and a reformed clergy, nor identifying with a single class or interest, as the prophets of the late fourteenth century had done, promised the joy of possessing divine favor in the form of power and glory for the Republic, if its citizens would serve the common good.

The dominance of these themes of civic concord combined with self-assertion abroad coincided remarkably closely with the period

---

[81] "E così facendo vedrete sempre questo vostro fortunatissimo imperio fiorire: vedrete questo amplissimo principato sempre magnificarsi: vedrete il trionfante nome di Firenze crescere nel mondo sempre in fama degnissima, e meritar venerazione di tutti i popoli." *Prose*, ed. Giuliari, p. 26.

[82] *Ibid.*, p. 44.

[83] Francesco Flamini, *La lirica toscana del Rinascimento anteriore ai tempi del Magnifico* (Pisa, 1891), p. 100.

[84] *Ibid.*, note, p. 215. Calderoni was substituting for the regular herald, Antonio di Meglio, who was ill (p. 213).

of Cosimo de' Medici's leadership, 1434-64.[85] By contrast, the prophecies of the years immediately following Cosimo's death in 1464 give voice once more to social discontent and to aspirations of civic freedom, sometimes even to direct attack upon Medici domination. One text, ascribed to the thirteenth-century poet, Jacopone da Todi but obviously composed much later, foretold the "cruel sentence" that would be passed in the year " '70," when the lovely lady, full of envious and rapacious citizens, would suffer from a general pestilence and her wicked inhabitants would be driven out by a dragon, against whom, in turn, all Christians would rise up. Florence, like the phoenix, would go up in flames before recreating herself with her own people, but "no physicians (Medici) will be found who will make trial of so many ills."[86] Ultimately, "honest government" would be restored to the city, but she would never recover her former power, for all the cities of Tuscany would recover their liberty and she would live in peace with all of them. The "cruel sentence"

[85] On the themes of civic liberty and glory in the contemporary humanist eulogies of Cosimo, see Alison M. Brown, "The Humanist Portrait of Cosimo de' Medici Pater Patriae," *Journal of the Warburg and Courtauld Institutes*, XXIV (1961), 186-221. Cosimo himself may have been instrumental in the projection of such themes in contemporary Florentine civic art. In a most interesting study Saul Levine argues that Donatello's bronze *David* was commissioned by Cosimo to symbolize his personal triumph in 1434 and that this reflects a similar meaning in the David and Goliath panel of Ghiberti's *Doors of Paradise* for the Florentine Baptistery, with the Jerusalem of the background an idealized Florence. (See Plate 3.) According to Dr. Levine this is part of the iconographic tradition from which the republican symbolism of the Savonarola period later emerged as well as part of the background for Michelangelo's portrayal of David the giant-killer guarding Florence's liberty against the enemies of the Republic in 1501. Saul Levine, *"Tal cosa*: Michelangelo's *David*—Its Form, Site and Political Symbolism" (Ph.D. diss., Faculty of Philosophy, Columbia University, 1969), especially pp. 110-11. For arguments against the contention—first advanced by Vasari—that the bronze *David* was commissioned by Cosimo de' Medici, and for a discussion of its meaning, see H. W. Janson, *The Sculpture of Donatello* (Princeton, 1963), pp. 81-86.

[86]   Medici non si truova
      Per far si gran pruova
      Di tanti mali

MS BNF Magl. VII, 40, fol. 46 verso. See also the pessimistic expectations in a brief "Epistola exortatoria in angustis temporibus," dated 1464, in MS BNF Magl. VII, 1081, fols. 53 verso–54 recto.

of the dragon doubtless referred to the Turkish attacks of the 1470's; the dragon was a conventional symbol for both Turks and Antichrist. In the prediction that "honest government" would return to Florence we have, perhaps, an echo of the republican conspiracy of 1466.[87] In this prophecy anti-despotism was linked with anti-imperialism in the manner of the Guelfs of old. More often, however, the aspirations for freedom in the period were coupled with ambitious dreams of Florentine power and spiritual leadership, as in the "Vision of the Holy Hermit of the Year 1400." This prophet saw the Florentine lion beset with difficulties: Pisa was continually trying to break her bonds; Arezzo would have liked to do the same; Lucca was menacing. Within Florence herself the "bad seed" was sown and the swords of the people would cut cruelly. In all of Italy there would be popular upheavals and great havoc. The emperor would come to Italy to be crowned and all would tremble, while the Castilians would come by sea. Tuscans and Lombards would become embroiled with them and the most terrible wars in history would take place. But Florence would be victorious: the "flowery lily" would grow, and those who disobeyed her would suffer; she would play a leading role in the New Church and she would have great wealth and power:

> Your power will spread to Rome
> And you will have that part of her
> That the New Church will grant you.

> You will be in complete harmony with her
> In perfect friendship
> Thus, all your paths will be guided.

> The pastor will leave his court

[87] On this conspiracy, called "del Poggio," see Guido Pampaloni, "Fermenti di riforme democratiche nella Firenze medicea del Quattrocento," *Archivio storico italiano*, CXIX (1961), 11-62, 241-81; A. Municchi, *La fazione antimedicea detta del Poggio* (Florence, 1911). On the other hand, see the poem of Niccolò di Cristofano Risorboli in praise of Piero di Cosimo de' Medici in which the traditional themes of liberty and the extension of Florentine hegemony are identified with Medici power, in Flamini, *La lirica toscana*, p. 145, n. 2:

> Tu se' el mio Petro, et sopra questa petra
> ò rinovato il tempio a libertate.

Where he ordinarily stays
And come to rest in the city of the flowers.

. . . . .

The city will grow in great measure
of riches and possessions
And will have pleasure and good government. . . .[88]

The troubled decade of the 1490's produced an outpouring of prophecies. The death of Lorenzo the Magnificent on April 8, 1492 was accompanied by signs and portents which, at least in retrospect, seemed to foretell the evils that came afterwards.[89] Lorenzo was succeeded as ruler of Florence by his son, Piero, who alienated the patricians whose support he needed and mismanaged the diplomatic balance which was the key to Florentine security. The peace of Italy was threatened by the growing rivalry between the great Italian states and by the impending invasion of Charles VIII of France. By the time Charles succeeded to the French throne in 1483 he was already being linked to the "Great Enterprise" of conquering Italy and crusading against the Infidel.[90] Prophecies in the tradition of the Second Charlemagne legend appeared, envisaging a great reli-

---

[88] Distenderassi tua potentia a roma
Et parte harai di quella
Che la chiesa novella   Tel consente.

Sarai cum lei daccordo pienamente
In perfecta amistade
Cosi tucte tue strade fieno scorte.

Partirassi el pastor della sua corte
Donde uso distare
Verrassi ariposare   Nella citta fiorita.
. . . . .
Crescera la citta per piu misure
Di richezza e d' havere
Staranno in piacere   Et buono stato

MS BNF Magl. VII, 40, fols. 36 verso–37; and Magl. VII, 1081, fols. 49 verso–53. I cite the latter, fol. 51 verso. The prophecy in the third stanza may refer to the residence of Pope Eugenius IV in Florence in the decade 1434-43.

[89] See, for example, the ending of Machiavelli's *Florentine History* and, for an illuminating discussion of the sixteenth century *elogia* of Lorenzo, Felix Gilbert, "Guicciardini, Machiavelli, Valori on Lorenzo Magnifico," *Renaissance News*, XI (1958), 107-14.

[90] Henri F. Delaborde, *L'expédition de Charles VIII en Italie* (Paris, 1888), pp. 312-18. See below, pp. 112-14.

gious reform and a universal French monarchy.[91] By 1492 the King and his counsellors were making their plans and laying the diplomatic groundwork for the invasion of Italy.[92] Among the Italians too, the impending invasion of the French preoccupied prophets as well as diplomats. In 1491 in Rome a street preacher "of unknown nationality, poorly dressed, like a mendicant," warned that the tribulations would begin in Rome in that very year. In 1492 they would spread to the rest of Italy; all the cities would lose their freedom and their territory. In 1493 the clergy would be deprived of their temporal power (*clericus absque temporali dominatione reperietur*) and the Angelic Pastor would come.[93] In the Kingdom of Naples a prophecy attributed to St. Cataldus, legendary bishop of Taranto, was "discovered"; it predicted the French invasion, a world war between believers and unbelievers, and the appearance of an avenging angel who would bring about a universal renewal in the year 1510.[94]

To the Florentines the prospect of the French invasion was an agony. Florence had been a "French city" since the days of the Guelf alliances of the thirteenth century. She honored Charlemagne as her second founder and her prophets linked her with the coming of a new Charles who would make the Florentine *giglio* flourish along with the French *fleur de lis*. The connection was based on material interest as well as political ideology: Florence's business connections with France were at least as old as her political ones;

---

[91] *Ibid.*, pp. 313-15.　　　　　[92] *Ibid.*, pp. 236ff.

[93] Stefano Infessura, *Diario della città di Roma*, ed. O. Tommasini, *Fonti per la storia d' Italia*, Vol. V (Rome, 1890), pp. 264-65. See also Paul O. Kristeller, "Marsilio Ficino e Lodovico Lazzarelli," *Annali della R. Scuola Normale Superiore di Pisa, Lettere, Storia e Filosofia*, 2nd ser., VII (1938), 237-62. On the tradition of the prophecy of the Angelic Pastor see Friedrich Baethgen, *Der Engelpapst* (Halle, 1933).

[94] Piero Parenti noted it in his Florentine history under May 1492. Parenti, *Storia fiorentina*, ed. Schnitzer, p. 4. It was also mentioned in Florence by Bernardo Vettori, who coupled it with Savonarola's prophecies and prophecies of the Crusade, in a letter to Piero Guicciardini, May 7, 1492. See the letter in Roberto Ridolfi, *Studi savonaroliani* (Florence, 1935), p. 107. For other contemporary references and the whole question of the genesis and fortune of the Cataldus prophecy, see Giampaolo Tognetti, "Le fortune della pretesa profezia di San Cataldo," *Bullettino dell'Istituto Storico Italiano per il Medio Evo e Archivio Muratoriano*, no. 80 (1968), pp. 273-317.

her merchants and bankers had more than their share of lucrative French markets for Florentine cloth and capital. To them a break with France was unthinkable. Yet a break with France was exactly what appeared to be coming. In the quarrel with King Ferrante of Naples, which had induced Lodovico *il Moro* of Milan to seek French intervention, Piero de' Medici had taken the side of Ferrante. Now, although continuing to protest his friendliness toward the French king, Piero refused to abandon his ally to the south. For over a year French emissaries in Florence had been working to gain the city's support for the enterprise, while from the French court the city's own envoys were advising Piero to grant the King's request for free passage for his army through Tuscany. But Piero went his own way.[95]

To the warnings of the diplomats were added the threats of the prophecies. The *Prophetia Caroli Imperatoris* castigated Florence for having deserted the French, for in doing so she had also abandoned the divine cause which the New Charlemagne would carry forward. Because of this desertion the invaders would destroy Florence as well as Rome.[96] While this prophecy was probably of French origin,[97] the same forebodings were expressed in its Italian counterparts. The Bridget prophecy, for example, appeared once again, predicting that the French king would bring about a renewal of the Church, but that Florence would suffer famine, foreign rule and a popular uprising in which many people would die. Florence would seek help from a league, but to no avail; she would grieve forever.[98] Other apocalypses predicted religious reform and world renewal but

---

[95] For the diplomatic sources on Florentine negotiations with France at this time see A. Desjardins and G. Canestrini, *Négociations diplomatiques de la France avec la Toscane*, vol. I (Paris, 1859). The standard history of the French expedition is H. F. Delaborde, *L'expédition de Charles VIII en Italie* (Paris, 1883). For a good summary of the Florentine situation on the eve of the invasion, see Schnitzer, *Savonarola*, vol. I, pp. 170-78, and below, pp. 118-31.

[96] *Prophetia Caroli Imperatoris con altre prophetie de diversi santi huomini* (n.p. or d.). Copy in BNF, Guicciardini, 2-3-57.

[97] This seems to be the same prophecy as the one entitled *La prophetie de Charles VIII*, attributed to Guilloche de Bordeaux. Schnitzer, *Savonarola*, vol. I, p. 165.

[98] This is a group entitled "Rasmo di Viterbo 1420." One version is in MS BNF Magl. VIII, 1443, fols. 27-28, another in MS BNF II, 130, fols. 153-54.

also omitted the traditional vision of a special role for Florence.[99]

At the end of August 1494 Charles VIII led his army over the Alps into Italy. Meeting no resistance, he reached the northern borders of Florentine territory by the end of October. Piero de' Medici's stubborn courage abandoned him; his capitulation and downfall quickly followed.[100] As the French army approached the city a certain "devout monk" recorded his prediction of the city's fate in a vision which, he said, he based on "the Prophet Daniel, St. John the Evangelist in the Apocalypse, St. Bridget, and other old prophets." The world, he wrote, stood at the beginning of the fourth age, the age of scourge which had been predicted to begin "after the year '76." The cities of Italy would be visited with great punishment. Florence, the lovely lady with her beautiful lily and her wise people, would weep for her beautiful daughter, Pisa, who would be seized by the proud lion. Many of her people would cover the ground with their blood, while the French king would camp just outside her San Frediano gate before entering to devastate her. Furious with their leaders, the people would rise up and overthrow the government, but "according to the prophet who speaks here" they would be set upon an evil path. After wreaking havoc in Florence the French king would go on to Rome where he would persecute the Bride of Christ and sack the city. For this, and for refusing to go on crusade against the Turks and pagans, he would be excommunicated; but after three and a half years he would see the error of his ways and fulfill his mission to establish Christianity among the pagans. At last, on the Mount of Olives he would give up his power, leaving to the Church a larger patrimony than even Constantine had done, while the Archangel Michael would come to announce an era of peace and religious reform under a new Emperor and a new pastor who would reign together in mutual love.[101]

This vision of the "devout monk" could have been written only

[99] "Versiculus hic qui in 76 psalmo Voce Mea ad dominum clamavi. . . ." MS BNF Magl. VII, 1081, fol. 45 verso; *Quest' e il Judicio Generale* (n.p. or d.); "De adventu antichristi," MS BNF Magl. XXXIX, 86, fol. 76 verso–78 recto.

[100] See above, pp. 27-28 and, in more detail, below, pp. 130-34.

[101] MS BNF Magl. VII, 1081, fols. 57 verso–60 verso; and Magl. VII, 40, fols. 18–32 verso.

at the moment in November when the French army was in fact approaching the San Frediano gate and the Florentines were awaiting their punishment for having abandoned their old Guelf alliance. Based on the Second Charlemagne prophecy, it reflects the Florentines' fear of this new Charles. Thus the monk turns on the French king, predicts his apostasy, even suggests that Charles VIII would play the part of Antichrist, persecuting the Church for three and a half years before finally submitting to the divine chastisement and fulfilling his apocalyptic role. For Florence the monk holds out no hope: the old Guelf partnership seemed dissolved forever; the promise of Florentine glory had come to nothing; the myth of Florence seems to have run its course.

It is very likely that "the prophet who speaks here" to whom the monk refers was the city's Advent preacher, Fra Girolamo Savonarola, who was indeed predicting that the Florentines would be set upon "an evil path." Never an advocate of the myth of Florentine glory, Savonarola had, on the contrary, long warned that God was preparing a scourge for all Italy in which Florence would go down with the others. Now he spoke with the authority of a prophet who had lived to see his own words come true, and so it was to him, in this time of deep trouble, that the Florentines turned to hear more of what God had in store for them.

II

The Making of the Prophet

AND SO, CHOOSING ME, USELESS AND UNWORTHY AMONG ALL HIS
SERVANTS, FOR THIS MINISTRY, HE ARRANGED FOR
ME TO COME TO FLORENCE

—Savonarola, *Compendium Revelationum*

DURING the three and one-half years of Savonarola's ascendancy
in Florence he maintained that he had a divine mission to begin
there the work of conversion which would lead to the reform of the
Church and the world. Many Florentines believed in this mission
too. How, in the midst of crisis, they came to believe it is a story
often told. How Savonarola himself came to believe it, how a repentance preacher, a "foreigner," a prophet of universal destruction and
doom, came to think of Florence as God's chosen city—these are
questions that have scarcely been asked, let alone answered. From
his own day to ours the crucial period of November-December 1494
has been seen as a turning point in Savonarola's life as well as in the
life of the city, for this was the time when he came into his own as a
prophet and a civic reformer. Everyone seems to have remained
unaware, however, that this was a turning point for Savonarola's
prophetic message as well as for his civic career; it was only during
those days of crisis that his millenarian vision took shape. The glorious prospect of his new vision was very different from the catastrophic sufferings with which he had been threatening the Florentines. Once Savonarola had established his credit as a true prophet
by successfully predicting the misfortunes of Florence and Italy, he
drew upon that credit to launch the Florentines on a program which
was based upon a very different kind of prediction.

If this was a paradox it was one of which Savonarola himself seems to have been less than fully aware. The first time he publicly reviewed the story of his prophetic mission was in his famous "Renovation Sermon" of January 13, 1495; already he had come to think of his illumination as complete from the very first, and of his mission to Florence as inseparable from that illumination:

> But I tell you, Florence, that this light has been given to me for you and not for myself; because this is not the light that makes man acceptable to God. And I want you to know that I began to see this more than fifteen years ago, perhaps twenty, but it is ten years since I have begun to talk about it. First at Brescia, when I preached there, I said something. Then God permitted me to come to Florence, which is the navel of Italy, in order that you might give notice of it to all the other cities of Italy; but you, Florence, have with your ears heard not me but God.[1]

The following summer, as his enemies in the city began to marshal their forces and Pope Alexander VI in Rome began to press him to give an account of himself,[2] Savonarola wrote and published his *Compendium Revelationum*, a summary of his visions and his prophecies which begins with a more detailed résumé of his career. Since this account has had so much influence on biographers and historians, and because it tells us so much about how Savonarola viewed himself and his career, we shall quote it at length:

> Almighty God, seeing that the sins of Italy continue to multiply, especially those of her princes, both ecclesiastical and secular, and unable to bear them any longer, decided to cleanse His Church with a mighty scourge. And since, as the Prophet Amos says, the Lord God does nothing without first revealing His secret to His servants, the prophets [Amos 3:7], He wanted this scourge to be foretold in Italy for the welfare of His chosen people, so that, forewarned, they might prepare, the better to withstand it. Since Florence lies in the center of Italy as the heart of a man, God deigned to choose her for the task of making the proclamation, whence it would be spread abroad to the other parts of Italy. And we have seen this come to pass in our time.

[1] Girolamo Savonarola, *Prediche sopra i Salmi*, vol. I, ed. Vincenzo Romano (Rome, 1969), p. 41.
[2] On the writing of the *Compendium Revelationum*, see Roberto Ridolfi, *The Life of Girolamo Savonarola*, trans. Cecil Grayson (New York, 1959), especially p. 135.

And so, choosing me, useless and unworthy among all His servants, for this ministry, He arranged for me to come to Florence on the orders of my superiors in the Year of our Lord, 1489. And in the same year, on Sunday, August 1, I began publicly to expound the Book of the Apocalypse in our Church of San Marco. During that whole year, preaching to the Florentine people, I continually set forth three things: first, that the renovation of the Church would come about in these times; second, that all of Italy would be mightily scourged before God brought about this renovation; third, that these two things would come about soon. I labored to prove these three conclusions by rational arguments, by figures from the Holy Scriptures, and by other analogies and parables that can only be derived from the Scriptures. I argued on the basis of this kind of reasoning for the time being and did not reveal that I had learned of these things from God in another manner, since it seemed to me that your minds were not yet ready for a revelation of mysteries. However, in the years following, judging that your minds were better prepared to believe, I sometimes disclosed to you some vision, not revealing that it was a prophetic vision, but only proposing it in the manner of parable. Then, because I was afraid, seeing that men on all sides were inclined to oppose and mock me, I frequently made up my mind to leave off and to preach other things, but I was unable to do so, for whatever other reading and study I turned to grew wearisome, and however much I thought and tried to preach about other matters the more I failed, until I grew angry with myself. I recall that while preaching in the Church of Santa Reparata in Florence in 1490 I decided to suppress a sermon on visions of this sort which I had prepared for the second Sunday of Lent, and to abstain from such matters thereafter. But, as God is my witness, I dragged through the whole preceding Saturday and the whole of the following night, sleepless, until daylight. At last every approach seemed closed to me and every alternative blocked, so that I absolutely knew not where to turn. At daybreak, as I was praying, wearied by my long wakefulness, a voice came to me: "Fool! Do you not see that God wants you to announce these things in this way?" Wherefore that morning I delivered a terrifying sermon.

My faithful listeners also know how I expounded the Scriptures according to the condition of the present times. One thing above all convinced the most intelligent and learned men, and that is that from the year 1490 until the year 1494, through every Advent and Lent with the exception of one in Bologna, I continually preached on Genesis, always beginning where I had left off in my last sermon either of

Advent or of Lent; and I was not able to arrive at the chapter on the Flood until after the present tribulations had begun. I thought that I would be able to explain the mystery of the building of Noah's Ark in a few days, but so many things about this building occurred to me every day that I spent the whole of Advent and Lent of 1494 on the secret meaning of it. Then, by God's will and guidance, leaving off where it reads, "Make it with lower, second and third decks" [Genesis 6:16], the following September, on the Feast of Saint Matthew the Apostle, I resumed with the next text, "For behold, I will bring a flood of waters upon the earth" [Genesis 6:17]. As soon as I began my sermon with the words, "For behold, I will bring a flood of waters upon the earth," many were astonished, suddenly realizing that God's secret impulse had given this part of Genesis to fit the times, since everyone knew then that the King of the Gauls had invaded Italy with his army. Among them was Count Giovanni della Mirandola, a man unique in our times for his intellect and breadth of learning, who was terrified upon hearing these words and later told me that his hair had stood on end.

But to return to my subject: in those first years I made predictions about the future with the support of Scripture alone, with reasons and a variety of parables, because the people were unprepared. Then I began to reveal that I knew these future events by a different light than that of the understanding of Scripture alone. At last I began to disclose the matter more openly, admitting that my words were divinely inspired. One of the things I repeated often was, "Thus says the Lord God, 'The sword of the Lord over the earth swiftly and soon,'" and another was "Let the just rejoice and exult, prepare your minds against temptation by reading, meditation and prayer, and free yourselves from a second death. And you, O slaves, worthless in your vileness, for now you may continue to besmirch yourselves. Let your bellies be filled with wine, your kidneys be rotted with excess, and your hands be stained with the blood of the poor, for this is your portion and your lot. But know that your bodies and your souls are in my hands and soon your bodies will be worn out by the scourges and your souls I will hand over to the eternal fire." These words were not from the Holy Scriptures, as some thought, but newly come forth from heaven just at that time. And since a single vision contains many words of this kind sent from heaven I only disclosed as much as seemed necessary—and that clothed in a vision—to show by whose command had come the words I was proclaiming publicly, lest the unbelievers laugh.

[Savonarola goes on to describe how, in a night during Advent of 1492, he had seen a vision: a hand holding a sword in the sky with the inscription *Gladius Domini super terram cito et velociter* (see Plate 4); a great voice issuing from three faces surrounded by a single light that called upon him to convert before the coming of the divine punishment; a multiude of angels in white descending from heaven to earth, offering men red crosses and white mantles which some accepted and some rejected; the hand brandishing the sword over the earth filling the air with dense clouds, swords, hail, frightful thunder, arrows, and fire, while on the lovely earth itself arose wars, plague, famine and innumerable other tribulations.]

After that [vision], I predicted, also by divine inspiration, the crossing of the Alps into Italy of some one like Cyrus [II Chronicles 36:2]. . . . I also warned Italy not to put her trust in her fortresses or towers, for he would conquer them against any resistance. To the Florentines I predicted—with special hints to those who were governing at the time— that they would choose a policy that would be contrary to their own safety and advantage while clinging to what is weaker and defeatist, and that they would lose all their good judgment just as if they were drunken. . . . I pass over those predictions I made privately about individuals. It was not seemly to reveal them, lest they stir up public scandal; but I did make them known at the time to some of my confidants. For example, I predicted the time appointed for the death of Innocent VIII and of Lorenzo de' Medici, also the revolution of the Florentine government at the time when the King of France would first approach Pisa, and many other things which, if I wished to recount them now would perhaps not be believed, since they were not generally made known at the time.

Then, as the King of the French was approaching and a revolution in the Florentine state was imminent, although His sword had appeared to me, as well as the great spilling of blood in this city, nevertheless, asking myself why God had especially chosen her as the place for these things to be predicted, I began fervently to hope that this prophecy was not without some conditions, that if the people were repentant most indulgent God might abate at least a part of His judgment. Thus, on November 1, All Saints Day, and on the two days following, I spared neither voice nor lungs, and (as everyone knows) I cried out so loudly from the pulpit as almost to wear myself out: . . . "O Italy, these adversities have come to you because of your sins, O Florence, these adversities have come to you because of your sins. O clergy, this tempest has arisen on your account." I repeated this continually, that Italy would be destroyed (*everteretur*) and Rome particularly, and declared these words revealed to me by the same spirit: "O nobles, O wise men, O humble folk, the mighty hand of God is upon you; neither power nor wisdom nor flight can withstand it. However, the Lord has been awaiting you, that He might show His pity to you. Convert, therefore, to the Lord your God with all your heart, because He is kind and compassionate. If you do not, He will avert his eyes from you forever."

[Savonarola goes on to recount his embassy on behalf of the city of Florence to King Charles VIII. In his address to the King he said that Charles was God's minister of justice, that he himself had long since been predicting Charles' coming, although God had not permitted him to mention the King by name. He urged Charles to fulfill his mission as God's agent by casting down the proud, lifting up the humble, overcoming vices, and reforming all that needed to be reformed. Finally, he asked the King's indulgence for the offenses of the Florentines, who did not know that Charles had been sent by God.]

. . . In the meantime the revolution of the Florentine state took place. Having, therefore, returned to the city, I began again to preach what all were able to understand with the aid of prayer and the yoke of repentance, how it was apparent that divine compassion had freed the Florentine people from its greatest perils. Continuing in this salutary vein, I said that the Florentines had still many dangerous shoals to cross, that they would yet be battered by other tribulations, and that all of Italy would be destroyed, but I did not reveal by whom, nor how, nor when. [I said that] there was no remedy for the prelates of the Church or the princes of Italy, but that repentance was all that remained. . . . I also added (since one barber would not suffice to scrape all of Italy clean) that others would come, this was certain. . . .

To this I added that the Turks and Moors would convert to Christianity in our time, saying: "many who are standing here will see this; this was revealed to me a long time ago." For in 1492 while I was preaching for Lent in the Basilica of San Lorenzo in Florence, I saw during the night of Good Friday two crosses. The first, a black one, stood in the midst of Rome, touching heaven, its arms extending to the whole world. On it were these words: *Crux irae Dei*. As soon as I had seen it the air grew dark with swift clouds and turbulent with a confusion of winds, lightning bolts, arrows, hail, fire, and swords. A vast crowd of people pressed together there so that only a few were left on earth. After a short time the air grew peaceful and clear, and I saw a golden cross in the midst of Jerusalem as tall and as shining as the other, so that it lighted up the whole world and filled it anew with flowers and joy. On it was this inscription: *Crux misericordiae Dei.* Quickly all the nations of the earth, men and women, gathered there to adore and to embrace it. I had many more visions, much clearer ones, on this theme, and I have frequently been supported with many visions and very clear illustrations of the other things I have spoken about, especially with respect to the renovation of the Church and the scourge. Further, I predicted that the city of Florence would be reformed to a better way of life and that this is the will of God and that the Florentine citizens would have to do it. Also I predicted, on behalf of God, that because of this the city herself would be more glorious, more powerful, richer than she had ever been before; and that this was intended by the divine will events themselves have proved. . . .[3]

Looking back from the summer of 1495, it must have seemed to Savonarola that all his past actions and utterances pointed straight to the crisis of November-December 1494 and that the coming of Charles VIII, the revolution in Florence, and the beginning of reform in the city confirmed what he had constantly been predicting and therefore proved that he was God's prophet, sent to Florence to preach the scourge and the renovation of the Church and the world. In the *Compendium* he was candid about his past inconsistencies; they were easily accounted for from the triumphant vantage point of 1495. If he had not always disclosed everything he knew, nor always confessed the prophetic source of his knowledge of the future, this was due to his very human weaknesses or to his consideration for the weaknesses of his audience. Sometimes, too, God had willed him to remain silent. If at first he had predicted worse tribulations for Florence than those she had actually suffered, this was because he had underestimated the full measure of the divine compassion. All this was now of slight importance compared to the conviction that from the first he had known that God had sent him to Florence to prophesy the renovation of the Church, the conversion of the world, and the future glories of this city.

[3] Savonarola published the work both in Italian and in Latin. I cite the Latin edition of Quetif, which is the most widely available. *Compendium Revelationum,* in Gianfrancesco Pico della Mirandola, *Vita R. P. Hieronymi Savonarolae,* ed. Jacques Quetif, 2 vols. (Paris, 1674), vol. I, pp. 225-45.

If, however, rather than look backward with Savonarola from the summer of 1495, we find our own way to the beginning of the story and work forward, we shall see things in a very different perspective. The *Compendium* account begins with Savonarola's arrival in Florence in 1489. This is misleading, although probably not intentionally so. Savonarola first came to Florence in 1482, not 1489,[4] and he remained there until 1487, at which time he was appointed Master of Studies in the *Studium Generale* of San Domenico in Bologna.[5] He was reassigned to Florence in 1490 (not 1489)[6] by his superiors at the request of Lorenzo de' Medici, and he began to preach on the Apocalypse to his brothers in San Marco. The beginnings of his career as a prophet coincided with neither his first nor his second arrival in Florence. Savonarola began preaching shortly after he first came to Florence in 1482, but he did not begin to prophesy then. When he did begin is a problem, for he himself gives conflicting accounts. In the "Renovation Sermon" of January 13, 1495, he says he had already begun "to see these things more than fifteen years ago, perhaps twenty"; this would take his first prophetic inspiration back to the years between 1475 and 1480. In the *Compendium*, however, he indicates that he began to prophesy before his arrival in Florence in 1489, but not long before. Still a third account comes from the record of his interrogation, when, in April 1498, he was imprisoned and put to the torture.[7] In his first published "confession" Savonarola tells how "about fifteen years earlier," that is, about 1484 during his first residence in Florence, while waiting for a fellow friar in the monastery of San Giorgio in Florence, he was thinking about a sermon he had been preparing when suddenly he conceived

---

[4] Joseph Schnitzer, *Savonarola*, trans. Ernesto Rutili, 2 vols. (Milan, 1931), vol. I, pp. 44, 49; Roberto Ridolfi, *Vita di Girolamo Savonarola*, 2 vols. (Rome, 1952), vol. II, pp. 90-91, nn. 45, 46.

[5] This has been established by Ridolfi, *Vita*, vol. I, p. 37 and n. 12.

[6] *Ibid.*, vol. I, p. 44. The discrepancy is less than it may seem, since, by the Florentine method of dating, the New Year began on March 25, and Savonarola returned to Florence in May or June. However, it is to be noted that Savonarola recalled the correct year in his first confession in 1498. Pasquale Villari, *La storia de Girolamo Savonarola e de suoi tempi*, 2 vols. (Florence, 1926), vol. II, appendix, p. cl. Villari published all three confessions in his appendix, pp. cxlvij-cxcviij.

[7] Ridolfi, *Vita*, vol. I, pp. 375-78.

of "about seven reasons" why the Church was soon to be punished and renovated.[8]

As we shall see, none of these dates coincides with the beginning of Savonarola's prophesying, although each of them is significant as referring to a stage in the development of his ideas. The earliest, 1475-80, coincides with his first years in the cloister; the second, 1484, was the year of the death of Pope Sixtus IV and a key year in much of the apocalyptic speculation of the time; the third, 1489, was in Savonarola's faulty recollection the year of his return to Florence. The first sermons in which Savonarola prophesied the coming tribulations were those he preached in the city of San Gimignano for the Lenten-season of 1486. They contain no message to, or special connection with, Florence; nor, from what we can tell from their remains, did they hold out the hope or promise of a great reform of the Church. Human sinfulness, the evil state of the Church, and the decay of Scriptural religion, he declared, led him to expect a great scourge, either of the Antichrist, war, sickness, or famine.[9] Although Savonarola was based in Florence at the time that he went to San Gimignano to preach, there is no record of his having repeated these baneful predictions in Florence then, nor is there any trace in the contemporary diaries and histories that the public took the slightest notice of this obscure San Marco friar.[10] After he left Florence, however, Savonarola preached in a number of north Italian cities, among them Brescia, where in 1489 he seems to have used the Book of Revelation as the basis for a prediction of the coming punishment of Italy.[11] Soon after this he returned to San Marco in Florence where

[8] Villari, *Savonarola*, vol. II, appendix, pp. cxlix-cl. On the reliability of the three confessions, see Roberto Ridolfi, "I processi del Savonarola," *La Bibliofilia*, XLVI (1944), 3-41; and the same author's "Ancora i processi del Savonarola," *La Bibliofilia*, XLVII (1945), 41-47.

[9] Ridolfi, *Life*, pp. 23-24. The drafts of these sermons are published by Ridolfi, *Gli archivi delle famiglie fiorentine* (Florence, 1934), pp. 79-81; and extensively described in his *Studi savonaroliani* (Florence, 1935), pp. 37-52. The material of these sermons contradicts Felice Tocco, who declared that Savonarola did not preach Antichrist or the end of the world. *Savonarola e la profezia* (Milan, 1892), p. 381.

[10] Ridolfi, *Life*, p. 25.

[11] The text was Revelation 5:8-9 which tells of the book of seven seals and the twenty-four elders who venerated the Lamb of the seven Spirits of God.

he began to expound "The Apocalypse of John," that is, the same Book of Revelation. Undoubtedly, in his account in the *Compendium* Savonarola transferred the first locus of his use of the Apocalypse from Brescia to Florence.

The *Compendium* résumé, then, is a foreshortening which, unlike that of Renaissance painters, obscures rather than clarifies our vision. By omitting the earlier stages of his life, or by telescoping them into later ones, the résumé gives the impression that the origins of Savonarola's preaching mission, his first prophetic inspiration, and his coming to Florence all coincided, that from the outset he was indeed the apostle to the Florentines. At the same time he had to explain why he had only begun to claim prophetic inspiration some years after his first revelation. This he did by making a distinction between content and manner; while the content, he maintained, had been the same from the beginning, he had only gradually revealed his divine inspiration because men's minds had been unprepared to hear such a startling truth. He says that after his visions of 1492 he began to reveal his divine illumination, but again, the evidence casts doubt upon the accuracy of the *Compendium* résumé. There is no indication in any of his surviving sermons that he had claimed such illumination—as distinct from the authority of the Scriptural prophets—before the crucial days of autumn 1494. The predictions of his 1493 sermons on the Psalm *Quam Bonus Israel Deus*,[12] for example, are exegetical rather than visionary.[13]

Savonarola's claim to Florentine leadership as well as his defense against both Florentine and Roman criticism depended upon his ability to fix his account of himself as the steadfast prophet and apostle to the Florentines in the minds of his readers. Yet, there seems little point in questioning his sincerity or in attributing to him deliberate distortion; events had so contrived, by the time he came to write the *Compendium Revelationum*, that he could well have come

---

The source of the report of Savonarola's preaching is *La vita del Beato Ieronimo Savonarola*, ed. Piero Ginori Conti (Florence, 1937), p. 15. (This is the life formerly attributed to Fra Pacifico Burlamacchi and will henceforth be cited as pseudo-Burlamacchi.) The true editor is Roberto Ridolfi; see Mario Martelli, *L'opera di Roberto Ridolfi* (Florence, 1962), p. 45.

[12] Psalm 72 in the Vulgate; 73 in the King James version.

[13] See the discussion below, pp. 94-95.

to think of himself in this way. However, the facts suggest a more complicated development, a less sure consciousness of his message and his role. The coming of the new Cyrus from the North, the conversion of the infidel, the establishment of *unum ovile et unus pastor*, and the rule of a *Papa Santo* were later additions to his prophecy. If this were merely a matter of the accretion of more detail in his predictions it would not be very significant to us, but it is something more than that. At a certain point Savonarola's apocalyptic vision of future tribulations became millenarian and this-worldly, his ascetic piety made room for a materialistic promise of riches and power. At a certain moment his Christian universalism narrowed to a partisan civic focus, with Florence taking shape in his mind as the New Jerusalem and the future of her government and worldly fortunes becoming part of the divine plan. In short, the very nature of Savonarola's eschatology underwent a radical transformation.

As with the prophecy, so with the prophet. The mendicant preacher who excoriated the wealthy and championed the poor became the solon of the bourgeois republic, promising new riches, power, and glory to the Arno city. The anti-humanist who disdained, if he did not condemn, secular philosophy and worldly learning became the friend and hero of Florentine philosophers and humanist poets. The Dominican champion of orthodox, Thomist theology became the herald of a new order in which Florence would succeed Rome as the first city of a reformed Christendom. The *forestiero* from Ferrara became the outstanding advocate of the Florentine myth.

It is necessary to study Savonarola's career to trace the stages of these transformations as well as to try to account for them—to see what were the influences and circumstances which caused Savonarola to alter his view of the world, future history, and himself. At the same time we must not oversimplify the process of change. We are not dealing with the simple progression from old to new positions but with the inner dialectic of a protean personality who, while absorbing new experiences and conceiving new ideas, did not entirely relinquish older values and convictions. Thus, in reading Savonarola's later sermons one senses the satisfaction he came to feel from moving men and influencing the course of events. But even in these sermons he continues to discourse upon the contemplative ideal and the obstacles to spirituality presented by the flesh, material riches, and an appetite for power and honors. Observers noted the contrast between the slight, mild friar of private conversations and the powerful figure in the pulpit, a contrast that is reflected in a comparison of his devotional writings with the sermons as we have them, recorded *viva voce*. The active life of the prophet-reformer came to dominate that of the contemplative ascetic, wistful for solitude, but Savonarola never fully resolved this conflict for himself, and the ambivalence is reflected in his vision of the future. He promised the Florentines both spiritual bliss and the satisfactions of power and riches as the rewards of their conversion to the Lord's work.

GIROLAMO SAVONAROLA joined the order of Friars Preachers in 1475, when he was a few months less than twenty-three years old.[14] The religious impulse that moved him to do so was neither sudden nor simple. Three years before joining the Dominicans Savonarola had already voiced his dismay at the wickedness of the world and the corruption of Peter's See in language as strong as any he was later to use in his sermons. In his canzone, *De ruina mundi*, laced with Petrarchan expressions, the twenty-year-old gives us some insight into his earliest religious preoccupations:[15]

> The pirate's hand has seized the scepter;
> Down tumbles St. Peter;

[14] For details on the Savonarola family and on Savonarola's early years, see Schnitzer, *Savonarola*, vol. I, pp. 1-15; Ridolfi, *Life*, pp. 1-4; Paolo Rocca, "La giovinezza di Gerolamo Savonarola a Ferrara," and Alfonso Sautto, "La casa dove nacque e abitò fra Girolamo Savonarola" (with illustrations), *Studi Savonaroliani, Atti e memorie della Deputazione Provinciale Ferrarese di storia patria*, n.s., vol. VII (Ferrara, 1952-53), part III, pp. 7-53, 75-82.

[15] *De ruina mundi* in Girolamo Savonarola, *Poesie*, ed. Mario Martelli (Rome, 1968), pp. 3-5. While the date 1472 is found in the earliest MSS, this has sometimes been disputed in favor of a date some twenty years later, most recently by Domenico Coppola, *La poesia religiosa del secolo XV* (Florence, 1963). Martelli reviews the entire question, concluding that 1472 is the correct date (*Poesie*, pp. 199-206) and I follow him. See also Mario Ferrara, *Savonarola*, 2 vols. (Florence, 1952), vol. I, p. 7, n. 14.

Filled with every vice and plunder;
By heav'n it must be split asunder.[16]

How it was that God did not punish such wickedness the young
poet could only explain by supposing that He was preparing still
worse punishment for the future, or that perhaps the Last Days were
imminent:

I think, O heavenly King, that your delay,
Foretells a still worse scourge for her great sin;
Even perhaps that the time begins
Which makes Hell tremble—the Final Day. . . .[17]

In the meantime, Savonarola's own counsel to himself was to avoid
the world and keep silent:

Flee palaces and meeting places,
Let few men know of what you think,
Be an enemy to the world, and from it shrink.[18]

Such gloomy thoughts and stern self-admonitions in such a young
man are hard to explain, especially since we are told that as a youth
he loved poetry and lute-playing, while much later he recalled that
he had never intended to become a friar.[19] Girolamo had not yet
made up his mind to renounce the pleasures of worldly society, but
apparently he was deeply affected by a disappointed love. It seems to
have been shortly before he wrote *De ruina mundi* that he proposed
marriage to Laudomia, illegitimate daughter of Roberto Strozzi of

[16] Ne le man di pirata è gionto il scetro;
A terra va San Pietro;
Quivi lussuria ed ogne preda abunda,
Che non so come il ciel non si confunda.

Poesie, pp. 3-4, lines 19-21.

[17] Ma credo che ritardi, o Re superno,
A maggior pena de' soi gran defetti
On pur ch'è forsi appresso, e tu l'aspetti,
L'estremo dì che fa tremar l'inferno.

Ibid., p. 3, lines 12-15.

[18] Fugi palazi e logie
E fa' che toa ragion a pochi dica,
Chè a tuto el mondo tu serai nemica.

Ibid., p. 5, lines 69-71.

[19] Schnitzer, *Savonarola*, vol. I, p. 12.

Ferrara. The girl contemptuously rejected him as her social inferior, and Girolamo replied with heated indignation.[20] This story has been dismissed as exaggerated and insignificant, primarily on the grounds that it is inconsistent with his already developed spiritual vocation.[21] This would be so if we were determined to maintain the dogma that the youthful Savonarola was already the mature prophet and reformer, aloof from the concerns of ordinary young mortals and wholly dedicated to his future tasks.[22] If we reject that dogma, however, this story of disappointed love on the eve of Girolamo's turn toward the spiritual life ought not be so easily passed over. The passion with which the future reformer denounced the pleasures of the world and the pessimism which led him to expect divine punishment cannot have been wholly unrelated to his own suffering and rejection. Besides, the story of Laudomia's refusal takes on added significance when we consider it in the light of still another story to which Savonarola's modern biographers have given scant attention.[23]

[20] The story was told by Fra Benedetto Luschino on the authority of Savonarola's brother Maurelio. Benedetto Luschino (Benedetto da Firenze), *Vulnera diligentis*, MS BNF Magl. XXXIV, 7, fols. 11 verso-12 verso.

[21] Ridolfi, *Life*, pp. 4-5. But not by either Schnitzer (*Savonarola*, vol. I, pp. 12-13) or Villari, who, while embellishing the story considerably beyond the known facts, sees it as an important experience in the development of Savonarola's religious mentality. Moreover, Villari cites the literature which has established that there was a Laudomia Strozzi, daughter of Roberto, and that the house of Roberto Strozzi was near that of the Savonarola. Villari, *Savonarola*, vol. I, pp. 15-17. Paolo Rocca repeats the story as told by Fra Benedetto and maintains that, contrary to Ridolfi, the incident is important in explaining Savonarola's personality: ". . . perchè mi sembra pure di trovare, in questa ferita interna, la sorgente nascosta della fierezza tutta Savonaroliana, in un cuore nobile e altero." "La giovinezza di Gerolamo Savonarola," p. 19. On the collection of Strozzi material in Ferrara, see Cecil H. Clough, "The Archivio Bentivoglio in Ferrara," *Renaissance News*, XVIII (1965), 12-19.

[22] It is at this point that Ridolfi makes the statement I have already quoted earlier: "Rarely if ever does one find in the adolescence of a great man, not merely the germs of his future actions and life, but also their whole and perfect image. . . ." *Life*, p. 5; see above p. 18. See also Mario Ferrara who, referring to *De contemptu mundi*, says, "Here are expressed Savonarola's first indications of prophecy, the eagerness which he already felt, before entering the cloister, to accomplish his divine mission in the world." *Savonarola*, vol. I, p. 18, n. 12.

[23] Ridolfi, *Life*, p. 7; Schnitzer, *Savonarola*, vol. I, p. 18; Villari does not mention it at all; nor, unfortunately, does Rocca.

This is the account of the striking dream that finally moved the young man to enter the cloister. The biographer known as pseudo-Burlamacchi tells us that for some time he had been troubled by the state of the world and by the thought that perhaps he himself should seek a better way of life. In this frame of mind he arrived at the age of twenty-two, "and remaining in this state of uncertainty for quite a while, [one night] while he was sleeping he felt a freezing water spill upon his head. This roused him at once and he awoke from his dream, that is, he took up a new life. Thus God came to his aid and in this way he decided that he preferred being a spiritual physician of the soul to a physician of the body. That was the water of repentance and with it was extinguished the carnal heat of desire, while its coldness froze in him every worldly appetite."[24]

This dream story indicates that Savonarola's yearning for another kind of life was based on a real, concrete conflict between flesh and spirit. The explicit, vivid imagery of being drenched in *una frigidissima aqua*, the water of repentance that extinguished *el calore carnale della libidine*, suggests that the conversion which decided Girolamo on a career in religion was his way of resolving a dual problem, defeat in love and the guilt of physical desire. As a young man who had strong feelings of his own worth (his proud reaction to Laudomia's refusal), he found a positive solution: he would be a physician of souls.[25] What was constant in Savonarola's nature, and what made him no ordinary man, was not a particular prophetic insight into the state of things, but this ability to translate personal experience and inner struggle into creative and effective terms.

For the time being, however, until new disappointments and new crises challenged him to seek new solutions, his resolve was to escape from the despised allurements of the world. Writing to his father the day after he left home to enter the Convent of San Domenico in Bologna, he catalogued the vices—"the wickedness of men, the carnal violence, the adulteries, the robberies, the pride, the idolatry, the

---

[24] Pseudo-Burlamacchi, *La vita*, pp. 7-8. "Its coldness froze in him every worldly appetite" is my translation of "la quale, fredda, lo raffrenava da ogni mondano appetito." See also Gianfrancesco Pico della Mirandola, *Vita R. P. Hieronymi Savonarolae*, vol. II, pp. 10-11.

[25] He had been studying medicine, although Ridolfi says he had given it up by this time in favor of theology. *Life*, pp. 3-4.

cruel blasphemies"—that had made him pray to *messer Iesu Christo* to remove him "from this filth" and that had made him determined to follow the Virgilian exhortation, *Heu fuge crudelas terras, fuge litus avarum* (*Aeneid* 3.44). Now Christ had shown him how to live "rationally, not as a beast among swine."[26] He also left behind a short Latin tract, *De contemptu mundi,* in which he repeated the same theme and again referred to the Last Days: "O you who are blind, judge now in your own case: judge yourselves whether these are the Last Days. Why, O soul, do you delay? Arise and fly here; flee Egypt and Pharaoh, since his heart has hardened against the Lord. . . ."[27] The same theme of escape from the iniquities of the world is expressed in his poem *De ruina Ecclesiae,* also written some time during 1475, the year of Savonarola's entry in the cloister. Lamenting the passing of the ancient days of fervent sanctity, sweet martyrdom, and contemplation of the Scriptures, and complaining of the transformation of the Church into "a false proud whore, Babylon," he tells himself at the end, "You, weep and be silent; this seems to be the better way."[28]

Whether Savonarola considered silence to be consistent with his vocation as a "spiritual physician of the soul" is not clear. Preaching would seem a natural outlet for this passionate puritan who could be so didactic and patronizing in his letters to his parents,[29] so unforgiving of the world's sins and so outspoken of them in his poetry. Had he aspired to a life of cloistered silence, it seems unlikely that he would have chosen the Order of Preachers. At any rate, his superiors must have decided that the young friar should pursue an active career, for after his novitiate he was enrolled in the Dominican *Studium Generale* in Bologna to study theology. That preaching was on Savonarola's mind is indicated by his correspondence with the

[26] My translations from Savonarola's letters are based on the texts in *Le lettere di Girolamo Savonarola,* ed. Roberto Ridolfi (Florence, 1933), pp. 1-2.

[27] In Ridolfi, *Studi savonaroliani,* pp. 235-38. Savonarola alludes to Exodus 7:3, 13, 14, 22.

[28] *Poesie,* p. 8, line 77.

[29] E.g., the last paragraph of his letter to his father, April 25, 1475: "I commend to you all my brothers and sisters, but especially I commend to you Alberto, whom I wish you to set to learning; if you let him waste his time, your responsibility will be a heavy one and your sin great." *Lettere,* p. 3.

well-known Bolognese humanist, Giovanni Garzoni. Savonarola had written to Garzoni, asking for advice on improving his preaching, and Garzoni had replied, holding up the model of some other preachers who had attained fame, including Vincent of Ferrer: "You have come to the city of Bologna as to a market of the good arts; if you persevere in this determination I have no doubt you will be a great orator. If you add philosophy and theology to oratory you will obtain immortal praise."[30] However, in a second letter, Garzoni took Fra Girolamo to task for having "declared war on Priscian" and predicted that if he persisted in this way both Savonarola and Priscian would be the losers.[31] Apparently Savonarola was already forming his own attitudes toward a preaching language; a simple unadorned style would later make his sermons a striking contrast to the humanist oratory of preachers who were popular with the members of the Laurentian circle.

Upon completion of his studies in Bologna, in 1479, Fra Girolamo was sent to his native city of Ferrara, apparently for further training at the University.[32] In 1482 he participated in a disputation held in conjunction with the meeting of the Lombard Chapter of his order in Reggio of Emilia. That occasion was doubly important for him: first, because he was heard in disputation by Giovanni Pico della Mirandola, who was to play such a significant role in Savonarola's Florentine career;[33] second, because the Reggio meeting marked the

[30] See Alessandro Gherardi ed., *Nuovi documenti e studi intorno a Girolamo Savonarola*, 2nd edn. (Florence, 1887), p. 38. For bibliography and a discussion of Giovanni Garzoni, see Charles Trinkaus, *In Our Image and Likeness: Humanity and Divinity in Italian Humanist Thought*, 2 vols. (London, 1970), vol. I, pp. 271-93 and nn. on pp. 433-43.

[31] *Ibid.*, p. 39.

[32] Schnitzer, *Savonarola*, vol. I, pp. 43-44. For the few details which are known about this period, see *ibid.*, vol. I, pp. 36-44; Ridolfi, *Life*, pp. 9-12; Celestino Piana, "Il diaconato di frà Girolamo Savonarola (Bologna, 1° marzo 1477)," *Archivum Fratrum Praedicatorum*, XXXIV (1964), 343-48; and, by the same author, "Il suddiaconato di frà Girolamo Savonarola (Bologna, 21 settembre 1476)," *Rinascimento* 2nd ser., VI (1966), pp. 287-94. A few details may also be gleaned from Dante Balboni, "Briciole Savonaroliane," *Studi Savonaroliani, Atti e memorie della Deputazione Provinciale Ferrarese de storia patria*, n.s., VII (Ferrara, 1952-53), part III, 61-73.

[33] On the meeting, see Eugenio Garin, *Giovanni Pico della Mirandola vita e dottrina* (Florence, 1937), p. 8. Garin thinks they met first in Ferrara. See also below, pp. 211-12.

end of his apprenticeship, the Chapter having elected him to the office of Reader in the Convent of San Marco of Florence. And so it was that Savonarola came to the Arno city for the first time, in the year 1482.

As Reader he expounded Scriptures to his brother friars, upon whom his strong emotion and his deep Scriptural learning seem to have rapidly made a lasting impression.[34] Unfortunately, we know nothing about the content of his teaching at the time or what books of the Bible he expounded.[35] Still more regrettable, we know little about the sermons he gave for his first preaching assignment, which came in Advent of the same year, to the nuns of the Benedictine cloister of the Murate. Apparently, he was not a great success: his Ferrarese speech and his style—or lack of it—do not seem to have impressed his audience favorably.[36] Two years later, preaching was still coming hard for him. While he was preaching the Lenten sermons in the Basilica of San Lorenzo, his audience dwindled, and, if Fra Placido Cinozzi, who was an admirer of Fra Girolamo and in the audience, is to be believed, Savonarola was thinking of giving up preaching, returning to teaching, and leaving Florence for Lombardy.[37] As Savonarola himself later recalled, he had no great

[34] *Annalia Conventus Sancti Marci de Florentia*, ms BLF Conventi soppressi S. Marco 370, fols. 153 verso–154 recto (pencilled numeration).

[35] Ridolfi cites the chronicler Bartolomeo Cerretani on Savonarola's apostolical method of preaching, *Life*, p. 16; but Cerretani was talking about Savonarola's later preaching. See Cerretani's *Storia fiorentina*, partly published in Joseph Schnitzer ed., *Quellen und Forschungen zur Geschichte Savonarolas*, vol. III, *Bartolomeo Cerretani* (Munich, 1904), p. 6.

[36] He also preached in the Church of Orsanmichele in Florence. Ridolfi, *Life*, p. 16.

[37] ". . . e, perché né in gesti né in pronunzia satisfece quasi a nessuno, in modo che mi ricordo, avendolo udito tutta la quaresima, all'ultimo restammo fra uomini, donne e fanciulli manco di xxv; onde vedendo questo, e anco essendoli detto da altri secondo che li udi' dire di poi più volte, al tutto deliberò di lassare stare il predicare e seguitare il leggere; e tornossi in Lombardia." *Estratto d'una epistola fratris Placidi de Cinozis Ordinis Praedicatorum S. Marci de Florentia, De vita et moribus reverendi patris fratris Hieronimi Savonarole de Ferraria, fratri Iacobo Siculo, eiusdem Ordinis vicarius generalis (sic), post mortem dicti Prophete*, in P. Villari and E. Casanova eds., *Scelta di prediche e scritti di fra Girolamo Savonarola* (Florence, 1898), p. 11. See also pseudo-Burlamacchi, *La vita*, p. 16, and the sixteenth-century account of the Ferrarese priest, Francesco Caloro. He says that Savonarola was inept when

gifts, *ne voce ne petto ne modo di predicare*, on the contrary his preaching had been unpleasing to everyone who heard him.[38]

This year of deep discouragement, 1484, was another turning point for Savonarola. Just as he had overcome discouragement and uncertainty nine years earlier by means of a sudden conversion (the dream of the water of repentance), so now he found himself again by means of an inspiration: the Church had to be scourged, and soon; there were "about seven reasons" why this must be so. This was the sudden illumination in the monastery of San Giorgio, already mentioned. Now Savonarola began to discover his prophetic voice and henceforth he thought no more about abandoning the pulpit. The next year, when he preached the Lenten sermons in the nearby town of San Gimignano, he added the third part of the prophecy, so that it took its classic form: the Church was to be scourged, then reformed, and soon.[39] Not that Savonarola's sudden prophetic inspiration can be explained merely by his need to find something striking to say; he was responding to events and ideas as well as to his own inner struggle. A key to the reconstruction of the background of the San Giorgio–San Gimignano prophecy is provided by Savonarola's own statement that the prediction came to him as he was pondering the meaning of Scripture rather than by direct divine illumination, *per ragione delle scripture* as he later put it.[40] What seems to have come to him so suddenly in San Giorgio was that certain Biblical apocalypses were about to be fulfilled because they were being confirmed by contemporary events. Unfortunately, he never recalled which Biblical texts these were, although a clue is provided by the text of his second series of San Gimignano sermons, those for Lent of 1486. This was Matthew 4:17—*Poenitentiam agite: appropinquavit enim*

---

he first lived in Florence, years before he had begun to prophesy; so much so, that his relatives, brothers, and intimate friends asked him to give up preaching; they were afraid he would dishonor his *patria*, his family, and the doctrine he preached. *Defensione contro gli adversarii de Frate Hier. Savonarola, prenuntiatore delle instanti calamitade et renovatione della chiesa*, published together with G. Savonarola, *Prediche sopra Amos e Zaccaria* (Ferrara: Giovanni Mazocco dal Bondeno, 1513), chap. III.

[38] Girolamo Savonarola, *Prediche sopra l'Esodo*, ed. Pier Giorgio Ricci, 2 vols. (Rome, 1955), vol. I, p. 50 (Sermon of February 11, 1498).

[39] Ridolfi, *Life*, p. 22.

[40] Villari, *Savonarola*, vol. II, appendix, p. cl.

regnum coelorum—which was Jesus' own first text when he began to preach after the temptation in the wilderness.

This was also a time when Savonarola was very concerned with the situation in the Church. His canzone, *Oratio pro Ecclesia*, of 1484 was written on the occasion of the death of Pope Sixtus IV (1471-84) "when the devil roused dissension in the Church" and when, after a short time, Innocent VIII (1484-92) was elected "not without wonder on the part of his flock, which feared a schism."[41] In July 1484, reports of miracles performed by an image of the Virgin Mary, similar to those that had been attracting the "whole world" to Bibbona in the Maremma since 1482,[42] came from the neighboring town of Prato. In the laud *O anima accecata* which is either by Savonarola or inspired by his preaching, these wonders are taken as signs of the coming tribulations:[43]

> You see a thousand signs
> at Prato and at Bibbona
> and since you do not choose
> to believe anyone
> your mind is prone
> to every vice:
> see the punishment
> that soon you will receive.
> Alas, alas, alas!
> All fear of God has gone.
>
> You see Italy in war
> and great famine;
> God lets loose the plague
> and His judgment extends everywhere:
> these are the fruits
> of your life,

[41] *Poesie*, p. 13.

[42] Luca Landucci, *Diario fiorentino del 1450 al 1516 continuato da un anonimo fino al 1542*, ed. Iodoco Del Badia (Florence, 1883), pp. 41-42.

[43] The laud is ascribed to Savonarola by Ridolfi, *Life*, p. 18; but Martelli gives good reasons for restoring it to the authorship of Feo Belcari to whom it is attributed in some of the older editions, *Poesie*, pp. 85-94. Nonetheless Martelli agrees that the poem is "an eloquent document of the impression that Savonarolan preaching had made on the mind and also the imagination of the now aged, elegant 'laudista' " (p. 90).

blind and lost
because of your weak faith.
Alas, alas, etc.

Astrologers and prophets,
learned men and holy,
knowing preachers
have predicted your laments;
you seek music and song,
because you are foolish,
steeped in sin
you have lost all virtue
Alas, alas, etc.[44]

Who were these astrologers, prophets, learned and holy men, and preachers who had predicted the coming suffering? Savonarola later confessed that his prediction of the speedy coming of tribulation and reform was based not upon the light of revelation, nor even upon the Scriptures, as he had written in the *Compendium*, but upon reasons that were "written in diverse places," and he mentioned *lo tracte di Daniele san Hieronymo: Sancto Augustino Origene: et San Tomasso.*[45] This is puzzling. Jerome, Augustine, Origen, and Thomas we know as theologians and Biblical exegetes; Daniel is the only prophet in the list, but this would take us back to the Scriptural authority that Savonarola had just disavowed in the first part of his statement. We might be tempted to ignore the entire statement as something Savonarola invented on the spot to satisfy his inquisitors; but on the assumption that no statement is entirely random let us

---

[44]
Tu senti molti segni	Vedi l'Italia in guerra	Astrologi e profeti
a Prato e a Bibona,	e la carestia grande;	uomini dotti e santi,
e par che tu non degni	la peste Idio disserra	predicator discreti
di credere a persona;	e 'l suo giudicio spande:	t'han predetti i tuoi pianti;
la mente tua è prona	queste son le vivande	tu cerchi suoni e canti,
a ogni vizio:	della tua vita	perchè se' stolta,
ecco el supplizio,	cieca e smarrita	ne' vizi involta
che presto viene a te.	per la tua poca fé.	in te virtù non è.
Omé, omé, omé,	Omé, omé, omé, etc.	Omé, omé, omé, etc.
timor di Dio non c'è.		

Poesie, p. 89. This text varies slightly from the one cited in Ridolfi, *Life*, pp. 18-19. On the wars and famines of this period in Italy, see Nino Valeri, *L'Italia nell'età dei principati dal 1343 al 1516* (Verona, 1949), pp. 611-29.

[45] Villari, *Savonarola*, vol. II, appendix, p. clxviij.

look a bit further. Savonarola referred not to the Book of Daniel but to *lo tracte di Daniele*, which suggests that—particularly since he had just disavowed Scriptural authority—he was alluding to one or more of the apocalypses that went under the name of the prophet Daniel and were so widespread in Italy at this time.[46] And indeed, in his San Gimignano sermons Savonarola referred to the prophets of his time as confirming his predictions: God multiplies his prophets today, he said, and even men far from holy are foretelling the future; this is the third reason for believing that the scourge is at hand.[47]

What gives these clues added weight, however, is the fact that the year 1484, the time of Savonarola's own prophetic awakening, was the *annus mirabilis* of contemporary prophetic speculation about religious change. *Astrologi e profeti, omini dotti e santi* as well as men of lesser degrees of holiness were predicting for that year some great turning point in the history of Christianity, indeed in the religious history of the world. By the fifteenth century the diverse sources of this speculation had swelled to a broad stream, so that we can distinguish its separate tributaries—Biblical prophetism, Joachism, astrology—only with great difficulty. However, the method by which 1484 was selected as the year of a great religious watershed appears to have derived ultimately from a non-Christian source: the Latin translation of the writings of the ninth-century Arab astronomer-astrologer, Albumasar, whose own ideas derived from still older Arab sources.[48] According to Albumasar, religions as well

---

[46] E.g., the Daniel prophecies predicting *flagello*, in MS BNF Magl. VII, 40, fol. 18; *I sogni di Daniele profeta* (Florence, n.d.). See *British Museum Catalog of Books Printed in the Fifteenth Century*, vol. VI, p. 687. There was also a prophecy attributed to Saint Thomas Aquinas, MS BNF II. VIII. 28, fols. 226–227 verso: "Sent to Master Roberto of the Order of S. Domenico by Frate Antonio da Orvieto." He might also have known the book of Giacomo Palladini di Teramo, Bishop of Florence from 1401-10, entitled *Somnium Nebugodonosor sive Statua Danielis*, which predicted the speedy coming of the millennium. Palladini di Teramo was tried for heresy in 1410. See Angelo Mercati, "Un vescovo fiorentino del primo Quattrocento millenarista," *Rivista di storia della Chiesa in Italia*, II (1948), 157-65.

[47] Ridolfi, *Studi savonaroliani*, p. 50.

[48] Franz Boll, *Sphaera* (Leipzig, 1903), pp. 413-19, 482-539. There is a brief review of the theme in Eugenio Garin, *La cultura filosofica del Rinascimento italiano* (Florence, 1961), pp. 155-58. On fifteenth-century interest in astrology

as people had their horoscopes; all the great world religions had their distinctive zodiacal signs, and the conjunction of certain planets in these signs marked important changes or stages in the respective destinies of these religions. Albumasar's theories had been diffused in the West at least since Roger Bacon's time, but in the late fifteenth century they were being employed in a particularly pointed application. It was widely held that the conjunction of Jupiter and Saturn marked the completion of an astrological Great Year and therefore heralded spectacular changes for Christianity.[49] The astrologer Paul of Middelburg, correspondent of Marsilio Ficino, used this notion as the basis of his calculation that great innovations in religion would begin in 1484,[50] and his calculations were taken over in a rather confused fashion by Johannes Lichtenberger, court astrologer to the Emperor Frederick III.[51] In Florence, no less an authority than the Platonist philosopher Cristoforo Landino predicted that a major astral conjunction heralded the return of Dante's mysterious *Veltro* to inaugurate religious reform on November 25, 1484.[52] The strange prophet Giovanni Mercurio of Correggio also appeared in Florence, although whether he did so before or after his sensational apparition in the streets of Rome in 1484, urging repentance before the coming *renovatio*, is not clear.[53]

A slightly different chronology of the same themes was provided by a Dominican contemporary of Savonarola. This was Giovanni

in Florence, see Benedetto Soldati, *La poesia astrologica nel Quattrocento* (Florence, 1906), especially chaps. II-IV.

[49] See the discussion and bibliography in G. Pico della Mirandola, *Disputationes adversus astrologiam divinatricem*, ed. Eugenio Garin, 2 vols. (Florence, 1946), vol. I, pp. 636-39; Lynn Thorndike, "Albumasar in Sadan," *Isis*, 45 (1954), 24-25; and the many references in the same author's *A History of Magic and Experimental Science*, 6 vols. (New York, 1923-41), especially vols. III and IV passim.

[50] Paul of Middelburg, Bishop of Fossombrone, was the recipient of Marsilio Ficino's famous letter of September 12, 1492, on the golden age. Ficino, *Opera* (Basel, 1561), p. 944. On Paul, see Aby Warburg, *Gesammelte Schriften*, 2 vols. (Leipzig, 1932), vol. II, pp. 514-15 and passim.

[51] Dietrich Kurze, *Johannes Lichtenberger*, Historische Studien, vol. 379 (Lübeck, 1960), p. 34.

[52] In his commentary on Dante's *Commedia*, cited in Villari, *Savonarola*, vol. I, p. 66.

[53] On Giovanni of Correggio, see below, pp. 199-202.

Nanni, or Annius, of Viterbo, theologian, historian, and charlatan extraordinary,[54] who in 1480 had published his *De futuris Christianorum triumphis in Saracenos,* a concatenation of the astrological theories of Albumasar, the theosophy of Hermes Trismegistus, the prophecy of Joachim of Flora, and his own interpretation of the Apocalypse.[55] His immediate inspiration may well have been the Turkish raids on the southern coast of Italy in 1480, since he identifies the Turk as the Great Beast of the Apocalypse and predicts that in the following year the tide would turn with the defeat of "the Turks and Mohammedans" and that in succeeding years the *resurrectio universalis* would get under way with the regeneration of the Church, the establishment of *unum ovile et unus pastor,* and the inaugural of "a new heaven and a new earth in the form of the holy city of Jerusalem and the tabernacle of God." After this earthly millennium there would be a second *resurrectio* of the dead at the end of the world.[56]

It would seem, then, that Savonarola's sudden vision of the coming tribulation and reform arose in the context of widespread contemporary speculation of the same kind and, further, that it was connected with the apocalyptic excitement of the year 1484. His reference much later to *lo tracte di Daniele* is a hint that by this time he may already have read some of the apocalypses that circulated under the names of famous prophets and religious figures of the past, although there is nothing in his early vision that connects him with the specifically Florentine versions of these apocalypses. In these texts, as in the more formal speculations of the philosophers, Biblical prophecy joins with astrology in predicting religious renovation. The laud *O anima accecata* also refers to *Astrologi e profeti* as a dual authority. Later, Savonarola would condemn astrology as a superstition and a pseudo-science, and he would carefully distinguish between true prophecy, which came only through God's illumination, and astrology, which was a vain attempt to predict contingent

[54] On Annius of Viterbo, see especially Garin, *Cultura filosofica,* pp. 188-89; and Roberto Weiss, "Traccia per una biografia di Annio da Viterbo," *Italia medioevale e umanistica,* V (1962), 425-41.

[55] *De futuris Christianorum triumphis in Saracenos* (Genoa, 1480); *GW* nos. 2017-24.

[56] *Ibid.,* Tract I, chap. II.

events. If the aforementioned laud was of his authorship, this would suggest that he had not made such a distinction between astrology and prophecy by 1484. Even if Savonarola did not write these lines, however, it is possible that he had not yet come to reject astrology. In 1484 his vision was new, his view of himself as God's special prophet no more than half-formed. Later, with the intensity that was to come from further inspiration and the confidence born of new success, he would insist that no one but a man directly illumined by divinity could know the future and that he was such a man, singled out to herald the coming New Era to Florence and the world. That conviction would allow no room for astrologers or other seers who claimed to know the future by human art.

SIN, DIVINE WRATH, repentance, renewal, and the Last Things—these had been the themes of Christian prophecy since its earliest days.[57] The Book of Revelation, the quintessential apocalypse, provided Christian eschatology with a vocabulary and much of the material for reading the "signs of the times" and calculating the time and manner of God's future acts.[58] On it, as well as on some older, Jewish sources, such as the Book of Daniel, some early Christian thinkers based a hope for a period of secular bliss, a millennium during which Christ would reign on earth. But millenarianism in particular and eschatological speculation in general were discouraged by the weighty authority of St. Augustine, who identified the millennium of the Apocalypse with the thousand-year history of the Church in Christ. Beyond this, according to Augustine, there was no earthly millennium nor any good in calculating the future: the Lord would bring on the Last Days and put an end to history when and how He chose to do so.[59] While neither the idea of an earthly millennium,

[57] I make no attempt to cite the massive literature. For an important recent discussion of the idea of Christian reform and related ideas in the Patristic period, see Gerhart B. Ladner, *The Idea of Reform, Its Impact on Christian Thought and Action in the Age of the Fathers* (Cambridge, Mass., 1959). For a recent, brief treatment of the millenarian theme, Ernest Lee Tuveson, *Millennium and Utopia* (N.Y.: Harper Torchbooks, 1964).

[58] On the imagery of the Book of Revelation, see Austin Farrer, *A Rebirth of Images* (Westminster, 1949).

[59] See the excellent brief description and the quote of a key passage from Saint Augustine in Heiko A. Oberman ed., *Forerunners of the Reformation*

nor movements inspired by it, disappeared in the centuries of Augustine's dominance, the greatest challenge to his eschatology came much later, with Joachim of Flora (d. 1202) and his vision of a New Age of the Spirit. Spreading outward from thirteenth-century Italy, especially through the agency of the Franciscan radicals, Joachite and pseudo-Joachite writings and ideas stimulated the apocalyptic imagination everywhere in Europe well into the Reformation and beyond.[60] The central thrust of Joachism was millenarian,[61] the expectation of the speedy coming of a New Age, the Spirit's earthly reign which would precede the onset of the Last Days.[62] This idea itself was subject to more than one interpretation and to a multitude of computational schemes,[63] as well as to extraneous influences from astrology and other sources. Besides, there were many who, while affected by and participating in the heightened eschatological excitement of the times, were little impressed by millenarian hopes and

---

(N.Y., 1966), pp. 9-19. Professor Oberman makes an interesting distinction between prophecy and apocalyptic, the first judging "the human condition on the basis of the acts of God," the second judging "the acts of God on the basis of the human [im]moral condition" (p. 12). The distinction is meaningful, although I use the term prophecy in the more general and less technical sense of prediction of God-ordained events to come.

[60] "His doctrine gave shape to the fears and hopes of humanity for centuries." Fritz Saxl, "A Spiritual Encyclopaedia of the Later Middle Ages," *Journal of the Warburg and Courtauld Institutes*, V (1942), p. 84.

On medieval millenarian movements before as well as after Joachim, see Norman Cohn, *Pursuit of the Millennium*, 2nd edn. (New York: Harper Torchbooks, 1961). On Joachim, see Leonard Bloomfield, "Joachim of Flora: A Critical Survey of His Canon, Teachings, Sources, Biography, and Influence," *Traditio*, XIII (1957).

[61] Various forms of the term are used: "millenarianism," "millennialism," "millenarism," "chiliasm."

[62] Some recent scholars have argued that Joachim himself was not as interested in the future as has been generally thought. See Bloomfield "Joachim of Flora," p. 209, for a review of these questions and the bibliography. When I refer to Joachism I include the thirteenth- to fifteenth-century writers who were inspired by him directly or through the pseudo-Joachite literature.

[63] Ladner, *Idea of Reform*, pp. 27-29. For the distinction between some types which also occur in this period, see Philip Schaff, "Premillennialism," *A Religious Encyclopedia or Dictionary of Biblical, Historical, Doctrinal, and Practical Theology*, vol. III (1891), pp. 1887-90; and G. Bardy, "Millénarisme," *Dictionnaire de théologie catholique*, vol. X, cols. 1760-63.

little inclined to follow the Joachites. Instead, they looked for signs that confirmed the presence of Antichrist among them or his imminent arrival in their midst, to be followed by Christ himself and the end of the world, and they preferred to go directly to the apocalyptical books of the Bible for guidance.

With the full knowledge that this is oversimplification, we roughly distinguish two currents of eschatological expectation in the later Middle Ages: one, optimistic, pointing toward the speedy coming of a reign of peace and joy after a strenuous divine scourging and purging; the other, pessimistic, holding out no hope that the divine scourge would bring about a collective spiritual renewal and offering men only the opportunity to repent before the onset of world destruction. In Savonarola's time both extremes were available to him: the optimistic current, in the works of his fellow Dominican, Annius of Viterbo for instance, and the many other apocalyptic writings already mentioned in the previous chapter; the pessimistic current was represented by such famous Dominicans as the powerful Manfred of Vercelli and St. Vincent Ferrer.[64] At different times, Savonarola drew upon each. In the early years of his preaching, those which we have just been examining, his message was entirely of the Vincentian type. Tribulation and the reform of the Church were the prelude to the Last Days which were at hand, not to the beginning of a millennial era. In his San Gimignano sermons of 1486, he warned of the coming divine scourge, *gladius domini cito et velociter*, and took as his text "Repent, for the Kingdom of Heaven is at hand"; while in a letter of December 5, 1485, to his mother, he had pointed out (in that patronizing tone Savonarola used with his parents) that God scourged His children in order that they put not

---

[64] "Eo tempore [1420] miro quodam incremento percrebuit opinio, et praevaluit doctrina quorumdam, etiam piorum, et doctorum virorum de Anti-Christi celerrimo adventu, inter quos potiores auctoritate, et virtute fuerunt sanctus Vincentius Ferrerius, miraculorum gloria, et praedicationis fructu celeberrimus, ac Manfredus Vercellensis, eiusdem Instituti: *vir venerabilis vitae*, inquit sanctus Antoninus, *peritus, et timens Deum*." Luke Wadding, *Annales Minorum seu Trium Ordinum*, 26 vols. (Rome-Quaracchi, 1731-1933), vol. X, p. 33. On Manfred in Florence, *ibid.*, p. 34. On Saint Vincent Ferrer, see also Johann von Döllinger, *Kleinere Schriften*, ed. F. H. Reusche (Stuttgart, 1890), pp. 462, 489-90.

their hopes in earthly things but that they might cut their worldly ties so that they would flee to His arms, to eternal life.[65] We have only a few notices concerning the sermons he gave between the time he left Florence in 1487 and his return in 1490, but from these it would appear that Savonarola persisted in his preaching of repentance and renunciation before the divine wrath.[66] When he returned he began to expound, as he later put it, "The Apocalypse of John," the Book of Revelation, with a restatement of his reasons, now increased to ten, for believing that the Last Days were at hand.[67] In the same year, preaching on John's First Epistle—that message of the last hour and the presence of Antichrist (I John 2:18) —he spoke of the universal conversion and reform which would come on the Day of Judgment.[68] Similarly, in his Lenten sermons of 1491, when he was already preaching to larger audiences from the pulpit of the Florentine cathedral, he announced that the evils abounding in the Church signified that the Day of Judgment was at hand. Like so many others of his time, he seems to have believed that the Turks were the Antichrist or one of the divine scourges that signified the imminence of the end.[69] This is not to say that Savonarola's ideas at this time were static. In the years between his return to Florence in 1490 and his emergence at the center of the political stage late in 1494, he seems to have been enriching his message by establishing it on a base of Biblical prophecy that was broader and deeper than his first efforts. For example, in one of his sermons on the Psalm *Quam Bonus Israel Deus*, which he probably gave in 1493,[70] he allegorized the generations of Adam in a prophetic sense:

[65] *Lettere*, pp. 5-11.

[66] On this period, see Ridolfi, *Vita*, vol. I, pp. 37-44 and nn.

[67] The summaries of these sermons are partially published by Villari, *Savonarola*, vol. I, appendix, pp. xv-xvj. The full text is in *Sermones sive magis lectiones super Apocalypsim*, MS BNF Conventi soppressi J. VII. 25, fols. 53-85.

[68] MS BNF Magl. XXXV, 110, fol. 78 recto. There is an 1846 edition of these sermons, but it is not complete; see Roberto Ridolfi, *Le prediche*, pp. 24-27.

[69] MS Florence Museo San Marco 480, fol. 54. On dating, see Ridolfi, *Studi savonaroliani*, pp. 81-82. Summaries of some of these sermons, including the "terrifying sermon," are included in Villari, *Savonarola*, vol. I, appendix, pp. xxviii-xxxiv.

[70] On problems of dating these sermons, see Ridolfi, *Vita*, vol. I, pp. 103-106 and nn.; and *Le prediche*, pp. 35-40.

Pray that Adam, who is the first father and signifies God, will know his wife again; [that is] pray that he will again have union with his church and that another seed will be born in place of Abel, Seth, who is interpreted *resurrectio*. Pray that he will raise up a people like Abel, that is, similar to the first Christian people. And that this people will generate another, that is, Enos, who is interpreted as man, who will begin to call upon the name of the Lord in truth. . . .[71]

A comparison of this passage with the discussion of the same Biblical material by St. Augustine provides an illuminating contrast. For Augustine the text is an allegory of the Incarnation and the founding of Christ's Church in the world. Abel signifies grief in the death of Christ; Seth, resurrection; and Enos, the Christian who calls upon the name of the Lord. The Genesis text, for Augustine, represents the life of the spirit in the City of God. For Savonarola, however, the text was the occasion for a vision of the future in which God, through a new union, would renew His Church, Enos signifying the new Christian who will again call upon the name of the Lord as did the Christians of old. Savonarola's position here is between the Augustinian and the Joachite. More concerned with the imminence of the Second Coming and the Last Days than was Augustine, he believes in a renovation of the whole Church; yet he does not subscribe to the Joachite millennial vision. In the same course of sermons he spoke again of the fire that would come at the end of the world, bringing with it a universal renovation; but whereas the Joachites taught that Enos would return at the end of the present age to preach as a prelude to the new reign of the Spirit, Savonarola held that Enos would return to preach against Antichrist at the end of the world.[72]

Although he disagreed with the Joachites, it is difficult to believe

---

[71] *Prediche nuovamente venute in luce . . . sopra il salmo Quam bonus Israel Deus* (Venice, 1528), fol. XCI verso. Autograph text in MS Florence Museo San Marco 480, fols. 1-51.

[72] Saint Augustine's discussion of the psalm is in *The City of God*, Book XV, chap. 18.

See Savonarola's explicitly anti-millenarian argument in his sermon of November 28, 1490, in which he says that past, present, and future are essentially equal in the world of time, that there is nothing new under the sun, and that human striving is vain because there is no new level that can be reached. MS BNF Magl. XXXV, 110, fol. 65.

that Savonarola was still entirely uninfluenced by current radical eschatologies in forming his views of the future. He adopted a seven-fold periodization of history and the idea of a World Sabbath which were characteristic of contemporary apocalyptic speculation. Already in the sermons of 1491 he used certain concepts and motifs that were common in radical apocalyptic thought. In his "terrifying sermon" of Lent of that year, he sees in Christ's leading the multitude to the mountain (Matthew 4-5) an allegory of the new conversion to a *magnus status*. In the new conversion, he says, the sun will illumi-nate the world, and after six days, when men have escaped the bonds of material things (*omnia corporalia*) and have been brought to the mountain of contemplation, they will have revelations and knowl-edge (*scientia*) of the Old and the New Testaments.[73] These refer-ences to the last age as one of contemplation and the revelation of new mysteries are perhaps mere echoes of contemporary Joachite speculation, but they are at least that. The latter point, especially, is reminiscent of the pseudo-Joachite doctrine of the Eternal Gospel which was condemned by the Church in the thirteenth century.[74] Evidently Savonarola was sensitive to the danger of being identified with the radical prophets of either the optimist or pessimist variety, since in the first of the sermons on the Apocalypse in 1490 he felt it necessary to deny that he had been influenced by the visions of *diversas prophethias Joachin, Sancti Vincentii, etc.* Nevertheless he continued to pursue certain ideas that had radical implications. In the 1491 Lenten sermons he speculated on the coming destruction of the Church, and he predicted that God would "change this order and liberate all of His own from the hands of the wolves," using

[73] Villari, *Savonarola*, vol. I, appendix, pp. xxxj-xxxij.

[74] On the Eternal Gospel and its condemnation, see Hastings Rashdall, *The Universities of Europe in the Middle Ages*, 2nd edn., ed. F. M. Powicke and A. B. Emden, 3 vols. (Oxford, 1936), vol. I, pp. 385-86. On the Joachite doc-trine of contemplation, see Herbert Grundmann, *Studien über Joachim von Floris* (Leipzig, 1927), pp. 128-34. One of Savonarola's sermons (Villari, *Savonarola*, vol. I, appendix, p. xix) contains the notation *mulier amicta sole*, the figure of the woman clothed in the sun (Revelation 12) which was popular with the Joachites. See Franz Kampers, *Kaiserprophetien und Kaisersagen im Mittelalter* (Munich, 1895), p. 19.

Jeremiah's imagery of the breaking of the wooden yoke of Babylon and its replacement with an iron one (Jeremiah 27-28).[75]

To be sure, all this does not add up to Joachism or to millenarianism of any variety. Nor, even as late as 1492 does Savonarola seem to have developed a consistent eschatological system of his own. The essential spirit of his preaching continued to be pessimistic in outlook, penitential in aim, and conservative with respect to the Church —despite a few radical-sounding statements of uncertain implication. This does, however, show us a Savonarola rather different from the traditional picture of the self-consistent, self-contained prophet with a vision fixed and whole. On the contrary, this Savonarola was tentative and eclectic, in touch with the radical apocalyptic thought of his time and prepared to take what he needed from it as well as from other sources.

It is just as important to discover what was not a part of Savonarola's vision at this time as to state what was. One thing he did not envision in 1492 was the idea of a special role for the city of Florence in the divine scheme. In his *Compendium*, Savonarola was to emphasize that God had sent him to Florence, the city chosen for the revelation of the prophecy of tribulation and reform; while in his exultant sermons of December 1494 and January 1495, he had already begun to describe the city's responsibilities in that elect role. But such ideas are not to be found before late 1494. The fact that Savonarola had his first apocalyptic inspiration in Florence—the San Giorgio experience of 1484—only underscores the point, for this is the only link between his early prophecy and the city of his future triumphs. He chose to express his new conviction in San Gimignano rather than in Florence, and there is no contemporary record of his ever having prophesied in the latter city before he left it in 1487, although later he was to say that God had sent him to Florence especially for that mission. When he returned in 1490, after having delivered apocalyptic sermons in Brescia and other cities of northern Italy, he began to prophesy immediately, but still without any special attention to

[75] See MS Museo San Marco 480, fol. 56; and "Ego indignus nuntio vobis quod deus mutabit ordinem istum peximum et liberabit omnes suas manu luporum," *ibid.*, fol. 61.

Florence. The spiritual community of which he spoke in his sermons on the Book of Revelation was the universal city of the faithful, not the city on the Arno; while in the letter to his mother dated January 25, 1490, he speaks of his mission to go to *diverse cittade* in order to save souls.[76] In his "terrifying sermon" of 1491, which marked his decision to persist in this apocalyptic mode of preaching and which had such a frightening impact upon his audience, he threatened his listeners not only with the destruction of Italy but even with an especially severe punishment for "this region."[77] If Florence was singled out it was not for glory but for special tribulation; no longer would she be called *Florentia*, he warned, but "turpitude and blood and a den of robbers."[78]

If Savonarola had not yet glimpsed his vision of Florentine election and glory, neither had he begun to think of himself as a political and social reformer, a conception which was to be closely related to that vision, as we shall see. After his return to Florence in 1490 he acquired the epithet, "Preacher of the Despairing," for he attacked social injustice from the start. The excesses of the rich, their oppression of the poor, and the injustice of the greedy which destroyed the happiness of the community, were among the reasons he gave for believing in the coming of divine punishment. He made pointed remarks about tyrants, who, like Nebuchadnezzar, Nero, and Domitian, must come to bad ends. He excoriated the *grandi* who spent huge sums on buildings by which they hoped to make themselves immortal, while at the same time they exploited the poor and violated the natural law of brotherly love. The poor, he said, had only their labor; they were burdened with taxes which went to pay for the rich man's palaces and whores; and they no longer received even

---

[76] *Lettere*, p. 12.

[77] ". . . et dico vobis quod Dominus confringet hoc vas Italie, et presertim in hac parte." Villari, *Savonarola*, vol. I, appendix, xxviij; and MS San Marco 480, fol. 57 verso, where "dicit Dominus" is added.

[78] "Non vocabitur locus iste Florentia, sed turpitudo et sanguis etc., et spelunca latronum, etc. [Jeremiah 7:11] Frange Domine, proice in torrentem lagunculam texteam etc." MS Museo San Marco 480, fol. 57 verso. Also, "Et tamen diabolus non cessit est in hac parte inveniri malitias." *Ibid.*, fol. 60. Apparently he had given similar warnings in Brescia, see pseudo-Burlamacchi, *La vita*, p. 15.

charity, so absorbed were the *grandi* in their sensual pleasures and in their games. Woe to the *ottimati*![79]

This was the warning cry of the moralist and repentance preacher, not of the political reformer or social radical. The world's corruption was the sign of the coming scourge, not the signal to overturn the world's governors. It was God who would punish injustice, not man. Palaces and treasures and fame and political power were all vain; there would be an end to everything.[80] To the poor Savonarola urged patience and a willingness to bear suffering in the expectation of divine help.[81] Convinced as he was of the vanity of human ambition and the imminence of the Last Days, he seems to have seen no point in dwelling upon the possibilities of reforming social institutions or of the long range improvement of the human condition.

WHILE SAVONAROLA did not assume the role of Florentine prophet and reformer immediately upon his return to the city in 1490, he was nevertheless creating the bonds of affection and admiration that were the foundation of that great mission. Having begun to preach in San Marco, he moved to the Cathedral during Lent of 1491 to accommodate a larger audience. Fra Placido Cinozzi, perhaps with some exaggeration, describes how his reputation was growing steadily, so that he became the foremost preacher in the city, outstripping all rivals.[82] Among these were the Franciscan Fra Domenico da Ponzo, who proclaimed a similar message of tribulation and repentance,[83] and Fra Mariano da Genazzano of the Order of Augustinian Hermits, whose polished sermons embellished with classical learning were the delight of the Medici *literati*.[84] More temperate than Fra Domenico, who incurred Piero de' Medici's displeasure for his demagoguery, more convincing than Fra Mariano, who finally lost the sympathy of his learned audience by making an exasperated

---

[79] "Ve vobis optimates," MS Museo San Marco 480, fol. 57 verso.

[80] MS BNF Magl. XXXV, 110, fol. 65 verso–66 recto.

[81] MS Museo San Marco 480, fol. 57 verso.

[82] Cinozzi in Villari-Casanova, *Scelta*, pp. 11-16.

[83] On Domenico da Ponzo and Savonarola, see below, pp. 126-28.

[84] On Fra Mariano della Barba da Genazzano, see D. A. Perini, *Un emulo di fr. Girolamo Savonarola: fra Mariano da Genazzano* (Rome, 1917).

ad hominem attack upon Savonarola's preaching,[85] Savonarola gained the admiration of both crowd and court. In the latter group were such men as the poet Girolamo Benivieni and his brother Domenico, canon of the Basilica of San Lorenzo and sometime professor of logic in the *Studium* of Pisa. Girolamo had been particularly close to Giuliano de' Medici, as he now was to Lorenzo, to Marsilio Ficino, and to Giovanni Pico. Both Benivieni brothers were early, ardent followers of Fra Girolamo, and later they became two of his most important apologists.[86] The poet Ugolino Verino became a Savonarolan admirer at least as early as 1491, when he dedicated his *Carmen de christiana religione* to the friar.[87] Still another influential supporter was Oliviero Arduini, philosopher and professor at Pisa, who, according to Cinozzi, when he heard Savonarola preach, told his students, "Let us take our books and follow behind this man, although we are unworthy to do even this." To such men, whose ears were tuned to the studied rhetoric of humanism, Savonarola's style was rude, but Gianfrancesco Pico describes how, enraptured, they listened to words which, as he put it, penetrated their hearts rather than their ears, words of the coming tribulation and reform of the Church. To those who had heard him preach before he had begun to prophesy, wrote Gianfrancesco, the change seemed a miracle.[88]

One of those who had heard Savonarola before 1490 was Giovanni Pico della Mirandola, the renowned young philosopher-prince (uncle of the aforementioned Gianfrancesco Pico) who may have been Savonarola's sponsor in the Medici circle. Pico and Fra Girolamo met some time between 1479 and 1482, either in Ferrara or in Reggio, as we have seen, and presumably their friendship began with that first meeting. Pico was in Florence between 1483 and 1485, so it is possible that the friendship took root during Savonarola's first visit to the city. At that time, however, their activities gave them little in common, for Pico was absorbed in his Kabbalistic studies and the

[85] Cinozzi, in Villari-Casanova, *Scelta*, pp. 14-15. Cinozzi says that Lorenzo de' Medici "ordered" Fra Mariano to deliver a sermon against predicting the future. Pseudo-Burlamacchi uses the same words, *La vita*, p. 28.

[86] See below, pp. 216-20.

[87] Gherardi, *Nuovi documenti e studi*, pp. 290-302.

[88] G. F. Pico, *Vita*, p. 27.

preparation of his ill-fated nine hundred theses. In 1488 Pico returned to Florence seeking a haven after the nine hundred theses had brought the wrath of the Church down upon him and, so the early biographers of Savonarola tell us, urged Lorenzo de' Medici to use his influence to have Savonarola recalled to Florence. The grounds for accepting the first part of this allegation—that Savonarola's recall was due to Pico's influence—will be examined later;[89] here let us consider the motives of the ruler of Florence, the Magnificent Lorenzo, since it has been established that Lorenzo did indeed intercede with the Dominican authorities to have Savonarola assigned to Florence.[90] Could he have had any motive beyond the desire to please his friend Pico to whom he had offered refuge? Savonarola's anonymous sixteenth-century biographer (pseudo-Burlamacchi) says that Pico prevailed upon Lorenzo by telling him of Savonarola's extraordinary piety and learning, and by suggesting that having such a man as Reader "in his own Convent of San Marco" would redound to Lorenzo's glory and honor, be helpful to the younger brothers who had a talent for learning, and thus bear fruit in God's Church, as well as give Pico himself immense pleasure. Moreover, he says, for just these reasons, Lorenzo acceded to Pico's request.[91]

The explanation is consonant with what we know of Lorenzo's character and purposes, as well as with the relationship of San Marco to the Medici. San Marco was the Medici's own convent, both in spirit and in substance. Lorenzo's grandfather, Cosimo, had been instrumental in obtaining the ecclesiastical decision expropriating its original occupants, the Benedictine Silvestrines, in favor of the Observant Dominicans in 1436. Cosimo's money paid for the rebuilding of the cloister under the direction of Michelozzo in 1442, and for the continued enrichment of San Marco with the paintings of Fra Angelico and the books of the humanist Niccolò Niccoli. He kept a double cell there for his own use and maintained close relations with its Prior, Antonino, the future Archbishop of Florence (1446-59) who was canonized in 1523.[92] However, by the time of which

[89] See below, pp. 210-12.
[90] The document is recorded in ASF Mediceo Avanti il Principato; see Ridolfi, *Vita*, vol. I, p. 43; and vol. II, p. 98, n. 26.
[91] Pseudo-Burlamacchi, *La vita*, pp. 16-17.
[92] Schnitzer, *Savonarola*, vol. I, pp. 75-81.

we are speaking, Antonino had been dead for over thirty years, and the Convent of San Marco had not seen his like again. If Savonarola was all that Pico said he was, he might help restore San Marco to the prestige it had had thirty years earlier. Glory and honor had their practical value for the city as well, for a Florentine Dominican house that achieved a position of spiritual leadership in Tuscany might be a useful instrument of Florentine regional consolidation, as indeed San Marco turned out to be. Admittedly, we are speculating about Lorenzo's motives; we can only point out that later events suggest that Lorenzo had such considerations in mind when he wrote to Savonarola's superiors in 1489. To borrow an apt comment from Joseph Schnitzer: "all Florence had long ago learned that the Medici did nothing for nothing."[93]

Lorenzo may soon have had second thoughts, however, for, as we have seen, Savonarola did not stop with criticizing the Church and clerical corruption, but made pointed remarks about tyrants, the luxurious living of the *grandi*, and their exploitation of the poor.[94] In a letter of March 10, 1491, to his confidant Fra Domenico Buonvicini of Pescia, who was preaching in Pisa, he discussed his situation in Florence:

> Our affairs go well, for God is doing wonderful things, although we are strongly opposed by some of the high and mighty [*apud maiores*]. But I will tell you all about that in detail when you return; it is not wise to write about such things now. Many have been afraid, and some still fear that the same thing might happen to me as to Fra Bernardino. Certainly our position here has not been without danger, but I have always put my trust in the Lord, knowing that the heart of the king is in the hand of God, and that He turns it in whatever direction He wills. . . . You also must take comfort and be steadfast, because our affairs go well, nor should you be troubled if many in this city do not run to hear us preach; it is enough to have announced such things to a few. In a small seed there is great power.

[93] *Ibid.*, vol. I, p. 137.
[94] Also, in his 1490 sermons on the First Epistle of John, "a quelli che vogliono reggere le cipta sotto li principi et gran maestri: che vivino bene. O quante iniustitie: quante iniquita et peccati si fanno per preghi et comandamento de principi: per non esser cacciata da quella potesta." MS BNF Magl. XXXV, 110, fol. 70.

. . . I announce very frequently the renovation of the Church and future tribulations, not absolutely, but always with a basis in the Scriptures, because in this way no one can reproach me unless he does not wish to walk in the way of righteousness. The Count steadily grows more devout (*Comes semper in Domino augetur*) and attends my sermons often. I cannot send you any alms, for although monies have come from the Count you must wait a little, for good reasons.[95]

Despite its guarded tone, the letter gives us a glimpse into Savonarola's mind. He felt some apprehension about displeasing Lorenzo—for surely he meant Lorenzo in his reference to Proverbs 21:1, "The king's heart is a stream of water in the hands of the Lord: he turns it wherever he will." The danger was exile, as he was aware. What the Medici gave the Medici could take away; Savonarola had in mind the case of Fra Bernardino da Feltre, the Franciscan preacher who had been forced to leave the city in 1488 after he had incited the populace against the Jews.[96] On the other hand, the letter offers no ground for inferring that a state of hostilities existed between Lorenzo and Fra Girolamo, or that the high and mighty who strongly opposed Savonarola included Lorenzo. Had this been the case it is doubtful that the friar could have escaped the banishment which had been Fra Bernardino's lot. So far, by his own admission, his following in the city was not large. Savonarola's criticism must have been an irritant to Lorenzo, who seems to have complained about it more than once,[97] but Lorenzo had little to fear from this preacher

---

[95] *Lettere*, pp. 15-16.

[96] On the ejection of Fra Bernardino from Florence in March 1488, see Landucci, *Diario fiorentino*, pp. 53-54; and below, p. 128. On this Franciscan, who was one of the advocates of the *Monte di Pietà*, or communal loan fund, see Gino Barbieri, *Il beato Bernardino da Feltre nella storia sociale del Rinascimento* (Milan, 1962); Luke Wadding, *Annales Minorum*, vol. XV, pp. 5-13, 37-46, 62-88, 98-99.

[97] According to pseudo-Burlamacchi, *La vita*, pp. 24-25, who is followed by Ridolfi, *Vita*, vol. I, pp. 67-68. Ridolfi rightly scores the "republican and Jacobin portrait of the Friar which many have painted and like to imagine" (*Life*, p. 50), but he does not note that in the first instance this picture derives from Savonarola himself, who took an extreme anti-Medicean stand after November 9, 1494, and who liked to recall his earlier pronouncements against tyranny. It is interesting to compare Guicciardini's observation that Savonarola's sermons did not please Lorenzo much, but that one of the reasons he did not

whose main preoccupations, reiterated in this letter, were the coming renovation of the Church and future tribulations. Far from suffering Lorenzo's opposition, Fra Girolamo writes that his situation is improving, his cause prospering, his fear of banishment diminishing. The Count, Giovanni Pico, was on his side, lending his prestige by his presence at Savonarola's sermons and giving him money for his work. In July, four months after he wrote this letter, the brothers of San Marco elected Savonarola their Prior, a clear indication of their faith in the man and in his future.

While Savonarola's election to the priorate presented him with his first opportunity to translate his hopes for reform into a program, it also forced him to consider more realistically what he could achieve. The obvious starting place for reform was the community of San Marco itself and this is no doubt what Lorenzo had intended; but San Marco, with its Medici connections, its elegant cloisters and extensive properties, seems at first not to have been Savonarola's idea of the proper setting for a life of repentance and spiritual renewal. For a time, apparently, he planned to take the brothers out of San Marco, out of Florence, into the chestnut forest of Montecavo, above Careggi, where they could live truly apart from the world. The younger brothers were enthusiastically in favor of the plan, but the older ones were afraid to exchange their familiar home for the discomforts and uncertainties of the Montecavo forests. Their strategy for blocking the move was to warn the families of the other friars that it was a perilous undertaking which would endanger the lives of their loved ones. Apparently they were successful in building up the opposition, and Savonarola was forced to give up his plan. As his biographer put it: "The servant of God, seeing that he was cheated out of his desire, was discouraged not at all, but turned to more moderate measures, less severe and rigid, and began to think how to get them to accept a more perfect life. . . ."[98]

The new, moderate way to perfection began to take shape in the spring of 1492. As Savonarola himself described it in a letter of the

---

prohibit the friar from preaching was that Savonarola *non lo toccava nel vivo*. Francesco Guicciardini, *Storie fiorentine*, ed. Roberto Palmarocchi, *Opere*, vol. VI (Bari, 1931), p. 108.

[98] Pseudo-Burlamacchi, *La vita*, p. 54.

following year to the Prioress of San Domenico in Pisa, a number of brothers as well as the Prior began, independently of each other at first, to think about separating San Marco from the Lombard Congregation of which it was a member house, as a first step toward reform. Fra Tommaso Busini was the most fervent advocate of the plan, while Savonarola himself, aware of the dangers and hostilities that such a step would create, was hesitant. He wrote that for many months he had prayed for guidance and called upon others for their prayers and advice, not only in the Convent but throughout Florence and beyond, until finally, convinced that he was moved by the Spirit to achieve the separation, he decided to go ahead. In his characteristic way, Savonarola once again turned a major disappointment into an opportunity and, after prayerful hesitation, found that the Spirit was moving him to take a new course. Even as he himself described it, the similarity with the decision to enter the Order twenty years earlier is striking: "And thus more than ever I was moved by the Spirit to accomplish this separation, which seemed to me more useful and necessary, and that for the love of God I had to leave fatherland and family and friends and honor and glory and embrace the cross of Christ, as it is written, 'Go from your land and from your kindred.' "[99]

And yet, while he might describe this as a new departure from family and friends, the proposed separation from the Lombard Congregation was, in a different sense, a turning back to the world. Faced with the opposition of his own Convent, Savonarola had been forced to abandon his own plan of taking the brothers and himself into the wilderness; in other words, he was forced to reconsider his more stringent, ascetic spirituality in favor of the compromise course of working for reform within the context of Florentine San Marco. The importance of this shift for Savonarola's development has been obscured, in the first instance by his own habit of looking back at his prophetic mission as all of a piece, in the second, by his biographers' adoption of his point of view. In fact, the decision to keep the San Marco brethren in Florence had for Savonarola two major implications. For one thing, it meant the virtual abandonment of his radical asceticism, a reconciliation with the world of the possible. He

---

[99] *Lettere*, pp. 33-34. The scriptural reference is to Genesis 12:1.

himself expressed this very clearly in a letter of May 22, 1492, which was just the time that he was considering the new course of action. Writing to Stefano da Codiponte, a novice in the Dominican house of St. Catherine in Pisa, who was disillusioned with the spiritual tepidity of the Convent life, Savonarola argued that the young man's expectations were unrealistic:

> In heaven everyone is good; in hell everyone is evil; but in this world we find both good and evil. Never will you find that there have been good [men here] without [also finding] evil ones. Many who are anxious to live good lives and, unmindful of what their elders say, seek what is impossible in this world, for they wish to be remembered among the saints by rejecting all human sin and imperfection. When they do not find this they draw back and wander off from their proper vocation; they are deceived by the devil; they are led into error and they fall away, never afterwards returning to the wisdom of truth. My son, to live well is to do well and to suffer evil and persevere unto death. Who but a perverse creature entirely destitute of God's grace lives badly among saints? . . . In the world you have lived among scorpions; in the cloister, however, you must live among those who are perfect, those who are making progress and those who are imperfect, but no longer among those who are purely evil.[100]

The advice to the novice was the fruit of Savonarola's own inner struggle and marks, we might say, the end of his own spiritual novitiate. Henceforward he would live where men were engaged in the struggle between good and evil, finding perfection sometimes, but not despairing if they were not always successful. He had sought for spiritual guidance and had been directed to wage the struggle not in the wilderness but in San Marco of Florence. Herein lay the second implication of his decision: from this time on his own future and the future of his mission were to be bound up with the city of Florence to a degree they had never been before. In adopting the image of the building of a new, spiritual city in a sermon of October, Savonarola seems to have been expressing this new commitment.[101]

The first practical step toward building the spiritual city was, then, the separation of San Marco from the jurisdiction of the Lombard Congregation. Since separation involved the closest cooperation with

[100] *Lettere*, pp. 17-18.   [101] Ridolfi, *Life*, p. 58.

the Florentine government, it seems most unlikely that Savonarola would have been considering it unless he already had some assurances from that direction. In his letter to the Prioress of San Domenico he indicated that in the many months during which he was seeking guidance for his decision he had consulted beyond the Convent. Did such consultations include the Magnificent Lorenzo or his surrogates? We do not know; nor do we know whether Lorenzo himself would have approved the step, since he died on April 8, 1492, while the San Marco brothers were still deliberating about their future course. We have already suggested that one of Lorenzo's motives in having Savonarola reassigned to Florence was to increase the prestige of the Convent of San Marco, and through it, his own, but we have no way of knowing whether, either then or later, Lorenzo contemplated a break from the Lombard Congregation. Considering that San Marco had rejoined the Lombard jurisdiction in 1474 during Lorenzo's own regime and that it was part of Lorenzo's policy to maintain good relations with the Duke of Milan, it is highly possible that he would have opposed the step. If so, the death of *il Magnifico* in April removed an obstacle from the new course on which the Convent was setting out, and improved relations between its Prior and the city government. We cannot overlook the fact that the decision to separate San Marco coincided fairly closely with the time of Lorenzo's death, or that his successor, Piero, reoriented Florentine policy by ignoring the old bonds of friendship with Milan and strengthening his alliance with the King of Naples. Furthermore, whatever the relations between *il Magnifico* and Savonarola may have been like, between Piero and Savonarola they were cordial. Piero and his younger brother Giovanni, the Cardinal and future Pope Leo X, worked hard to secure papal approval for the separation of San Marco from the Lombard Congregation.[102] Their advocate in the Curia was Cardinal Oliviero Carafa of Naples; their

---

[102] ". . . la Signoria et etiam el magnifico Piero habiano assai scripto al Reverendissimo Cardinale quanto desiderano questa cossa. . . ." Savonarola, *Lettere*, p. 46; Francesco Guicciardini, *Scritti autobiografici e rari*, ed. Roberto Palmarocchi, *Opere*, vol. IX (Bari, 1936), p. 50. On Savonarola's work for Dominican reform, see Joseph Schnitzer, *Savonarola im Streite mit seinem Orden und seinem Kloster* (Munich, 1914).

chief opponent, the spokesman for the Duke of Milan.[103] Obviously, the issues went beyond those of internal monastic politics to the politics of the realignment of Italian states after the death of Lorenzo. San Marco as a member of the Lombard Congregation was a possible outpost of Milanese influence in Florence, and it was part of Piero's new policy to reduce that influence. On the other hand, San Marco as the nucleus of a new congregation would serve the Florentine state in a similar way. It was more than diplomatic rhetoric when the Signoria of Florence described the separation as a matter involving the will and the interest of the Florentine people,[104] just as it was more than gratuitous invective when some of the brothers of St. Catherine of Pisa earlier denounced Savonarola as an agent of the Medici for trying to win them over to his reforming plans.[105]

Milanese opposition notwithstanding, the Florentines, through Cardinal Carafa, contrived to secure a Papal brief on May 22, 1493, that annulled San Marco's membership in the Lombard Congregation. The Milanese did not give up: they succeeded in winning agreement for a compromise by which the execution of the brief was delayed, but the crucial battle had been won by Florence and San Marco. Savonarola was perfectly aware that he owed everything to Piero de' Medici's support and that as Prior of the Convent he was, in a sense, Piero's steward. Writing to Piero on May 26, the same day on which the compromise delaying execution of the Papal order was reached, he assured him of the complete harmony of their respective interests and of the loyalty of "your convent": "Magnificent Piero. I told those Fathers of ours that my intention and the intention of the Convent was to do everything as Your Magnificence wished it, just as you stated in your declaration, my interpretation of which I stated to those Fathers. I am always ready to do whatever you wish. I recommend your convent to you. The grace of the Lord Jesus be with you. Amen."[106]

<hr/>

[103] Schnitzer, *Savonarola*, vol. I, pp. 144-45; Romeo de Maio, *Savonarola e la curia romana* (Rome, 1969), especially chap. II.

[104] Letter of the Signoria to the Cardinal of Naples, June 10, 1493, in Villari, *Savonarola*, vol. I, appendix, p. xlvij. For other documents, see *ibid.*, pp. xl-lij.

[105] C. Lupi ed., "Documenti pisani," *Archivio storico italiano*, 3rd ser., XIII (1871), 180.

[106] *Lettere*, p. 30.

By a Papal brief of August 13, 1493, Savonarola became the first Vicar General of the new Tuscan Congregation, later renamed the Congregation of San Marco, which included San Domenico of Fiesole, the Dominican houses in neighboring Prato and Sasso, and St. Catherine of Pisa. This was the outcome of unceasing efforts on the part of Savonarola, his brethren in San Marco, and the political agencies of the Florentine state. In Siena the reformers failed utterly; the friars of the Convent of Santo Spirito in that city violently attacked Savonarola and his companions who had gone there in June 1494 to effect union with San Marco.[107] But—unlike Siena— Prato, Sasso, and for the time being Pisa, were under Florentine rule, so the union of their Dominican houses with San Marco was achieved.

Three letters of late April to the Florentine ambassadors in Rome not only show the extent to which Savonarola was involved in the negotiations regarding the creation of the new Congregation, but also reveal the mixture of deference and confidence with which he now dealt with the instrumentalities of the state power. "All our trust," he writes, "lies first in all-powerful God, then in you. Wherefore, if we have sent letters there [to Rome] this is not because we are not confident of your diligence, but to defend and reinforce Your Magnificences, since you might be thought, for love of us, to be too importunate in this matter. . . ."[108] If, however, the ambassadors feel that they need additional letters from the Signoria or from others, they need only let Savonarola know and he will see to it.[109] Thus, the successful outcome of the fight for separation and the establishment of a new Congregation marks a further stage in the continuing domestication of Savonarola as a Florentine.

Since his return to Florence four years earlier he had undergone major changes in circumstances and outlook. Even his Ferrarese speech, it has been observed, underwent "Florentinization."[110] Having come to identify the beginnings of reform with the reform of San Marco—and come to see God's hand in it—he had also come to

---

[107] Ridolfi, *Vita*, vol. I, pp. 112-15 and nn.
[108] *Lettere*, p. 42.   [109] *Ibid.*, pp. 44, 45.
[110] On the "Florentinization" of Savonarola's language, see Jean Nicolas, "La 'Florentinisation' de la langue de Savonarole," *Les Langues Modernes*, 52 (1958), 78-85.

terms with both human weakness, as manifested in the less ardent brothers of San Marco and other houses, and with human power, as manifested in the government of the city. No longer a simple itinerant friar—Francesco Guicciardini pointed out that the separation from the Lombard Congregation held Savonarola in Florence, unlike other frati who changed location from year to year[111]—he now occupied posts of dignity and responsibility as Prior of San Marco and as Vicar General of the new regional jurisdiction. No longer merely the "Preacher of the Despairing" he had close relations with the Archbishop of Florence,[112] while he counted among his best friends and most enthusiastic supporters many of the leading lights of the city's intellectual and artistic life, beginning with Giovanni Pico della Mirandola, the Benivieni brothers, and Ugolino Verino. Some of these prominent men of the world, members of important patrician families of Florence, even joined him in the cloister. San Marco now included among its brothers such men as Zanobi Acciaiuoli, who had been educated in the Medici household and was later to serve as Pope Leo X's librarian, Giorgio Antonio Vespucci, a lover of learning from the famous Florentine family, and Pandolfo Rucellai, who as Fra Santi Rucellai was to achieve renown as an Hebraicist and Biblical translator.[113] In making San Marco available as a gathering place for scholars, artists, and literati, Savonarola was continuing a Medici tradition; but it was under his leadership that it came to be called, in good humanist fashion, *Accademia Marciana*.[114]

The shrewd Florentine observer, Piero Parenti, himself no friend of Savonarola, reported that the friar's success in the reform of San Marco increased his reputation in the city.[115] It also initiated Savona-

---

[111] Cited in Schnitzer, *Savonarola*, vol. I, p. 179, n. 1.

[112] See "Vita e Memoria di Fra G.S. raccolte da Giovanni di Poggio Baldovinetti," MS BNF Palat. Baldovinetti 115 (1734), fol. 15 recto.

[113] On these and other important recruits, see Schnitzer, *Savonarola*, vol. I, pp. 417-18.

[114] Piero Crinito, *De honesta disciplina*, ed. C. Angeleri (Rome, 1955), pp. 104-105. On the sixteenth-century notion of the *Accademia Marciana* as a school for artists, see André Chastel, *Art et humanisme à Florence au temps de Laurent le Magnifique* (Paris, 1961), pp. 19-25.

[115] Piero Parenti, *Storia fiorentina*, ed. Schnitzer, *Quellen und Forschungen*

rola's growing dependence upon the favor of the Florentine citizenry, for, just as Fra Girolamo predicted, the struggle for the independence and reform of San Marco made him enemies as well as friends. He need hardly have had prophetic powers to make such a prediction. At the time of the separation he had already been summoned to appear before the Vicar General of the Lombard Congregation and had refused, on the grounds that he was no longer subject to that jurisdiction.[116] Later he would need the protection of the city walls against the Pope himself. So long as he could demonstrate that his prophetic mission was a boon to Florence he was on solid ground. This took a shrewdness in judging the mind of his new compatriots and a flexibility in adapting his purposes to theirs which are saved from the suspicion of charlatanism by his sincere belief in his own divine inspiration.

---

zur Geschichte Savonarolas, vol. IV, *Savonarola nach der Aufzeichnungen des Florentiners Piero Parenti* (Leipzig, 1910), pp. 4-5.

[116] Ridolfi, *Life*, p. 63.

III

The Prophet and the City

YOU KNOW THAT YEARS AGO
GREAT TRIBULATIONS WERE ANNOUNCED
BEFORE THERE WAS ANY NOISE OR SMELL OF THESE WARS LAUNCHED
BY THE MEN FROM OVER THE MOUNTAINS WHICH WE ARE NOW
WITNESSING. YOU ALSO KNOW THAT NOT TWO FULL
YEARS HAVE PASSED SINCE I SAID TO YOU:
Ecce gladius Domini super terram cito et velociter.
NOT I, BUT GOD WAS RESPONSIBLE FOR THIS
PREDICTION TO YOU, AND BEHOLD,
IT HAS COME AND IT
IS COMING.

—Savonarola, Sermon of November 1, 1494

WHILE, in Florence, Savonarola was laboring to build his new reform Congregation and prophesying a *renovatio* of the Church, far to the North, in France, another enterprise was taking shape in which visions of renewal also played a vital role. By the end of the 1480's and with Charles VIII's assumption of personal rule,[1] the ancient royal dream of Italian conquest came to the fore again.[2] In Charles the idea of an Italian expedition became a governing passion to which he was seduced by dreams of glory, lust for power, and apocalyptic fantasies. Neapolitan exiles at the French court and Milanese envoys combined to recall to Charles the ancient Angevin

---

[1] That this was a gradual process of emancipation and self-assertion on Charles' part is clear from the standard accounts: Henri F. Delaborde, *L'expédition de Charles VIII en Italie* (Paris, 1888), pp. 199ff.; John C. Bridge, *A History of France from the Death of Louis XI*, 5 vols. (Oxford, 1931-6), vol. I, pp. 236-42.

[2] Delaborde, *L'expédition*, pp. 214-21ff.

rights to the *Regno*. French courtiers who saw glorious opportunities for their King and for themselves in an Italian expedition pressed their suit at court; religious reformers and dreamers stirred up the old fantasies of a Second Charlemagne: after conquering Italy and restoring French power in Naples and the true religion in Rome, Charles would cross to the East, conquer the Infidel and reduce the world to a single sheepfold under one shepherd.[3]

With the incessant comings and goings of merchants, diplomats, clerics, scholars, and adventurers of all sorts between the two countries, rumors of the coming French enterprise reached Italy very quickly.[4] By the same means the apocalyptic contagion spread, and we cannot always tell in which of the two countries the infection arose. The chief prophetic influence on Charles himself seems to have been exercised by the Calabrian hermit Francesco di Paola, who lived as an exile in France. This holy man had been close to Charles before his accession to the throne and continued as a trusted adviser at court. Anxious for a renewal of the Church, he taught Charles to think of himself as a divine agent and seems to have encouraged him to undertake the Italian enterprise as the first step toward the great renovation.[5] Another prophet close to the King was the royal physician Jean Michel, who reported seeing Charles in a vision as the reformer and conqueror of the world.[6] Guilloche de Bordeaux

[3] For all this, see *ibid.*, chaps. III-VIII.

[4] Piero Parenti in Florence, under the date June 1492, wrote: "Stavansi cosi le cose adormentate e novità alcuna perlo terre di Italia non si scopriva benche qualche portento ogni giorno di nuovo si divulgassi: siccome quello che piu huomini di Pietramala sopra ad Arezzo dissono havere sentito, cioè passare moltitudine di gente d'arme a piei e a cavallo in certo luogho di nocto. la qualcosa con effecto vana essere sicompresa." *Storia fiorentina*, ms BNF II. IV. 169 fol. 132 verso. On the general awareness of the coming French invasion in Italy, see Nino Valeri, *L'Italia nell' età dei principati* (Verona, 1959), pp. 726-33.

[5] Some of the contemporary sources are cited by Delaborde, *L'expédition*, pp. 314-15. It is interesting to note that in the early sixteenth century it was believed that Francesco di Paola had himself prophesied the coming of the prophet Savonarola. For the apocryphal letters in which the predictions occur, see S. Francesco di Paola, *Centuria di lettere*, ed. Francesco di Longobardi (Rome, 1655), pp. 297-322.

[6] Delaborde, *L'expédition*, p. 317. Text in I. de la Pilorgerie, *Campagne et Bulletins de la Grande Armée d'Italie commandée par Charles VIII 1494-95* (Nantes-Paris, 1866), pp. 431-33.

circulated a "Prophecy of Charles VIII" according to which Charles would become the universal monarch and establish a world order under the Cross until, in the thirty-fifth year of his reign, he would receive an angelic crown on the Mount of Olives.[7]

The French predictions had their counterparts in the Italian oracles of warning and foreboding, as we have seen,[8] so that when Charles came to Italy in the fall of 1494 he came with the aura of one who had long been expected, as the chosen instrument of God's avenging wrath. As Delaborde remarked, "Whatever may have been the credence given to these oracles, it is certain that at the beginning of 1494 there reigned in Italy a kind of mysterious anxiety."[9]

Charles came with a mighty army as well. With some forty thousand effectives and a hundred siege guns which the Italians found particularly *stupenda*, his was a conquering force the likes of which had never been seen or bargained for by Charles' Italian allies.[10] For Florence, as we have already seen, the coming of Charles VIII swiftly set off a chain of traumatic consequences. It stripped the Florentine state of key ports and border towns, leaving her in a weakened and precarious position. It brought down the Medici regime of sixty years by a revolution which, however many welcomed it, opened a Pandora's box of troubles. As the French army advanced, Florence had, under the vacillating leadership of Piero de' Medici, first taken a posture of noncooperation, then of abject submission to the juggernaut, and it seemed that she would be overwhelmed and overrun.

The apocalyptic dimension of Florence's peril was the persistent theme of Savonarola. Preaching almost daily in the Cathedral to swollen and frightened crowds, he reminded the Florentines that for almost two years he had been warning them of the coming of the divine sword: *Ecce gladius Domini super terram cito et velociter.*[11]

---

[7] Delaborde, *L'expédition*, p. 317.

[8] See above, pp. 62-66.

[9] Delaborde, *L'expédition*, p. 317.

[10] *Ibid.*, pp. 324-27. The size of the army was exaggerated three-fold.

[11] *Prediche sopra Aggeo*, ed. Luigi Firpo (Rome, 1965), p. 12. According to his own account, these words first came to him on April 5, 1492; Roberto Ridolfi, *Vita di Girolamo Savonarola*, 2 vols. (Rome, 1952), vol. I, pp. 73-75 and n. 20.

The French invasion was the divine tribulation he had prophesied in these words which he had had from God: "I, the Lord, speak in my zeal, that the days will come when I shall unsheath my sword over you. Convert before my wrath is fulfilled. For tribulation is coming to you and you will want peace and shall not find it."[12] Each November day seemed to bring confirmation of these terrible words a step nearer, and as it did so the Florentines drew closer to their prophet. On November 5, they sent an embassy headed by Savonarola to the invader's camp with "free and absolute authority to do and say whatever you decide for the safety of this City."[13] The city's salvation was still in doubt when Charles entered Florence on November 17, and when negotiations between the King and the city fathers stalled—Charles insisting on restoring the now tamed Piero de' Medici to his former position—Savonarola was delegated to persuade the King to accept terms more favorable to the new republic.[14] Bartolomeo Cerretani reported that when Savonarola came into the King's presence he drew a silver crucifix from his bosom and said that God had elected Charles His minister to do great deeds for the Christian Republic; that He wanted Charles to show his kindness to the city of Florence (*che lui benificassi la cipta fiorentina*); that the King's delay in the city was displeasing to Him; and that He wanted Charles to speed on his way to the conquest of Naples as soon as possible. When the King heard these words, says Cerretani, he was awed (*stupefacto*) because Savonarola was held in great repute as a holy and true prophet, and he promised that he would

---

[12] *Prediche sopra Aggeo*, pp. 12-13. Savonarola seems to have been inspired here by various passages from Ezechiel.

[13] ". . . e ingegneretevi fare tutte queste petizioni migliori che vi sarà possibile per là Città nostra; dandovi in questa parte libera autorità e assoluta di fare e dire tutto quello che vi occorrerà per la salute di questa Città." "Instructions données aux ambassadeurs envoyés a la rencontre de Charles VIII," in G. Canestrini and A. Desjardins, *Négociations diplomatiques de la France avec la Toscane*, 6 vols. (Paris, 1859-86), vol. I, p. 600. Besides Savonarola the members of the embassy were Piero Capponi, Tanai de' Nerli, Pandolfo Rucellai, and Giovanni Cavalcanti. *Ibid.*, p. 598.

[14] Ridolfi, *Vita*, vol. I, pp. 131-34 and nn. In his *Compendium Revelationum*, Savonarola reported what he said to the King. In Gianfrancesco Pico della Mirandola, *Vita R. P. Hieronymi Savonarolae*, ed. Jacques Quetif, 2 vols. (Paris, 1674), vol. I, pp. 237-43.

do this forthwith.[15] The report of the interview given by Savonarola's anonymous sixteenth-century biographer is even more colorful: Savonarola threatened the King with God's wrath and Charles burst into tears.[16] Savonarola himself later reported a more sober but no less decisive exchange with the King,[17] and when, on November 25, the treaty of reconciliation was signed between Charles VIII and the Florentine republic,[18] the friar received much of the credit for having used his holy authority to save the city from destruction.[19]

Thus once the French had departed on November 28, it was as the savior of the city and her special prophet that Savonarola spoke to the Florentines. Continually urging a "universal peace" so that the Florentines could turn to the major work of repentance and reform, he heralded the city as the chosen center of divine illumination and himself as the man sent by God, not only to warn Italy of the tribulations which had now come, but also to lead her out of the abomination of desolation. To restore peace to Florence and to make her worthy of God's election as the starting place of the divine work, he championed a plan for reforming the republican government, and he came to be hailed as the protector of civic peace and the founder of the city's new-found freedom. In the worst days of her crisis Florence was uplifted by the Savonarolan message of a rebirth of freedom and spirituality, while to many the new atmosphere of piety and repentance seemed the most wonderful of all the signs that they were living again in the days of prophecy. As Savonarola explained it, past, present, and future were united in his prophetic vision: God had ordained that he come to Florence, prophesy, and found a new order. In his *Compendium Revelationum*, written the

[15] Bartolomeo Cerretani, *Storia fiorentina*, ed. Joseph Schnitzer, *Quellen und Forschungen zur Geschichte Savonarolas*, vol. III, *Bartolomeo Cerretani* (Munich, 1904), p. 27.

[16] Pseudo-Burlamacchi, *La vita del Beato Ieronimo Savonarola*, ed. Piero Ginori Conti (Florence, 1937), p. 74.

[17] In his sermon of October 28, 1496: *Prediche sopra Ruth e Michea*, ed. Vincenzo Romano, 2 vols. (Rome, 1962), vol. II, pp. 325-26.

[18] Text in Gino Capponi, ed., "Capitoli fatti dalla città di Firenze col re Carlo VIII a dì di Novembre 1494," *Archivio storico italiano*, I (1842), 363-75.

[19] "Ab eo [Hieronymo Savonarolae] civitas florentina in adventu Regis Caroli octavi, Gallorum Regis, quam depopulandam decreverat, miserante Deo, servata est." Quoted from the Chronicle of San Marco by Ridolfi, *Vita*, vol. II, p. 128, n. 21.

following summer, he reviewed the whole story: how the Lord had sent him to Florence; how, in Advent of 1492 he had had the vision of the hand holding the sword of judgment; how he had then predicted that one would come like a new Cyrus from beyond the mountains and that the "Turks and Mohammedans" would be converted to Christianity in those times; how, also in 1492, he had had a vision of two crosses in the sky, the black cross of God's wrath over Rome, the golden cross of God's mercy over Jerusalem; and how, finally, in addition to the renovation of the Church and the coming tribulations, he had prophesied Florence's reformation according to God's will. He did not hesitate to remind his readers that it was through him, speaking with divine authority, that the peace of the city had been restored and the constitutional reforms adopted in the previous months. Having done God's will, Florence would be "more glorious, richer, more powerful than ever before."[20]

There is no reason to doubt that Savonarola himself believed this account of things as sincerely as his own most devoted follower. Indeed, he had ample reason for believing that it was true. His visions had not played him false; the tribulations had come, both to the city and to Italy, and Charles VIII had arrived with the aura of the apocalyptic reformer of the Church and the new crusader who would conquer the East. Savonarola's own role in the reform of the Florentine state was such as to recall his earlier castigation of tyrants and to lend validity to his claim that he had introduced the *governo popolare*.[21] For the rest, only the future could say whether he was right or wrong in prophesying the fulfillment of God's plan. But, however sincere, Savonarola's own account was better as prophecy than as history. It passes too vaguely over the details of his coming to Florence and over the origins of his prophesying, as we have already seen, and it obscures the details of his earlier activities in the city. Most important of all, it ignores completely—perhaps because he himself was unaware of them—the fundamental changes that

[20] *Compendium Revelationum*, especially pp. 233-34, 244-45.

[21] For the passages where Savonarola claimed to have introduced the new government by divine inspiration, see Nicolai Rubinstein, "Politics and Constitution in Florence at the End of the Fifteenth Century," *Italian Renaissance Studies*, ed. E. F. Jacob (London, 1960), p. 155, n. 1.

took place in the nature of his prophetic vision and his program for the city. In order to understand all this it is necessary once more to retrace our steps, to follow in greater detail the events leading up to the crises of November-December 1494 and to assess Savonarola's role in them.

THE CLASSIC PORTRAIT of Florence at the time of Lorenzo de' Medici's death in 1492 derives mainly from the city's two most famous historians, Niccolò Machiavelli and Francesco Guicciardini. In bringing the eighth, and last, book of his *History of Florence* to a close with Lorenzo's death, Machiavelli describes how the city was at the height of her prosperity due to the wise policy of *il Magnifico*, for "it was throughout his aim to make the city prosperous, the people united, and the nobles honoured." Notwithstanding the misfortunes he suffered in his own business affairs because of the misconduct of his employees, Lorenzo bent his efforts to beautify the city, showered favors on the learned, founded a college in Pisa for the city's youth, and built a monastery for his favorite preacher, Fra Mariano da Genazzano. His wisdom benefited all Italy as well, for he knew how to keep the peace and when he died he was mourned by everyone, for in all Italy there was no one to take his place. "Heaven gave many unmistakeable signs that ruin would follow his decease, among such signs was the destruction of the highest pinnacle of San[ta] Reparata by lightning."[22]

Guicciardini also drew his picture in strong, bright colors, although he tempered it with a few shadows. At Lorenzo's death, he wrote, the city was at peace; its citizens were united and the Medici regime so powerful that none dared oppose it. The Florentines took their delight in spectacles and festivals; the city had plenty of food, business was good, and men of learning were well provided for. Florence enjoyed glory abroad and tranquillity at home. Much of her well-being was due to the wise rule of Lorenzo who had about him "a number of noble and prudent citizens" who dealt with important matters and among whom the honors of the city were distributed; but Lorenzo was chief of state. He followed his own

[22] Niccolò Machiavelli, *History of Florence*, trans. W. K. Marriott (London, n.d.), pp. 358-60.

counsel even when it went against the will of the others, and he took good care to see that no one might become so important in the city as to give him cause for fearing them. At the time of the war with Naples and the Papacy (1478-80) while Lorenzo was absent on his peace-making mission to the King of Naples, some men at home summoned their courage to demand that the distribution of offices and the assessment of taxes be decided upon by councils rather than "by the will of the few," but when Lorenzo returned from Naples in triumph he took measures to tighten still further his hold upon the government, and he made his own position stronger and more stable than ever. Thus, concludes Guicciardini, under Lorenzo the city was not free, although it would have been impossible to have had a better or more pleasing tyrant. While his death was welcomed by those whom he had kept down, even many whom he had offended were sorry, for now they did not know what to expect, and the mass of the people grieved his death.[23]

In contemplating these portraits of the death of a hero and the end of an age we must keep in mind that they were written in the sixteenth century, after the trials and troubles of the intervening years had induced in many Florentines a certain nostalgia for the "golden age of Lorenzo."[24] Besides, Guicciardini and Machiavelli hoped that by holding up Lorenzo as the model of prudence and wise moderation for the Medici of their own time they might be able to influence the restored Medici government in the proper direction. In fact, after writing the account summarized here, Guicciardini composed a eulogy of Lorenzo which omitted the shadowy accents altogether and which, like Machiavelli's portrait, derived from the eulogy composed between 1517 and 1519 by Niccolò Valori.[25] Even Guicciardini's first picture is somewhat overdrawn in favor of wishful thinking and political propaganda. Business was not quite so good,[26] the citizens not quite so united, the city not quite

[23] Francesco Guicciardini, *Storie fiorentine*, ed. Roberto Palmarocchi *Opere*, vol. VIII (Bari, 1931), pp. 30, 52-54, 80.

[24] On the artistic treatment of the legend, see Chastel, *Art et humanisme à Florence au temps de Laurent le Magnifique* (Paris, 1961), pp. 11-12.

[25] Felix Gilbert, "Guicciardini, Machiavelli, Valori on Lorenzo Magnifico," *Renaissance News*, XI (1958), 107-14.

[26] On economic conditions in Florence at the end of the century, scholars are

as tranquil as Guicciardini maintained.[27] The widespread interest in preachers of repentance and prophecies of coming tribulations antedate Lorenzo's death, while some of Florence's learned circle were already beginning to show signs of a spiritual malaise that shakes our confidence in Marsilio Ficino's famous description, in 1492, of the Florentine age of gold.[28] Still, hindsight gives us no warrant to exaggerate the tensions in Laurentian Florence any more than it justifies sixteenth-century historians exaggerating the well-being of that age; tensions there were, but they were outweighed by the generally favorable material conditions, by Florence's secure position in Italy, and by the strong but relatively moderate hand of a prudent and experienced manager. When Lorenzo died on April 8, the succession passed to his eldest son, Piero, with the goodwill of most of the city's leading men.[29]

---

in marked disagreement. The decline in prosperity of the Medici themselves is not to be attributed merely to mismanagement by Lorenzo's "servants," as Machiavelli indicated, but also to more general difficulties in Italian foreign trade, as Raymond de Roover shows in *The Rise and Decline of the Medici Bank* (Cambridge, Mass., 1963), passim. More recently Richard Goldthwaite has made a good case for a high level of prosperity in Florence at this time by emphasizing the confidential outlook and the continued high level of investment activity of certain businessmen, rather than concentrating on the objective factors that ultimately led to decline. *Private Wealth in Renaissance Florence: A Study of Four Families* (Princeton, 1968), pp. 237-41 et passim.

[27] Louis F. Marks shows the rising tide of complaint in the Florentine councils in the 1480's against the government's tax policies. "The Financial Oligarchy in Florence under Lorenzo," *Italian Renaissance Studies*, ed. E. F. Jacob (London, 1960), pp. 123-47, especially p. 145. Nicolai Rubinstein's summation seems accurate: "There remained throughout the period of Medici ascendancy an undercurrent of dissatisfaction, which was revealed time and again, in narrow majorities for Medici legislation. Exceptional circumstances were required to make it a serious danger to the regime." *The Government of Florence Under the Medici (1434-1494)* (Oxford, 1966), p. 231. This is not inconsistent with Parenti's remark that, at the time of the transfer of government from Lorenzo to Piero "La citta in segreto dolendosi della contribuita riputatione a Piero, dubitando un altra volta e con piggiore grado d'avere a incorrere nella servitu, assai dispiacere sosteneva. Tuttavolta temporeggiava." Piero Parenti, *Storia fiorentina*, ed. Joseph Schnitzer, *Quellen und Forschungen zur Geschichte Savonarolas*, vol. IV, *Savonarola nach der Aufzeichnungen des Florentiners Piero Parenti* (Leipzig, 1910), p. 3.

[28] See below, pp. 189-92.

[29] Rubinstein, *Government of Florence*, p. 229.

If all was not perfect in Lorenzo's Florence, the situation deteriorated rapidly after he died, and in this sense the midnight premonitions that accompanied his death were prophetic. Piero lacked the delicate touch required to govern a city which, after sixty years of Medici domination, still had a self-conscious political elite and an explosive populace. Some members of the ruling group had resisted Lorenzo's tightening of his hold on the machinery of state and seem to have expected a relaxation after he was gone. Guicciardini mentioned Bernardo Rucellai as one man who dared criticize Lorenzo and said that Bernardo and Paolantonio Soderini hoped to persuade Piero to use his authority more moderately, to avoid the tyrannical methods that had caused ill feeling toward his father, and to move in the direction of a *vita civile*.[30] Piero Parenti similarly indicates that the political leaders resented Piero's efforts to make himself as powerful as his father, who "with a single gesture was able to bend all the other citizens to his will."[31]

One of the causes for resentment against Lorenzo in his later years had been his tendency to supplant older members of the ruling circle with young, unknown men and others whom the *ottimati* regarded as their inferiors. The most important of the new men were the brothers Bernardo and Ser Piero Dovizi of Bibbiena, who emerged from rural obscurity to become trusted servants of Lorenzo and were roundly hated for it by the *ottimati*, who accused them of arrogant behavior.[32] Even more than had his father, Piero de' Medici favored the Dovizi to the exclusion of the "men of quality" and the "friends of the state," and this is mentioned frequently in the contemporary sources as a major cause of his ruin.[33] In this practice of supplanting the citizens of the city who were rich and powerful in their own

[30] Guicciardini, *Storie fiorentine*, pp. 84-88.

[31] Parenti, *Storia fiorentina*, fol. 151 recto.

[32] Bernardo Dovizi da Bibbiena, *Epistolario*, ed. G. L. Moncallero, 2 vols. (Florence, 1955-65), vol. I, p. 142.

[33] "Metteva innanzi gioveni e gentilotti favoriva questi contro alla voglia di alquanti antichi principali et huomini di matura età parendoli che questi tali antichi da lui non riconoscessino." Parenti, *Storia fiorentina*, fol. 132 verso. Also Guicciardini, *Storie fiorentine*, p. 86; Giovanni Cambi, *Istorie*, in *Delizie degli eruditi toscani*, ed. Ildefonso di S. Luigi (Florence, 1770-89), vol. XXI, pp. 10-11; Cerretani, *Storia fiorentina*, MS BNF II. III. 74, fol. 180; Rubinstein, *Government of Florence*, p. 230.

right with men whose dependent position required them to be sub-servient, the *ottimati* saw a conscious policy of further undermining republican independence in favor of despotic control. They may have been right; but in Piero's case, at any rate, what seemed conscious design was more likely due to sluggish indifference. Piero had an unfortunate propensity for exacerbating his father's minor offenses into outrageous blunders. Basically uninterested in the exacting tasks of governing,[34] he lacked the flexibility to abandon profitless courses as well as the imagination to devise new ones.

This tendency to compound earlier grievances can be seen in another issue that disturbed the *ottimati*—the question of preferment to Church offices. Ecclesiastical benefices were an important source of prestige and income for the sons of patrician families, and the Medici were in a position to influence their distribution. Piero Parenti, the acute observer who was himself a well-born Florentine, writes that Lorenzo's second son, the Cardinal Giovanni (later Pope Leo X) whom Pope Alexander VI appointed his legate in Tuscany, incurred hatred in Florence because "he took possession of every benefice that fell vacant." In this way, concludes Parenti, the Medici "usurped the ecclesiastical as well as the civil power."[35] In point of fact, it was Lorenzo who had begun this practise of hunting for bene-fices to enlarge Giovanni's ecclesiastical patrimony, not only in Tuscany but all over Italy.[36] Piero continued the practise, at the con-tinual urging of Giovanni, even to the point where it affected his freedom of action in dealing with the Pope, as we shall see.[37]

Piero had succeeded his father in April 1492. As early as June, Parenti noted a general dissatisfaction with Piero and an expectation of change.[38] By the following May it was reported in Italian diplo-

---

[34] For example, his neglect of affairs is evident in the correspondence of Dovizi, who had to apologize for troubling Piero with letters to be read: *Epistolario*, p. 28; see also, p. 21, n. 4.

[35] Parenti, *Storia fiorentina*, ed. Schnitzer, p. 7.

[36] G. B. Picotti, *La giovinezza di Leone X* (Milan, 1927), Chapter II, "La caccia dei benefizi," pp. 67-159.

[37] For a letter from Giovanni to Piero in which he complains of Piero's neglect of his interests and those of his friends, see Picotti, *La giovinezza*, appendix I, 626-28; for Giovanni's requests for favors and help in securing benefices, see especially pp. 630-31, 633-34, 637.

[38] Parenti, *Storia fiorentina*, fol. 133 recto.

matic circles that Piero's regime had split into several factions and that even the Medici family was divided against itself.[39] Just before this, in April, Parenti described the situation in the city as tense, the "good citizens" waiting "with ears perked up" for some event which they might use to bring about a restoration of "true liberty." In June the opportunity seemed to have come. A squabble that began in the Franciscan cloister of Santa Croce and involved Giorgio Benigno— a former tutor of Piero's whom Piero had unsuccessfully supported for the generalship of the Order[40]—turned into a full scale riot. Members of prominent families including the Alberti, Serristori, and Corsi took arms and rode their horses through the city streets, trying to raise the populace against Piero.[41] But the attempt was premature; as yet there was no grievance sufficiently widespread as to gain popular support for an uprising led by disgruntled patricians.

But such a grievance was in preparation. If the reliance upon new men and the disregard of the older ruling clique was the beginning of Piero's ruin, what finally accomplished it was his bungling of Florentine foreign policy so that the city found herself in the perilous position of November 1494. Where Lorenzo had skillfully walked the tightrope of equilibrium between the great Italian powers, Piero plunged heavily into a one-sided alliance with the King of Naples. Why he did so has never been satisfactorily explained. Most contemporary accounts simply describe him as rash and stubborn in not taking the good counsel of older, more experienced citizens. Guicciardini attributes Piero's behavior to a tyrannical and haughty nature which made him suspicious of "men of quality" and his father's friends.[42] Even if true, this does not explain Piero's choice of allies. No doubt it was the web of family loyalties that entangled him in a disastrous Neapolitan alliance: Piero's wife and his mother were both members of the powerful Orsini family, and Virginio Orsini counted upon him for support in his quarrels with the Pope, who was Orsini's overlord for certain territories in the Roman *campagna*. Already in the time of Lorenzo the Magnificent, Virginio

---

[39] Rubinstein, *Government of Florence*, pp. 230-31.
[40] See below, pp. 242-43.
[41] Parenti, *Storia fiorentina*, fols. 145-47.
[42] Guicciardini, *Storie fiorentine*, pp. 83-85.

Orsini had acted as intermediary in negotiations for a *rapprochement* between Florence and Naples, and he seems to have played the same role with respect to Piero.[43] Here, too, the greed of the Medici for church benefices exacted its price. Pope Alexander VI, who inclined toward the side of the Aragonese of Naples against the French claims to the *Regno*, blocked Piero from acquiring new ecclesiastical preferments for his brother Giovanni until, in the spring of 1494, Piero assured the Pope of Florentine support for Naples.[44] With Giovanni bombarding Piero with complaints that he was being neglected and demands for more patronage for himself and his friends, Piero had found it impossible to resist the Pope's pressure. Thus he spurned repeated overtures from the French envoys who were trying to gain his guarantee that he would allow their army passage through Florentine territory, and he ignored the signs that his policy of favoring the Neapolitan against the French king was "universally displeasing" to the Florentines. As late as October 1494, when Charles VIII had already entered Italy with his army, envoys and letters from the French camp attempted to unlock Piero from his deadly embrace with Naples, but Piero held firm.[45] Already Florentine businessmen had been expelled from the rich markets of

[43] For the summaries of some of the relevant letters in the time of Lorenzo, see *Catalogue of the Medici Archives Consisting of Rare Autograph Letters Records and Documents 1084-1770 . . . the Property of the Marquis Cosimo de' Medici and the Marquis Averardo de' Medici*, Sale Catalogue of Christie, Manson, and Woods (London, 1917), nos. 45, 207, 222, 344, 422. See also the indices in P. G. Ricci and N. Rubinstein, *Censimento delle lettere di Lorenzo di Piero de' Medici* (Florence, 1964) and Marcello Del Piazzo ed., *Protocolli del carteggio di Lorenzo il Magnifico per gli anni 1473-4, 1477-92, Deputazione di Storia Patria per la Toscana Documenti di storia italiana*, ser. 2, vol. II. For the relevant correspondence of Piero's government, see the registers in Marcello Del Piazzo, "I ricordi di lettere di Piero di Lorenzo de' Medici," *Archivio storico italiano*, CXII (1954), 378-432; CXIII (1956), 101-42. Piero's relations with Virginio Orsini are covered by Parenti, *Storia fiorentina*, fols. 143ff, and by Guicciardini, *Storie fiorentine*, pp. 87-88.

[44] Picotti, *La giovinezza*, pp. 95-96. The question of papal assent to the Florentine efforts to unite the Pisan and Fiesolan Dominican houses with San Marco was also involved in the negotiations between Piero and Alexander VI. See Romeo De Maio, *Savonarola e la curia romana* (Rome, 1969), p. 51.

[45] Parenti, *Storia fiorentina*, fol. 180. Earlier efforts were made in February and August. For the documents of the embassies between the two states, see Canestrini and Desjardins, *Négociations*, vol. I.

Lyons, and the blow was felt at home not only by merchants and bankers but also by workers who were thrown out of their jobs. This, added to the danger of a domestic uprising, observed Parenti.[46]

In contrast to the mounting opposition of Florence's leading citizens, however, there is no evidence that the general populace was ready to revolt before the crucial autumn of 1494. The failure of the patricians to make a rebellion out of the Santa Croce riots of June 1493 must have taught them that it would take something more catastrophic than a monkish quarrel to overthrow Piero. Unrest among the rank and file seems to have expressed itself unpolitically at first, in a visible but vague religious excitement, a mood of confused and contradictory expectations, and of mounting hatred of the Jews. When Parenti remarks that the people of Florence were putting their hopes in the promises of preachers who were telling them that God would bring men to the good life by means of a great scourge, it comes as a surprise to learn that he was not talking about Savonarola but about two Franciscan rabble-rousers, Bernardino da Feltre and Domenico da Ponzo.

Fra Bernardino was a famous preacher of repentance who staged bonfires of vanities and advocated the establishment of a *Monte di Pietà*, a public loan fund—two measures which Savonarola later incorporated into his own program.[47] Because of his incitement of the populace against the Jews, Fra Bernardino had been expelled in 1488, but in May of 1493 he was allowed to re-enter the city. The *Otto di Guardia e Balìa*, the magistracy in charge of public security, gave him a license to preach accompanied by a warning not to incite the people to dangerous acts (*novità*), but the magistrates quickly thought better of it and forbade the public from attending his sermons. Despite the ban a crowd gathered on May 20 to hear Fra Bernardino preach, whereupon his fellow Minorite, Domenico da Ponzo, persuaded Piero de' Medici to rescind the order of the *Otto*. Ten thousand people heard Fra Bernardino that day, if we are to believe Parenti.[48] On May 28, the Feast of the Holy Spirit, after Mass and a popular procession, he preached again in front of the Loggia

---

[46] Parenti, *Storia fiorentina*, ed. Schnitzer, p. 7.
[47] On Bernardino da Feltre, see above, p. 103.
[48] Parenti, *Storia fiorentina*, fol. 143 recto.

della Signoria, adjacent to the Palazzo della Signoria, and he continued to preach publicly until July, when after a public burning of vanities he left the city again, disappointed because he had failed to achieve either the expulsion of the Jews or the establishment of the *Monte di Pietà*.[49] His fellow Franciscan, Domenico da Ponzo, was also a stormy figure, a popular agitator constantly at odds with the authorities who alternated between allowing him to preach and threatening him with expulsion. Fra Domenico was suspected of being an agent of Lodovico il Moro, Duke of Milan. If the suspicion was justified—as is likely—this would explain the apparent inconsistency of his behavior toward Savonarola: for while Piero was still in power and favoring Naples against Milan, Domenico endorsed Savonarola and called him a holy man; afterward, when Savonarola emerged as the chief spokesman for the French alliance and Lodovico reversed himself to become a leader of the anti-French coalition, Domenico became Savonarola's bitter enemy.[50]

With apocalyptic excitement steadily mounting in Florence between 1492 and 1494, the crowds flocked to hear Fra Domenico da Ponzo in the Cathedral, Fra Bernardino da Feltre (who returned to Florence in 1493), an unnamed Dominican preacher in Santa Maria Novella,[51] and Fra Girolamo himself in the basilica of San Lorenzo, which stood almost directly behind the Medici Palace. Those preachers who offered milder fare lost their audiences, a fate which apparently befell the preachers of Santo Spirito and Santa Croce[52] as well as the former Medici favorite, Fra Mariano. The message of *flagello* and repentance was the order of the day, with particular attention to what Florentine reformers charged was the special Florentine vice—sodomy.[53] Everyone knew of the frightening portents that accompanied the death of Lorenzo il Magnifico.[54] The

---

[49] Parenti, *Storia fiorentina*, ed. Schnitzer, p. 5.

[50] *Ibid.*, pp. 3-4; and below, p. 228.

[51] Letter of Niccolò di Braccio Guicciardini, April 7, 1492, in Roberto Ridolfi, *Studi savonaroliani* (Florence, 1935), appendix IV, p. 262.

[52] "Per ora [a] santta Croce non vi va X vuomini e santto Ispiritto ve ne va comunalemente, o meno; . . ." *Loc. cit*; see also p. 104, n. 2.

[53] *Ibid.*, p. 263.

[54] Luca Landucci, *Diario fiorentino del 1450 al 1516 continuato da un anonimo fino al 1542*, ed. Iodoco Del Badia (Florence, 1883), p. 64.

preacher of Santa Maria Novella reported that a flaming tower had been seen crashing to the ground.[55] During the night of April 4-5, a great wind and hail storm blew up, thunder rolled, and a lightning bolt tore a huge rent in the side of the cupola of the Cathedral. Savonarola announced that this was a sign of the coming Godly scourge. Fra Domenico da Ponzo more boldly warned that this signified that if the Florentines failed to reform themselves by next August the streets would run with blood; if this were not true they could cut off his head. "Everyone is terrified," reported Niccolò Guicciardini in a letter to Piero Guicciardini, "especially myself. May God help us."[56] Shortly afterward, he reported that Savonarola was daily repeating his warnings that "all of us will be found out by God's scourge, and soon, and that we need not make plans to escape by talking, or by going into the country or to Rome or to France or any other place, because we will be found anywhere. And this morning I understand that he said that God has given His decision, so that there is nothing left to do, but that we must prepare, because soon we will be found out, and that all the same he believed that prayer and contrite hearts and humility may ward off this scourge."[57]

And yet, while Savonarola had emerged as one of the city's most rousing preachers of repentance, as well as the favorite of some of Florence's leading men, he is mentioned very little in the Florentine chronicles before the autumn crisis of 1494. Piero Parenti, doubtless the most astute and best-informed of the contemporary chroniclers, barely mentions him before that fateful November, although he reports the doings of Fra Bernardino and Fra Domenico in some detail.[58] Only with the onset of the November crisis, as Savonarola moved to the center of the civic drama, would this change. When we consider the point of view from which Parenti, Cerretani, and, to a lesser extent, the other chroniclers were writing, this apparent neglect becomes understandable, for they were observers of Florentine politics and public affairs, and from the standpoint of their

---

[55] Ridolfi, *Studi savonaroliani*, p. 262.

[56] *Ibid.*, p. 262. [57] *Ibid.*, p. 264.

[58] Parenti mentions him twice, briefly, before November 1494: once, when Savonarola visited the dying Lorenzo; again, on the occasion of the separation of San Marco from the Lombard Congregation.

interests Savonarola was not as important in 1492 and 1493 as he later was to become. By comparison the two Franciscans whose preaching had more radical social and political implications which were likely to lead to public turmoil and embroilment with the authorities seemed much more important. In that frenetic and rabble-rousing company Savonarola was a relative moderate; his criticisms of social injustice and tyranny were generalized and conventional; his remedy was conservative. In contrast to Fra Bernardino da Feltre he does not seem to have attempted to stir up the mob against the Jews, or to have criticized the government's policy in allowing them to reside in Florence, or to have supported the alternative policy of establishing a *Monte di Pietà*. To the poor he counselled patient acceptance of suffering; to all, reform of their individual lives.

This is partly explained by the fact that Savonarola's position in the city was very different from that of the two Franciscans. He was no itinerant preacher but the Prior of San Marco, the head of a new congregation, the collaborator of Piero de' Medici, and the friend of influential men like Pico and the Benivieni brothers. As sensational as his prophetic message might be, he had no small stake in public order. His friends and his solid position would hardly have protected him if the Signoria or Piero de' Medici had thought him dangerous to the peace or security of the state. Apparently they did not: in the summer of 1494 when there was fear of public turmoil the government silenced the preachers whom it considered potentially danger-ous, but Savonarola was not one of them.[59] Pro-French plots were discovered; anti-Medicean literature was distributed in which the French king was called upon to liberate Florence from tyranny; Piero's own cousins, Lorenzo and Giovanni di Pierfrancesco de' Medici, were expelled under suspicion of having treated with Lodo-vico Sforza of Milan; another riot broke out in protest against another Medici relation, Simone Tornabuoni. Yet as late as Septem-ber 1494—that is to say, before the revolt—Piero Parenti could write that although there was now a universal desire in the city to throw off the Medici yoke, there was no leader to be found whom the peo-ple might follow: *ma capo non si scopriva il quale seguisseno.*[60]

[59] Parenti, *Storia fiorentina*, fol. 164 recto.
[60] *Ibid.*, fol. 179 recto.

Through all this Savonarola continued to preach. By not becoming involved in street politics he survived where the more turbulent preachers fell afoul of the regime, and in surviving he came to dominate the public's attention as *the* prophet who had predicted the coming of divine tribulations. In his *Compendium Revelationum* he was to recall that after his vision in Advent of 1492 he had begun to prophesy the coming of a new Cyrus from beyond the mountains. Since none of the pre-1494 sermons which survive contain any mention of this prophecy we have only his own retrospective testimony for this, although it would be difficult to understand why he was hailed as a prophet in 1494 had he not been publicly predicting something of the sort.[61] By the fall of 1494 all the accumulated warnings of the past four years concentrated on this one cataclysmic event. Charles was not only the new Cyrus, he was *flagellum Dei*, God's scourge; his expedition was *il diluvio*, the Flood; and he wielded *gladius Dei*, the sword of God's vengeance. In those days of apocalyptic fulfillment and of fear few people, certainly not the prophet himself, were likely to have reflected carefully on what had been said. It was enough that here was a man of God who for some time had been telling them to build the Ark of repentance against the coming Flood, enough that the dreams and visions of the past few years were dreams and visions no longer, but hard, terrifying reality.

The sudden thrust of Charles VIII to the border of Tuscany in October was reality. When resistance was offered Charles sacked the town of Fivizzano. This had its calculated effect: in Florence the fear grew intense.[62] Rumors flew: although Piero de' Medici had held firm in his alliance with the King of Naples despite rising opposition in Florence,[63] when his youngest brother, Giuliano, went off on a mission to the Pope, some said it was a move to get him out of harm's way, others whispered that Giuliano had been sent to guard

---

[61] Ridolfi makes this point, although he seems to hold that the coming of Charles VIII was not widely discussed before Lent 1494. *Vita*, vol. II, p. 111, n. 4.

[62] Parenti, *Storia fiorentina*, fol. 187 recto.

[63] In May, Parenti said the people were *universalmente* displeased by Piero's negative reply to the French ambassadors. *Ibid.*, fol. 159 verso. On the anti-Neapolitan views of the city's "governors," see fol. 172.

a treasure which Piero was smuggling out of Florence.[64] Piero appealed to Venice for help and for a time it seemed that the Serenissima might be stirring; but Venice had not the slightest intention of coming to Florence's rescue; as usual she kept out of quarrels which did not touch her vital interests.[65] Earlier, the King of Naples had sought to land troops at Livorno and march them eastward to meet the French in the Romagna, but Piero had forestalled this in order to prevent Tuscany from being used as a battleground.[66] Now Florence was left to stand alone against the oncoming French army.

If she *would* stand. Piero had good reasons for doubting that his fellow citizens would support him against the French, whom many Florentines looked upon as their liberators. Already in July, Siena had risen against her Medici-supported despot, Jacopo Petrucci, and had set up a popular regime.[67] In Florence the pro-French party was led by Piero's own cousins, Giovanni and Lorenzo di Pierfrancesco, who now slipped out of the city to the camp of Charles VIII.[68] Piero redoubled the troops at the Bargello palace and mounted a night guard against a possible uprising.[69] North of the city the border fortresses of Sarzana, Sarzanello, and Pietrasanta stood between Florence and the French. If anything could save the city now it would be the show of a firm determination to resist; but this was a waiting game that required steel nerves and Piero was not up to it. On October 26, he left Florence for the camp of Charles VIII. Writing back to the Signoria he tried to create the impression that he was repeating his father's dramatic and bold action of sixteen years earlier, when during the war with Naples and the Pope Lorenzo had gone directly to the Neapolitan court to make peace. But the gesture turned out to be a disastrous parody, Piero demonstrating once more

[64] *Ibid.*, fol. 185 recto.

[65] The Florentine ambassadors to Venice were Gianbattista di Lorenzo Ridolfi and Paolantonio Soderini, selected on June 26. *Ibid.*, fol. 165.

[66] *Ibid.*, fols. 162 verso–163.

[67] The Sienese "restored a popular government of true liberty," says Parenti, *ibid.*, fol. 168 verso.

[68] Villari, *La storia di Girolamo Savonarola e de' suoi tempi*, 2 vols. (Florence, 1926), vol. I, p. 222.

[69] Parenti, *Storia fiorentina*, fol. 187 verso.

that he was unworthy of his father's inheritance.[70] When he reached the King's camp near Sarzanello he gave in to all of Charles' demands—surrender of the border strongholds, both Florentine ports, Pisa and Livorno, and, so it was soon rumored in Florence, a subsidy of 200,000 ducats. On October 31, Piero's minister Bernardo Dovizi had already written from Florence that the city was *franzese tucta*,[71] but the news of Piero's capitulation was the last straw.

If Piero's anti-French policy had been contrary to Florentine interests, his capitulation was even more so. The ports were vital links in Florence's commercial life-line, while the border-towns were hard-won gains in the city's continuing effort to achieve territorial consolidation and a guarantee of her independence. In Piero's absence the Signoria took charge, calling a meeting (*pratica*) of all former Standard-bearers of Justice (*Gonfalonieri di Giustizia*) together with all those whose names had been drawn for that executive office.[72] In short, this was a meeting of the political leaders of Florence, many of them Medicean supporters who now began to change their colors —*volgere mantello* as Parenti put it—and as such it was the beginning of the revolt against Medici rule. In the *pratica* Piero Capponi insisted that it was now necessary to put an end to tyranny and return to a free popular government, and on November 5, the Council of One Hundred met "to make provisions as a free city." On the advice of Piero Capponi they chose Fra Girolamo Savonarola and four other citizens, including Capponi himself, for an embassy to King Charles with instructions to put the blame for the city's previous anti-French policy upon one man, and thus to repudiate Piero de' Medici as the head and spokesman of the Florentine government. In this way Savonarola was first brought into the rebellion against the government of Piero de' Medici.

[70] See Piero's letter in Canestrini and Desjardins, *Négociations*, vol. I, pp. 587-88; and the comparison of Lorenzo's and Piero's actions in Rubinstein, "Politics and Constitution," p. 149.

[71] Dovizi in Florence to the Duke of Calabria, October 31, 1494, *Epistolario*, pp. 235-36; also, that the city was in *tanta mutatione et tanto diversa da quella che la lasciai . . . (loc. cit.).*

[72] See the account of the revolt in Rubinstein, "Politics and Constitution," pp. 148-51.

The appearance of the new Cyrus, which made an exile of Piero, had made a prophet of Fra Girolamo. He had ascended the pulpit of the Cathedral on September 21, resuming the exposition of the Book of Genesis on which he had been preaching intermittently for two years. His starting place was the text of Genesis 6:17—*ecce adducam aquas super terram* ("lo, I will bring the waters over the earth")—and he proclaimed it in triumph. For years, he reminded his listeners, he had been saying that God's scourge was coming to cleanse the Church and to punish wicked Italy, and now it had come to pass.[73] In the main this was the same message he had been preaching all along: the Florentines must labor to build the spiritual Ark of prayer and repentance; only then would they have protection with which to withstand the trials to come. But in one respect there was a difference, a shift in emphasis which is the first sign of the transformation which the Florentine crisis had begun to work in him. As the Flood seemed to be concentrating its force upon Florence, singling her out as the special object of divine punishment, so it seemed that he, Fra Girolamo, had been chosen to speak to Florence as to no other city. Before this time his prophecy had been for all of Italy, indeed for all of Christendom; only Rome as the center of the Church had been singled out for special treatment. On November 1, still preaching from the Cathedral pulpit, he began his sermons for Advent.[74] Now he spoke as the prophet of Florence; God had illumined him so that Florence could be illumined. God had wanted him to be as a father to this city and so Savonarola spoke to Florence as to a daughter.[75]

Nevertheless, even as the Florentines now called upon him as their

---

[73] *Sermons super Archam Noe* (Venice, 1536). On these sermons on Genesis in which Savonarola concentrated on the Flood story, see Roberto Ridolfi, *Le prediche del Savonarola cronologia e tradizione del testo* (Florence, 1939), pp. 40-46.

[74] *Prediche sopra Aggeo*. The first six sermons in this collection are based on Biblical texts other than Haggai. See the editor's remarks, pp. 491-94.

[75] *Prediche sopra Aggeo*, pp. 1-23. "Potete cognoscere se io sono in luogo di vostro padre, perchè el padre tesaurezza per el figliuolo e di tutto quello che ha lo fa partecipe; così ho fatto io verso di te, Firenze: tutto quello che io ho studiato e affaticatomi tutto el tempo della vita mia, sì della verità della fede, sì del ben vivere cristiano, tutto l'ho sparso in te, come buon padre a' suoi cari figliuoli." *Ibid.*, p. 16.

holy man to intervene with the new Cyrus, Savonarola resisted becoming involved politically. He took on the ambassadorial responsibility with reluctance, and only with special conditions. At first he refused it altogether; then, after entreaties and prayer, he accepted with the stipulation that he did not intend to discuss the status of private persons—an obvious reference to Piero de' Medici—but only to implore the King publicly for the safety of the city.[76] Savonarola was making it plain that he was embarking upon a mission of charity, as befitted his priestly function, not of rebellion. Whether his reluctance was a matter of loyalty to Piero, of prudence in the face of a venture whose outcome was still uncertain, or of unfamiliarity with and unsuitability for the new role that was being thrust upon him is difficult to say; perhaps it was some of all three. Savonarola had not been involved in the earlier agitation against Piero, and nothing had occurred to change the good relations between the two men. Besides, although the revolution was already launched, its success and even its direction were still unclear; the outcome would only be decided when Piero had returned to Florence. In addition to these practical reasons, however, and most important, was Savonarola's own understanding of his mission. Everything he had said until then, and everything he was to say for some time to come, suggests that he still thought of his prophetic mission in purely spiritual terms. To remain above faction and to keep aloof from the world of politics was more than a tactic or a pose, it was part of his continuing conviction that the Republic of which he was herald was not of this world.

But events moved independently of Savonarola's will.[77] After he

[76] "Epso da prima al tutto ricuso," says Parenti, *Storia fiorentina*, ed. Schnitzer, p. 9. "Accepto frate Jeronimo con prima notificato chome di stati di private persone ragionare non volea, bene in publico pregare per la citta si contentava et voleva." *Ibid.*, p. 10; Cerretani, *Storia Fiorentina*, ed. Schnitzer, p. 11. In the *Compendium Revelationum* Savonarola says he consulted with the fathers of his Order and other important citizens, and was persuaded by them as well as by considerations of charity (p. 237). He does not mention the stipulation reported by Parenti.

[77] This account is based on the following sources: Parenti, *Storia fiorentina*, fol. 190 recto–197 recto; Cerretani, *Della storia fiorentina*, ed. Leopold von Ranke, *Historisch-biografische Schriften*, in *Sämmtliche Werke*, 2nd edn., vol. 40-41 (Leipzig, 1878), pp. 338-40; Landucci, *Diario*, pp. 74-75.

and the other ambassadors left Florence on November 5, the revolt of the civic leaders gathered momentum as more of Piero's friends abandoned the Medici regime, deciding that it was "time to turn to the public good." Excitement mounted still further upon the return of Piero's cousins and rivals, Giovanni and Lorenzo di Pierfrancesco. At this point it was learned that Piero himself had got wind of trouble and was hurrying back to Florence. This frightened the rebels who were not at all certain that they were masters of the city. Piero returned on November 8, was greeted by a few friends, and together with some soldiers made for the communal Palace, where he exchanged words with the members of the rebellious Signoria. Both sides realized that the showdown would come the following day, after each had had an opportunity to rally all its forces. Piero collected his loyal troops outside the city walls, while the insurgents drew together with their arms inside the Palazzo della Signoria. The next day, November 9, Piero returned only to find that he was barred from entering with his armed followers, while from the Palace windows he could hear the rallying cry, "Popolo e libertà!" Uncertain what to do, he faltered, turning back toward the Church of Orsanmichele a few hundred feet away, where he encountered a hostile crowd which had begun to rally to the cries and the ringing bells in the Palace. With difficulty he made his way back to the Medici Palace on the Via Larga. His brother, the Cardinal Giovanni, and his Tornabuoni cousins tried to raise a counter force in the streets until more loyal troops could arrive from Pistoia and the valley of the Mugello, but the Signoria quickly spread the word that it would hang anyone caught helping the Medici and offered a reward for the capture or assassination of Piero or Giovanni. Taking a few loyal followers, the two sons of the Magnificent Lorenzo rode out of the Bologna Gate and into exile. For the first time in sixty years Florence was without Medici leadership.

So it was that when Savonarola returned to Florence the revolution was an accomplished fact which he could no longer ignore,[78] and his next sermon shows how quickly he absorbed this fact into

[78] The date of his return to Florence is uncertain. Ridolfi places it between November 9-11. *The Life of Girolamo Savonarola*, trans. Cecil Grayson (New York, 1959), p. 85.

his own scheme of things. Likening the Florentine people to the man who had been assaulted and wounded by robbers on the road to Jericho (Luke 10:33-5), he explained that Florence was under the special care of Christ the Samaritan: "He, I say, O Florence, has had pity upon you and has brought you His help, . . . has put on your wounds the oil of His compassion and the wine of contrition for the tribulations to heal you; He has placed you in the stable, that is, He has restored you to his Church and given you into the hands of the stablekeeper, that is, the preacher; and the two pennies that He has given him with which to take care of you are the Old and the New Testament. . . ." Moreover, he continued, this revolution would have cost Florence much blood if God had not mitigated it in His mercy. They had only to compare their experience with upheavals that had taken place in other cities of Italy or would in the future. In the affliction which was coming to all Italy it was too much to expect that some part would not touch Florence as well, but with the penitence, prayer, and fasting which Savonarola as their father imposed upon them from that time until Advent, they would have consolation.[79]

Savonarola, in his new authority as spiritual father of Florence, here commands the city which God has singled out for His special care. Here for the first time he acknowledges that the cause of the revolutionaries is the cause of the Lord, that the Medici government was a government of robbers, of devils, who had held captive and wounded the Florentine spirit. Its overthrow was the first step in freeing the Florentines from the grip of sin and vice, and mercifully God kept the revolution from turning into a disastrous bloodletting. But what the next step was to be, Savonarola did not yet reveal; just as before, his message was to repent and to convert in preparation for the flood of divine wrath. Of Florence's many material problems he had little to say; his mission was entirely spiritual. For years he had been warning all Italy, including Florence, of the coming destruction. There were to be no exceptions, no place would escape; only God's elect, wherever and whoever they might be, would sail

[79] *Prediche sopra Aggeo*, pp. 63-64. November 9, the date assigned to this sermon by the editor, is probably erroneous. Ridolfi thinks it was November 11. See n. 78 above.

safely in the Ark to shores untouched by the Flood. With Charles VIII in Tuscany, in command of the Florentine strongholds and ready to descend upon the city, it seemed that the vial of divine wrath was about to be poured out upon Florence, and Savonarola could only offer her the consolation of repentance and prayer. And yet there is also a note of hope: God might soften His wrath if he saw that His people were turning to Him. In a passage of the *Compendium Revelationum*, which sheds some light on the way Savonarola's prophetic inspiration arose in response to practical situations, he recalls that at the time when the King of the French was approaching and a revolution in the Florentine state had seemed imminent, he had seen a sword over the city and the spilling of much blood. Nevertheless it had seemed to him that God had specially chosen Florence for the announcement of these things, and so he had begun to hope that the prophecy might not be unconditional, that if the populace could be induced to repent God might remit some of His punishment. God might further soften His wrath if He saw that this people was listening to its prophet. They must continue to build the Ark of repentance in which to ride out the onrushing Flood.[80]

The Flood came very soon. Charles VIII entered the city on November 17. All Florence put on a face of rejoicing, welcoming him as the liberator,[81] but underneath the mask there was fear. Charles had entered with lance upraised and canopy overhead in the pose of a conqueror, and he quickly made it clear that he intended to treat the city as a defeated enemy. He gave no sign that he harbored any kindly feelings toward her as an old friend of his own people, or that he had been softened by the recent embassy of Savonarola and his companions. He demanded the overlordship of the city and—impossible of conditions—the restoration of Piero de' Medici who, by surrendering the subject cities and fortresses, had put himself in the King's good graces. Charles had little sympathy

[80] *Compendium Revelationum*, pp. 236-67. The sermons in which he communicated his new hopes are in *Prediche sopra Aggeo*, pp. 1-60.

[81] On Charles VIII in Florence, see Guicciardini, *Storie fiorentine*, pp. 102-104; Cerretani, *Storia fiorentina*, ed. Schnitzer, pp. 21-28; Parenti, *Storia fiorentina*, fols. 199 verso (partly in Schnitzer ed., pp. 12-18); Landucci, *Diario*, pp. 79-84.

with Florentine aspirations for a restoration of the free republic, evidently believing that a dependent Medici regime would be easier to manage. Also, it was being said in the city that Piero's wife, Alfonsina Orsini, and other pro-Medicean leaders had suborned some of the French counsellors. The Florentines, however, led by Piero Capponi, refused the King's demands, which they saw as tantamount to their personal and collective ruin. According to Cerretani, Charles threatened to blow his trumpets and Capponi countered by threatening to toll the city's bells.[82] In the streets citizens clashed with French soldiers. Savonarola was again called upon to plead the city's cause with the King, and on November 21 he exhorted Charles to remember that he was God's instrument for the doing of great deeds and that by lingering in Florence he was incurring the Lord's displeasure. Whether it was due to the threats of Capponi or exhortation by Fra Girolamo, Charles did modify his demands and the parties came to terms. A formal agreement restored the traditional friendship between the two parties.[83] The French promised to restore Pisa to Florentine hegemony and to return the fortresses as soon as practicable, while Florence agreed to pay the French a subsidy of 120,000 ducats. Charles VIII left Florence on November 28, bound southward for the conquest of Naples.

Even to such a realistic observer as Parenti, the departure of the French army with no more damage done than the loss of ten lives on both sides seemed *mirabile,* a miracle the likes of which he had never seen, due equally to divine providence and to the brave Florentine stand for liberty.[84] (And, he pointed out, to the promise of help from Lodovico Sforza of Milan, who was now turning against the French enterprise which he had fostered.) Luca Landucci credited Savonarola as the agent of divine intervention, and in this Landucci seems to have expressed the common view.[85] Savonarola emerged from this latest crisis with greater prestige than ever.

[82] Cerretani, *Storia fiorentina,* ed. Schnitzer, p. 24; but it is doubtful whether these famous words were ever spoken. See Schnitzer, *loc. cit.,* n. 3.

[83] See above, n. 18.

[84] Parenti, *Storia fiorentina,* fol. 206 verso.

[85] Landucci, *Diario,* pp. 87-88.

IV

Florence the New Jerusalem

. . . I ANNOUNCE THIS GOOD NEWS TO THE CITY, THAT FLORENCE WILL
BE MORE GLORIOUS, RICHER, MORE POWERFUL
THAN SHE HAS EVER BEEN.

—Savonarola, Sermon of December 10, 1494

IN HIS campaign to win the Florentines to repentance and moral
reform Savonarola had always been hampered by certain difficulties:
his focus was universal while that of the Florentines was civic; he
spoke of the spirit, but they were chiefly concerned with bread; he
dwelt upon Last Things, while they were reluctant to reflect upon
their own mortality. And he did not offer much in the way of
concession; if there was a discrepancy between his vision and theirs,
it was they who must change, for Savonarola spoke with the authority of the Scriptures and of prophecy. But while the difference
between them was still, as he himself put it, the difference between
concern for superficial "matter" and concern for essential "form,"
the time was ripe for a reconsideration on both sides. The upheavals
of November had wrenched Florentine civic life out of its normal
course, made the future of the city uncertain, and called into question the assumptions by which most Florentines lived. Trade and
industry had suffered serious shocks, jeopardizing the livelihood of
the poor and the profits of the rich. With the rebellion of Pisa and
the loss of the border fortresses, much of the work for the consolidation of the Florentine territorial state had been dissipated and even
reversed, the advantage now passing to Florence's rivals in Tuscany,
the Lucchesi and the Sienese. Florence was vulnerable to the expansionist efforts of the non-Tuscan states on her borders. Her position

as the arbiter of the Italian equilibrium had been declining since the latter days of the Magnificent Lorenzo: since the moment of Piero's reconciliation with Charles VIII, now confirmed by the new government, this position was gone; Florence was isolated among the Italian states, accused by the anti-French powers of endangering "Italian liberty," and liable to attacks from the newly formed Italian coalition.[1] The solution of these difficulties had not been made easier by the overthrow of the sixty-year Medici system of managed republicanism. "Popolo e libertà" was the general cry once again and a free republic the universal goal; but liberty was attended by uncertainty, confusion, and the prospect of more domestic violence. What was the free republic? The Florentines had in their history a number of definitions from which to choose; these ranged between the *governo popolare*, the short-lived democracies of the thirteenth and fourteenth centuries, and the *governo stretto*, the pre-1434 oligarchy. The Medici system had sprung out of their failure to make an adequate choice in the past; what would help them to make the right decisions now?

Amid such diversities and uncertainties Savonarola emerged not only as the Republic's prophet but also as her protector. The coming of the new Cyrus had validated his claim to divine inspiration, and his success with Charles VIII had given him an additional authority and bound him still closer to his adopted city. While the French armies were approaching the city, Savonarola was still insisting that the Florentines were about to feel the scourge of the divine wrath, and he filled his sermons with alarms and reproaches: "O Florence, Florence, Florence, for your sins, for your cruelty, for your greed, for your lasciviousness, for your ambition, you have yet to suffer many adversities and much grief."[2] In those dark days before the descent of the French it seemed that Florence had lost God's grace: "O Florence, Florence, your cup is full of holes; it no longer holds the grace and oil of the Holy Spirit."[3] There was only the protection of God's saving Ark of forgiveness; those who repented

---

[1] On the gravity of Florence's position, see Guicciardini, *Storie fiorentine*, ed. Roberto Palmarocchi, *Opere*, vol. VI (Bari, 1931), pp. 100-101.

[2] *Prediche sopra Aggeo*, ed. Luigi Firpo (Rome, 1965), p. 21.

[3] *Ibid.*, p. 33.

might still find consolation or perhaps some mitigation of the divine tribulations. But then, marvelously, the Flood did not engulf Florence; the departure of the French army on November 28 was a triumph both for the city and for Savonarola, who on November 23, had already announced that the Ark was being closed.[4] Now, disregarding his earlier forecasts of doom, he rejoiced in this demonstration of divine love for the city, which he first saw simply as the gratuitous gift of a merciful God: "God has loved you, Florence, wherefore He has acted compassionately toward you, for no other reason—*e non per alcuna sua utilità*—than for His love, out of true friendship and to help you, although He has no need of you at all."[5]

In the days and weeks following the closing of the Ark Savonarola preached frequently, mainly exhorting his listeners to take up a new life in spirit now that they were free in body.[6] They must govern their new state through prayer and good actions;[7] they must give up usury, helping those in need out of love rather than greed;[8] they must drive out *gl'incantatori e le superstizioni e divinatori* and restore the divine cult.[9] But Savonarola seems also to have been searching for a context in which he could offer the Florentines more than a spiritual refuge in these days of mounting political crisis, an objective that would give them a definite cause for which to strive as well as consolation and hope. After announcing the closing of the Ark he had gone to the Book of Psalms for the texts of his next seven sermons;[10] but while he was preaching on Psalms his thoughts were turning to the rebuilding of the Temple in the time when the Jews had returned from their captivity in Babylon.[11] New events in

---

[4] *Ibid.*, p. 93.

[5] *Ibid.*, p. 112.

[6] E.g., *ibid.*, pp. 144-45.

[7] *Ibid.*, p. 134.

[8] *Ibid.*, pp. 162-63, 140-41.

[9] *Ibid.*, p. 129.

[10] I.e., *ibid.*, sermons VII-XIII.

[11] Savonarola did not turn to Haggai as soon as the revolution in the Florentine state took place, as Ridolfi maintains he did. *Vita di Girolamo Savonarola*, 2 vols. (Rome, 1952), vol. II, p. 123, n. 10. Firpo, the latest editor of these sermons, notes that Savonarola turned instead to Psalms for the texts of his next sermons (see n. 10 above) and only began to expound Haggai on December 15, although he had already begun to think about the significance of Haggai in connection with the reform of the state in his sermon of December 8. *Prediche sopra Aggeo*, pp. 493-94. The implications of this fact are important: the period from the coming of the Flood (Charles' occupation of

the public life of Florence inspired him to new insight into God's purposes. On December 2 the people were summoned to the Piazza della Signoria for a *Parlamento*—the traditional assembly of the rank and file convoked to consider major constitutional changes—and they shouted their approval of the uprooting of the Medici system.[12] This event's impact on Savonarola was immediately voiced in his preaching: he had begun to see why God had sent him to Florence to construct the Ark and to understand what the Ark was for. Those who had been sheltered in the Ark, he declared in his next sermon, on December 7, were God's elect.[13] The Ark was designed not merely for the protection of the repentant, it was—as it had been in the days of Noah—God's instrument for the great renewal: "Just as the world was renewed by the Flood, so God is sending these tribulations to renew His Church with those who shall be in the Ark. . . . And thus says our Psalm, 'Sing to the Lord a new song,' that is, O elect of God, O you who are in the Ark, sing a new song because God wants to renew His Church."[14] Who were those who would dwell in the Ark? The revolution of the state had provided the answer—the Florentines—for it was a political conversion now, and not a spiritual one, that showed that they were ready to enter the Ark, wherefore God had spared them. The uprooting of the Medici government begun on December 2 was a godly work; the Florentines had made a beginning by transforming themselves materially, in the flesh, now they must prepare for the essential transformation of form, in the spirit.[15] Florence must sing the canticle of the Lord because He had saved her, not for herself (as Savonarola had previously said) but for Him, because she was the Lord's: "Florence, God has saved you in this misfortune.

Florence) on November 17 to the intensification of the constitutional crisis in mid-December was for Savonarola a period of transition in his prophetic self-realization during which he finally came to choose this Biblical text for its application to the Florentine political situation.

[12] Rubinstein, "Politics and Constitution in Florence at the End of the Fifteenth Century," *Italian Renaissance Studies*, ed. E. F. Jacob (London, 1960), pp. 152-54; and on the institution of *Parlamento*, his *Government of Florence Under the Medici (1434-1494)* (Oxford, 1966), pp. 68-69.

[13] *Prediche sopra Aggeo*, pp. 123-42.

[14] *Ibid.*, pp. 125-26.   [15] *Ibid.*, p. 126.

But note well that it is said: *Salvavit sibi*, that is, the Lord has saved you for Himself; it is not said for you. Not for you, because you must understand that no one is to make himself great, nor to say, 'Florence is mine.' She is the Lord's, and if anyone disregards this God will shut him out."[16]

The meaning of Florence's escape from destruction, and with it the meaning of Savonarola's mission, was becoming increasingly clear to him: Florence was a chosen city; God had elected her to help Him accomplish His great plan of renewal. Soon even this inspiration grew into one more thrilling: not only was Florence *a* chosen city but *the* chosen city, destined to become the center of a new, more glorious age. And Savonarola had been sent to show her the way. On December 15, he began to expound Haggai, the Jewish prophet who had preached to the children of Israel after their liberation from captivity in Babylon. The Jews, he said, had begun to rebuild their Temple, but then they had faltered. Haggai had intervened to persuade them that the time for the rebuilding was come and to show them the way. Likewise he, Savonarola, was there to show the Florentines how to build their new Temple, a new order in Florence, more glorious than the first (Haggai 2-4; 8-10). Florence too could become a holy city, a new Jerusalem: "the man who is just and compassionate God will always treat compassionately in his every need; be sure then that you are compassionate toward the poor, and if your city has such citizens as we have said there must be, blessed will you be, Florence, for you will soon become that celestial Jerusalem (*quella Jerusalem superna*)."[17]

---

[16] *Ibid.*, p. 134. Note the change from his previous sermon in which he had said that God had saved Florence for no other reason than out of His love (see n. 4 above). In this present sermon he also tries to deal with his earlier prophecy of the coming of the *flagello*: "I have told you many times in the past, Florence, that, although God has prepared a great scourge for everyone, nevertheless, on the other hand God loves you and wishes you well, and therefore it can be said that in you is verified the saying, *Misericordia et veritas obviaverunt sibi* [Psalm 85:10, Rev. Standard; 84:11, Vulgate], that is, mercy and justice [sic] have met together in the city of Florence. And the scourge has come from one direction and mercy has come to meet it from the other and *iustitia et pax obsculatae sunt* and have embraced each other . . ." (pp. 133-34).

[17] *Ibid.*, p. 151.

But it was in his sermon of December 10, that Savonarola's vision of Florence in her glory took wings: ". . . I announce this good news to the city, that Florence will be more glorious, richer, more powerful than she has ever been. First, glorious in the sight of God as well as of men: and you, O Florence, will be the reformation of all Italy, and from here the renewal will begin and spread everywhere, because this is the navel of Italy. Your counsels will reform all by the light and grace that God will give you. Second, O Florence, you will have innumerable riches, and God will multiply all things for you. Third, you will spread your empire, and thus you will have power temporal and spiritual. . . ."[18]

To Florence leadership in Italy and the world for the renovation of religion! To Florence new glory, wealth and power surpassing all her other achievements! Let the Florentines grasp this opportunity which God held out to them and their troubles would be overcome. God would not let His city languish in want nor suffer humiliation; indeed He would raise her above all others. But it was up to them to justify the election of their city and to establish her right to leadership. Let everyone "reform his conscience" by confessing and communicating, beginning with "the civic leaders and leading citizens." Let each man make restitution for his transgressions by helping his neighbor. Let each put the common good before his own. In this way Florence would become "a city of God and not of Florence."[19] By following the advice of their Noah and governing well, her leaders would make the Ark "a good instrument for the renewal."[20] If the Florentines followed these two counsels—personal reform and love for the common good—they would reap joys spiritual and temporal: your city will be called the city of God and will be richer, more powerful and more glorious than ever it was and she will reform all of Italy.[21] Here again the breathtaking declaration with its twofold promise to Florence: Florence the vital

---

[18] *Ibid.*, pp. 166-67. Contrast this with his exhortation of November 16, the day before Charles' entry into Florence: "This is the time to begin to live in simplicity as I have told you many times, and you who are the leaders, you ought to be the first to begin to live in simplicity and to put down every manner of pride, because against this pride God has prepared and sends these tribulations which are now beginning to come to Italy" (p. 83).

[19] *Ibid.*, p. 168.   [20] *Ibid.*, p. 173.   [21] *Ibid.*, pp. 187-88.

center of a worldwide spiritual reformation; Florence, richer, more powerful, more glorious than ever.

Now other parts of the Scriptures also took on new meaning as Savonarola found further textual prefigurations of the New Day and of Florence's mission. The story of the Sunamite woman in II Kings 4[22] he now read not only as referring to the Incarnation and to the reform of the Church in general, but also to Florence, "the Florentine Church," and the new reform to come.[23] In his first sermon on Haggai, on December 15, Savonarola turned back to the seven-day scheme of the Apocalypse which he had expounded four years earlier, investing it with a new, more precise interpretation. St. John tells us in the Apocalypse that he saw four horses whose colors were white, red, black, and pale (Revelation 6). These signify the four states of the Church. The white horse was the state of the Apostles; the red, of the martyrs; the black, of the heretics. The pale horse, which is neither white nor black, but colorless, signifies the state of the tepid. This is our present state, and we have been in it for a long time, but it is coming to a close. The fifth state, of Antichrist and of conversion, will soon begin. Already Florence has seen the beginning of the new light and she must prepare for the renovation of the Church. God has come to Florence to reform her so that she may be the cause of the reform of many other peoples: in the coming age the Turks and Infidels will convert to Christianity, men will rest in the renewed Church (*Chiesa renovata*), turning from worldly affairs to the love of godly things, and the church will be glorious throughout the world.[24]

The contrast between this and Savonarola's message of a few weeks earlier, not to speak of the previous four years, is striking. From the start of the invasion crisis in October, through the revolt in Florence, the passing of the French armies, and the revolutionary actions of the December 2nd *Parlamento*, Savonarola's prophetic vision had undergone a steady change, until the transformation could hardly have been more complete. His apocalyptic warnings of tribulation and doom had given way to promises of divine love and favor. Instead of the Last Days men could look forward to a new

---

[22] IV Kings 4 in the Vulgate.   [23] *Prediche sopra Aggeo*, pp. 196-98.
[24] *Ibid.*, pp. 234-40.

age of piety, love, and peace. This was something more than an adjustment of details, it was a fundamental transformation of Savonarola's eschatology. His earlier exhortations to reject the world had given way to the conviction that the world could be—indeed, would be—transformed, with the regeneration not only of the individual penitent but of society itself. The preacher of repentance had become a prophet of the millennium, exchanging his earlier radical pessimism for an even more radical optimism. The new Cyrus, whom Savonarola had originally seen only as God's avenging sword, had now become the new Charlemagne, God's instrument of renewal and Florence's special benefactor. And what a metamorphosis in Florence herself! No longer must she expect to suffer the common fate; for now she knew that she would be triumphant, the new city of the millennial age. This changed attitude toward Florence is at the heart of Savonarola's new inspiration. The events of the past weeks had illuminated him with the understanding of his own labors, made perfect sense of them by showing him that God had intended all along to build the New Jerusalem in this city to which He had summoned His servant and performed many wonderful things.[25] These events had shown Savonarola how to connect Florence's destiny with the universal design and thus to speak to her people more intimately than he had ever been able to speak to them before. But if the prophet had found his city, his New Jerusalem, the city had also found her prophet, who was ready to acknowledge the validity of her own special dream, for by no means the least part of his new message was the promise that Florence would enjoy temporal as well as spiritual greatness, that she would be richer, more powerful, more glorious than ever. And he left no room for doubt as to what he meant; again and again Savonarola assured the Florentines that their temporal concerns were compatible with God's holy aims. They would not only recover Pisa "despite the world," they

[25] On Florence as the New Jerusalem, see, e.g., "As for the fourth part of the reform, which I told you you must make, see our Psalm which says: *Aedificans Hierusalem Dominus* [Psalm 147:2, Rev. Standard; 146:2, Vulgate]; the Lord wants to build here a new Jerusalem so that this city will no longer be Florence as she has been up to now, but a Jerusalem holy and peaceful, if you want it to be." *Ibid.*, pp. 340-41.

would also gain possessions they had never had before.[26] Florence would spread her empire to many places,[27] and those who resisted her would be conquered and fall under her dominion, and her light would spread as far as the land of the Turks.[28] Preachers would arouse the people of other cities to go to Florence, where they would find both the true light and the model form of government. And Florence would possess the inheritance of these other cities, dissipated by the devil, by sin, by tyrants, by famine, and by war. And when the wicked are dead and the tyrants spent, then many good people will come to Florence and fill all the roads and fields of her land with their goodness.[29]

These promises, which are in such striking contrast to Savonarola's own former puritanism and other-worldliness, reveal how he had come around not just to a millenarian fantasy,[30] but to the particular variety of millenarian fantasy which had long been entertained by Florentines. The myth that celebrated Florence both as the New

[26] "And I tell you that you will have Pisa back despite all the world, and other possessions [*dell' altre cose*] will come under the Florentines that have never been yours before. . . . If your neighbors knew what is going to happen to them and had seen it with their eyes as I have seen it in my mind's eye, they would weep the whole day." *Prediche sopra i Salmi*, vol. I, ed. Vincenzo Romano (Rome, 1969), pp. 203-204.

[27] ". . . and out of you will come the reformation of all Italy. And Florence will become richer, more powerful than she has ever been and will spread her empire [*imperio*] in many places." *Prediche sopra Aggeo*, p. 213.

[28] ". . . and you will begin to extend yourself through all of Tuscany and outside of Tuscany. Some will come whom it will not be necessary to fight, and they will say, 'we wish to be governed by you,' and they will come under your dominion, so that this light will spread as far as Turkey, and the Turks will convert to the faith of Christ to the praise and glory of our Lord. . . ." *Prediche italiane ai Fiorentini*, vol. III², *Quaresimale del 1496*, p. 188.

[29] *Ibid.*, pp. 196-97.

[30] In his sermon of January 13, 1495, called the "Predica della Rinnovazione" because in it he sums up all his previous preaching on the renovation of the Church, Savonarola cites "the abbot Joachim and many others" who "preach and announce that in this time this scourge must come." *Prediche sopra i Salmi*, vol. I, p. 45. This is his most explicit use of Joachim as an authority. He also says, "and therefore God will give his vineyard, that is, Rome and the Church, to others to be cultivated, because at Rome there is no love [*carità*] left but only the devil." *Ibid.*, p. 48.

Jerusalem and as the New Rome in a dual mission of spiritual and political leadership was one with which Florentines of every class would have been familiar, for it had been cultivated by humanists, preachers, the Ciompi rebels, and civic chroniclers in the particular form that suited each best. Savonarola's particular version of it was not simply his response to recent events, but also the expression of an ever deeper involvement in Florentine life, which was now climaxed by his intervention in the constitutional crisis that followed the overthrow of the Medici.

Only gradually, however, did Savonarola turn his attention to the constitutional problem. In the same sermon of December 7, in which he insisted that laws should be passed to prevent the recurrence of tyranny, and in which he exhorted Florence to become a new city, he discussed his conception of reform: "Now, as to the reform of something that is composed of matter and of form, you should recognize that, following the order of natural things, its reform consists first and principally in the form and secondly in the matter. Man is composed of form and matter, that is to say, of soul and body, and the body is made for the soul. Therefore it is necessary that the reform begin in the soul."[31] And further on: "Reform yourselves first inwardly, if you wish to reform yourselves outwardly, and if you wish to make good laws accommodate yourselves first to the law of God, because all good laws derive from the eternal law to the observance of which we must seek the grace of the Holy Spirit."[32] And then, referring to the famous dictum attributed to Cosimo de' Medici: ". . . and what mad and evil men say is not true, that the state is not governed by paternosters, because the states of true Christians are ruled by prayer and good actions. That is the saying of tyrants, not of true princes."[33] This was a neat shot which found a double mark: in the Medici tyranny and in its cause, the unchristian divorce of politics from morality. And yet, in this same sermon, in the very midst of his defense of a Christian politics, Savonarola, almost casually, first took public notice of the mounting crisis in the Florentine government.

[31] *Prediche sopra Aggeo*, p. 126.   [32] *Ibid.*, p. 133.
[33] *Ibid.*, p. 134.

WITH THE DEPARTURE of Charles VIII and his army from Florence on November 28, the political leaders of the city turned to the work of consolidating the revolution.[34] On November 30, a *pratica*, or advisory meeting of principal citizens, was held and recommended the following measures: the preparation of a new electoral list of citizens eligible for public office (*squittinio*), the selection of twenty commissioners (*Accoppiatori*) who would elect the Signoria "by hand" (*a mano*) until the new *squittinio* was ready, and the calling of a general assembly of the people (*Parlamento*) to approve the new program. On December 2 the *Parlamento* met and dutifully approved the agenda set out for it; those councils and commissions that had been the main instruments of Medici domination (*Cento, Settanta, Otto di Pratica, Dodici Procuratori*) were abolished; the old councils of the *Popolo* and the *Comune* were restored, and the other arrangements decided upon in the *pratica* were ratified. Further, the hated *gabelle*—direct taxes levied mostly on the sale of commodities—were abolished, and a Council of Ten (*Dieci di Libertà e di Pace*) was appointed to manage the campaign for the recovery of Pisa which, with the apparent complicity of her French garrison, had just revolted against Florentine rule. The architects of the *coup d'état* of November 9—for it was largely the same leaders who were in control of these arrangements who were now elected as the *Accoppiatori*—considered that the matter of Florence's new government had been settled.

They were mistaken. They had underestimated the weaknesses of their own position and had failed to take into account the extent of democratic expectations which they themselves had aroused among the people. Nor did they correctly calculate Savonarola's growing importance. In prestige and in mass appeal Fra Girolamo stood without rival, and he had for his audience, if not for his following, virtually the entire Florentine population. No matter that his original aims had been apolitical; perhaps precisely because he had remained

[34] On the constitutional reforms of the new republic: Rubinstein, "Politics and Constitution," and his "I primi anni del Consiglio maggiore di Firenze (1494-1499)," *Archivio storico italiano*, CXII (1954), 151-94, 321-47; Felix Gilbert, *Machiavelli and Guicciardini: Politics and History in Sixteenth-Century Florence* (Princeton, 1965), Part I; Antonio Anzilotti, *La crisi costituzionale della repubblica fiorentina* (Florence, 1912).

aloof from the revolt, it was inevitable that he was now drawn into the domestic crisis. Besides, Savonarola was, as we have seen, beginning to grasp the importance of the political revolution for the success of the religious renovation of which he had so long dreamed and which now seemed so close to fulfillment, and therefore he could not hold himself aloof any longer.

What drew him into politics, finally, was the mounting tension in the city following the *Parlamento* of December 2. The *Parlamento* had performed as expected. It was easy to gain the assent of an unorganized crowd for a program already formulated and presented by skilled speakers while armed soldiers blocked the entrances to the Piazza della Signoria and mingled with the people. But it was another matter to maintain the same people in a state of passivity once they had returned to their homes. A prospect of freedom had been raised by the leaders themselves, with their cry of "popolo e libertà," and by Savonarola, who was telling the Florentines that they had recovered their liberty by the will of God. The people's determination had already been tested and tempered in the crisis of November 17-28, when Charles VIII had threatened to restore Medicean government. The brave stand they had taken then, buoyed up by their spirit of liberty as well as by their trust in God, filled Piero Parenti with admiration: "for this I cannot praise the generous spirit of our people enough. With the King of France in their midst, surrounded by many thousands of his men and by many very powerful citizens who are Medici supporters, they dared to oppose his will in order to preserve their liberty and courageously to resist his dishonorable demands."[35] Now, after December 2, Parenti writes, the people felt betrayed, they considered the *Parlamento* "false and fraudulent" and they grumbled that affairs were not being managed *popularmente*. The "good citizens" complained that they had taken up arms to regain their liberty only to preserve in power the same men who had ruled before, with the exception of a few.[36]

If the *primati* (as Parenti called the principal men) had been

[35] Parenti, *Storia fiorentina*, MS BNF II. IV. 169 fol. 207.

[36] Piero Parenti, *Storia fiorentina*, ed. Joseph Schnitzer, *Quellen und Forschungen zur Geschichte Savonarolas*, vol. IV, *Savonarola nach der Aufzeichnungen des Florentiners Piero Parenti* (Leipzig, 1910), p. 21.

united among themselves they might have been able to withstand this mounting pressure from below, but united they were not. Personal animosities divided two of the most important leaders of the November upheaval, Piero Capponi and Francesco Valori: each had his own following, each was ambitious for power and eager to secure offices for friends and relatives. Moreover, the group as a whole now faced a challenge from another quarter—from those who were returning from exile, embittered against those who had waxed fat under the Medici, but even more bitter at finding these people still in power. Of former Medici supporters there were two groups, those who, like Capponi and Valori, had turned against Piero and led the revolt of November 8-9, and those who still continued to hope for a Medicean restoration. In this latter group were such *primati* as Bernardo Del Nero, Agnolo Niccolini, Niccolo Ridolfi, Pierfilippo Pandolfini, Lorenzo Tornabuoni, and Iacopo Salviati. This die-hard group suffered the greatest amount of odium, but in the eyes of the former Medicean exiles the leaders of the revolt against Piero were almost equally detestable, since they too had supported the Medicean regime until just a few weeks earlier. Therefore, since the latter were afraid that a general anti-Medicean reaction would sweep them away too, they now opposed further repressive measures against the *Bigi*, or Greys, as the Medici supporters now came to be called; but this tactic gave further substance to the suspicion that they themselves were disguised Mediceans.

The situation grew more and more tense. With neither of the city's major problems solved—neither the reconquest of Pisa nor the recovery of Florentine commercial and industrial activity—the people grew increasingly restive after December 2, and the patricians more fearful. Some of the *primati* now began to try to find ways to pacify the citizenry, but none of them seemed willing to go to the heart of the matter, which was their own monopoly of power and offices. Suddenly a few of them broke ranks, led it seems by Paolantonio Soderini.[37] A member of an old *popolano* family long prominent in public affairs,[38] Soderini now came forward to champion

[37] Francesco Guicciardini, *Storie fiorentine*, ed. Roberto Palmarocchi, *Opere*, vol. VI (Bari, 1931), pp. 106-107.

[38] Rubinstein, *Government of Florence*, pp. 158, 214-15; Gene A. Brucker, *Florentine Politics and Society 1343-78* (Princeton, N.J., 1962), pp. 30, 38, 125, et passim.

popular reforms against the oligarchy. Resentment and personal ambition may have been among his motives, for he was one of the few leaders of the revolt against Piero who had been omitted from the all-important commission of *Accoppiatori*, his personal rivals, Capponi and Valori, having leagued against him.[39] Alone, the *primati* converts to constitutional reform might not have made much headway, but, as Guicciardini puts it, help came from an unexpected quarter. Savonarola, who had previously given little concrete advice on questions of the new government, now revealed himself as a partisan of further constitutional revision. From the pulpit he called for the introduction of reforms modeled on the constitution of Venice, and he suggested that the Sixteen *Gonfalonieri*, or Standardbearers, who formed one of the two Colleges advisory to the Signoria, submit proposals for a new law which would embody the needed reforms. Later Savonarola was to claim that he had originated the new government which resulted from this constitutional crisis and that the government was the work of God.[40] In this way he came to identify the new *governo popolare* with the "new city" of his prophecy.

It is very likely, however, that the initiative for constitutional reform and for the idea of using the Venetian model was not Fra Girolamo's but that of a group of *primati* led by Paolantonio Soderini, and that Savonarola merely endorsed the plan and gave it his all-important public support. In addition to the testimony of Guicciardini, we have the report of the reliable Parenti, who indicates that the idea originated among the *primati* themselves, some of

[39] Cerretani, *Storia fiorentina*, ed. Joseph Schnitzer, *Quellen und Forschungen zur Geschichte Savonarolas*, vol. III, *Bartolomeo Cerretani* (Munich, 1904), p. 32. Guicciardini, *Storie fiorentine*, pp. 107-108. Guicciardini actually gives two different explanations of Savonarola's intervention in the constitutional crisis. Here he reports the belief that Paolantonio, out of anger and in order to change the government (*mutare lo stato*), persuaded Savonarola and "used him as an instrument to preach that a government of one people be established." Elsewhere he says that Savonarola's intervention was *uno aiuto non pensato* (p. 108) and that he gained so much support for a free and popular government that the leaders were not able to resist, although privately they were very displeased and began to hold consultations on further reform (pp. 109-10). This seems to be Guicciardini's own explanation.

[40] For the references to Savonarola's claims, see Rubinstein, "Politics and Constitution," p. 155, n. 1.

whom went to Savonarola with the proposal that he support a Venetian-style reform. In this way, according to Parenti, they intended to preserve themselves in power while at the same time forestalling a popular revolt; but Savonarola incorporated their suggestion into a more general proposal that embraced spiritual reformation and a universal amnesty. According to Parenti, whose account reports the gist of Savonarola's sermons, Savonarola said "it was necessary that virtue be exercised and vice eliminated and for this the Signoria had to take measures to purge [the city of] gaming, lasciviousness, sodomy, usury, and other defects, and to see that virtuous works be undertaken.

"If this were observed [Savonarola is reported to have continued], the people, restored to goodness, would be receptive to God's grace and thus we would go forward from good to better; we would have abundance of every good, we would become rich, we would increase the state and our empire and at last live in felicity. Further, all the rest of Italy would follow our example of good living. But in order to arrive at this goal it was necessary to grant pardon to every wrongdoer up to the present time. Since God had forgiven us we ought truly to forgive each other; but from this time forward whoever broke the law should be justly punished.

"Next, in order that the old might pass away and the new be established, a new form of government should be adopted and the old abolished. Nevertheless, he approved what the Signoria had done up to that time, in order that the acts of the *Parlamento* [i.e., abolishing the Medici system] not be considered illegal, etc. As to the adoption of a new system, he favored our looking at the Venetian type, that is, a government by elections, but that we ought to deliberate about it. Each of the *Gonfalonieri* of the Companies should have its own people consult in a specified place and report within three days to their leaders. Each of these leaders, four to a quarter, should then confer and reduce their plans to a single one, next, report the four plans for each quarter to the Signoria, who would then call a general council, where the plans would be reported and discussed, and whichever is accepted ought to be adopted."[41]

[41] Parenti, *Storia fiorentina*, ed. Schnitzer, pp. 26-27. On the use of the Venetian constitution as a model see below, pp. 248-62.

Savonarola's earliest public statements on the issue of constitutional reform seem to bear out Parenti's contention that he was brought into the plan for revision "in the Venetian mode" after it had been conceived by others. He first raised the issue in his sermon of December 7, almost as a footnote to a more extensive discussion of spiritual reform,[42] as follows: "And so, being established in the fear of God, He will give you the grace to find a good form for this new government of yours, so that no one may make himself its head, either as the Venetians do it, or in some better way to which God will inspire you. In order that God may illuminate you in this I exhort all the people to pray and to fast for three days, and then to come together in your councils to choose a good form for your government. And now I have said enough about the form in order that you reform yourselves as I have just suggested; let us now speak about the matter."[43] Clearly Savonarola was here referring to a discussion that was already under way; otherwise he could not have introduced the subject in such an abrupt and almost casual manner. His approach to it was oblique and he quickly turned back to what he considered the main problem of Florentine life, that is, the moral reformation.

At the same time, however, there is a shift in his terminology which shows that the question of the Florentine constitution was becoming much more important in his religious scheme of things. Earlier, even in the very same sermon, he had identified "form" with the law of God, the things of the spirit which take precedence and are determinative, while he had identified "matter" with the things of the body, those things which are outward and were made for the soul.[44] Now, however, in beginning to discuss the need for constitutional reform, he suddenly used these terms in a different way; those things having to do with the manner of government are the "form"; those having to do with the Spirit are the "matter." Thus, while things spiritual and moral are still determinative, containing "all the virtue of governing,"[45] by transposing his terms and equating modes of government with "form," Savonarola had given the question of the constitution a new importance, one in keeping with his new

[42] *Prediche sopra Aggeo*, pp. 123-34. [43] *Ibid.*, p. 135.
[44] See above, pp. 141, 147. [45] *Prediche sopra Aggeo*, pp. 136-37.

vision of the constitutional reform of the Florentine government as a part of God's plan which will come about through His grace. A few weeks later, on December 25, after a reform law had been adopted, he would say that in laying the foundation of a new government, Florence had changed her form and was no longer the Florence of the past.[46] But in the meantime his reorientation toward politics proceeded fitfully. While he preached at least four other times during the week following December 7, he did not mention the issue of constitutional reform and made only the following bare reference to the city's political problems: "O Florence, this sick man is the Florentine people; sick first of all in spiritual things, then as to its mode of government (*ordine civile*), and in other ways as well. All these ills the physician has cured; this is the Savior who has come to treat you."[47] For the most part, he continued to discuss the spiritual requirements for building "a city of God and not of Florence."[48]

At last, on December 14, Savonarola turned his full attention to constitutional reform and delivered "his first great political sermon."[49] He began by establishing a theoretical framework which is recognizably Thomist. Man, he said, is a social animal and therefore he has had to congregate either in cities or in castles or in villages to satisfy his common needs. Every society that wishes to live well has had to choose a form of government and has chosen either a government headed by one man, a government led by a few, or a government of all the people together. One-man government is best when the head is a good man because it produces the most unity, but when he is wicked this is the worst form of all. The character of the governed is also an important consideration. In regions where there are extremes of temperature—hot regions where men are thin-blooded and timid, and cold regions where they have much blood and little sense—government by one man is best. In temperate zones where men have both spirit and good sense (*dove abonda sangue ed ingegno*) they do not suffer the rule of a single man with patience; everyone wishes to be the head, to command rather than be commanded; hence dissension and discord arise among the citizens.

[46] *Ibid.*, p. 363.   [47] *Ibid.*, pp. 165-66.   [48] *Ibid.*, p. 168.
[49] The phrase is Rubinstein's, "Politics and Constitution," p. 164.

Such is the case of Italy, and this has been shown by the history of Rome as well as the other cities of Italy, including Florence. Thus the sacred doctors have taught that in those regions government of the many is better than one-man government. And this is most true of Florence, where men are high-spirited and intelligent; but it is necessary that such a government be well-ordered, otherwise the people of Florence will always be in dissension and in faction, and one group will drive the others out and declare them rebels.[50]

Having established this rather flimsy theoretical base for a popular regime, Savonarola went on to remind the Florentines of what he had told them some days earlier: that they stood on the threshold of the fifth age of the Church, in which the Turks and pagans would accept baptism; that Florence would be the center of reform and of empire if they opened their ears and listened to his advice for the common good of the city. The Florentines must repent and reform; the Magnificent Signoria must discipline the clergy, driving out bad priests and monks and seeing that those who remain live good and simple lives; the Signoria must pass laws against sodomy (for which, he charged, Florence had become infamous throughout Italy), against poetry and gaming and drinking and the indecent dress of women and all those things which are pernicious of the soul's health. Taxes must be reformed so that they fall upon property and not arbitrarily, and the imposts (*gabelle*) must be modified. Limits must be set on the size of dowries so that they do not impoverish families: five hundred ducats for the greater families and three hundred for the families of artisans. Above everything else, it was necessary that no one be allowed to become the sole head of the city, because a people under a tyrant is like water which has been held under pressure; when it finds a hole through which to escape it rushes out impetuously and ruinously. Tyrants are given to people as punishment for their sins, and out of His mercy God removes them when the punishment has done its work. Then, returning to the problem of the constitution, Savonarola warned the Florentines to "take care that no such person tries to make himself head in your city and guard the common good. And how you are to do this, I will tell you as God has inspired me to do. I have told you in these recent

[50] *Prediche sopra Aggeo*, pp. 210-11.

days that when a people wants to do a thing according to nature every consideration is directed to the form of that thing, and therefore I told you that you should choose a good form for your new government and above all that no one think of making himself its head, if you wish to live in liberty. The form with which you have begun cannot stand if it is not revised in a better fashion. I believe that there is no better [form] than that of the Venetians and that you should follow their example, leaving out some things which are not suited for your needs, such as the doge (*come è quella del duce*). Thus I also believe it would be well, in order to inspire everyone to behave virtuously, that the artisans in some way be made eligible for office (*che gli artefici fussino in qualche modo beneficiati*) and, being honored, become accustomed to behave well. And therefore it would not be misguided to have the major offices chosen by election and the minor ones by lot."[51] With the conviction that God had inspired him to announce a particular form for the new government, Savonarola's equation of Florence with the "new city" of his apocalyptic vision was complete. Much was still to be done; the citizens had yet to give themselves wholly to the fulfillment of the great task, and Savonarola reflected this uncertainty by continuing to insist that the prophecy of Florentine glory was contingent upon the Florentines' obeying the divine command.[52] But from this time on political reform became a central part of his prophetic message, and as the reforms were achieved his promise became more and more certain.

At the outset, however, there was opposition to reforming the constitution, and in dealing with it Savonarola became increasingly insistent that the reform of the state was an absolute command:

---

[51] *Ibid.*, pp. 212-26. Savonarola must have been sensitive about the question of who had originated the reform plan and whether he was acting independently in proposing it. In his next day's sermon (December 15) he said, "And what I told you yesterday in my sermon, don't think that anyone persuaded me to do so." *Ibid.*, p. 248.

[52] E.g., "What I told you is absolutely certain (*certissimo*), and if you do what I have told you to do, Florence, you will have those three things I said: you will be more powerful, richer, more glorious than ever. But, if you don't do it, I tell you, city of Florence, that I see a great evil hanging over you and your ultimate inundation." *Ibid.*, p. 261.

"Thus I say to you, Florence, that this is the time to build the new house of God and to renew your city, but just as there is opposition to all of God's work (as you know, the rebuilding of the Temple of God in Jerusalem had opposition), in the same way you see that opposition has appeared, with the argument that this is not the time to make another reformation. But I tell you that God wants you to do it and requires that you renew your city and the state, and that your city become the city of God, no longer of Florence as it has been up to now. And everything depends upon the form that you choose; for when the form has been changed the city will be changed."[53] What he had initially relegated to the indifferent sphere of outward things—the form of the state—Savonarola now made the basic condition for the fulfillment of the spiritual renewal of the city. Here the implication of his shift of terminology referred to earlier becomes fully apparent. What had formerly been secondary matter had now become not only form, but the determinative form: "everything depends upon the form that you choose, for when that form has been changed the city will be changed."

But not the city alone; the reformation of Florence was merely the initial step in the fulfillment of the entire millenarian vision: "Believe then, Florence, that this is the time of the reformation of the Church and of your city, as I have told you. And as you have seen part of these things come about so all the more you must believe the rest. Believe, I say, that this is the time that the gentile peoples— that is, the infidels and pagans—will reform, especially that this will take place in our age, and that many who are present here will see it. But first it is necessary that we reform ourselves, and the instruments for this are already being prepared. If you do not want to believe me, I wish to demonstrate to you through Holy Scripture and by the prophecies of Saint John that this is true. Only let me rest a little and you will see that the end of the fourth state, the beginning of the fifth state of the Church, has come."[54] In the fifth state Antichrist would appear, but with the renewal of the Church and the conversion of the infidel the Christians would fight with Antichrist and overcome him,[55] and the Lord would build a new

[53] *Ibid.*, pp. 231-32.   [54] *Ibid.*, p. 234.   [55] *Ibid.*, pp. 235-37.

Zion which would appear in all its glory.[56] That this new Zion was Florence, that Florence was to be the center of the New Age of love and of contemplation but also of *imperium* was now Savonarola's principal theme: "*Ascendite in montem,* climb high in contemplation of Christ and of his works. *Portate ligna,* said Haggai to the people of Jerusalem, bring wood with which to rebuild the temple of God. Likewise you, citizens, bring your counsels and take counsel with charity and love to rebuild your temple, that is, your new government and new order (*governo e reggimento*). Learn to make your laws from the laws of God. His is complete union and complete love; so should your reform be all full of charity and love. See how Christ rules and governs his Christian people with love and charity. Do you likewise. *Aedificate domum,* said the Lord through the mouth of Haggai, that is, build the house of the Lord and rebuild my temple. *Et acceptabilis mihi erit et gloriabor,* and it will be a thing most pleasing to me and in this temple my name will be glorified.

"And thus I say to you, Florence, build your new government and your reform in praise of the Lord and Florence will be His, and in this way God will be glorified in all the world. Your domestic laws, Florence, make them all love, union, and charity. Your external law, because not everyone is good, but for the most part bad, must be a bridle to restrain those who wish to do you harm."[57] The old warning of the speedy coming of the Last Days had now been superseded by a vision of the imminent World Sabbath: "And through all Italy the fame of Florence will spread and will reach the Turks and they will be converted. They will be better than the Christians are today because among them we see greater simplicity and a greater disdain for the things of the world and more good faith (*lealtà*) than among Christians. Then will come the seventh day *ubi Deus quievit ab omni opere quod patrarat.*

"God rested, says St. Augustine, that is, he rested and ceased from his labors. And thus will men rest in the church renewed, converting themselves to the love of divine things and almost ceasing from the labors of the world, and the Church will be glorious in all the world."[58]

[56] *Ibid.,* p. 238.   [57] *Ibid.,* pp. 292-93.   [58] *Ibid.,* pp. 319-20.

V

Savonarola and the Millennium

... AND THE CHURCH WILL BE SO FULL OF LOVE THAT ANGELS WILL
CONVERSE WITH MEN, BECAUSE THE CHURCH TRIUMPHANT WILL LOVE
THE CHURCH MILITANT. YOU CANNOT BELIEVE HOW MUCH
CHARITY AND LOVE ANGELS HAVE FOR MEN; THEY
NEVER GROW ANGRY, AND WHEN THEY SEE
MAN PURGED OF HIS SINS
THEY STAY WITH HIM
ALWAYS.

—Savonarola, Sermon of March 13, 1496

IN the three and a half years of life remaining to him after the
upheavals of November and December 1494 Savonarola continued
to urge upon the Florentines his vision of the great renewal which
would come *cito et velociter*, within the lifetime even of his older
listeners. Scripture, particularly the Book of Revelation and the
Prophets, continued to be his guide; but he now read Scripture in
the clearer light of recent events—the French invasion, the revolution in Florence, the reconciliation between Florence and her old
ally, and the beginnings of a new civic order in which he himself
was a central figure. Moreover, he now gave to Scriptural apocalyptic
a new interpretation which, while typically millenarian in its general
outlines, was imprinted with special features that derived from the
Florentine situation as well as from his own passionate inspiration.
Savonarola was no apocalyptic exegete of Hildegard of Bingen's or
Joachim of Flora's type; he was not interested in constructing
prophetic-historical systems. His vision of the future was meant to
inspire the Florentines to undertake reform and to persist in the
work of renewal. He was first and always a reformer, but a reformer

who had little faith in the ordinary means of exhortation and Scriptural teaching. The world was so evil that reform was impossible without some deeper process of regeneration and renewal. As he told his listeners, he had come to see that by itself Scriptural exposition could bear no fruit because God's light had been removed from the Church in their time; therefore God had to intervene to bring about a great cleansing and renovation.[1] Thus, while Savonarola sought confirmation in the Scriptures for his teaching, he relied essentially upon his own inspiration—the divine illumination of which he frequently spoke—to initiate his understanding of God's purposes, and it was characteristic of the man that he found such illumination when he needed it. In other words, the prophet grew out of the reformer as the millenarian out of the prophet. Savonarola was primarily a preacher, not a theologian; he was concerned most of all with changing the world, not explaining it. Day after day he wrestled with the *tiepidi*, the shallow Christians who put their religious stock in ceremonies and superficial forms; from day to day his prospects for achieving reform suffered setbacks or managed small victories, and his own mood fluctuated accordingly between pessimism and optimism. This was reflected in his preaching. From such an approach we would neither expect a thoroughgoing theoretical system or flawless consistency, nor do we find them. Those who have discovered inconsistencies and contradictions in Savonarola's preaching and have taken these as proof of insincerity or demagoguery have missed this point. Experience, not logic, is the key to under-

---

[1] See the very important passage in *Prediche italiane ai Fiorentini*, ed. Roberto Palmarocchi and Francesco Cognasso (Perugia-Venice, 1930-35), vol. III¹, *Quaresimale del 1496*, p. 286, where he speaks of his earlier mistake of believing that by itself exposition of the Gospel would bring about reform: "Io confesso il mio errore; io fui ancora io già involto in questo errore, ma poi fui fatto vedere che non si faceva frutto e non era buona piova. Essendo adunque mancato il cibo buono dell'anima, è mancato la piova della terra della Chiesa. La piova del cielo è quando la viene di sopra, cioè quando Idio manda le sue illuminazioni, le quali sono cessate nella Chiesa in questi tempi." In Savonarola's thinking, reform was always the dominating idea, the goal; prophecy was always the means. To put this another way Savonarola was essentially a reformer who became a prophet. On this point I find myself in disagreement with Cantimori who, in his review of Schnitzer's biography, asserted the contrary. See above, pp. 12, 18.

standing his prophetic message, just as passion rather than calculation is the key to understanding the character of the man. Not even
in the two treatises where he discussed his prophecies did he attempt
to elaborate the apocalyptic schemes of his sermons.[2] He wrote these
works to uphold the orthodoxy and legitimacy of his preaching and
his prophecy, not to expound an apocalyptic view of history. To the
extent that he concerned himself with theory it was mainly to prove
that latter-day prophetic illumination, namely his own, was still
possible and valid.

This is not to say that Savonarola was altogether indifferent to
apocalyptic theory or system. He had some knowledge of traditional
eschatological speculation, and he referred to a variety of apocalyptic
schemes based on Biblical symbolism. His favorite had always been
the sevenfold division which derived from the Book of Revelation,
an interpretation in which, he said, he followed the exposition of
alcuni antiqui.[3] According to this scheme there were to be seven ages,
or states of the Church, in all before the Day of Judgment. Three
had already passed; the present was the fourth state; three more
were to come. Each of these states was marked by great evil and by
renewal. Thus, the first state, which encompassed the time "from
the beginning to Christ," saw the introduction of the Gospel and of
Christianity; the second, the martyrs of the Church; the third, the
heretics who were opposed by the Doctors. The fourth state was the
present, the age of indifference, of spiritual shallowness, dominated
by the *tiepidi*, and it was almost at an end. Already the tribulations
had begun; soon the Church would be renewed.[4] The approaching
fifth state was to be the time of the preachers of Antichrist and
would be followed by the coming of Antichrist himself, while the
last state he described merely as the age "after Antichrist," which
would end with the Last Judgment. In regard to the three future

[2] I.e., the *Compendium Revelationum* in Gianfrancesco Pico della Mirandola, *Vita R. P. Hieronymi Savonarolae*, ed. Jacques Quetif, 2 vols. (Paris,
1674), vol. I; and his *Dialogus de veritate prophetica* (Florence: Bartolomeo
de' Libri, 1497). Hain no. 14339. On the *Dialogus*, see Roberto Ridolfi, *Vita
di Girolamo Savonarola*, 2 vols. (Rome, 1952), vol. II, p. 193, n. 23.

[3] *Prediche italiane ai Fiorentini*, vol. III[1], p. 286.

[4] E.g., *ibid.*, pp. 286-87; *Prediche sopra Ruth e Michea*, ed. Vincenzo
Romano, 2 vols. (Rome, 1962), vol. I, p. 188.

states Savonarola was not very clear, for while he maintained that each age was marked by a great renewal, so that the coming renovation of the Church would apparently be succeeded by further states of decline and renewal before the End, at other times he seemed to be saying that the next renewal would be the ultimate one, the last millennium, which would end with the Second Coming and the Day of Judgment. He seemed to be telescoping the three future states of the Church into one great age which would experience the ultimate war of the good against Antichrist, the final defeat of the latter, and the reconciliation and regeneration before the Last Days.[5]

As we saw earlier, Savonarola sometimes used a fourfold scheme based on the vision of the four horses of the Apocalypse, in which the present state precedes the ultimate regeneration. The white horse represented the first state, of the Apostles; the red horse the second state, of the Martyrs; the black horse was the state of the Heretics; the pale horse, the present state, of the *tiepidi*. Soon after this must come the renovation of the Church.[6] In still another variant of the fourfold scheme, Savonarola interpreted the story of Lazarus (John 11) in a millenarian sense that had special relevance for Florence. Here the four days between the time Lazarus fell sick and the time of his resurrection were the four days of recent Florentine history: the first day represented the time when the Medici and their cohorts ruled the city (*quando la brigata si stava*); the second day represented the time when God lifted up His servants and it was announced that they must repent to prepare for the coming scourge (this was the time of Savonarola's appearance on the scene); the third day represented the time when the tribulations began to appear; now, in the fourth day, there would be a war of all and it would be said, "Lazarus, come forth." Thus, the resurrection of Florence, the present-day Lazarus, he equated with the final age of regeneration.[7]

[5] E.g., *Prediche sopra Aggeo*, ed. Luigi Firpo (Rome, 1965), pp. 238-39; and p. 250, where he somewhat inconsistently said, "Noi siamo nel principio del quinto stato della Chiesa."

[6] Girolamo Savonarola, *Prediche sopra i Salmi*, vol. I, ed. Vincenzo Romano (Rome, 1969), pp. 48-51.

[7] *Prediche sopra Ezechiele*, ed. Roberto Ridolfi, 2 vols. (Rome, 1955), vol. II, pp. 173-74.

Still, Savonarola was less interested in apocalyptic speculations per se than he was in rousing his listeners to action, and his theology of history was never more than the sketchiest of improvised frameworks for the more important program of renewal. At times he seems to have conceived of the process of history as an ebb and flow of good and evil in which each state of the Church repeated the same pattern of sin and renewal, a pattern which would only be complete with the return of Christ and His Last Judgment. At other times, however, he seems to have regarded the coming renewal as the last one before the End, thus conceiving of history as a spiritual progression toward ultimate perfection. This characteristic looseness of thought stems from the spontaneous way in which Savonarola's prophetic inspiration arose and from his own attitude toward it. In the example given here we see his more recent millenarian vision superimposed upon his older eschatology. The sevenfold scheme of periods of decline and renewal dates from his earliest exposition of the Book of Revelation in 1490, when he had urged repentance and reform within the context of the speedy coming of Antichrist and the Last Days. The fourfold scheme, according to which the world stood on the threshold of the final age of universal regeneration was the result of his more recent inspiration and expressed his new millenarian optimism.[8] But, believing as he did in the validity of his prophetic illumination, it would have been difficult for him to discard entirely his own earlier views; he was bound to see a basic continuity and consistency between what he had thought and said in 1490 and what he was thinking and saying in 1494. For this reason Savonarola merely added his newer views to his older ones and gave them a different emphasis; for example, while continuing to use the older sevenfold scheme and to maintain that the world was in the fourth state of the Church, he gave the coming age much more importance as a period of worldly regeneration than he had done earlier.[9]

[8] Compare these views with those in his earlier sermons on the First Epistle of St. John, where he said that the universal conversion and reform would come at the Day of Judgment. Ms BNF Magl. XXX. 110, esp. fols. 78 recto–81 (30 November 1490).

[9] In a sense he did the same thing in his political thought, that is, he superimposed Florentine republican ideas upon a Thomist base. See Nicolai Rubin-

This reluctance to discard earlier modes of thought indicates a deeper problem in Savonarola's thinking. The conflict of apocalyptic systems—or perhaps we should say, the failure to recognize the conflict between them—reflects a fundamental and persistent ambiguity of values inherent in Savonarola's new millenarianism. While he continued to repeat to the Florentines those promises of earthly joys that were such a striking part of his new vision, he also continued to insist that material blessings were wholly irrelevant to the truly spiritual life. The following passage from a Lenten sermon of 1497 shows this persistent inconsistency: "Behold my Florentines constantly [concerned] with those temporal things. Let such things alone. I do not mean to say that you will not have these things I have told you of, or rather that God has told you of; but is it not enough that God has illuminated you? If Florence were to be ruined and to lose her liberty and all her temporal possessions, would it not be enough that she has the light of God which can lead to Paradise? This is enough, and if you are Christian you will not look for anything else but this light."[10] Was this reproach directed to the Florentines alone or to himself as well? Did Savonarola ever feel that in promising riches and power to the Florentines he had compromised his own commitment to the life of the Spirit? Perhaps not, since he believed that he was only God's spokesman, and that whatever he had promised was part of God's plan. Besides, in his more recent view Florence had to have temporal power in order to do the Lord's work; the great enterprise of renewal was still the all-important objective, the justification and purpose of the city's divine election. Nonetheless, between Savonarola the puritanical reformer and Savonarola the civic prophet there was an underlying disharmony which he never resolved. This becomes still more apparent as we press further in our examination of his millenarian vision.

Millenarianism has been divided into two types according to the believer's view of the relation between the millennium and the Sec-

stein, "Politics and Constitution in Florence at the End of the Fifteenth Century," *Italian Renaissance Studies*, ed. E. F. Jacob (London, 1960), pp. 159-60; and Chapter IX below.

[10] *Prediche sopra Ezechiele*, vol. II, *Giorni festivi del 1495*, p. 71; also *Prediche italiane ai Fiorentini*, vol. II, p. 269.

ond Coming. One type, called premillenarianism, refers to the belief that Christ's Second Coming will precede the millennium. The other, called postmillenarianism, refers to the belief that the Second Coming will follow the millennium and only then initiate the Last Days. Premillenarianism, which is less common in Christian eschatology, has been said to reflect a pessimistic view of the ability of human agencies to bring about man's regeneration, for in this view regeneration must come about through cataclysmic, superhuman means, by Christ or some other divine agency of deliverance at the end of time. On the other hand, postmillenarianism implies that the Christian agencies of the world are able to bring about the millennial order, achieving it within historical time and before the return of Christ. It has been suggested that "pre- and postmillennialism correspond, in the secular sphere, to the revolutionary and reformist attitudes to social change."[11]

In form, Savonarola's new vision belongs to the more usual postmillenarian type, for whatever time-scheme he used he always placed the age of regeneration within historical time, before the Second Coming and the Last Judgment, and he came increasingly to rely upon such human institutions as the French monarchy and the Florentine state to initiate the new order. But the usefulness of characterizing Savonarola's thinking as optimistic or pessimistic, as radical or conservative, is doubtful. Such a classification depends to a large degree upon which elements of his vision we single out for attention. In describing how the new age was to come about and what it would be like, Savonarola always insisted on the need for, and the certainty of, divine intervention. The Church was so corrupt, rulers so tyrannical, men so indifferent to the demands of the spiritual life, that not even the preaching and teaching of the Gospel could by themselves provide an adequate remedy. Therefore God had to intervene to visit the sword of tribulation upon the earth and bring men to repentance. On the other hand, the Lord had chosen to carry out His work by means of human, temporal agencies. The hand that would wield the divine sword—that had already begun to wield it—

[11] George Shepperson, "The Comparative Study of Millenarian Movements," *Millennial Dreams in Action*, ed. Sylvia Thrupp, Comparative Studies in Society and History (The Hague, 1962), pp. 41-45.

was a human hand, belonging to King Charles VIII of France; indeed Charles himself was the sword.[12] The King's role was not merely punitive, it was also messianic: God had elected him "to be His minister in this ministry of the renovation of the Church, begun in this time,"[13] and after the renovation of the Church, he was expected to conquer the Mohammedans and convert Islam to Christianity.[14] This prophecy, it will be recalled, had been circulating in France and Italy for some time before Savonarola made it a key part of his own millenarain vision. It was, moreover, part of a much older apocalyptic tradition in which French kings were cast in the role of a Second Charlemagne who would bring about a renovation of the Church, go to the East, convert the Infidel, unify the world in a single sheepfold under one shepherd, and at last lay down his crown on the Mount of Olives.[15] If, as is highly unlikely, Savonarola had previously been ignorant of this tradition, he could have heard it proclaimed in Marsilio Ficino's oration welcoming Charles VIII to Florence on November 17.[16] What is interesting, however, is not so much Savonarola's adoption of these ideas as his suddenly taking them over in the midst of the November crisis, when events seemed to urge them upon him, and his superimposition of them on his older, more pessimistic view. Only when Charles had actually arrived in Tuscany, when Savonarola himself was charged with the task of deflecting the conqueror's wrath from the city, and when these efforts were crowned by the restoration of friendship between Charles and Florence did Savonarola begin to envision for Charles a messianic role in partnership with Florence herself. Such a role accommodated imperfectly with his older conception of Charles as the new Cyrus, the instrument of God's wrath who would carry

[12] *Prediche italiane ai Fiorentini*, vol. II, pp. 45-46.

[13] *Le lettere, di Girolamo Savonarola*, ed. Roberto Ridolfi (Florence, 1933), p. 48.

[14] *Ibid.*, p. 209.

[15] See above, pp. 112-14; also, Samuel Krauss, "Le roi de France Charles VIII et les esperances messianiques," *Revue des études juives*, 51 (1906), 87-95.

[16] Marsilio Ficino, *Opera omnia*, 2 vols. (Basel, 1561), vol. I, pp. 961-63. See also below, p. 187. On the widespread belief within Italy in Charles VIII's divine mission and the evocation of the New or Second Charlemagne legend, see also Joseph Schnitzer, *Savonarola*, trans. Ernesto Rutili, 2 vols. (Milan, 1931), vol. I, pp. 188-90.

the children of Israel into bondage; nevertheless, the ambiguity remained, as we shall see.

For the moment, however, we must consider the other messianic agency which featured even more importantly than the French king in Savonarola's new vision of the coming regeneration—that is, the city of Florence herself. Just as he transformed the new Cyrus into the new Charlemagne, the avenger into the deliverer, so he transformed Florence "the den of robbers" into Florence the new Jerusalem, the center of the great renewal. In doing so he employed a symbolic language of mixed, although predominantly Biblical, origins. The Lord, wishing to renew the world, decided to begin in Florence, and as He had once before come to Jerusalem, so now He came to Florence, *città novella*.[17] Florence was the elect of God, the city of God where the Lord was gathering a group (*la brigata*) and drawing it to Himself as in no other city.[18] Her very tribulations, greater than those of any other city, were a sign of her election.[19] Florence had lived through sixty years of captivity (the sixty years of Medici rule), but still she suffered; everyone spoke ill of her; everyone persecuted her; but the years of her captivity were seventy, and the fifth age (when, presumably, she would enjoy her ultimate liberation) was at hand. The Lord loved Florence; she was His bride and He illuminated her; He would bring her consolation soon. The Lord was jealous of His bride and withheld Pisa from her as a hostage so that she might not fall in love with another and forget Him; but when she had become completely united in Him she would have the joys of the bride.[20] The Lord had promised, "I must return into the Florentine Church, to build my temple there. Jerusalem will be visited again and the wicked of Rome reproved."[21] The Lord wants to build a new Jerusalem here, so that this city is no longer Florence but a Jerusalem holy and peaceful.[22] Zacharias asked a man (who

[17] *Prediche italiane ai Fiorentini*, vol. III², p. 363.

[18] *Prediche italiane ai Fiorentini*, vol. III¹, pp. 126-27. "The city of Florence is the city of Christ and the city of God," *Prediche italiane ai Fiorentini*, vol. II, p. 290.

[19] *Prediche italiane ai Fiorentini*, vol. III², p. 195.

[20] *Ibid.*, vol. III², pp. 270-72.

[21] *Ibid.*, pp. 273-74.

[22] *Prediche sopra Aggeo*, ed. Luigi Firpo (Rome, 1965), p. 341; also, pp. 144-45, 151.

was the Savior) where he was going with his measuring line, and he replied that he was going to measure Jerusalem and Judah. In the same way the Lord will measure Florence to see whether she is fit to spread the light to others, for the judgment and the measure of God must commence in the house of God, which is Florence, the first to be illuminated.[23] Just as Jerusalem shall be inhabited without walls (Zacharias 2:4) so Florence shall be inhabited without walls, that is, the elect of God will not be contained within a single city, but will be diffused everywhere and there will be so much unity and love as to dispel the wall of avarice, the towers of pride, the battlements of vainglory, and all those other false defenses which surround the city of the devil.[24] In Florence has been fulfilled the prophecy of Zacharias 9:9: "Lo, here is your King who has come down to you." Nor should the Florentines doubt that today the angels will come to be with them; their humble King will be seated over the great and the lowly and clothed in Scripture.[25]

Leaving aside for the moment the important question of what Savonarola conceived Florence's millennial role to be, let us first try to follow his explanation of why Florence was chosen. The question of Florence's election was clearly a problem for him, and he returned to it time and again, now maintaining that Florence was God's chosen city on account of certain superior virtues and qualities, now insisting that she had no particular merit, indeed that she had less virtue than other places. Florence, he said, was chosen despite her sins;[26] just as Jerusalem had had more wicked Scribes and Pharisees than other places, so Florence had more wicked people than there were elsewhere;[27] Florence was "beloved of Christ," but not for her merits. Why then did Christ liberate Florence? *Quia ipse voluit*, because he wished to do so.[28]

And yet Savonarola was not content with this explanation, although theologically speaking it was consistent with the idea of God's freedom and omnipotence. If from a religious point of view

[23] *Prediche italiane ai Fiorentini*, vol. III², p. 291.
[24] *Ibid.*, p. 293.
[25] *Ibid.*, p. 365; also vol. II, pp. 319-20, 324.
[26] *Prediche sopra Aggeo*, pp. 63-64.
[27] *Prediche sopra Ezechiele*, vol. I, p. 44.
[28] *Ibid.*, vol. I, p. 78; and *Prediche italiane ai Fiorentini*, vol. II, pp. 436, 446.

God's choice of Florence was a mystery, from a politico-historical
and a geographical point of view it was no mystery at all: Florence
was the obvious choice because she was the organic center of Italy.
Repeatedly he described the city as the head or the heart or the navel
of Italy; sometimes he combined the images, as "head and heart"
or "heart and navel."[29] All meant the same thing: Florence was the
vital center from which flowed movement and life to the other members of the body. If she should die, all of Italy would die.[30] In this
view Florence's special position was prior to and the reason for, not
the consequence of, divine election. Savonarola made it perfectly
clear that Florence was chosen as the setting for the prophesying of
tribulations *because* she was the heart of Italy: "I have not preached
here to Florence alone, but to all of Italy. And we have stopped here
in Florence because she is the heart of Italy and God has wanted
it this way because from here the voice goes out and all Italy hears
it, as from the heart the vital spirits are diffused throughout the
body."[31] And again, ". . . I have told you that as you are the center
and the heart of Italy, God wants the light to come out of you.
Do you think that God has led you thus far without reason?"[32]
Both geography and the special qualities of the Florentine people
accounted for this natural preeminence. In the most literal sense the
city's function as the vital center of Italy derived from the fact that she
was located in the center of the country; "since Florence is situated
in the middle of Italy as the heart in a man, God decided she was
worthy to be chosen for the task of proclamation, so that from her
it would spread throughout all the other parts of Italy as we see it
happening now."[33] But it was more than an accident of geography
that made Florence the heart and head of the Italians. In a country
made up of spirited people the Florentines were particularly favored
with *sangue ed ingegno*, with spirit and intelligence, and this is what

---

[29] E.g., *Prediche sopra i Salmi*, vol. I, pp. 41, 204, 236; and *Prediche italiane
ai Fiorentini*, vol. II, pp. 301, 366.

[30] *Prediche sopra Ezechiele*, vol. I, p. 231.

[31] *Prediche italiane ai Fiorentini*, vol. III¹, p. 408; also p. 73; and vol. II,
p. 324.

[32] *Ibid.*, vol. II, 301.

[33] *Compendium Revelationum*, p. 226. For a comment on this by one of
Savonarola's critics see below, p. 232.

made them so difficult to rule and why they were best off under a free regime,[34] a regime which was to serve as the model for all other peoples.[35]

These two conceptions of the election of Florence were logically and theologically incompatible. If God's choice of Florence was a function of His inscrutable will, then any explanation in terms of geographical necessity or civic virtue was not only gratuitous but impertinent. The root of the difficulty, of course, was the same as of most of the difficulties inherent in Savonarola's doctrine; the contradiction stemmed from the fact that his prophetic message had undergone a major transformation during the great civic crisis without a corresponding reexamination of the eschatological principles on which it was based. Having for four years treated Florence along with other governments instituted by men as the deserving recipients of God's forthcoming vengeance, he now had to justify his new view, that Florence had been selected as the agent of the coming millennium. He could do it either by stressing God's gratuitous decision or by celebrating Florence's special qualities. By employing both strategies at the same time Savonarola was compounding the inconsistency and befuddling the deeper problem of the relation between divine and human agencies in the coming work of regeneration. But Savonarola was neither logician nor theologian; he was a visionary reformer who was secure in his faith that all contradictions were only apparent, protected by his own conviction that he was the inspired spokesman of a truth beyond all human reasoning.

Besides, formal explanations of why Florence had been chosen were much less important than the conviction that she *had* been so chosen, a conviction that seemed to be established beyond doubt by having a prophet in her midst and by her acceptance of the proffered *lume interiore*. ". . . and just as Isaiah in the fortieth chapter spoke and prophesied of Christ, so this which I expound on this chapter has to do with Florence; those were then the elect of God, so are these now, and therefore God will treat them in the same way."[36]

---

[34] *Prediche sopra Aggeo*, pp. 211, 218-19.

[35] For Savonarola's analysis of the need for a popular regime, see below, Chapter IX.

[36] *Prediche italiane ai Fiorentini*, vol. III², p. 194.

The Florentines had begun to demonstrate their election by turning against tyranny, and they were continuing to demonstrate it by taking the first steps toward making their city into the city of God. By October 1495 Fra Girolamo was moved to say that the Florentines had demonstrated *el ben vivere essenziale* which was the simplicity of the true Christian. Never before, he observed, had so many people converted to the good life. Maidens went about veiled; widows lived virtuously; married women lived chastely with their husbands. The youth were reformed and the entire city was transformed, full of fervor. Gaming, sodomy, and blasphemy had been banished.[37] The Florentine people had reformed themselves by accepting Savonarola's urgent suggestion of a "universal peace," a general amnesty for all ex-Mediceans, and the Law of Appeal, without which Florence would have been set ablaze and tyranny even worse than before would have returned. There remained the fulfillment of the promises of "great spiritual goods, glory both eternal and temporal, and vast territorial acquisitions";[38] for God had made a covenant with His people: they would reform still further and maintain His work and His state, and He would give them riches and glory. Then the preachers would arouse the people of other cities and send them to Florence where the true light shone and tell them to adopt her form of government.[39] The Lord had promised to make Florence the most famous country in the world.[40] In Florence Zacharias' prophecy had been fulfilled.[41] In Florence the renewal of the Church had begun.[42]

But if Florence was to extend a spiritual as well as a temporal hegemony throughout Italy, perhaps throughout the world, what of Rome? In the new state of the Church what place was reserved for the See of Peter? Did Savonarola foresee *la chiesa fiorentina*, as he called it, taking over Rome's authority? Some passages in his ser-

---

[37] *Ibid.*, vol. II, pp. 434-35; and *Lettere*, p. 116.

[38] "... gran territorio molto più che avessi mai," *Prediche italiane ai Fiorentini*, vol. II, p. 435.

[39] *Ibid.*, vol. III², p. 196.

[40] "... la più egregia terra di tutto il mondo," *Prediche sopra Ezechiele*, vol. II, p. 262.

[41] *Prediche italiane ai Fiorentini*, vol. III², p. 365.

[42] *Ibid.*, p. 585.

mons would seem to support such an interpretation. Christ's promise to return to Jerusalem was to be understood, he said, as a promise to return to the "Florentine Church."[43] The reign of Rome is finished and the reign of Christ has begun.[44] Jerusalem must be chosen again and Rome reproved.[45] God will give "the Church and Rome to others to cultivate, because at Rome no charity is left, only the devil."[46] To those who said that Rome must not be destroyed because she had so many holy relics, Savonarola would reply that Jeremiah had warned the Israelites that even Jerusalem, the temple of the Lord, which had many more holy objects than Rome, had not been safe from the divine wrath.[47] Rome, he warned, would be turned "upside down" and lose everything.[48] God will give the territory of the Church as well as of Jerusalem to Florence.[49] Savonarola denied that by prophesying the rejection of Rome and the election of Jerusalem he had fallen into doctrinal error.[50] He did not mean, he explained, that the Roman Church was to change its form, but that the wicked Romans would be *reprobati e spenti* while the flower of the Christians would be found in the region of Jerusalem. The Roman Church would not disappear; there would be no change in the faith,[51] nor would there be two Popes; but under one Pope,

[43] *Ibid.*, p. 273; and *Prediche sopra Giobbe*, ed. Roberto Ridolfi, 2 vols. (Rome, 1957), vol. I, p. 281.

[44] *Ibid.*, vol. II, p. 380.

[45] *Prediche italiane ai Fiorentini*, vol. III², pp. 205, 274.

[46] *Prediche sopra i Salmi*, vol. I, p. 48.

[47] *Prediche italiane ai Fiorentini*, vol. III², p. 205.

[48] *Ibid.*, vol. II, pp. 264, 301.

[49] *Prediche sopra l'Esodo*, ed. Pier Giorgio Ricci, 2 vols. (Rome, 1955-56), vol. II, pp. 133, 136.

[50] It is worth noting that in his polemic against Savonarola, Rafaello da Volterra accused him of having called for the abandonment of the city of Rome: "Urbem Romam quam omnes Christiani venerantur, ac religionis causa penit fugiendam esse, minimeque adeundam dicebat. His igitur persuasionibus atque exemplis, non procul aberat a condenda nova hereseos secta, nisi divina providentia subvenisset." MS BNF Magl. VIII, 1443, fol. 147 verso–148.

[51] Despite the evidence of the manuscripts, Ridolfi suggests that where Savonarola speaks of not changing *fede*, we should read *sede*. The difference is significant, for if Savonarola said there was to be no change of *sede* then he would have been denying what he seems to have implied elsewhere, that is, a movement of the center of the Church away from Rome. If, however, he

Jerusalem would flourish in the Christian life more than any other region, and all the Christians of the world would live in the Roman faith under a holy Pope (*una Papa sancto*), the successor of St. Peter. For even if the Pope is not in Rome, he does not lose his jurisdiction; on the contrary, he is always the Roman bishop and in him is united the universal Church[52]—*ubi Papa, ibi Curia.*[53]

By distinguishing between Roman leaders and the Roman Church, between Rome as a place which might be abandoned and Rome as the symbol of Christ's leadership which would last to the Judgment Day, Savonarola attempted to put an orthodox face on his vision of the loss of Roman primacy in the age to come. To papal authority Savonarola professed his obedience and his submission; at the same time he made it clear that he considered himself bound only so long as the Church of Rome was in harmony with the Church Catholic. What was the Catholic Church? On this there were diverse opinions among theologians, he observed, "but let us avoid these disputes and say this: the Catholic Church most properly speaking is defined as those Christians who live good lives and have God's grace; less properly, it is made up of those who have faith only, and there is a much greater number of this latter group than of the former." It was this latter Church, the "Roman Catholic Church," he continued, against which the devils of Hell would not prevail, which would be renewed as he had promised, and to which he submitted himself.[54] Thus for Savonarola the true church was neither the Church of the hierarchy on the one hand nor the invisible community of the Elect on the other. Nor was it even the community of the faithful. Savonarola's true Catholic Church was a visible community of saints who were in possession of divine grace because *vivan bene*, because they lived good lives. It existed every-

---

was denying that the *fede* of the Church was to change, he was merely maintaining his doctrinal orthodoxy and leaving open the possibility of a movement from Rome. While, as Ridolfi says, the manuscript "f" and "s" were easily confused, I see no grounds for making such a change. Ridolfi recognizes the implications of his suggestion and obviously prefers a reading that strengthens Savonarola's orthodoxy. See his note in Savonarola, *Lettere*, p. cxi.

[52] *Ibid.*, p. 102.
[53] *Prediche italiane ai Fiorentini*, vol. III¹, pp. 424-25.
[54] *Ibid.*, vol. III², p. 564.

where and it would ultimately pervade the world. St. Augustine would no doubt have called Savonarola a Donatist. Luther might have regarded him as one of the *Schwärmer*. While neither epithet would have been entirely accurate or fair since Savonarola denied neither the authority of the Roman bishop nor the sacramental powers of the priesthood,[55] each would have had a point: Savonarola seems to have subordinated both Sacrament and Word to Charity—the love of Christ upon which the Christian life of virtue was based. Moreover, he had come to believe what neither Augustine nor Luther could ever believe but which went hand in hand with radical sectarianism—that such love was to be the basis for a new millennium of spirituality, when "the angels would come to live together with men and the Church Militant would join together with the Church Triumphant,"[56] when the world would be united in one sheepfold under a single shepherd,[57] when as on the seventh day all would be at peace in the renewed Church, when men would be converted to the love of divine things, practically ceasing from all worldly labors, and the Church would be glorious throughout the world.[58] In those days, "everyone will be consoled in the spirit and say 'come to the preaching' and lead each other to things spiritual; and the world will be filled with sweetness and inhabited once again by those hermits of Egypt, as I have told you on other occasions; and the Cross will be adored in the midst of the world; and we will have triumphs and joys in this world and glory in the next."[59]

In a community where each would minister unto the spiritual needs of the other and the world would return to the simple life of the hermits of old, the role of the Church would surely be very different from its present one. Although, like most millenarian visionaries, Savonarola did not describe the coming terrestrial paradise in any further detail, even from these rather vague landmarks we can discover certain features which show his dependence upon the

---

[55] E.g., where he says that the sacraments are the foundation of the Church, *Prediche sopra Aggeo*, p. 206.

[56] *Prediche italiane ai Fiorentini*, vol. III², p. 199; also p. 67.

[57] *Ibid.*, p. 206.

[58] *Prediche sopra Aggeo*, pp. 319-20.

[59] *Prediche italiane ai Fiorentini*, vol. III², p. 322.

themes of the so-called Joachite tradition—that is, the broad stream of apocalyptic materials that had been accumulating for more than two centuries. That Savonarola was widely or deeply read in the materials of the Joachite tradition is doubtful. We have already noted the references he made to "the abbot Joachim and many others," to "some ancients," and the like. These references prove only that Savonarola had knowledge of certain Joachite ideas, but they do not suggest that the acquaintance was either direct or extensive. On the other hand, we are on firmer ground in identifying Savonarola's millenarian prophecy as another variant of the Second Charlemagne prophecy, which was itself a variant of the Joachite tradition and was well established in the Florentine literature of popular prophecy.[60] This we can do by recognizing certain common themes as well as by noting the striking similarity in vision between Savonarola's millenarian prophecy and the existing Florentine messianic tradition. Of such themes perhaps the signal one is his repeated prediction of the coming of a *Papa santo e buono*, a *Sommo Sacerdote*, a *Pontefice nuovo*.[61] The prediction originated with Joachim of Flora's prophecy of the coming of an Angelic Pope,[62] but Savonarola's usage corresponds more closely to the terminology of later Joachites.[63] Another expression he shared with the Florentine prophecies was *cito et breviter*, or *cito et velociter*, his favorite way of emphasizing the speedy coming of the new age,[64]

---

[60] See above, Chapter I; also, pp. 88-97.

[61] *Lettere*, p. 102; *Prediche italiane ai Fiorentini*, vol. III², pp. 313-14, 320, 528; also, vol. II, p. 321. Savonarola did not mean merely a pope who was a holy man but a supernatural one. See especially vol. III², p. 313, where he describes the "Papa santo e buono" as "uno instrumento sopranaturale . . . in questa renovazione della Chiesa, che è cosa sopranaturale."

[62] On the Joachite idea of the *Papa Angelico*, see especially Friedrich Baethgen, *Der Engelpapst* (Halle, 1933); on the Joachite use of other terms such as *papa sanctus* and *dux novus*, see K. Burdach and P. Piur, eds., *Briefwechsel des Cola di Rienzo* in *Vom Mittelalter zur Reformation*, vol. II, part V (1929), pp. 307-309.

[63] E.g., the prophecy that begins "Lievassi l'orsa. . . ." See above, p. 58.

[64] A similar expression, *cito et breviter*, is identified as deriving from the pseudo-Joachite *Commentary on Jeremiah* by J. Rohr, "Die Prophetie im letzten Jahrhundert vor der Reformation als Geschichtsquelle und Geschichtsfaktor," *Historisches Jahrbuch* XIX (1898), p. 34. Rohr apparently believed the *Commentary* was an authentic work of Joachim, however. Both *cito* and

while his earlier vision of *flagellum Dei*, the sword of God's wrath, recalls the same expression employed in the prophecies of Daniel, St. John, St. Bridget, "and others" which circulated in Florence in this period.[65] His frequent use of the image of Florence as a lion with a fever which would abate we find repeatedly in the Florentine prophecies,[66] along with his image of the Florentine lilies extending themselves over the world.[67] Even Savonarola's frequent references to the Florentines as a people of unusual *sangue ed ingegno* seem to have been the echoes of a traditional theme found in both apocalyptic and other forms of civic patriotic expression.[68]

---

velociter are, of course, found in the Scriptures in passages dealing with repentance and punishment (e.g., Revelation 2:16, 3:11, 11:14, 22:7), but I do not find in Scripture the combination of the two as used by Savonarola.

[65] E.g., ms BNF Magl. VII, 1081, fol. 60 recto, which has the phrase "[the French] faran flagello depreti e defrati." The common Scriptural source may be Isaiah 10:26: "Et suscitabit super eum Dominus exercituum flagellum. . . ."

[66] E.g., *Prediche sopra i Salmi*, vol. I, pp. 187, 197, 201; *Prediche italiane ai Fiorentini*, vol. III², p. 186. See the earlier cited prophecies of Antonio da Rieti and the "Romito Santo" in Chapter I above, and the fourteenth-century poem "Nel tempo ch'l lione era infermato" in *Poesia del Duecento e del Trecento*, ed. Carlo Muscetta and Paolo Rivalta (Turin, 1956), p. 824.

[67] ". . . vidi Florentiam totam florere liliis, quae per minas et pinnulas extra maenia undique late diffundebantur . . . ," *Compendium Revelationum*, p. 358. The figure of the lilies spreading their foliage may have derived from Joachim of Flora's *Concordia*, Book V, col. 84 where it is a symbol of the Third Age. *Il libro delle figure dell'abate Gioachino da Fiore*, L. Tondelli, M. Reeves, and B. Hirsch-Reich eds., 2 vols., 2nd edn. (Turin, 1953), vol. I, p. 194. See also Douie, *The Nature and Effect of the Heresy of the Fraticelli* (Manchester, 1932), p. 217; and Herbert Grundmann, "Die Papstprophetien des Mittelalters," *Archiv für Kulturgeschichte*, XIX (1928), 122. The lily itself, of course, was a common symbol of the city of Florence.

[68] For similar expressions in prophecies, see ms BNF Magl. VII, 1081, fol. 59 recto; in the preaching of San Bernardino of Siena, see Iris Origo, *The World of San Bernardino* (London, 1963), p. 183 (from a sermon in Florence in 1424). Compare Savonarola's phrase *sangue ed ingegno* with Gregorio Dati's *arte e ingegno* in Hans Baron, *The Crisis of the Early Italian Renaissance*, 2nd edn. (Princeton, 1966), p. 180. In his eulogy of Lorenzo Magnifico Guicciardini says that it would have been mad to deny Lorenzo's *ingegno grandissimo e singulare*, he having so long and so successfully ruled Florence, "sendo questa una città liberissima nel parlare, piena di ingegni sottilissimi e inquietissimi." There is also an intriguing likeness between Savonarola's explanation that God had chosen Florence because she was the heart of Italy and had the most intelligent men with the Hermetic idea that Egypt was the

In general structure as well as in language, Savonarola's vision corresponded to that of the Second Charlemagne type. As we have already seen, in fourteenth-century Florence the Second Charlemagne prophecy was absorbed into a developing messianic strain of civic patriotism. Older themes of Florence the daughter of Rome, of Florentine religious and republican restoration by Charlemagne, together with her Angevin-Guelf political orientation, all constituted a favorable ground for the reception of the Second Charlemagne prophecy. In the merging of patriotic and millenarian themes Florence came to share the central role in the messianic world design with the French king.[69] To this civic tradition belongs Savonarola's newer vision of a divinely ordained partnership between Florence and Charles VIII.

On the evidence we cannot accept Savonarola's conviction that his prophetic message was fundamentally unvarying from the beginning, however sincerely he may have held it. For the same reasons, we cannot agree with his devotees' belief that his inspiration was unique and essentially free of such outside influences as the Florentine prophecies. Savonarola's adoption of a millenarian scheme was the climax of a period of increasing involvement in and identification with a distinctly Florentine point of view, the crucial turning point of which came during the weeks of November and December 1494. This was no simple process. Savonarola could not have adopted this peculiarly Florentine ideology without at the same time altering a whole framework of related views. For example, his earlier universalism narrowed to a focus on Italy as the stage of the divine drama and the Florentines as its leading players. His earlier other-worldly asceticism, his attacks on the pursuit of wealth, glory, and power gave way before his new vision of a richer, more glorious, more powerful Florence.

---

favored country because it was the heart of the earth, had the best climate (the temperate climate also played a part in Savonarola's evaluation), and produced the most intelligent men. See A.-J. Festugière, *La révélation d' Hermes Trismégiste*, 4 vols., 3rd edn. (Paris, 1949-54), vol. I, p. 85. The Hermetic dialogues were, of course, already known in Florence through Ficino's Latin and Tommaso Benci's Italian translations, but I have no evidence that Savonarola was familiar with them.

[69] See above, Chapter I.

Nowhere can we better observe the progress of this transformation than in Savonarola's step by step modification of his views on the relation between repentance, divine judgment, and the future of the city. At first he had called upon all Christians to repent in order that God might be moved to soften His wrath somewhat in the coming days of universal destruction.[70] Then, during the November crisis, as he later wrote, he began to hope that the Florentines' change of heart might induce God to relax the dread decree, at least with respect to themselves.[71] In December he first announced that Florence was to gain new riches, power, and glory, although for a time he continued to insist that this promise was conditional upon their further reformation.[72] By the following May 17, however, he was saying that the promise was unconditional; Florence would have her glory in any case, although first she must undergo some tribulations, whether few or many would depend on how well or badly she behaved.[73] In his next sermon, on May 24, 1495, Savonarola revealed that he had had a vision of the Virgin who had confirmed this,[74] and a few months later in his *Compendium Revelationum*, he reported at length his conversation with the "glorious Lady":

> If my people should ask whether these promises are absolute and will be completely fulfilled, or whether they are conditional, that is, whether they will be fulfilled according to their good or evil actions, what shall I say?
>
> She replied: Know, my son, that they have been granted absolutely and certainly and it will be altogether thus; for without any doubt God will find and produce the means whereby these promised blessings will attain their fulfillment.[75]

[70] See above, pp. 71-72.

[71] ". . . coepi vehementer sperare prophetiam hanc sine conditione non esse. . . ." *Compendium Revelationum*, p. 236.

[72] E.g., *Prediche sopra i Salmi*, vol. I, pp. 7-8 (January 6, 1495).

[73] "Firenze, io ti dico e ti protesto un' altra volta che, se tu arai delle tribulazioni, sarà per tua gloria. Guarda se gli è fermo e chiaro quello che io ti dico, . . . Sicché, Firenze, abbi fede, perché arai tutto quello che ti è stato promesso; ma, prima, delle tribulazioni, e tanto più e tanto meno, quanto peggio o meglio farai." *Ibid.*, pp. 199-200.

[74] *Ibid.*, p. 203.

[75] *Compendium Revelationum*, p. 359.

In this new belief in the absolute certainty of the coming blessings Savonarola remained firm, although he sometimes explained that God was delaying the fulfillment of His promises, in particular the reconquest of Pisa, until the Florentines had proven themselves worthy of their election.[76] Underlying this alternation of views was something more fundamental than propaganda. Savonarola's understanding of God's intentions with respect to the temporal order, and therefore his whole conception of his own prophetic mission, was undergoing transformation. As he came to believe in the speedy coming of a new era of spiritual bliss and temporal glory he had to change his views on the nature and function of repentance. No longer did he see repentance as a last resort, a final preparation that might bring the sinner a modicum of spiritual consolation during the Last Days. With the dawning possibility that the Day of Judgment could be postponed, repentance took on a different meaning for him, as the means whereby God's anger might be averted and a new day established. This, however, was an intermediate step to his belief in the unconditional promise of earthly regeneration, and when he had taken that final, millenarian, step the function of repentance changed still further. If God was to bring about a new era, men must cooperate in the godly work. Savonarola thus came to see his mission as one intended not only to announce the divine intention but also to lead men toward renewal and the building of the New Jerusalem. Inevitably, in the context of the new situation in Florence, to which Savonarola had begun to address himself in December, he came to relate spiritual conversion to civic peace-making, to concern for the *bene commune*, even to constitutional reform. In short, "repentance" took on a new significance for him as something more than a conversion of the heart; it came almost to be equated with the action of building the City of God in Florence and a necessary prelude to Florentine glory.

Through transformations such as these we can mark where Savonarola departed from his earlier Catholic universalism as he formulated an ideology centered in Florentine messianic republicanism and imperialism. We have already seen that the elements of such an

[76] *Prediche sopra Ezechiele*, vol. I, p. 248.

ideology had long since been present in Florence, and we have suggested that Savonarola absorbed them into his own scheme of things, albeit with something less than perfect consistency. What we have called the "myth of Florence," the fantasy of a glorious civic destiny in which religious leadership and territorial imperialism were usually combined, was, after all, no unique phenomenon. It had parallels in French Joachism, from which it derived some of its themes, and in the rising Muscovy state's contemporary ideology of the Third Rome, to draw examples from either end of the European spectrum.[77] Seldom, however, before the Reformation at least, were the implications of such ideologies as they related to the ideal of the Catholic Church fully worked out; no doubt the implications were consciously avoided. This seems to have been the case in Florence.[78] At certain crucial times in her history the mythology of a special Florentine destiny helped to sustain the city, as during the War against Pope Gregory XI in 1375 and in the subsequent drawn-out struggle against Giangaleazzo Visconti of Milan; but the sectarian implications of these outbursts of religious patriotism were neither sustained nor elaborated into ideologies that outlived the moments of crisis. In this respect the Savonarola episode was different. Fra Girolamo did not merely repeat the ideas and slogans of the past; to the patriotic tradition which he embraced he gave as much or more than he received. Most of all, he gave himself. For the first time Florence had a prophet who was truly her own, a mediator who spoke for her to the Virgin, interpreted God's will, and confirmed to the Florentines what they had long suspected—that theirs was a city of destiny, that they were a chosen people. The importance of Savonarola's charismatic qualities of leadership cannot be overestimated: neither millenarian beliefs nor a patriotic mythology by themselves created an ideology, much less a movement. Such move-

[77] For a discussion of "the specifically religious forms of ethnocentrism"— sacred nation, messianic ruler, etc.—see Werner Stark, *The Sociology of Religion: A Study of Christendom*, 3 vols. (London, 1966-67), vol. I.

[78] Warman Welliver's thesis, in his *L'impero fiorentino* (Florence, 1957), already referred to, that Lorenzo the Magnificent was bent on creating a Florentine religious and political empire, undoubtedly exaggerates the extent to which this was a conscious and concrete program.

ments always formed around a prophet.[79] Most apocalyptic fantasists took refuge behind the protective cover of a famous name or anonymity instead of openly claiming direct divine inspiration. This is why we find many more apocalypses, prophecies, and revelations of Daniel, Joachim of Flora, and St. Bridget of Sweden than they themselves ever conceived or wrote down, and more which are anonymous or pseudonymous than those that went under the name of real historical people. Moreover, while many felt themselves called to prophesy, few were chosen. As we have seen, Savonarola was not the only prophet in Florence at the time of the upheavals against Piero de' Medici. The two Franciscans Bernardino da Feltre and Domenico da Ponzo matched him in vehemence and outstripped him in the ability to stir up a crowd against the real or imagined enemies of the people. By comparison Savonarola was a moderate, and this was undoubtedly a major reason for his greater success. He spoke to all classes in the interest of the *bene commune*; he offered no extreme solutions, nor did he challenge specific communal policy, as in the matter of the Jews and the establishment of a *Monte di Pietà*; he did not move in advance of events but in their train, as a healer of domestic discord and bodily and spiritual suffering. "Consolation" was a word constantly on his tongue. When at last he intervened in the constitutional crisis he held out an exciting, indeed a fantastic, vision of the millennium; but the core of that vision was a program of reforms which were on the whole concrete, moderate, and familiar. The genius of Savonarola's millenarianism was that it gave expression to constitutional, political, and religious aims that were

[79] "A millenarian revolt never formed except round a prophet—John Ball in England, Martinek Hauska in Bohemia, Thomas Müntzer in Thuringia. . . . Wherever the career of such a prophet can be traced, it turns out that he had been obsessed by apocalyptic fantasies for years, before it occurred to him, in the midst of some social upheaval, to address himself to the poor as possible followers. And what he then offered them was not simply a chance to improve their material lot—it was also, and above all, the prospect of carrying out a divinely ordained mission of stupendous, unique importance." Norman Cohn, "Medieval Millenarism: Its Bearing on the Comparative Study of Millenarian Movements," *Millennial Dreams in Action*, p. 38. This fits the case of Savonarola quite well, with the exception of the special appeal to the poor. On Savonarola's social views, see Chapter VII below.

widely shared and provided a basis for civic order and harmony rather than further conflict and disruption—which, as we shall see, is not to say that harmony was achieved in the years of his ascendancy.

It was not, however, the pragmatic, but the prophetic nature of Savonarola's program that gave it such fascination and compelling power. Here too Savonarola gave his unique stamp to existing material. In its most general aspect the authority of his prophetic message stemmed from its Scriptural foundation. While he might claim direct divine illumination and borrow the language and themes of Florentine ideology, he always presented his message as a further elucidation of the word of God already revealed in the Bible.[80] His method of preaching was to build a course of sermons on a particular book of the Bible, not to expound it systematically but to draw upon it for moral teachings and prophetic ideas that had relevance for the existing situation. After his return to Florence in 1490, when he expounded "the Apocalypse of Saint John" to his brothers in San Marco, Savonarola chose almost exclusively books of the Old Testament, although he would intersperse material from the Christian Gospel and the Fathers as well.[81] The religious experiences of the ancient Jews provided him with a rich stock of material for the construction and legitimation of his own prophetic message. The dramatic confrontation between an elect but errant people and their angry but forgiving Father, the vital mediating work of the Jewish Prophets, inspired and inspiring men of God, the visions of the messianic redemption of Israel—these came to be the basic sources of his own doctrine. The Florentines were cast in the role of the Chosen People; Rome was Babylon; he himself was now Noah, the builder of the Ark which would ride out the Flood, then Haggai, prophet of the reconstruction of the Lord's Temple in Jerusalem

[80] "La sua fonte era la stessa Sacra Scrittura, l'immenso tesoro e la passione della sua vita. Specialmente si sentì attratto con forza irresistibile dai profeti del vecchio Testamento; in continuo contatto con essi, anche egli divenne profeta." Schnitzer, *Savonarola*, vol. II, p. 203. With this last statement I am unable to agree. The genesis of Savonarola's prophecy was not simply a response to his reading of the Prophets, as I have been trying to show. Moreover this statement contradicts Schnitzer's own better judgment, that Savonarola's prophetic impulse stemmed from his reforming passion.

[81] On Savonarola's emphasis on the Old Testament and his early interest in it, see *Prediche italiane ai Fiorentini*, vol. III², p. 215.

after the return from captivity. While he undoubtedly drew upon Florentine patriotic themes and prophecies for his message of the city's future glory, it was to the Scriptures that he went for illustration and verification, and it was from Scripture that he developed his own formulation of the vision, giving it a more solid base in religious history than it had ever before had in Florentine ideology. His application of the Genesis story of a covenant between God and Israel added a new dimension to the Florentine concept of civic election. The Florentines, he said, could be a seed like the ancient Israelites if they had "a lively faith warmed by the heat of love." God had made a covenant with His people; if they reformed He would give them riches and glory; He would maintain their new state and government; and other peoples would come to receive their light from Florence.[82] Just as the Jews were the elect of God in former times, so now were the Florentines, and God would behave toward them in the same way.[83] Here the whole Florentine millenarian fantasy is subsumed in a single, powerful, and Scripturally authoritative idea: the Florentines were the latter-day Israelites; their election, their religious mission, and their glorious future both spiritual and temporal were all prefigured in Holy Scripture. Savonarola saw his own illuminations and the predictions of other latter-day prophets as restatements of that ancient revelation, their accuracy and application confirmed by the divinely ordained events of November and December. To those who might object that Scripture related things that were of the past and completed, not things that were to be fulfilled in the future, he replied that he would not have set himself to expound Scripture if he had not had "another light" which showed him how to interpret the Scriptural mysteries.[84]

Savonarola was a self-conscious and explicit evangelical reformer. He saw himself as a reviver of Scripturalism after ages of neglect. The Scriptures had been abandoned to the dust and were unknown, he declared. He should not be denied his place among those who, on the eve of the Reformation, were seeking to reestablish Christian

[82] *Ibid.*, p. 196.

[83] ". . . quelli allora [the Jews at the time of the Prophet Isaiah] furono li eletti di Dio, così son questi [the Florentines] adesso; però farà loro Idio el medesimo." *Ibid.*, p. 194.

[84] *Ibid.*, pp. 215-19, for an extensive discussion of prophecy and Scripture.

faith and piety on a foundation of the Gospel;[85] yet his was not the evangelical faith of the Erasmian or Lutheran varieties. Savonarola advocated neither a simple Biblicism which provided a moral code nor a priesthood of all believers in which the Word was available to anyone who would approach it in faith. The Bible was not to be put into the hands of Everyman; it had to be expounded by those who were skilled in a complex exegetical method: "If one wishes to interpret [*dichiarare*] the figures of Holy Scripture, he must know that Scripture has two senses; one is literal, the one intended by him who composed and wrote the literal word; the other is mystical and is expressed in three modes, allegorical, tropological, and anagogical."[86] But not even skill in the fourfold exegetical method was enough to reveal all the mysteries contained in Scripture. Only the prophet illuminated by God could uncover the history of the future recorded therein; Savonarola's Biblicism was inseparably linked with his prophetism and inevitably subordinated to it: "And this I have not by Scripture nor by the revelations of any man who is under heaven."[87]

[85] *Ibid.*, pp. 215, 316. Contemporaries regarded him as a Biblicist without parallel. E.g., Ridolfi, *Vita*, vol. I, p. 23 and notes. ". . . introduxe quasi nuovo modo (di pronuntiare il verbo d'iddio) coe al apostolescha sanza dividere el sermone, non proponendo quistione, fugendo el chantare gl'ornamenti d'eloquentie, solo il suo fine era exporre qualchosa del vechio testamento et introdurre la semplicita della primitiva chiesa." Cerretani, *Storia fiorentina*, ed. Joseph Schnitzer, *Quellen und Forschungen zur Geschichte Savonarolas*, vol. III, *Bartolomeo Cerretani* (Munich, 1904), p. 6.

[86] *Prediche sopra i Salmi*, vol. I, p. 45.

[87] "E questo io non l'ho per scrittura, né per revelazione di uomo che sia dal cielo in giù." *Ibid.*, p. 32. "Insuper ex futuris, multisque particularibus mihi revelatis, occulta scripturarum per comparationem quandam invicem didici: quae sine consimili argumento nunquam cognoscere potuissem." *Dialogus de veritate prophetica* (Florence, Bartolomeo de' Libri, 1497), sig. b fol. 7 verso.

VI

Savonarola and the Laurentians

HIS SPIRIT WAS VERY GREAT, HIS LEARNING AS OUTSTANDING AS
ANYONE'S IN TWO CENTURIES, A GREAT PHILOSOPHER AND AN
EXCELLENT THOMIST, A UNIQUE ORATOR, MORE PERSUASIVE THAN
ANYONE OF HIS TIME, AND AMONG THE MODERNS THE LEADING
INTERPRETER OF THE INTIMATE SECRETS OF SACRED
AND DIVINE SCRIPTURES. IN EATING, DRESS,
MANNER, AND SPEECH HE WAS MOST HUMBLE,
THE DIVINE HERALD OF THE WORD
OF GOD, THE MOST POWERFUL
EXPONENT OF THE PRIMITIVE
CHRISTIAN LIFE.

—Bartolomeo Cerretani, *Storia fiorentina*

THIS judgment of the Florentine chronicler Cerretani[1] is a summary of the many things that Savonarola was to many men—philosopher, theologian, preacher, Biblicist, prophet, and simple man of
God teaching the primitive Christian way by the example of his
own humility. That such a judgment was not shared by all his contemporaries Cerretani readily acknowledged. There were many, he
admitted, who found Savonarola "of a singular pride" and who
maintained that he had confessed in the presence of witnesses to
being a false prophet to whom God had never revealed anything.

[1] Cerretani made this judgment after Savonarola's death. *Storia fiorentina*,
ed. Joseph Schnitzer, *Quellen und Forschungen zur Geschichte Savonarolas*,
vol. IV, *Bartolomeo Cerretani* (Munich, 1904), pp. 77-78. Cerretani also recognized Savonarola as the founder of Florentine liberty: ". . . et qui comincio
ne le menti degl'huomini a introdurre un vivere publico et universale, ilche
da molti fu volentieri udito." *Ibid.*, p. 29.

Marsilio Ficino, dean of Florentine philosophers, was the most eminent of these. Shortly after Savonarola's execution Ficino wrote an apology to the College of Cardinals for himself and "the many Florentines" who had been deceived by "the Antichrist Hieronymus of Ferrara, the greatest of hypocrites."[2] According to Ficino, Savonarola had simulated virtue and concealed his vices, he had a "Luciferean pride," and he had mixed his prophecies with lies in order to deceive the people. In contrast to Cerretani's description of the spiritual blessings brought to Florence by this man of God, Ficino alleged that Savonarola had brought sedition, deadly enmities, a neglect of public affairs, and grave losses, that he had imbued people with pride and heretical stubbornness, that he had "demented and stupefied" them.

Yet the vehemence of Ficino's attack is that of a disillusioned believer rather than the dispassionate analysis of a skeptical bystander like Machiavelli.[3] The Apology was written because Ficino along with many other "intelligent and learned Florentines" had believed in Savonarola, although he claimed that he had been only "briefly deceived" and had quickly come to his senses, so that for the past three years (that is, since 1495) he had been working against this "monster" both openly and secretly. In a letter of December 12, 1494, to Giovanni Cavalcanti, Ficino acknowledged that for four years Savonarola had been warning of the dangers threatening Florence, and that these dangers had actually come to pass and yet had been miraculously averted. The city's escape he attributed to the friar's warnings and counsels of repentance, and he concluded that Savonarola was God's chosen, a man of understanding, sanctity, and wisdom, whose advice all should follow.[4] This was two weeks after

[2] "Apologia Marsilii Ficini pro multis Florentinis ab Antichristo Hieronymo Ferrariense hypocritarum summo deceptis ad Collegium Cardinalium," *Supplementum Ficinianum*, ed. Paul O. Kristeller, 2 vols. (Florence, 1937), vol. II, pp. 76-79. The letter bears no date, but Ficino refers to the burning of Savonarola, which took place on May 23, 1498.

[3] On Machiavelli's attitude toward Savonarola, see Gennaro Sasso, *Machiavelli: Storia del suo pensiero politico* (Naples, 1958), pp. 9-18; and Roberto Ridolfi, *Vita di Niccolò Machiavelli* (Rome, 1954), pp. 15-16.

[4] Marsilio Ficino, *Opera omnia*, 2 vols. (Basel, 1561), vol. I, pp. 961-63. Ficino himself had interpreted the signs attending the death of Lorenzo il

Charles VIII's departure, at that exciting moment when Savonarola was triumphantly claiming that his prophecies had come to pass. Ficino himself composed an oration to welcome Charles VIII in which he addressed the French king as *Carolus Magnus Gallorum Rex*—no doubt a testimony to the Florentine tradition of the New Charlemagne—and heralded the King as the messenger of Christ, *Rex Pacificus,* who would recover Jerusalem from the cruel barbarian.[5] We do not know whether Ficino actually delivered this oration; if he did it was the last time that he involved himself publicly in the affairs of the post-Medicean republic until he addressed his Apology to the Cardinals; and the evidence of his subsequent letters suggests that he was telling the truth when he said that his ardor had quickly cooled.

In another letter to Cavalcanti, dated only eight days after the first, Ficino referred to a recent discussion with Cavalcanti and Gerardo Gianfigliazzi on how to distinguish between the friends and the enemies of God, and he cited Plato to the effect that men who claim divine gifts will show it in their characters. Moreover, he said, God, who provides for everything, sees to it that in the long run the hopes of good men succeed while those of the wicked only appear to do so.[6] Savonarola is not mentioned; however, given the moment, December 20, just when Savonarola was bringing the constitutional reform fight to a victorious climax, the reference is unmistakeable[7]

Magnifico as divine warnings of the great dangers which threatened the Florentine people. *Ibid.,* p. 931.

The attribution of the Apology to Ficino has been challenged by E. Sanesi, *Vicari e canonici fiorentini e il "caso Savonarola"* (Florence, 1932), pp. 15ff; and defended by Kristeller, *Supplementum Ficinianum,* vol. I, p. cxli; and by Raymond Marcel, who also reviews the whole question of Ficino's relation to Savonarola, satisfactorily, on the whole, despite a few factual errors, in *Marsile Ficin (1433-1499)* (Paris, 1958), pp. 555-79. To Marcel's evidence of Ficino's sometime admiration for Savonarola we might add the testimony of Cerretani, who said that Ficino attended Savonarola's sermons with "no little admiration." Cerretani, *Storia fiorentina,* ed. Schnitzer, pp. 8-9.

[5] Ficino, *Opera,* vol. I, pp. 961-63.

[6] *Ibid.,* p. 964. The Biblical reference is to Matthew 7:15-20. According to Arnaldo Della Torre, this conversation had taken place on the previous day. *Storia dell'Accademia Platonica di Firenze* (Florence, 1902), p. 832.

[7] Both Gianfigliazzi and Cavalcanti (Ficino's *amicus unicus*) were *ottimati,* politically active in the previous regime, and not Piagnoni.

and shows that Ficino's eventual rejection of the Savonarolan enterprise was something more than a last-minute change of heart based on opportunism or fear.[8] Ficino was a life-long beneficiary of Medici patronage who, now a man in his sixties, found himself in an entirely new and uncomfortable situation: his protectors in exile, their former friends—and his—under suspicion, and he himself confronted by a new spiritual and political climate for which he was both emotionally and intellectually unprepared. Public agitation and tumult created an atmosphere in which he found it difficult to breathe, and it is no wonder that during this time he often sought the clearer airs of his villa at Careggi.[9] His philosophy of the contemplative life, developed under three generations of Medici domination in Florence,[10] had little relevance for this new era of political activism. His Platonic theology comprehended little of the personal, conversionist demands of Savonarolan piety with its dominant themes of repentance and reform. True, in his letter to Cavalcanti he had adduced the authority of Plato in support of the prophet who brought men to repentance for their sins in the face of God's wrath, but even then he had dwelt upon his ideal of withdrawal from public affairs, citing Plato's *Phaedrus* as the model for the God-filled man who meditates on divine matters, steeps himself in the mysteries, keeps himself apart from human pursuits, fears the multitude, and hides from the crowd. Such a man, Ficino pointedly wrote, a prophet and a priest, is far above human wisdom.[11]

Yet, for all his reservations and despite its bitter denunciation of the friar, Ficino's Apology shares certain premises with the Savona-

---

[8] It also shows that Ficino did not suddenly turn against Savonarola after the execution of his good friend Bernardo Del Nero in the summer of 1497, as is usually suggested. See Marcel, *Marsile Ficin*, pp. 569-70.

[9] "Nam Italia ferme tota, certe Tuscia omnis, praesertim Florentia, externis pariter et internis quotidie tumultibus agitatur." *Opera*, vol. I, p. 963. Also quoted by Marcel, *Marsile Ficin*, p. 549, n. 2.

[10] On the *vita contemplativa* and the decline of the ideal of the active life during the Medici period, see Eugenio Garin, *L'umanesimo italiano* (Bari, 1952), Chap. III.

[11] In an earlier letter he had raised the question whether anyone who concerned himself with public affairs could achieve or keep himself in the exalted state necessary for prophetic knowledge. *Opera*, vol. I, p. 892.

rolans: a belief in the permeation of the world by demonic as well as by angelic powers, a preoccupation with Antichrist, a conviction of the validity of prophecy. Indeed, notwithstanding the personal and philosophical obstacles which stood in the way of an alliance between Florence's greatest philosopher and her greatest prophet, there was no one who was more instrumental than Ficino in providing the materials from which the bonds of affection between Savonarola and the Florentine intellectual community were forged. This was recognized by some of Ficino's own pupils who became Savonarola's disciples and linked the two *magistri* in their writings, even after Ficino's violent denunciation.

As did so many others of his time, but with more authority and influence than most, Ficino regarded the world with that mixture of foreboding and hope which darkened the mood of the last decades of the fifteenth century.[12] Ficino had set forth his theory of the decline and crisis of Christianity in his treatise *Della religione cristiana*. He held that when knowledge and wisdom were separated from faith, and faith became vulgarized as a consequence, the Church fell upon evil days, an age of iron: "O happy age when, especially you Jews and Christians preserved whole this divine union of wisdom and piety! O wretched times when this union of Pallas and Themis was finally dissolved!" Ficino had called for a reformation based on a revival of philosophy which would be as much a divine gift as revealed religion: "Above all I pray that some day we will liberate philosophy, sacred gift of God, from impiety, if somehow

---

[12] This mood has been described so often as not to warrant extended discussion here. See especially, Eugenio Garin, "L'attesa dell' età nuova e la 'renovatio,' " in *L'attesa dell' età nuova nella spiritualità della fine del Medioevo*, Convegni del Centro di Studi sulla Spiritualità Medievale, vol. III, 16-19, October 1960 (Todi, 1962), pp. 11-35; André Chastel, "L'Apocalypse en 1500," *Bibliothèque d'Humanisme et Renaissance Mélanges d'Augustin Renaudet*, XIV (1952), 122-40; and his "L'Antéchrist à la Renaissance," *Cristianesimo e Ragion di stato. L'Umanesimo e il demoniaco nell' arte*, Atti del II Congresso Internazionale di Studi Umanistici, Roma, 1952 (Rome, 1953), pp. 177-86.
Professor Garin, who has done more than anyone else to call attention to the prevalence of apocalyptic themes in Italy in this period, says, "It is not difficult to find in the later fifteenth century the two themes united, even in the same author: on one hand, the signs of Antichrist and the imminent cataclysm; on the other, the golden age." "L'attesa," pp. 13-14.

we can."[13] Plato himself, Ficino wrote in a letter to Cardinal Bessarion, had prophesied that the time would come when the mysteries of theology would be purified by precise discussion, just as gold is purified by fire; and Ficino claimed that this was the time.[14] He did not conceive of this revival of philosophy in the cause of religion as taking place only on the intellectual level, but on the spiritual and moral levels as well. To be sure, he regarded contemplation as the highest activity of life, and the direct intuition of God the supreme act of contemplation; but such an experience, while humanly possible in this life, was infrequent and limited only to the few most gifted contemplatives.[15] The basis of this experience, however, was love, and love was available to all. Through love of our fellow man, which Ficino identified with the Pauline concept of charity, we express a common love for God and participate in the essential unity which is God. Through love we not only move toward the divine, but we attain to what is most human in ourselves. And, finally, through love we transcend the barriers between men. Again and again, in his letters as well as in his treatises, Ficino returned to the idea that lover and beloved, friend and friend, become one in their mutual love. Even the Academy, those famous meetings with friends and disciples in the gardens of the Medici villa at Careggi, he regarded not as a mere school but as a community bound together by spiritual ties.[16]

This Ficinian theme of the unity of lover and beloved is especially interesting because of its reverberations in the literature of the Savonarolan movement, even in Savonarola's own homilies. Here, for example, in one of Savonarola's sermons, its echo sounds: ". . . to be compassionate makes man happy because to do good is very delectable. I will prove it to you: when someone shares with others freely what he has, it is a sign that he loves that other person whom he thus honors or for the love of whom he gives such a gift, and, *since love is unitive and transforms the lover into the beloved*,[17] to be a generous giver is a delectable thing (*et ideo amicus dicitur alter ego*),

[13] *Della religione cristiana* (Florence, 1476), pp. 7-8. See also Marcel, *Marsile Ficin*, pp. 583-86.

[14] *Opera*, vol. I, pp. 616-17.

[15] Paul O. Kristeller, *Il pensiero filosofico di Marsilio Ficino* (Florence, 1953), pp. 237-40.

[16] *Ibid.*, pp. 301-306.   [17] My italics.

that is, the friend becomes one with his friend. This is the origin of the fact that charity makes you love God more than yourself and your neighbor as yourself."[18]

Savonarola probably did not learn such themes directly from the master. The icy breeze that soon extinguished Ficino's brief flare of enthusiasm for Savonarola blew from San Marco as well as from Careggi. To the friar, Ficino must have been the very embodiment of those paganizing tendencies in contemporary thought which he so deplored in his writings and sermons. In both media he condemned astrology,[19] and astrology was Ficino's stock in trade;[20] while, in attacking the Neoplatonists' efforts to effect a synthesis of Platonism and Christianity, Savonarola was spurning Ficino's life work.[21] It is not surprising, therefore, to find no mention of Ficino by Savonarola, no indication that he read Ficino's works, nor any reference in the contemporary Piagnoni sources—usually so quick to recite the names of the great men who followed in Savonarola's train —of a meeting between the two men.[22] They were rivals. Among the members of what we might call the "Laurentian circle" a new,

---

[18] Savonarola, *Prediche sopra Aggeo*, ed. Luigi Firpo (Rome, 1965), p. 160.

[19] For a typical statement contrasting astrology with Christian belief in free will, see *Prediche italiane ai Fiorentini*, ed. Roberto Palmarocchi and Francesco Cognasso (Perugia-Venice, 1930-35), vol. III¹, *Quaresimale del 1496*, p. 410; for the distinction between astrology and true prophecy, see *Compendium Revelationum*, in Giovanni Francesco Pico della Mirandola, *Vita R. P. Hieronymi Savonarolae*, ed. Jacques Quetif, 2 vols. (Paris, 1674), vol. I, pp. 258-59. In the following excerpt Savonarola may have had Ficino himself in mind: "people of this kind, who frequent the houses and gatherings of great men as their satellites and adulators, do not praise the true and living God but are quicker to praise vain things, such as the astrologers and poets and philosophers and others of this kind, and they hold these things almost as their gods." *Prediche sopra Aggeo*, p. 182.

[20] On Ficino's use of astrology, see especially Kristeller, *Ficino*, pp. 334-37 (where prophecy is also discussed); D. P. Walker, *Spiritual and Demonic Magic from Ficino to Campanella* (London, 1958); Hans Baron, "Willensfreiheit und Astrologie bei Marsilio Ficino und Pico della Mirandola," *Kultur- und Universalgeschichte, Festschrift Walter Goetz* (Leipzig-Berlin, 1927), pp. 144-70; and many important references in the writings of Eugenio Garin.

[21] On Savonarola's distinction between Plato and the Platonists and his rejection of the latter, see Eugenio Garin, *La cultura filosofica del Rinascimento italiano* (Florence, 1961), pp. 201-12. See also, *Prediche sopra i Salmi*, vol. I, ed. Vincenzo Romano (Rome, 1969), pp. 255-56, for an attack on Plato.

[22] Apart from Cerretani's statement on Ficino's attendance at Savonarola's sermons cited in note 4 above.

stricter, more somber Christianity had been growing, perhaps in reaction to the untimely death of their great patron and protector, Lorenzo de' Medici.[23] One of its effects, as we shall see, was to polarize the group, with Giovanni Pico and Girolamo Benivieni voicing the new, more somber mood and Ficino holding firm in his old ways and beliefs. Stepping up to supplant Ficino as mentor and spiritual guide of the group was Savonarola, less the cause of the new mood than its beneficiary. And to the Savonarolan movement the new converts came, like the Israelite despoilers of the Egyptians, bringing their Ficinian ideas as well as their individual talents and enthusiasms. Younger, less cautious, and perhaps less critical than Ficino, they readily saw in the prophecies of Savonarola the promise of the *renovatio* long heralded by their Platonic master.

ONE OF THE DISCIPLES of Ficino who rallied to the cause of the Savonarolan *renovatio* was Giovanni Nesi. Nesi's spiritual odyssey is interesting.[24] Born in 1456, he had been influenced by Donato Acciaiuoli, who has been described as one of the last great representatives of the Florentine tradition of civic humanism which slowly, grudgingly, and never completely, receded before the mounting pressures of Medicean despotism.[25] That Nesi was at first an Aristotelian like Acciaiuoli is manifest in a sermon he wrote in 1478 on charity, in which he defined love as "a feeling and movement of the soul which induces us to love God for Himself."[26] After Acciaiuoli's

[23] See below, p. 212.

[24] So far as I know, no study of Giovanni Nesi's life and thought exists, although there are some notices in Garin, *L'umanesimo italiano*, pp. 135, 137-39, 143-44. Nesi MSS are to be found in the principal Florentine libraries and will be referred to below.

[25] See the important essay by Garin, "Donato Acciaiuoli cittadino fiorentino," in *Medioevo e Rinascimento* (Bari, 1954), pp. 211-87; and his "I cancellieri umanisti della Repubblica fiorentina da Coluccio Salutati a Bartolomeo Scala," reprinted in *La cultura filosofica*, pp. 3-37. For evidence of the continuation of themes of political liberty, however, see Claudio Varese, *Storia e politica nella prose del Quattrocento* (Turin, 1961), pp. 133-48 et passim; and the texts published by Emilio Santini, "La Protestatio De Justitia nella Firenze Medicea del Sec. XV (Nuovi testi volgare del Quattrocento)," *Rinascimento*, 10 (1959), 33-106.

[26] ". . . uno affetto et movimento d'animo il quale ci induce ad amare iddio per se." MS BRF 2204, fol. 155 recto.

death in that same year (a key year in the evolution of the sterner dictatorship of Lorenzo il Magnifico),[27] Nesi published a treatise, *De Moribus*, which, while still in the vein of his earlier Aristotelianism and still embracing an ethic of political activism, suggests a shifting orientation in its praise of Medicean rule.[28] By the time Nesi composed another oration on charity in 1486 we can see that his transition to Ficinian Platonism was complete. Explicitly criticizing the syllogistic and rationalistic approach, he asserts the primacy of the will over the intellect, extolls the human mind which can become divine through divine love, and enjoins it to fly with angel's wings to the nest of the immortal pelican, the celestial Jerusalem, where it sees the highest good face to face.[29] Indeed, Nesi employed that same theme of lover and and beloved which was so characteristic of Ficino and which was later repeated almost word for word by Savonarola: "I finally transform the lover into the beloved and the beloved into the lover; the first, because, dying in himself, the lover lives in the beloved; the second, because the beloved, recognizing himself in the lover, in loving the lover loves himself."[30] Very possibly Nesi was the medium through whom Savonarola was introduced to these themes; if so, however, it was probably later, after Savonarola's

[27] On the Pazzi conspiracy and the importance of the events of the year 1478 for Lorenzo's concentration of power, see Nicolai Rubinstein, *The Government of Florence Under the Medici* (London, 1968), pp. 195-201. On the impact upon thought in Florence, see Garin, *L'umanesimo italiano*, chap. III.

[28] *De Moribus*, MS BLF (Plut.) LXXVII, 24.

[29] *Oratio de charitate habita in Collegio Magorum* (Florence, 1486). The Company of the Magi was "the most famous [lay religious fraternity] in Florence, in which all the members of the Medici family took part, and in which [Donato] Acciaiuoli is thus also seen to have been a member." Della Torre, *Storia dell'Accademia Platonica*, p. 328. For a ground-breaking study of lay religious fraternities in late Quattrocento Florence, see Paul O. Kristeller, "Lay Religious Traditions and Florentine Platonism," in his *Studies in Renaissance Thought and Letters* (Rome, 1956), pp. 99-122. Also, Garin, "Desideri di riforma nell' oratoria del Quattrocento," reprinted in *La cultura filosofica*, pp. 166-82. Before I had seen Professor Kristeller's article, I gave some attention to the confraternities in my doctoral dissertation, "Prophecy and Humanism in Late Fifteenth Century Florence" (University of Iowa, 1957), pp. 102-106.

[30] *Oratio de charitate*, sig. b, fol. 1 recto. Also quoted in Garin, *L'umanesimo italiano*, p. 143. On Nesi's admiration for Ficino, see the extract in Kristeller, *Supplementum Ficinianum*, vol. II, p. 266.

return to Florence in 1490, for Nesi's oration of 1486 gives no hint of Savonarolan influence and therefore no suggestion that he knew the friar at that early date. In the oration he discusses prophecy, but only in the context of Ficinian Neoplatonism, maintaining that prophetic knowledge resulted from a purification of the eyes of the mind with a supercelestial fire, so that prophets knew not only the present but also the future condition of mankind.[31] Here Nesi was concerned with modes of cognition, not with eschatology. But this was during the heyday of the Laurentian circle, before the death of Lorenzo, the French invasion of Italy, the expulsion of the Medici, and the Prior of San Marco's triumphant rise to prominence.

Ten years later, when the Savonarolan movement was at its peak, we find Nesi among its outstanding spokesmen. In some sonnets from this period he wrote about his spiritual life in terms which strongly suggest an experience of religious conversion, especially in his lines *ad se ipsum*. Lamenting his past, the self-deception of his previous life, his enclosure for forty years in a moral prison, he recalls himself to the true pole of existence where the sun provides more light.[32] The persistence of Neoplatonic themes is self-evident. In another sonnet we even find the old theme of the lover and the beloved, now, however, doing service for Nesi's new preoccupation with conversion and the reform of religion.[33] But Nesi's quintessential Piagnone work, and by all odds the most fascinating document produced by any of the former members of the Laurentian circle, is his *Oraculum de novo saeculo*, an apologetic and messianic tract which he cast in the form of an oracular dream.[34] The *Oraculum* is a veritable encyclopedia of occult symbolism (astrological, Hermetic, and Neopythagorean, to mention only some) of Neoplatonism, and of Christian apocalyptic applied to Savonarolan reform and Florentine patriotic fantasy. Through its extravagant, difficult, symbolic language, we are introduced to the strange, exalted world of a Ficinian Piagnone no longer content with the mere

[31] *Oratio de charitate*, sig. a, fol. 3 recto.

[32] Giovanni Nesi, *Ad se ipsum*, 10 October 1497, MS BRF 2962 fol. 21 recto (new pagination).

[33] *Ibid.*, fol. 37 recto (7 November 1497).

[34] Florence, 1497; Hain no. 11693. The colophon records that Nesi completed the work in 1496. I have used the copy in BRF 554.

rhetoric of philosophical piety, but unable to abandon its charms for the simpler, more literal Biblicism of his new spiritual master.

Nesi addressed the *Oraculum* to his friend Gianfrancesco Pico della Mirandola, nephew of the famous Giovanni Pico and a philosopher and Savonarolan in his own right.[35] Nesi wrote that he had been thinking about how Platonicus Aeneas (Ficino), in whose teaching Platonism and Christianity were so intimately blended, had taught him that before we can hope to govern a republic each of us must make ourselves into a kind of model city. This led Nesi to reflect upon something which, he said, he had read in Plato himself —that in time one who was holier than man would come to open all the fountains of truth—and he remembered that St. Augustine had admitted most of Plato's teachings into Christian doctrine. Then, falling asleep, he dreamed that he saw a man standing on the moon, waving a wand and sowing dragon's teeth while rays from the sun struck his head and a cupbearer daubed his tongue with divine nectar, so that words which came from it seemed more divine than human. These words struck the members of his audience with different effects, some good, some bad; but those who were spared were illuminated with learning and joy. Passing through a flowering meadow[36] and taking up the cap of liberty, they entered their city and renewed it with divine laws, using as their model the celestial Jerusalem.

Then he saw a cross suspended in mid-air as a symbol of liberty, and inscribed upon it were these words: "*Ego constitutus sum rex super syon sanctum vestrum.*"[37] Close by in a temple sat a prince who predicted the coming of a hero carrying one bronze and one gold tablet; on the first would be inscribed the fate of the city, on the second its laws. At the same time a Samian with white hair and golden thigh was announcing the ancient precepts of Magna Graecia,[38] while the *imperium* of the city was increasing, until at

---

[35] On whom, see below, pp. 220-226.

[36] The play on words here is important: *in prata quaedam virentia atque florentia.*

[37] Psalms 2:6. For the same theme in Savonarola's political thought, see below, Chapter IX.

[38] E.g., Do not cut your fingernails near the sacrifices
Cover blood with stones
Abstain from eating beans

last it enjoyed the threefold good from the bosom of Jupiter. The dreaming Nesi exulted in the glory of his *patria*. Chosen from among all peoples, its inhabitants were almost more than human. The walls of the city were rising about a community in which the love of the seraphim, the truth of the cherubim, and equality of the thrones would rival each other. In building their city the citizens must copy the republics founded by Pallas Athene, one amidst the Greeks, the other amidst the Egyptians, as Plato had described in his *Republic*. It would be the same as the prophet's vision of the celestial Jerusalem descending to where the renewal was taking place and where men were singing the Vergilian refrain:

> Magnus ab integro saeclorum nascitur ordo.
> Iam redit et virgo: redeunt saturnia regna
> Iam nova progenies coelo demittitur alto.[39]

Other strange sights appeared: a goose turned into a swan and heralded great changes; a worm arose in Asia out of its parents' bones and turned into a phoenix; the phoenix nested with a lion in the city of the sun; six eagles appeared, one of which purged its eyes on a *gagate* stone and mated with the phoenix to produce a race of fledglings, while the rest were scattered throughout the world to bring captives back to the sun. All this confused Nesi so that (still dreaming) he invoked divine help; whereupon the great emperor sent down a bird, the *picus*, sacred to Mars, great in the taking of auspices, the son of Saturn. Nesi recognized the *picus* as Giovanni Pico who explained to him that the orator whom Nesi had seen standing on the moon was Girolamo Savonarola, the Socrates of Ferrara, divinely appointed for Florence, the center of Italy. Pico then described Savonarola's achievements in reforming the government of the city, spreading its *imperium*, and divulging the mysteries. He praised Savonarola as a profound student of Plato and Plotinus, of Kabbalah and the Bible, who knew many more senses of the Scripture than he had yet revealed. The swan which had ascended to the city of the sun was sent to rouse Pico's own nephew,

---

[39] Vergil, *Eclogue* IV. On the return of the reign of Saturn and the golden age as a propagandistic theme of the Laurentian circle, see E. H. Gombrich, "Renaissance and Golden Age," *Journal of the Warburg and Courtauld Institutes*, XXIV (1961), 307-308.

Gianfrancesco, for the fateful battle to come. The worm which had turned into a phoenix signified the rebirth of religion, while the nest in the city of the sun was Florence, where many sons would be born in the cross of the Lord. The sun in the house of Aries signified Christ, who would be chosen King of that Etruscan city whose horoscope was Aries and whose sign was Leo, while the turning of the Great Year marked the conversion of the Church Militant. Legions of Christians led by priests would come forth to recover the faith and recapture the Holy Land. In Florence everything would take fire and send fiery missiles throughout the world.

Before returning to heaven Pico turned to address his nephew Gianfrancesco, urging him to ascend to the upper circle where he would learn the meaning of the ultimate mysteries, receive deeper insight into the human condition, and learn to interpret the signs. Nesi himself then appealed to Gianfrancesco to study the dream and come to the *novissimum convivium*: "Lo, in the divine name I now call you to the new era (*novum illud saeculum*); I rouse you to the golden age (*ad auream illam aetatem*) which is more pure, more precious than all the others, undiminished by mold or age. Come to Florence, where Christ alone reigns, where the light from heaven has been directed, the light from that archetype of the world which will illuminate all who are languishing in earthly squalor."

The summary presented here is only a pale shadow of the florid symbolism of the *Oraculum*, but it is enough to discern Nesi's intention. In addition to presenting the essence of Savonarola's prophecy of imminent *flagellum* and *renovatio*, and to celebrating Florence as the divinely chosen center of the new era, Nesi was trying to show that Savonarola's mission heralded the fulfillment of all that Ficino and his followers had hoped and worked for. As Nesi saw it, the millennium announced by Savonarola would be a new start as well as a climax, an initiation into man's ultimate enlightenment, when spiritual renewal and moral perfection would at last permit man to open all those mysteries to which he was heir. This legacy included the wisdom of Zoroaster, the ancient Egyptians, and the Greeks, as well as the Jews and Christ. The idea was best expressed in those writings which were ascribed to Hermes Trismegistus. They had been translated into Latin by Ficino and into Italian by his pupil

Tommaso Benci.[40] According to the Hermetic teachings, spiritual and moral perfection made man a very god in wisdom and power. All the great world religious systems were said to have contributed to this end, but their real lessons had to be learned by study as well as practised by worship, and their esoteric doctrines were available only to an elite. Ficino had given this idea of a single universal tradition of wisdom its classic Renaissance interpretation; his doctrine of *pia philosophia* was based on the notion of a harmony not only of Christianity with Platonism but also of Christianity with the entire philosophical tradition.[41] On this foundation he had built his hopes that the new age would see a regeneration of human wisdom and of human virtue. Hermes Trismegistus put it another way, but it was the same idea:

> TAT ... I know not, thrice-greatest one, from what womb a man can be born again, nor with what seed.
>
> HERMES My son, the womb is wisdom, conceiving in silence; and the seed is the true god.[42]

Because a universe which is open to man's knowledge is also malleable by man's will, Hermeticists emphasized human power through the various forms of prophecy and magic, and the theme of deification. These themes fascinated the Renaissance Hermeticists for whom "the dignity of man" was more than a rhetorical topic or an aesthetic ideal.[43] For Ficino, man was "a kind of God,"[44] who

[40] Ficino's translation of the *Corpus Hermeticum* is in his *Opera omnia*. On Benci's Italian translation, see Kristeller, *Supplementum Ficinianum*, vol. I, pp. 98-103. The *Corpus* was, of course, not the work of the legendary thrice-great Hermes but of Alexandrian Neoplatonists of the third century of the Christian era. See A.-J. Festugière, *La révélation de Hermès Trismégiste*, 4 vols. (Paris, 1950-54), vol. I, p. vii.

[41] Kristeller, *Ficino*, pp. 16-20; also Delio Cantimori, "Anabattismo e neo-platonismo nel XVI secolo in Italia," *Reale Accademia Nazionale dei Lincei Rendiconti delle classe di scienze morali, storiche e filologiche*, 6th ser., 12 (1936), pp. 521-61.

[42] *Hermetica*, ed. and trans. Walter Scott, 4 vols. (Oxford, 1924-36), vol. I, p. 239. See also Festugière, *La révélation*, vol. IV, pp. 210-57.

[43] See especially Garin, *Medioevo e Rinascimento*, pp. 150-91. The Hermetic origin of the celebration of man as an earthly god is pointed out by Wilhelm Kroll in A. F. von Pauly and G. Wissowa, *Real-encyclopädie der classischen Altertumswissenschaft*, s.v. "Hermes Trismegistos" (1913), 792-823; and by

knew the past, present, and future, while for Giovanni Pico della Mirandola, whose *Oration on the Dignity of Man* is the most famous Renaissance version of the theme, man's freedom consisted in just this ability to make himself God-like through contemplation.[45] Through such media as the sermons prepared for the meetings of the confraternities, the disciples of Ficino and Pico gave wider currency to these themes. Pierfilippo Pandolfini, for example, whom Ficino called *delphicus totus*,[46] used the theme of human dignity and power in a sermon before the Company of the Magi,[47] while Giovanni Nesi talked about Christ as man deified through the power of love in his *Oratio de charitate* before the same group.[48]

Nesi's *Oraculum*, however, was not the first case of a contemporary employing the Hermetic apparatus to legitimize a living prophet of renewal. It had at least one precedent in the humanist Lodovico Lazzarelli's enthusiastic endorsement of the prophet Giovanni da Correggio. Giovanni, who had first appeared in the streets of Rome in 1484 (that year of great expectations) calling for repentance in preparation for the coming *renovatio*,[49] turned up again in Lucca in June 1949 when he tried to gain permission from Piero de' Medici to enter Florence. Not surprisingly, considering the trouble Piero was having from popular preachers and prophets at that very moment, Giovanni was denied.[50] It seems, however, that he had made an earlier appearance in the city, sometime between 1480 and 1487, and had been attacked as a false prophet in an epigram by Naldo Naldi, a Florentine poet and friend of both Ficino and Gio-

---

Festugière, *La révélation*, vol. I, p. vii. According to Klibansky the Hermetic dialogue *Asclepius* introduced the idea of man's centrality and earthly divinity into twelfth-century Western thought. Raymond Klibansky, *The Continuity of the Platonic Tradition During the Middle Ages* (London, 1939), p. 33.

[44] "Homo igitur qui universaliter cunctis et viventibus, et non viventibus providet, est quidam Deus." Ficino, *Opera*, vol. I, p. 296.

[45] On the differences between Ficino's and Pico's conceptions of man the microcosm, see Garin, *L'umanesimo italiano*, p. 140.

[46] Della Torre, *Accademia Platonica*, p. 583.

[47] BNF ms Magl. XXXV, 211 fol. 109 verso.

[48] "Per te [love] è il verbo humanato. L'huomo deificato." *Oratio de charitate*, sig. b, fol. 2 recto.

[49] Kristeller, "Marsilio Ficino e Lodovico Lazzarelli," *Studies*, pp. 221-47.

[50] Kristeller, "Ancora per Giovanni Mercurio da Correggio," *ibid.*, pp. 249-57.

vanni Nesi.[51] But Lodovico Lazzarelli, who as a student of Hermetica was dependent upon Ficino,[52] had no such hesitation about
embracing Giovanni da Correggio as his spiritual father. While Giovanni called himself Mercury, after his master in ancient theology,
the thrice-great Hermes (or Mercurius) Trismegistus, Lazzarelli
called himself Enoch, after the prophet who had walked with God
(Genesis 5:22) and who had later become known as one with access
to the divine secrets and even as the inventor of writing and
astronomy.[53] In his *Epistola Enoch*,[54] Lazzarelli described Giovanni
Mercurio's wonderful appearance in Rome on Palm Sunday 1484:[55]
"dressed in a double-draped black silk toga, a golden girdle, scarlet-
booted, and bedecked with a headband of purple hue, he was
mounted upon a black quivering steed." On his brow, over his
crown of thorns, were the words, "This is my son Pimander whom
I have elected"; and on his chest and back was the sign of the Thau,
"name and sign of the highest God."[56] Giovanni's discourse, in Lazzarelli's telling, was more wonderful than anything of any bygone
age, full of esoteric wisdom bearing the Christian message of
redemption,[57] and its effect upon Lazzarelli was to cause him to
exchange the profane muses for the sacred ones.[58] In Lazzarelli's
Crater Hermetis, the mixture of Hermetic with Christian messianic
themes is even more bizarre: the *crater* of Hermes is the chalice of

[51] For the epigram, see Naldus Naldius, *Epigrammaton liber*, ed. Alessandro
Perosa (Budapest, 1943), p. 56; reprinted in Kristeller, *Studies*, pp. 255-56.
Naldi's friendship with Nesi is indicated in the poems which the latter
addressed to him, e.g., MS BRF 2962.

[52] Kristeller, *Studies*, pp. 227-28.

[53] Philip Schaff and J. J. Herzog, *A Religious Encyclopedia*, 4 vols. (New
York, 1891), vol. II, pp. 739-40.

[54] From the title of the apocryphal book, cited by Lazzarelli. See Kristeller,
Studies, p. 231.

[55] *Epistola Enoch de admiranda ac portendenti apparitione novi atque divini
Prophetae ad omne humanum genus*, ed. Mirella Brini, in *Testi umanistici
su l'Ermetismo*, ed. E. Garin, M. Brini, C. Vasoli, P. Zambelli (Rome:
Archivio di Filosofia, 1955), p. 34. The text has the date 1485, but see *ibid.*,
p. 45, n. 28.

[56] *Ibid.*, pp. 37-38.   [57] *Ibid.*, p. 35.

[58] *Ibid.*, p. 44. Also, in three prefaces addressed to Giovanni Mercurio he
speaks of himself as "once a poet but now, by a new regeneration, a son of
the true wisdom." Kristeller, *Studies*, pp. 242, 244, 245.

Christ;[59] Pimander and Christ are one and the same;[60] Christ's message of salvation is the ancient wisdom of the Delphic Apollo, "know thyself." "I am a Christian," he declares, "and I am not ashamed also to be a Hermetic."[61] Reaffirming the identity of the classical golden age as the Christian millennium, Lazzarelli looked forward to the World Sabbath, the reign of the pious, and the establishment of *unum ovile et unus pastor.*[62] Yet at the same time he conceived of prophecy, as would Nesi in his *Oraculum,* as a form of power which makes man one of the gods:

> Happy beyond measure is he who knows
> The fruits of his fate and who will have brought
>   them freely to pass.
> For he ought to be counted among the gods,
> And not lower than the highest of them.[63]

As Giovanni Mercurio was Lazzarelli's ideal Hermetic model, so Savonarola was Nesi's. Interpreter of the mysteries of all ages and peoples, spiritual father whose divine eloquence, like the sun's rays, generated a lifegiving power, Savonarola appeared in Nesi's *Oraculum* surrounded by even more Hermetic symbols than was Giovanni Mercurio in Lazzarelli's *Crater Hermetis.* Standing on the moon, his head encircled by a lunar aureole,[64] he marked his listeners with the same figure of the Thau that the prophet Giovanni Mercurio wore on his chest and back. Magical stones,[65] geometrical figures, and astral symbols embellished the picture of a *magus* announcing the coming of the Great Year which was also the new era of Christian

---

[59] *Crater Hermetis,* ed. M. Brini, *Testi umanistici,* pp. 54, 56.

[60] *Ibid.,* p. 54.　　　　　　　[61] *Ibid.,* p. 56.

[62] *Ibid.,* pp. 66-69. The similarity to Joachite ideas is pointed out by Signorina Brini in her edition of *Epistola Enoch,* p. 26.

> [63] Felix ille nimis qui sua noverit
>   Sortis munera, perfecerit et libens.
>   Inter namque deos connumerandus est,
>   Nec diis est superis minor.

Ibid., p. 67.

[64] For the Hermetic origins of this figure see Festugière, *La révélation,* vol. I, p. 67. On illumination and regeneration in Hermetic thought (e.g., Nesi's theme of solar regeneration), see *ibid.,* vol. IV, pp. 241-57.

[65] Joan Evans, *Magical Jewels of the Middle Ages and the Renaissance* (Oxford, 1922), especially pp. 205-206.

millenarianism. The obscure Pythagorean symbols Nesi himself explained in a letter to another sometime Savonarolan, the Camaldolese monk, Paolo Orlandini;[66] they were moral precepts. The injunction against the eating of beans, for example, should be understood as an admonition to live chastely.[67] And lest the *Oraculum* left any doubt that Savonarola was an Hermetic seer, Nesi underscored the identification in a poem of December 3, 1497, in which the prophet appears in the vault of the heavens where "with his wand in his hand [he] seems another Hermes."[68] In another poem of the same date Nesi describes the *frate* "born in Arabia, a worm from the bones of his father," as having come to initiate the universal tempest and the Great Year.[69]

Whether Nesi was influenced by Lazzarelli in his own Hermeticization of Savonarola is difficult to say; the striking similarities may indicate no more than common sources and a common enthusiasm. At least they show, however, that Nesi's endorsement of Savonarola was in the vein of contemporary Neoplatonic syncretism and that the Hermetic revival, whose center was Florence and the Ficinian circle, was an important factor in the enthusiastic reception of the Savonarolan movement.

But what could Savonarola have made of this spectacle of himself decked out as the wand-bearing Hermes or as "the Socrates of Ferrara" who knew the secret lore of the Kabbalah? What could he have said of followers who read the coming of the new era in the conjunction of the planets which signaled the beginning of the Great Year? Giovanni Pico had encountered Savonarola's disapproval when he tried to defend the study of ancient pagan philosophers against the friar's warning that they were dangerous to the cause of true religion.[70] To Savonarola, Nesi's *Oraculum* could only have appeared

---

[66] On whom see below, pp. 362-71.

[67] *Symbolum nesianum*, in Paolo Orlandini, *Eptathicum seu opus theologicum et morale*, MS BNF II. I. 158 fols. 270 recto–280 verso.

[68] MS BRF 2962, fol. 66 recto (new pagination).

[69] *Loc. cit.*

[70] See the account by the contemporary humanist Piero Crinito, who was present, in his *De honesta disciplina*, ed. Carlo Angeleri (Rome, 1955), pp. 104-105. Pico maintained that there was agreement between the ancient philosophies and Christianity. When he was finished, Savonarola embraced him saying that Pico was the expert in such matters.

a wild travesty. Leaving aside the obvious differences of style and language, we can go into the heart of the matter by considering their contrasting views of prophecy. Savonarola had always explicitly denied any relation between the person of the prophet and his prophetic powers, often taking the story of Balaam and his ass as his text.[71] In his view, prophecy was a gift of God unrelated either to the prophet's morals or to his wisdom, and apart from such a gift no man had any power to see the future. Moreover, prophecy was historical, that is, it dealt with that part of the divine economy which God had not yet brought to pass but which He would effect in His own way according to His own will. As such the purpose of prophecy was exclusively religious and Christian: it was given to men that they might prepare spiritually to receive God's judgment upon them. Even those "private" prophecies which Savonarola claimed to have had (the deaths of Innocent VIII and Lorenzo de' Medici, for example) were related to his mission of preaching repentance. On the other hand, for Nesi, prophecy was something more than the foretelling of certain divine acts. It was less historical than mystical, poetical, and theosophical. Nesi does not seem to have distinguished between the power of predicting contingent events and the power of perceiving certain higher truths, penetrating the mysteries of the universal order and the meaning of life. Whereas for Savonarola prophecy was a divine agency through which man was induced to humble himself before his God, for Nesi it was a means whereby man attained to power over his destiny and thereby made himself God-like. The phrase *Novit qui colet* with which Wilhelm Bousset summed up the kernel of Hermetic philosophy[72]—that is, "He who is pious knows the mysteries"—might be taken as the theme of Nesi's *Oraculum*; but for Savonarola the order would have had to be reversed—through knowledge of God we come to worship Him.

The difference between Nesi's conception of prophecy and Savonarola's was more than a difference of personal inclination, for Nesi was expressing ideas shared by a generation of Neoplatonists whose doctrinal home was Ficino's Academy, while Savonarola was

[71] "The word that God puts in my mouth, that must I speak." Numbers 22:38.

[72] Wilhelm Bousset's phrase, quoted by Festugière, *La révélation*, vol. I, p. 360.

expressing ideas which derived from a very different set of premises and a very different, Biblical, scholastic, and, however indirectly, Joachite tradition. And yet we must attempt to understand the *Oraculum* in terms of the spirit in which it was written, for it was designed not to display the differences between the Ficinians and Savonarola but to celebrate what they had in common. Despite Nesi's syncretist orientation he made it quite clear that he considered the Christian revelation as the epitome of universal wisdom. The sixth eagle of philosophy made its nest with Christ the phoenix, and it was from this coupling that the "new race" was to emerge. The prophet, for all his Hermetic trappings and his Kabbalism, was the interpreter of the wisdom of the Bible, and his message was the Christian message of personal conversion and redemption. After all, the new era to which Nesi and Pico summoned Gianfrancesco Pico was, notwithstanding its contamination by classical and Neoplatonic elements, a Christian, millennial vision of the future.

The *Oraculum* reveals one other bond with the Savonarolan enterprise. Fundamental to the whole structure of Nesi's vision was the conception that the new era was to be built first as a kind of model city in which the celestial Jerusalem would be merged with the Platonic republic by citizens who prepared themselves as microcosmic ideal republics by means of the double enlightenment of Platonic wisdom and Christian virtue. Repeatedly Nesi declared that the scene of this wonderful construction was Florence, whose people were chosen above all others, and that Florence was the nest of the eagle and the phoenix out of whose mating a new race of fledglings would spread throughout the world. It was to Florence that he urgently summoned Gianfrancesco Pico, for there he would find "the new feast," there the new era would begin; in Florence Christ alone reigned and from Florence the fire would be lit which would send its sparks throughout the world. Nesi's apotheosis of his city was Ficinian in its dependence upon the theme of Florentine intellectual superiority and reached far back in time to connect with the old myth of Florence as the center of *renovatio*. At the same time he drew inspiration from the Piagnone version of the civic myth. His association of the "three-fold good" with the extension of the Florentine *imperium* echoes the three-fold Savonarolan promise, "more glorious, richer, more powerful than ever before"; and the way in which he connected the *renovatio* with the recovery of Florentine political liberty was characteristic of the rhetoric of the post-Medicean *governo civile*.

WHILE NESI was the only one of Ficino's disciples who publicly depicted Savonarola as an Hermetic seer, he was by no means the only one of them who embraced Savonarola's cause or became its public champion. Savonarola appealed to many of the Florentine Platonists, some of whom served and fought for him with the best weapons they had, with *frottola, canzone*, political tract, and philosophical dialogue. Like Nesi these others experienced Savonarola's call to repentance and glory as a religious conversion, but unlike him they seem to have found it necessary to abandon not only old ways of life but also some of their old ways of thought. For example, Girolamo Benivieni, one of the bright lights of Lorenzo's *brigata* of poets, friend of Lorenzo's murdered brother Giuliano, friend and pupil of Marsilio Ficino, Angelo Poliziano, and Giovanni Pico— in short, the very epitome of the Laurentian courtier-*literatus*[73]— responded to Savonarola's preaching as though he had awakened from the mortal dangers of his "boyish" activities, his "inept writing," and his "blindness."[74]

Benivieni had his first spiritual crisis at the age of eighteen,[75] when

---

[73] See the biography by Caterina Re, *Girolamo Benivieni fiorentino* (Città di Castello, 1906); and the shorter study by A. Pellizzari, *Un asceta del Rinascimento, della vita e delle opere di Girolamo Benivieni* (Genoa, 1906). Neither is entirely satisfactory, however. For a brief but valuable sketch with bibliography see Cesare Vasoli's article "Girolamo Benivieni," *Dizionario biografico degli Italiani*, 9 vols. (Rome, 1960-67), vol. VIII, pp. 550-55.

[74] Girolamo Benivieni, *Opere novissamente rivedute et da molti errori espurgate con una canzone dello amore celeste et divino, col Commento dello Ill. Conte Giovanni Pico Mirandolano distinto in libbri III* (Venice, 1522), p. 73 recto.

[75] ". . . circha a glianni della nostra salute MCCCCLXX et nel decimo octavo della mia eta io caddi, quale senefussi la cagione Dio elsa, ma io volentieri in occasione della mia salute la referisco, caddi dico in una grave, e come la experientia ha dipoi manifestamente demonstro, perpetuo valitudine. Dalla violentia della quale gia qualche volta nel corso di piu anni combattuto ad tanta debilita di corpo e anxieta di mente pervenni, che per el tedio della vita presente ad epsa morte converso non senza lachrymabile e affectuosa

the murder of Giuliano de' Medici turned him toward God.[76] Three years later, in 1481, he wrote: "Death every hour terrifies me, threatens me. Fear presses my anguished mind. Pale my face, frozen my heart in my cold breast."[77] Later he used to say that from his thirty-fifth year onward he constantly believed that the hour of departing this life was at hand.[78] The onset of this latest depression came just about the time that Benivieni, together with his brother Domenico and his friend Giovanni Pico, began to attend Savonarola's sermons in San Marco[79] and seems to have lasted a lifetime, reaching full crisis at the time of the death of his beloved Pico on November 17, 1494, the day of the French army's entry into Florence. For these reasons, the assertion of Benivieni's biographer that Savonarola converted Benivieni from a life of "religious indifference"[80] cannot be true. Benivieni's was a troubled spirit; he went through several periods of depression about which he talked and wrote freely. Savonarola's early preaching with its warnings of doom may well have deepened his malaise, but it was Pico's death that cast him into the depths of despair and was a turning point in his life. He later wrote that, while mourning Pico and thinking of abandoning his unpub-

---

obsecratione cosi exclamando dixi." Girolamo Benivieni, *Commento di Hieronymo Benivieni cittadino fiorentino sopra a piu sue canzone et sonetti dello amore et della belleza divina* (Florence, 1500); Hain no. 2788, fol. LXXV. I used copies in New York Public Library and BNF. In both, pagination is defective.

[76] Girolamo Benivieni, "Buccolica" in *Buccoliche di diverse* (Florence, 1482), Coppinger no. 6137, fol. 76 recto.

[77] *Opere*, p. 97 recto.

[78] [Anonymous] *Vita di Girolamo Benivieni* MS BNF II. I. 91, p. 267. Caterina Re attributes this biography to Antonio Benivieni, Girolamo's grand-nephew, who died in 1598. Re, *Benivieni*, p. 14.

[79] Girolamo Benivieni, *Lettera mandata a Clemento VII* (1530) I used Jacopo Nardi's copy: MS BRF 2022, fol. 8 verso. Benivieni here recalls that the three friends attended Savonarola's sermons when he came to Florence and began to preach in the Church of San Marco, in 1488. However, since Pico did not return to Florence until June 1488 and Savonarola had already departed from the city in 1487, the time when Benivieni began to frequent Savonarola's sermons probably should be moved forward to 1490 or soon thereafter—that is, after Savonarola's return to Florence in that year. Consequently, whether this coincided so closely with the onset of his sense of impending death as he seems later to have believed, is a moot point.

[80] Re, *Benivieni*, pp. 3, 102, 307.

lished writings to the dust, it pleased God to make him see that nothing happened on this earth without a reason, and that God must have had a motive for allowing him to outlive Pico, when according to human logic Pico ought to have outlived him. Therefore he decided to humble his pride and to submit to the yoke of divine will, making every use of his life for God.[81] From that time on, he continued, he dedicated every effort to the cause of piety and religious reform. With this recovery, which coincided with the onset of Savonarola's new millenarian optimism, Benivieni became the chief publicist of the Savonarolan movement, writing songs in which he celebrated the familiar themes, some to be sung in the religious processions of the Piagnoni, as the Palm Sunday procession of 1496.[82]

Before discussing Benivieni's Savonarolan writings, however, we must explore his "conversion" further, and this takes us into the question of his relations with Giovanni Pico and the crisis of the Ficinian circle. Benivieni had been one of Ficino's followers; in fact he had written a *Song on Divine and Celestial Love* which was a synopsis in verse of Ficino's commentary on Plato's *Symposium*.[83] When he became friends with Giovanni Pico, he asked Pico to write a commentary on his *Song*, and Pico did so. Shortly thereafter both men had second thoughts about publishing their joint enterprise

---

[81] *Commento . . . sopra a piu sue canzone et sonetti dello amore . . .* fol. I verso, and fol. LXXVIII (incorrectly numbered LXXVIIII) where he employs the familiar theme of the Laurentian circle, of the lover and the beloved: "Intendi vero quello che sidice, cio e che lanima dello amante viva in uno certo modo e si truovi in ello amato: e che per questo quando lo affecto e reciproco in due corpi sia per unione di amore una sola anima: Se questo e dico vero adviene. Et e necessario che se luno di epsi due corpi cosi da amore perla anima informati muore che lui cosi morendo privi anchora in gran parte laltre di sua vita. Cio e della propria sua anima: perche essendo epse due anime dello amante e dello amato in ello amore reciproco per se tanto unite che luna non possa essere senza laltra, e che per questo piu veramente sidica che le sieno una che due anime, e necessario che ella separatione delluna sisepari anchora laltra. Et pero morendo luno di epsi due corpi, e consequentemente partendosi lanima di quello tira anchora seco in uno certo modo e conduce lanima dellaltro."

[82] Pseudo-Burlamacchi, *La vita del Beato Ieronimo Savonarola*, ed. Piero Ginori Conti (Florence, 1937), p. 128.

[83] Most recent edition together with his prefatory letters: Giovanni Pico della Mirandola, *De hominis dignitate, Heptaplus, De ente et uno*, ed. Eugenio Garin (Florence, 1942), pp. 453-58.

because, according to Benivieni, they had come "to lack some of that spirit and fervor" with which they had written it, since it now seemed unfitting that one who professed the laws of Christ should write of divine love as a Platonist and not as a Christian.[84] Benivieni added that these doubts began to trouble them shortly before Pico's death, which would seem to suggest that they were moved to repentance by Savonarola's preaching; and Benivieni's sharp new distinction between Platonism and Christianity further suggests Savonarola's influence, since, as we saw earlier, this was the same distinction made by the friar. But there is a difficulty with this explanation: since Pico wrote his *Commentary* to the *Song* in 1486,[85] if the onset of their religious scruples followed an interval of at least four years,[86] why had they not published it before? Was there some other prior reason for their reluctance? Apparently there was. In his *Commentary* Pico was very critical of certain of Ficino's philosophical ideas; he explicitly maintained, for instance, that in interpreting Plato on the subject of love Ficino had committed many errors which he, Pico, would shortly expose and correct.[87] We can be sure that this was very embarrassing to Benivieni as well as annoying to Ficino. After Pico's death Ficino himself asserted that it had been Pico's last wish to leave this youthful work unpublished,[88] and so it remained until 1519, long after Pico and Ficino were dead, when Benivieni published it without the offending passages.[89]

---

[84] *Opere*, pp. 3 verso–4. Benivieni finally published the work in 1519, after much urging by his friends, he says. In the introduction to the published version, however, he carefully distinguished between the Platonic and the Christian treatment of love, and he asked his readers to excuse his error if anywhere he departed from the truth of Christ to follow Plato's doctrine. *Ibid.*, p. 4 verso. See also Pico della Mirandola, *De hominis dignitate*, ed. Garin, p. 15.

[85] Eugenio Garin, "Marsilio Ficino, Girolamo Benivieni, Giovanni Pico," *Giornale critico della filosofia italiana*, X (1942), 94. Pico's *Commentary* is published together with Benivieni's *Canzona* in Pico, *De hominis dignitate*, ed. Garin, pp. 461-581.

[86] That is, the interval between the completion of Pico's *Commentary* and Savonarola's return to Florence in 1490, after which they began to attend his sermons.

[87] For a discussion of this criticism, see Pico, *De hominis dignitate*, ed. Garin, p. 17.

[88] *Ibid.*, pp. 12-13.

[89] *Ibid.*, pp. 16-17. Garin also points out that Pico had already incorporated

The critical issue here is the question of the relations between Pico and Ficino, the two greatest figures in Florentine intellectual life at the time Savonarola came upon the scene. Pico had taken up residence in Florence in 1484 and seems to have been cordially welcomed by Ficino, who treated the twenty-year-old philosopher-prince with all the enthusiasm and respect due a learned colleague.[90] For his part, however, Pico, with all the brashness of precocious youth, was no more hesitant about criticizing Ficino than he was about challenging the orthodoxies of the Catholic faith in the nine hundred theses he was preparing to defend in Rome,[91] or than he was in running off with Margherita, the wife of Giuliano Mariotto dei Medici, a tax official in Arezzo.[92] Ficino was generous: the kidnapping of the errant wife he excused as the act of a hero running off with a nymph, not to be judged by the standards of ordinary mortals,[93] while two years later, when Pico was seeking refuge after the abortive and disastrous episode of the nine hundred theses in Rome, it was Ficino who wrote to Pico on behalf of Lorenzo the Magnificent inviting him to return to Florence to "be happy and be Florentine."[94] Pico did return and the two men resumed their friendship, but the kind of Laurentian idyll with which Ficino had beckoned Pico was becoming less and less possible for him. Increasingly in those last years of his short life he was attracted by a more austere religious ideal, and this, in addition to the philosophical issues which arose between him and Ficino,[95] could not fail to estrange them still further. Pico spent his time writing religious poetry, a commentary on the Psalms, and a treatise on the creation story in Genesis—his

---

substantial parts of his *Commento* into his *Heptaplus* (*ibid.*, p. 12) which suggests that it was principally Benivieni who was trying to avoid offending Ficino further.

[90] On the relations between the two men, see Marcel, *Marsile Ficin*, pp. 466-79; and Eugenio Garin, *Giovanni Pico della Mirandola* (Florence, 1937), pp. 6-7.

[91] Pico completed the theses and the *Oration on the Dignity of Man*, which was to be their preface, in the fall of 1486. *Ibid.*, pp. 29-30.

[92] On May 10, 1486. *Ibid.*, p. 25.

[93] *Apologus Marsilii Ficini de raptu Margarite nymphe ab heroe Pico*, in Kristeller, *Supplementum Ficinianum*, vol. I, p. 56.

[94] Ficino, *Opera*, vol. I, pp. 888-89.

[95] Garin, *Giovanni Pico*, pp. 21-23, 55-59, 78-79.

Heptaplus. "The Count of Mirandola has come to rest with us here," wrote Lorenzo de' Medici on June 13, 1489, "where he lives a very holy life and is like a monk, has written excellent works of theology and continues to do so, recites the ordinary of a priest and observes the fasts and the strictest continence, lives without much of a household, only what is necessary, and in my opinion offers an example to other men."[96] Pico's nephew, Gianfrancesco, who was much with him during this time, described the conversations in which Pico confessed that he wanted to preach as a barefoot mendicant in the squares and market places of Italy.[97] Pico's letters to Gianfrancesco were full of pious, often gloomy thoughts—of the pride and wickedness of those who would not see the truth, of the prodigies and signs that confirmed the truth of the Gospel, and of the need to keep always in mind the imminence of death. "Finally, I want you to keep in mind—I talked to you about this so often when you were here with me—the two things you ought never to forget: one, that God's Son died for you and the other, that you will also die shortly, even if you live a long life."[98]

Pico's recent escapades and tribulations had much to do with this penitential mood, as he indicated in his letter of October 15, 1486, to Andrea Corneo da Urbino.[99] Pico had learned what his brashness could cost him. In challenging both doctrinal orthodoxy and sacramental piety, he had suffered swift ecclesiastical censure, exile, and imprisonment. Even so, many would have said that he was lucky; the intervention of his powerful friends had protected him from the full fury of the Inquisitors and brought him to a safe refuge in

[96] In Pico, *De hominis dignitate,* ed. Garin, pp. 29-30.

[97] Gianfrancesco Pico della Mirandola, *Ioannis Pici . . . Vita,* in *Opera Omnia Ioannis Pici Mirandulae Concordiaeque Comitis TheologorumEt Philosophorum Sine Controversiae Principis,* 2 vols. (Basel, 1572-73), vol. I, fol. *7 recto. Thomas More translated part of the *Ioannis Pici . . . Vita.* See *Giovanni Pico della Mirandola: His Life by His Nephew Giovanni Francesco Pico . . . Translated from the Latin by Sir Thomas More,* ed. J. M. Rigg (London, 1890).

[98] *Opera,* vol. I, pp. 340-43. Also his letter of May 5, 1492, in Eugenio Garin, *Prosatori Latini del Quattrocento* (Milan, 1952), pp. 824-33.

[99] *Opera,* vol. I, pp. 376-78; and Garin, *La cultura filosofica,* pp. 231-89.

Florence.[100] Now he was inclined to dwell upon the still more frightening punishments which awaited the unrepentant sinner:

> But if our debts are weighed in the scale of equity
> And if the standards of Your justice are maintained
> Who is there who can bear the fearful scourge
> of the living Avenger. . . ?[101]

Both Pico's and Savonarola's early biographers, including Gianfrancesco Pico who composed lives of both men, declare it was Pico
who persuaded Lorenzo de' Medici to have Savonarola recalled to
Florence.[102] There is no reason to doubt this; it is understandable
that Pico would have wanted Savonarola at his side to help him
carry out his resolve to live a life of penitence and religious dedica-
tion. As mentioned earlier, Pico and Savonarola had met some years
before, either in Ferrara or in Reggio Emilia, and they may have
renewed their acquaintance during their earlier stay in Florence.[103]
But there is good reason to doubt that Savonarola converted Pico to
religious orthodoxy,[104] since, as we have just seen, Pico's "conver-

---

[100] On these events, see Garin, *Giovanni Pico*, pp. 25-36. The Papal breve
pardoning him was not forthcoming until June 18, 1493. *Ibid.*, p. 46. See also,
the same author, "Giovanni Pico della Mirandola," Comitato per le cele-
brazioni centenarie in onore di Giovanni Pico, Conferenza tenuta a Mirandola,
February 24, 1963 (n.p., 1963), p. 35.

[101] Quod si nostra pari pensentur debita lance:
      Et si judicii norma severa tui,
      Quis queat horrendum viventis ferre flagellum
      Vindicis, et plagas sustinuisse graves?

"Deprecatoria ad Deum," *Opera*, vol. I, p. 339.

[102] Pseudo-Burlamacchi, *La Vita*, pp. 16-17. This is accepted by most modern
authorities including Garin, *Pico della Mirandola*, pp. 42-43; and Roberto
Ridolfi, *The Life of Girolamo Savonarola*, trans. Cecil Grayson (New York,
1959), p. 29.

[103] See above, pp. 83-84, 211-12.

[104] As has been widely maintained. See Garin, *Pico della Mirandola*, pp.
42-43, for references. Garin himself rejects the contention on the grounds that
this does not take into account the profound change in Pico since at least
1486, on one hand, and the continuity of his philosophical ideas, on the other.
Ridolfi agrees that Savonarola was not the principal cause of Pico's "profound
transformation," yet he believes that Savonarola's influence was already at
work on Pico—apparently stemming from their earlier contacts. *Loc. cit.*

sion," if such it was, antedated Savonarola's return to Florence, as did Benivieni's. While both men became enthusiastic associates of the Dominican and adopted some parts of his penitential style, each of them was responding to his own life experiences and his own religious impulses and needs. Moreover, there was a reciprocal influence at work; the Florentine milieu of the 1490's had as much to do with the development of Savonarola's new prophetic message as he had to do with impressing his particular religious style upon the city in that decade.

Not that every member of the Laurentian and Ficinian circles had the same religious outlook. Ficino, as we have already seen, did not share with his younger friends their preoccupation with repentance and conversion. Whatever combination of ingredients was essential for the making of Piagnoni, Ficino did not have it.[105] The rallying of Laurentian *literati* and philosophers to the Savonarolan cause was a further elaboration of differences which were already beginning to be felt among the members of the group, differences that had roots in the philosophical, religious, and perhaps personal issues that divided Ficino and Pico. The theme of personal religious conversion was part of the Savonarolan style, and men like Benivieni and Nesi appropriated it; but their turning to Savonarola requires a more complicated explanation than the one they offered, an explanation that takes into account the influence of Ficino's own religious-philosophical teaching, the growing estrangement from the heterodox elements in that teaching, and the mood of pessimism which grew in Florence after the death of *il Magnifico*. Was it to conversion by Savonarola or was it to his own prior philosophical convictions that Pico owed the inspiration for his famous *Disputationes adversus astrologiam divinatricem*? His nephew Gianfrancesco wrote that

[105] Nor, I would contend, did Angelo Poliziano, greatest of the Florentine humanists of the Laurentian era, despite the fact that he spent the last weeks before his death on September 24, 1494, as a lay brother of San Marco. For what I think is a psychologically perceptive as well as a charming characterization of Poliziano, see Alan Moorehead, "The Angel in May," *The New Yorker Magazine* (February 24, 1951), pp. 34-65. Mr. Moorehead is incorrect, however, in saying that Poliziano lived to see the beginnings of the destruction in Florence—the looting of the Medici Palace, etc.—since these events did not take place until after Poliziano died.

the *Disputationes* was part of a larger work against "the seven enemies of the Church" which his uncle planned to write,[106] and Giovanni Nesi said that Pico often consulted with the friar and had his help in preparing the attack.[107] Later, as the astrologers rallied to their own defense, it became one of their stock arguments that Savonarola, fearful of the astrological predictions of the coming of false prophets, had turned Pico against the astral sciences and persuaded him to write a refutation.[108] Pico's sympathizers as well as his enemies found it simpler to ascribe his position on astrology to religious conversion than to deal with the complexities of his thought; but this position was not an about-face; it was consistent with his earlier philosophical and religious views.[109] In his *Heptaplus*, which he completed in 1489, he had already stated some of his views and indicated that he would treat the subject at greater length in a future work.[110]

In the *Disputationes* Pico was attempting to establish a distinction between "natural astrology," which was his term for the scientific study of the movements of the heavens, and "judicial" or "divinatory" astrology, the art of predicting man's destiny from stars, which he regarded as superstitious. His main argument against judicial

[106] Gianfrancesco Pico, *Ioannis Pici . . . Vita*, fol. *4 verso. This attack embarrassed Ficino, as we see from his letter of August 20, 1494, to Poliziano (Ficino, *Opera*, vol. I, p. 968) and from Poliziano's reply (reprinted in Kristeller, *Supplementum Ficinianum*, vol. II, pp. 278-79). Poliziano too referred to Pico's book as part of an attack against the seven enemies of the Church.

[107] Nesi, *Oraculum*, sig. b, fol. 8 verso.

[108] Beginning with Luca Bellanti, *Responsiones in disputationes Joannis Pici Mirandulae comitis adversus astrologos* (Florence, 1498); *GW* no. 3802. See the remarks of Garin in his edition of Giovanni Pico della Mirandola, *Disputationes adversus astrologiam divinatricem*, 2 vols. (Florence, 1946-52), vol. I, pp. 1-6.

[109] Baron, "Willensfreiheit und Astrologie," p. 155; Lynn Thorndike, "Marsilio Ficino und Pico della Mirandola und die Astrologie," *Zeitschrift für Kirchengeschichte*, 46 (1928), 584-85; Eugenio Garin, "Recenti interpretazioni di Marsilio Ficino," *Giornale critico della filosofia italiana*, II (1940), 299-318; and his *Giovanni Pico della Mirandola*, pp. 169-93; Paolo Rossi, "Considerazioni sul declino dell' Astrologia agli inizi dell' età moderna," *L'opera e il pensiero di Giovanni Pico della Mirandola*, Convegno internazionale sull' opera e il pensiero di Giovanni Pico della Mirandola nella storia dell' umanesimo Mirandola, September 15-18, 1963 (Florence, 1965), pp. 315-31.

[110] *Heptaplus*, ed. Garin, pp. 296-98.

astrology was that the heavenly bodies were only causes in a "universal" sense; that they generated motion and heat and light for the sustenance of life, but that the individual stars did not influence the lives and characters of individual men through the virtues and powers which judicial astrology attributed to them. Therefore, he reasoned, a knowledge of the positions and motions of the heavens could not possibly give men a knowledge of future contingent events.[111] Nor would Pico accept the compromise of those who would reconcile astrology with the Christian doctrine of Providence by arguing that the stars were God's agents for producing specific effects in the sublunar world. The ascription of only universal effects to the stars was far more consonant with the "honor" of God.[112] Pico deplored the habit of ascribing miraculous happenings or whatever passed human understanding to the action of the stars rather than to God and His angels.[113] Impious astrologers tried to subordinate religion as well as law to the action of the heavens, believing they could predict how long each religion would endure, and so reduce religion to the status of a natural phenomenon.[114] This, of course, was an attack upon Albumasar's doctrine that epic changes in the world's religions were forecast by the conjunction of Jupiter and Saturn. The belief was popular in Florence, as we have seen, and Giovanni Nesi, notwithstanding his admiration for Pico, was to use it in his *Oraculum*. For his part, Pico was never loath to criticize ideas which were dear to his friends on that account alone.

While Pico had planned the *Disputationes* before Savonarola's return to Florence, he had only begun to write it in 1493[115]—that is, when his friendship with the friar was in full bloom—and certain passages suggest that he had the Savonarolan enterprise in mind as he wrote. In attacking judicial astrology he seems to have been attempting to clear the way for a purely Biblical conception of prophecy. Against those who confused the false divining arts with prophecy by calling Moses an astrologer and trying to predict the

---

[111] *Disputationes*, ed. Garin, vol. I, pp. 174-80.

[112] "Quanto igitur causa universalis particularibus causis divinior et eminentior, tanto nos, sicuti verius, ita honorificentius de caelo sentimus quam astrologi." *Ibid.*, p. 194.

[113] *Ibid.*, pp. 126, 442.   [114] *Ibid.*, pp. 128, 542-48.

[115] *Ibid.*, p. 594.

coming of Antichrist by the stars he expressed his indignation.[116] All such attempts had failed in the past, he pointed out, and would continue to fail. The events announced by the Prophets were neither made nor foretold by the heavens; therefore, even if astrology were in other respects valid it would not be able to predict such things.[117] In this connection he raised the moral issue of prophecy: it was important to attribute human misfortune to God's punishment of the wicked and his testing of the good, rather than to the actions of the stars, which were morally neutral. In an obvious reference to Savonarola's prophecy he alluded to the *flagellum* which was "very close to our own times." This was not a human scourge but "the wrath of God and the devastation of the world."[118] To be sure, there was a place for wisdom in making conjectures about the future, since events were to some extent due to human choice; but only those who were truly filled with the spirit could foresee the future accurately.[119]

At the very moment when all Florence was turning to Savonarola as the man whose divine inspiration enabled him to foresee the future accurately, he was at Pico's deathbed. Giovanni Pico died on November 17, the day of Charles VIII's entry into Florence. Although he had resisted his own professed inclinations and Savonarola's urging to enter the Order,[120] his body was dressed in the habit of the Friars Preachers and buried in the convent church of San Marco, near his friend Poliziano who had preceded him by a few weeks in untimely death. In this way, Gianfrancesco Pico later reported the prophecy made by a certain nun in 1492, that Pico would become a Dominican at the time of the lilies (that is, the time of the entry of the army of the *fleur de lis*), was fulfilled.[121] Gianfrancesco Pico also reported that just before his uncle died he told his grieving friends how the Queen of Heaven had come to him in the night to refresh his feverish body and to comfort him with the assurance of salvation.[122] Savona-

---

[116] *Ibid.*, p. 614. [117] *Ibid.*, pp. 122-24.
[118] *Ibid.*, p. 446. [119] *Ibid.*, p. 454.
[120] On the contention of Fra Giovanni Sinibaldi that Pico deceived Savonarola on this score, see Ridolfi, *Vita*, vol. II, pp. 133, n. 11.
[121] Gianfrancesco Pico, *Ioannis Pici . . . Vita*, fol. *8 recto. This was Suor Lucia (Camilla Rucellai). Joseph Schnitzer, *Savonarola*, trans. Ernesto Rutili, 2 vols. (Milan, 1931), vol. I, p. 205.
[122] Gianfrancesco Pico, *Ioannis Pici . . . Vita*, fol. *7 recto.

rola too had a revelation about Pico's death, which he reported to his congregation on November 23: "I want to reveal a secret to you which I have not wanted to tell you before this because I was not as certain of it as I have been for the past ten hours. Each of you, I believe, knew Count Giovanni of Mirandola who lived in Florence and died a few days ago. I tell you that his soul, through the prayers of the *frati* and others and because of the good works which he performed in his lifetime, is in Purgatory. *Orate pro eo*: he was late in coming to religion in his lifetime, although it was hoped that he would, and therefore he is in Purgatory."[123]

WITH PICO GONE and Ficino retired into solitary contemplation at his villa in Careggi, the work of proclaiming the Savonarolan *renovatio* was left to their friends and disciples. In this work Girolamo Benivieni at last discovered his life's mission. His world-weariness, his depression, his grief over the death of Pico all fell away as he found himself again in the task of building the New Jerusalem. In his song for the Palm Sunday procession he exalted Florence as the City of God, the center of the New Age:

> Arise, O New Jerusalem and see
> your Queen and her beloved son.
> In you, City of God, who now sit and weep
>
> Such joy and splendor will yet be born
> as to decorate both you and all the world
> In those days of bliss
>
> You will see all the world come to you,
> devoted and faithful
> folk, drawn by the odor of your holy lily.[124]

While Benivieni was composing songs for Piagnoni celebrations he was also engaged in purging his earlier poems of those elements which he now considered to be "unfitting . . . for one who professed the laws of Christ." In the 1494 edition of his *Buccolica*, for example,

---

[123] *Prediche sopra Aggeo*, p. 104. A longer version, containing more praise for Pico, given by his nephew who says he was present at this sermon, is in his *Ioannis Pici . . . Vita*, fol. *7 recto.

[124] Girolamo Benivieni, *Commento sopra a piu sue canzoni*, fol. CXIII verso (incorrectly numbered CXII).

he omitted the reference to classical authority which is in the edition of 1481, while he replaced classical terms with Christian ones, such as "heaven" for "Jove, eternal God."[125] In later editions he provided each of his eclogues with a commentary demonstrating that the classical allusions were really spiritual allegories. For instance a description of two shepherds discussing a change of pastures became a demonstration of the superiority of celestial over sensual love.[126] In the *Canzone dell'amore celeste e divino*, for which Pico had written the offending commentary, Benivieni used numerous classical figures which later troubled him, as for example, the image of the heart filled with divine love appealing to Apollo.[127] Later, however, he declared that one ought not to invoke Apollo or the Muses or any other gentile figures, but only the Holy Spirit.

Benivieni's new literary puritanism might be dismissed as superficial display, designed to demonstrate his religious conversion; but it was more than that. In the commentary to his other songs we see that he was wrestling with the real problem of how to relate his mystical Neoplatonism to his new religious militancy. His solution was to conceive of the progress of the soul from a private love of God to love expressed in civic action. Benivieni divided his *Commento* into three parts, each corresponding to a state of the soul's travail in reaching God through love.[128] In the first part he interprets the poems to show how the soul (the lover) comes to know its Creator through sensible creatures.[129] In the second part the soul is unhappy because, having had a glimpse of the beatific vision through earthly creatures, it is now "ruined" by divine love.[130] At this stage the soul may suffer a decline because desiring to go directly to its

[125] In *Bucoliche elegantissimamente composte da Bernardo Pulci fiorentino et da Francesco De Arsochi senese et da Hieronymo Benivieni fiorentino et da Iacopo fiorino De Boninsegni senese* (Florence, Antonio Mischomini, 1494), sig. g fol. 1 verso. See Re, *Benivieni*, pp. 247-48. A comparison of the two editions reveals many other examples.

[126] *Opere*, fol. 80.

[127] "Dell' infiammato cor s'inclini Apollo," in Pico, *De hominis dignitate*, ed. E. Garin, p. 454 (Lucca, 1731), p. 2. The *Opere* cited for Pico's Commentary (n. 126 above) does not contain Benivieni's poem.

[128] *Commento . . . sopra a piu sue canzone et sonetti dello amore et della belleza divina*, fols. I-II verso.

[129] *Ibid.*, fol. III recto.   [130] *Ibid.*, fols. XLII verso–LXXIII verso.

lover it can do so only through intermediaries. In the third part, however, the soul achieves its union with the divine and is rewarded with the vision of God.[131] The songs Benivieni wrote for the public celebrations of the Piagnoni are in the third part of the work and his commentary relates them to the final revelation. In other words, the Savonarolan poems express the resolution of the soul's crisis. For Benivieni, then, the tension between mystic contemplation and social action is resolved in this third stage where the soul's striving to attain the object of its love is satisfied by the prophet's vision—the vision of Savonarola—and is directed to prepare for Christ's kingdom in Florence, the chosen city. It would seem, then, that the three sections of the *Commento* also correspond to the stages of Benivieni's own spiritual biography: his glimpse of the beatific vision in Neoplatonic philosophy, his spiritual crisis (or series of crises), and his resolution in converting to the cause of Savonarola and the Florentine millennium.

In his commentary on the third part, Benivieni expressed his belief in the superhuman nature of Savonarola's prophecy, taking over almost word-for-word the language of the friar's sermons and of his *Compendium Revelationum* (for which Benivieni wrote an introduction).[132] Savonarola's prophecy was the instrument of God's providence and the preface to the new age. The reform of morals in Florence, and especially the achievements resulting from Savonarola's organization of the youth as guardians of public morality, were the proof of this, for how else, other than by divine inspiration, could their great success in purifying Florence be explained?[133] The city, like the soul, must be prepared to receive Christ. Compassion (*pietà*) and justice, embracing each other, bring peace and happiness and prepare the way for the Virgin who will act as the city's guide in the union with Christ.[134] Christ has decided to be king and lord of Flor-

---

[131] *Ibid.*, fols. LXXII verso–CXLII verso.

[132] E.g., compare the passage of the *Compendium*, pp. 225-26, with that of the commentary in *Commento . . . sopra a piu sue canzone et sonetti dello amore et della belleza divina*, fol. CXI recto.

[133] *Commento . . . sopra a piu sue canzone et sonetti dello amore et della belleza divina*, fol. CXI verso.

[134] *Ibid.*, fols. CXVIII-CXVIV (incorrectly numbered CXVI, CXVII).

ence even for temporal affairs, and where Christ is king there can be no tyranny. Therefore, through this prophet, Christ warns whoever presumes to make himself tyrant of this city that he is usurping that which belongs to God.[135] Florence is a new city because God, having chosen it as His own, has rebuilt it with a new form of life and a new government.

These last remarks are part of the commentary Benivieni provided for the poem quoted earlier, "Arise, O New Jerusalem." All the peoples and all the nations, he continued, would conform to Florence's true religion—*a tuo culto e alla tua solo* [*sic*] *vera religione*—and there would be *unum ovile et unus pastor*.[136] From contemplation and the perfervid mystical vision, Benivieni passed directly into the enthusiasm of militant civic patriotism. In this millennial reign, he wrote, Florence would make good her recent losses of territory and extend her hegemony. But this would be a benevolent *imperium* since Florence was the city of the elect and of the true religion. Now Florence was derided and humiliated by the peoples of Italy, but the time would come when the odor of her sanctity would spread throughout the world and people would come to see her felicity and to share it by receiving her holy laws and the true mode of governing and living. Because Florentine rule would be moderate and just, her empire would become very powerful. Florence's neighbors had ungratefully rejected her protection, and therefore she must begin again to extend the leaves of her gentle lily. All who returned voluntarily to rest between the paws of the Florentine lion would be blessed with rewards both temporal and spiritual, but any who disdained her future glory would be cursed.[137] At the point in his *Commento* when Benivieni reached the climax of Florentine imperial glory, he seems to have realized that he had compromised the religious mysticism of the earlier poems, for he now posed the rhetorical question whether the promises made to Florence ought to be publicized or kept secret; and he resolved this difficulty by voicing the hope that wherever the songs went they might at least be received

---

[135] *Ibid.*, fol. CXVIII verso (incorrectly numbered CXVI).

[136] *Ibid.*, fol. CXIII recto (incorrectly numbered CXII).

[137] *Ibid.*, fols. CXIII recto (incorrectly numbered CXII)–CXIIII.

in faith, if not with the pure vision which God had vouchsafed to his new prophet.[138]

Despite his constant expectation of an early death, Benivieni lived to the age of ninety, dying in 1542. This means that he witnessed the fall of Savonarola, the restoration of the Medici in 1512, and the rise and fall of the last republic of 1527. He saw two Medici, both sons of his own former patrons, ascend the papal throne, and he witnessed the first stages of the Protestant rebellion and Catholic reform. Constantly torn between his preference for a life of contemplative quiet and his commitment to work for the cause of religious renewal, between his natural pessimism and his persistent belief that Savonarola's prophecy would be fulfilled, Benivieni was to play a modest role in some of those great events. But this phase of his life and work belongs to a later chapter, when we shall examine the Savonarolan legacy and its heirs in the era of reform which came only after the friar himself was gone.

AFTER GIOVANNI PICO della Mirandola died his friend the Carmelite poet Battista Spagnoli of Mantua wrote to Gianfrancesco Pico to predict that the nephew would follow in the footsteps of his illustrious uncle.[139] In some senses Gianfrancesco (only five years his uncle's junior) fulfilled the prediction, although he also struck out on paths of his own. In these pages he has already been mentioned as the biographer of both Pico and Savonarola, the two men whose lives made the greatest impression upon him, and as the friend to whom Giovanni Nesi addressed his *Oraculum*. He was also a close friend of Girolamo Benivieni and in his own right one of the most important apologists of the Piagnone movement. Even more important, he was the first serious exponent of philosophical scepticism since Antiquity,[140] and this was not unrelated to his great enthusiasm for Savonarola, as we shall see.

---

[138] *Ibid.*, fol. CXV recto.   [139] Pico, *Opera*, vol. II, p. 1296.

[140] In this respect he is just coming into his own as a subject of study. See Richard Popkin, *The History of Scepticism from Erasmus to Descartes* (New York, 1964), pp. 19-22; Charles B. Schmitt, *Gianfrancesco Pico della Mirandola and His Critique of Aristotle* (The Hague, 1967). Some important notices in Garin, *L'umanesimo italiano*, pp. 169-71. I briefly discussed Gianfrancesco's scepticism in my dissertation, "Prophecy and Humanism," pp. 249-54.

When Giovanni Pico opted for "a quiet and happy life of study in sacred theology and the liberal arts" he sold his property and title in Mirandola to Gianfrancesco at a price which the latter regarded as no more than a gift.[141] But the princely estate kept the nephew at home no more than it had the uncle; Gianfrancesco too had a thirst for learning and religion, and he was much in Florence during the Savonarola years. Hurrying to Florence at the news of his uncle's mortal illness, he remained to edit Giovanni Pico's works (including the *Disputationes*), to take part in the struggle on behalf of Savonarola, and to develop his own philosophy.[142] In his writings on Savonarola he expressed himself in the style of a hagiographer, giving currency to the stories about prophecies of Savonarola's coming,[143] to the miracle tales that sprang up after Savonarola's death,[144] and to the parallels between the life of the friar and the life of Christ.[145]

But Gianfrancesco's profounder tribute to the Dominican prophet is to be found in his philosophical works. He was much influenced by Savonarola's *Compendium Revelationum* with its insistence that prophecy was far above the level of human cognition, that it was an infusion of light which was sometimes accompanied by exterior visions, sometimes not. Savonarola had told him privately, he said, that his own prophecy originated in the divine mind and came to him either as "intelligible species," as "visions of the imagination," or as "perceptions which were hidden to the eyes of the body."[146] In his treatise *De studio divinae et humanae philosophiae* of 1496,

[141] Quoted in Garin, *Pico della Mirandola*, p. 41. For the terms of the sale, see Gianfrancesco, *Ioannis Pici . . . Vita*, fol. *6 recto.

[142] He arrived after his uncle's death, but in time to be present at Savonarola's sermon. *Loc. cit.*

[143] Gianfrancesco Pico della Mirandola, *Vita R. P. Hieronymi Savonarolae*, ed. Jacques Quetif, 2 vols. (Paris, 1674), vol. II, pp. 151-53; hereinafter referred to as *Vita Savonarolae*.

[144] To some of which he said that he was a witness. Gianfrancesco Pico della Mirandola, *De iniusta excommunicatione pro Hieronymi Savonarolae innocentia* (n.p. or d.), fol. 22; *Vita Savonarolae*, p. 212 and Chap. 25.

[145] *Ibid.*, Chap. 30.

[146] ". . . aut per species intelligibiles aut per visiones imaginarias aut per rerum sensatarum notas corporis oculis delatas." *Defensio Hieronymi Savonarole Ferrariensis Ordinis Predicatorum adversus Samuelem Cassinensem* (n.p., 1615), Chap. 3; copy in BNF Guicciardini 3-10-8. Compare the passage in Savonarola's *Compendium*, pp. 222-25, upon which he was obviously drawing.

Gianfrancesco tried to distinguish between philosophy and faith and between the usefulness of the former as contrasted with the indispensability of the latter.[147] *Scientia*, or philosophy, is good, he wrote, since, as Aristotle and many others have shown, it is concerned with knowledge of the highest truth or the highest good, but it begins in a consideration of individual material things and moves toward God step by human step. One cannot reach the highest stage of contemplation without divine help. Therefore, what is usually called metaphysics, or first philosophy, or divine philosophy, Gianfrancesco preferred to call human philosophy. Sacred philosophy, on the other hand, is the true wisdom; it starts in God and finishes in God; it is not achieved by human intelligence but by divine revelation.[148] While sacred philosophy is necessary to human life, human philosophy is not.[149] One can avail himself of sacred philosophy for the contemplation of God by reading the Bible, both Old and New Testaments, which were offered to mankind for his illumination.[150]

It appears that Gianfrancesco was pulling apart the two poles of philosophy and divine revelation which the Ficinian syncretists had tried to bring together in their Platonic theologies and their theosophical harmonies, and that in doing so he was at least to some extent influenced by Savonarola's teachings on the preeminence of Biblical authority and prophetic revelation. He did not shrink from disputing the authority of his own uncle, despite the respect and reverence in which he continued to hold him.[151] In his early work Gianfrancesco did not go so far as to deny the possibility of any human intellectual certainty, but only to separate the objects of human experience from the objects of faith. Nevertheless, in making this distinction he was denying the possibility of a theology in the

[147] *De studio divinae et humanae philosophiae*, in Pico, *Opera*, vol. II, pp. 1-39.

[148] *Ibid.*, pp. 5-6.   [149] *Ibid.*, pp. 7-9.

[150] *Ibid.*, pp. 38-39. Only with the gracious light of faith can the divine verities of Scripture be understood, he said in a later work, *On the Imagination*, trans. Harry Caplan, Cornell Studies in English, no. 16 (New Haven, 1930), p. 85.

[151] On his continuing admiration for his uncle while explicitly dissenting from his efforts to reconcile the ancient philosophers, see the notices gathered by Charles B. Schmitt, "Gianfrancesco Pico's Attitude toward His Uncle," *L'Opera e il pensiero di Giovanni Pico*, pp. 305-13.

scholastic sense, for if knowledge about God could be attained only through revelation then the Thomistic notion of a natural theology based on human reason and experience must be discarded as meaningless. These sceptical implications he carried still further in later works, particularly in his *Examen vanitatis doctrinae gentium*, completed in 1515, in which he was to become the first Renaissance thinker to make use of the writings of Sextus Empiricus.[152] Sextus Empiricus and the other Pyrronists, he wrote, were not useful for any contribution to Christian truth but for refuting the dogmas of the gentile philosophers, for in the resulting suspension of human judgment, faith comes into play.[153]

In this way, despite his divergence from the philosophical syncretism of his uncle, Gianfrancesco believed that he was continuing Pico's struggle against the pseudo-scientific enemies of the Church. His publication of Pico's *Disputationes* was a contribution to that fight;[154] but he also made an independent contribution in a work which shows that while taking his departure from Giovanni Pico he conceived of the whole question of truth in terms closer to those of Savonarola. This was his treatise *De rerum praenotatione* which he completed in 1502. Disputing the notion that future contingent events could be known through any human means, he emphasized that prophecy was a religious phenomenon, given to man in no circumstances except for his eternal felicity.[155] Among those thinkers whom he attacked in this regard were Avicenna, who thought man could "drink of the mysteries" and see the future; Maimonides, who taught a theory of prophecy that related it to poetic inspiration;[156]

---

[152] A work attributed to Sextus Empiricus, *Contra Arithmeticos et astrologos*, was in his uncle's library. See Pearl Kibre, *The Library of Pico della Mirandola* (New York, 1936), no. 1044. Pico's great collection of books remained with the brothers of San Marco until its sale to Cardinal Domenico Grimani in 1498. *Ibid.*, pp. 17-18.

[153] *Examen vanitatis doctrinae gentium*, in Pico, *Opera*, vol. II, pp. 851-53.

[154] The fight against astrology continues, he wrote after Pico's death. *Epistolarum*, in Pico, *Opera*, vol. II, p. 1285. On his resolve to continue the struggle against the enemies of the Church, see *ibid.*, p. 1286.

[155] *De rerum praenotatione*, Book II, chap. III, in Pico, *Opera*, vol. II, pp. 411-18.

[156] *Ibid.*, pp. 283-84. On Maimonides and the idea of poetic inspiration, see J. L. Teicher, "The Mediaeval Mind," *Journal of Jewish Studies*, VI (1955), 9-11.

and Moses of Narbonne, whose commentary on the Jewish *Book Baḳir* discussed the origins of prophecy through the possible intellect,[157] a proposal that Gianfrancesco called "silly and impossible." This was more than a theoretical attack upon remote enemies separated by centuries: at that very time there was in Florence a revival of interest in just those Arab thinkers who were particularly known for theories of the divining and magical arts.[158] Avicenna especially seems to have had a vogue, fostered by the lectures and writings of Andrea Cattani[159] and Antonio Benivieni, brother of Girolamo.[160] According to Gianfrancesco, Avicenna had asserted that one "could, by the purity of his spirit, bring about a union of his intelligence with God so that he could imbibe the mysteries, foresee the future, and by the action of his imagination dominate matter and make the very elements tremble."[161] Gianfrancesco was well aware that this was akin to the Hermetic notions of the *magus* and the seer so dear to the Ficinians; but in his own view imagination

[157] On Moses of Narbonne, a medieval Jewish commentator and translator of Arabic philosophical works, see Isaac Husik, *Judah Messer Leon's Commentary on the "Vetus Logica"* (Leyden, 1906), especially p. 23.

[158] Garin attributes the Florentine revival of interest in Avicenna to Ficino (*La cultura filosofica*, p. 115) and discusses this question in general (pp. 111-18). On the influence of Avicenna on the thought of Ficino, see Marjan Heitzman, "L'agostinismo avicennizante e il punto di partenza della filosofia di Marsilio Ficino," *Giornale critico della filosofia italiana*, 2nd ser., XVI (1935), 295-322, 460-80; XVII (1936), pp. 1-11. Garin, however, modifies this view considerably. For Savonarola's denial that prophecy is a natural virtue in the human intellect, see his sermon of 1496, *Prediche sopra Ezechiele*, ed. Roberto Ridolfi, 2 vols. (Rome, 1955), vol. I, pp. 275-77.

[159] Andrea Cattani, *Opus de intellectu et de causis mirabilium effectuum* (n.p. or d.). Garin says this was probably published in Florence around 1504. *Medioevo e Rinascimento*, p. 42. Tractatus III, "De praenuntiatione quae vigilanti continget atque de natura prophetae," is a lengthy discussion of prophecy which contains what seems to be a favorable reference to Savonarola: "potest ulterius talis homo orationibus et supplicationibus ac sacrificiis ex forti sua imaginatione super improborum urbes Dei flagellum convertere, ac efficere."

[160] See notices of him as well as of Andrea Cattani in Garin, *Medioevo e Rinascimento*, pp. 42-45. Antonio Benivieni was also mentioned by Savonarola in his trial statement as one who had the keys to San Marco in his capacity as a physician. Pasquale Villari, *La storia di Girolamo Savonarola e de' suoi tempi*, 2 vols. (Florence, 1926), vol. II, appendix, p. ccxxx. He also signed the letter to the Pope on Savonarola's behalf.

[161] Pico, *Opera*, vol. II, p. 418; also *On the Imagination*, p. 37.

was the lowest of the mental faculties.[162] He recognized three faculties of the mind: imagination or fantasy, which forms images from the sense impressions of the material world; reason, which investigates the likenesses of the sensible objects formed by the imagination; and intellect, which contemplates the intelligible things which are absolutely removed from even a likeness to matter. Intellect is highest, but is weak in man and belongs more truly to the angelic order. Reason is truly human, but it is often subject to fantasy which, dependent upon the senses, is the lowest part of the mind. Intellect chooses among the objects dealt with by reason and can, although with difficulty, contemplate sublime things. The surer guide, however, is faith, without which the intellect is not strong enough to have its own vision. Prophecy, which appears to the fantasy in the form of visions, is a pouring into the intellect by God, a divine engraving of the signs of the future. It is entirely distinct from "imaginative vision," the very misleading and dangerous creations of fantasy, which have nothing to do with divinely inspired prophecy.

It seems ironic that not long before this Giovanni Nesi had addressed his *Oraculum* to Gianfrancesco, clothing his arguments in the Hermetic terms which Gianfrancesco found so objectionable. Was Nesi ignorant of Gianfrancesco's views, or had Gianfrancesco not yet expressed them? Either is possible, but neither is likely. In 1496 Nesi was working on his *Oraculum* and Gianfrancesco on *De studio divinae et humanae philosophiae*, the first of his attacks on a too-confident human philosophy. It is difficult to believe that the two friends did not exchange views or that neither knew what the other was up to. Besides, the divergence of views went back earlier, to the disagreements between Marsilio Ficino and Giovanni Pico. As the exponent of what might be called "the Hermetic view" of Savonarola's prophetic mission, Nesi was still the disciple of Ficino, while, as the champion of what might be called "the Biblical-Prophetic view," Gianfrancesco was the disciple of Giovanni Pico. Neither position was quite so clear-cut, of course; Nesi felt he was drawing upon Pico's ideas as well as on Ficino's; Gianfrancesco consciously dissociated himself from some of Giovanni Pico's positions while at the same time carrying on his uncle's campaign against the super-

---

[162] *On the Imagination*, pp. 55-57.

stitious pseudo-sciences. Both Giovanni Nesi and Gianfrancesco Pico, despite widely divergent views on such fundamental questions as the relation between human reason and faith, the existence of an esoteric wisdom within the reach of man, and the nature of the coming new era, were ardent Savonarolans, united by their faith in the friar, their own common desire for religious *renovatio*, and their belief that the new age was at hand. The Savonarola movement provided a forum for discussion, a testing ground, so to speak, for the philosophical and religious ideas of the great teachers of the Laurentian circle. Gianfrancesco's religious scepticism is less well-known than the Neo-platonic mysticism of Girolamo Benivieni or the Hermeticism represented here by Nesi; but it was to have an important career in the coming age of Reformation. As a leader of the enlightened reaction against the contamination of Christian thought by ancient and Arabic philosophy, Gianfrancesco was inspired by Savonarola, as well as by his uncle, to a rededication to the Jewish-Christian God and the religion of Biblical revelation.[163]

---

[163] For a judicious estimate of the influence of Gianfrancesco's ideas in the Papal Bull "Apostolici Regiminis" of 1513, see Felix Gilbert, "Cristianesimo, Umanesimo, e la bolla, 'Apostolici Regiminis' del 1513," *Rivista storica italiana* LXXIX (1967), 979-83.

1. Botticelli, *Mystic Nativity*. Reproduced by courtesy of the Trustees, the
National Gallery, London.

2. Botticelli, *Magdalene at the Foot of the Cross*. Reproduced by courtesy of the Fogg Art Museum, Harvard University.

3. Ghiberti, Baptistery, Florence. East doors, David and Goliath panel, detail. Photograph by courtesy of Dr. Saul Levine.

4. Medallion. Obverse: Savonarola; reverse: Florence under God's scourge.
Reproduced by courtesy of Fratelli Alinari.

VII

Savonarola: For and Against

BUT NOW I AM COMPELLED TO WRITE ABOUT MY PUBLIC PROPHECIES,
ESPECIALLY THE MORE IMPORTANT ONES, BECAUSE MANY WHO HAVE
HEARD THEM FROM ME IN THE PULPIT HAVE TRIED TO DESCRIBE
THEM, BUT BEING INEXPERT WRITERS IN LATIN THEY
HAVE BUTCHERED THE TRUTH OR CONTAMINATED IT
WITH MANY ERRORS; OTHERS HAVE USED THE
VERNACULAR TO DISSEMINATE MY WORDS,
BUT, WHETHER OUT OF STUPIDITY OR
INTENTIONAL MISINTERPRETATION OR
MALIGNITY THEY HAVE MADE
ADDITIONS, SUBTRACTIONS,
AND DISTORTIONS.

—Savonarola, *Compendium Revelationum*

I

TO the kind of polemics referred to in the above passage from Savonarola's *Compendium*, few of the issues discussed in the last chapter were directly relevant. Benivieni's mystical commentaries, Gianfrancesco's religious scepticism, and Nesi's Hermeticism touched on, but did not speak directly to, the issues of belief and commitment and political allegiance as most Florentines would have understood them. For the most part, with the exception of some of Benivieni's songs, the Laurentians addressed themselves to members of their own circle of philosophers and *literati*, while the more immediate, practical questions were these: Was Savonarola a true prophet or a charlatan and a heretic? Was he a bringer of peace and love or a demagogue and a rebel against the Church? Was he the champion of Florentine liberty or its subverter? How could one arrive at sound answers to

227

such questions, and how could one believe in Savonarola and yet remain a faithful son of the Church?

Most of these questions were raised publicly by those who disapproved or doubted Savonarola's claims of divine prophecy, or by those who opposed his political influence in Florence. Even before the events of 1494, some of these questions had been asked by Fra Mariano da Genazzano, the favorite preacher of the Laurentians. They were also asked by Fra Domenico da Ponzo, onetime admirer of Fra Girolamo, who returned to Florence after the overthrow of the Medici as an agent of Lodovico *il Moro*.[1] They were asked, answered, and asked again throughout the brief term of Savonarola's ascendancy, and, indeed, well into the next century.[2] Savonarola's contemporary opponents have, for the most part, been harshly treated by his modern biographers, who are inclined to impugn their motives as well as to belittle the quality of their arguments.[3] Most of the anti-Savonarolan writings do, in fact, contain some wild charges which are difficult to accept as the considered opinions of intelligent men of good faith. For example, Giovanni Francesco Poggio Bracciolini, son of the famous humanist, a canon of the Florentine Cathedral chapter and a student of canon law, pounced upon Savonarola as soon as he was imprisoned on April 8, accusing him of causing the death of Carlo Strozzi, after promising to cure him of an illness, and darkly hinting at his complicity in the deaths of others.

---

[1] In addition to the evidence of letters from Lodovico Sforza to Fra Domenico and to Lodovico's ambassador in Florence, dated January 24 and 29, 1495, respectively (cited in Joseph Schnitzer, *Savonarola*, trans. Ernesto Rutili, 2 vols. [Milan, 1931], vol. 1, p. 260, n. 18), there is a letter from Fra Domenico himself to Lodovico, dated January 17, in Florence. In it Fra Domenico says he is at the orders of the Duke. This letter, which is apparently a holograph, is in the Pierpont Morgan Library, New York City, and seems to have hitherto gone unnoticed by historians.

[2] See below, pp. 360-61.

[3] Anti-Savonarolan literature has received relatively little attention. The starting point is Joseph Schnitzer's "Die Flugschriftenliteratur für und wider Girolamo Savonarola," *Festgabe Karl Theodor von Heigel* (Munich, 1903), most of which he incorporated in his biography of Savonarola. The short work by Cassandra Calogero, *Gli avversari religiosi di Girolamo Savonarola* (Rome, 1935), is useful but highly unsympathetic to the anti-Savonarolans, as are the many notices in Roberto Ridolfi, *The Life of Girolamo Savonarola*, trans. Cecil Grayson (New York, 1959).

To Bracciolini, Savonarola was "another Antichrist," insanely given over to the power of Satan.[4] While we would regard such charges as vicious and absurd, the ascription to Savonarola of demonic powers was, after all, analogous to his own and his friends' belief in his angelic powers. To Savonarola's own declarations that he had had "secret intelligences" and visions of the Virgin, the obvious reply of sceptics was not—as it would be today—to deny that such things were possible, but to charge that his visions were from the Devil. To Giovanni Nesi's characterization of Savonarola as a moon-based seer who used the science of the Kabbalah to bring about the reform of Christianity, Bracciolini could well reply that Savonarola used the Kabbalistic art to subvert the Church.[5] For us to accuse the anti-Savonarolans as a group of malice would only compound one partisanship with another. The controversy surrounding Savonarola was passionate; few on either side were scrupulous in their choice of weapons, but these were always the weapons of the age, an age

[4] Giovanni Francesco Bracciolini, *Contra fratrem Hieronymum Heresiarcham libellus et processus* (Nuremberg: Ambrosius Huber, n.d.); Hain no. 14478 sig. a fol. 1 verso. Another work by Bracciolini, which I have not been able to see, is *Refutatorium errorum Fratris Hieronymi Savonarolae* (Leipzig: Thanner, 1498); Copinger no. 13722; Reichling, fasc. III, p. 165. In 1500 Bracciolini was exiled for five years from Florence on charges that he had favored, and claimed that God favored, the cause of the Pisans, and that he had insulted the King of France by saying that the King could only harm, not help, the city. According to Parenti the charges were brought by Frateschi out of revenge for Bracciolini's part in Savonarola's destruction. Piero Parenti, *Storia Fiorentina*, ed. Joseph Schnitzer, in *Savonarola nach der Aufzeichnungen des Florentiners Piero Parenti, Quellen und Forschungen zur Geschichte Savonarolas*, vol. IV (Leipzig, 1910), pp. 294-95. For another attack upon Savonarola as Antichrist, see *Epistola di Frate Leonardo da Fivizano dell'ordine di Sancto Augustino a tutti e veri amici di Iesus Cristo Crocifixo*, ed. Achille Neri, *Il Propugnatore*, vol. XII, part II (1879), pp. 230-40. Fra Leonardo was an Augustinian of Santo Spirito in Florence. See A. Neri, "Un avversario di G. Savonarola," *Archivio storico italiano*, 4th ser., V (1880), 478-82; also Massimo Petrocchi, *Una "Devotio Moderna" nel Quattrocento italiano?* (Florence, 1961), pp. 37-38, 54-64. His *Epistola* is dated May 12, 1497, and is a reply to Savonarola's "A tutti gli eletti di Dio e fedeli Cristiani" of May 8, *Le lettere de Girolamo Savonarola*, ed. Roberto Ridolfi (Florence, 1933), pp. 122-28.

[5] "Hec est illa tua scientia Cabalica quam iam pridem edoctus paraveras cum plerisque complicibus novam sectam inducere ecclesiam subvertere." *Contra fratrem Hieronymum*, sig. a 5 verso.

in which demons were real and the birth of a new Antichrist was a frequent event.

In addition to the belief that Savonarola was demonic, certain other charges were common in the anti-Savonarolan tracts. One was that Savonarola plotted the establishment of a new religious sect. To some Fra Girolamo was another Mahomet, who "with the tail of a scorpion smote the flock of Christ with dreams and visions, seducing the crowd to [believe in] a new sect so that he might be called the originator of great deeds."[6] Francesco Altoviti, who had lived in exile as an enemy of the Medici[7] but was equally hostile to the new republic, wrote that the Ark to which Savonarola had summoned the Florentines was a schismatic heresy which aimed to subject the world to new religious laws of poverty and simplicity.[8] Giuliano de' Gondi, in a *pratica* of March 14, 1498, expressed his fear that Savonarola had founded "a new sect of Fraticelli like the one that formerly existed in this city" and aspired to make himself its Angelic Pope.[9] Raffaello da Volterra charged, after Savonarola's fall, that "he used to say that everyone ought to abandon and not even go near the City of Rome which all Christians venerate and which is the very source of religion (*ac religionis causa*). And with such arguments and promptings he would have founded a new heretical sect, if divine providence had not intervened."[10] The kernel of truth in these charges was contained in Savonarola's repeated predictions that Rome would be punished, perhaps abandoned in favor of a new cen-

[6] [Anon.], *Epistola responsiva a frate Hieronymo dellordine de frati predicatori delamico suo* (n.p. or d.). On dating (after July 13, 1495) and errors in cataloging, see Roberto Ridolfi, *Vita di Girolamo Savonarola*, 2 vols. (Rome, 1952), vol. II, p. 159, n. 18.

[7] While Altoviti claims to have been an enemy of the Medicean tyranny, there was a Francesco Altoviti whom Cardinal Giovanni de' Medici recommended to his brother Piero as "a friend of the family." See the résumé of Giovanni's letter in G. B. Picotti, *La giovinezza di Leone X* (Milan, 1927), p. 644.

[8] Francesco Altoviti, *Defensione contra alla Archa di Fra Girolamo* (n.p. or d.), sig. a fols. 2 recto–3 verso. Probably written in the spring of 1497 and published in Florence by Francesco di Dino; *GW* no. 1588 (but the biographical information therein is erroneous).

[9] C. Lupi, ed. "Nuovi documenti intorno a Fra Girolamo Savonarola," *Archivio storico italiano*, 3rd ser., II, part I (1866), p. 44.

[10] MS BNF Magl. VIII 1443, fol. 148 recto.

ter, a new Jerusalem, and in his exaltation of Florence as the center of a Christianity renewed and triumphant. These were dangerous prophecies, as Savonarola was well aware, and they grew more dangerous in the retelling.

Just as in the tense days of the struggle with another Pope a century earlier, when the air had been filled with the prophecies of the original Fraticelli, some Florentines turned for advice to a holy man of Vallombrosa.[11] Sometime early in 1496 a delegation from Florence visited Angelo Fondi, a hermit of Vallombrosa called Angelo the Anchorite, to ask his opinion concerning the prophecies of the new "*fraticello* in Florence who claims that he has been in Paradise and that the Church will be reformed." Angelo gave his answer in a letter to the Signoria and people that May.[12] He could not believe, he told them, that Savonarola, a man learned in Scripture, had really declared that Jerusalem would replace Rome. This was part of the false Jewish messianic belief and he himself rejected it. As to whether Savonarola had really been in Paradise, and whether he was really a prophet, Angelo believed that both were possible and had good precedents; but this would only be known by watching Savonarola's life and works. He himself, he continued, made no claims to the gift of prophecy, nor had he been in Paradise; he was earth-bound and a sinner; he interpreted Scripture with the light of the intellect, not through visions: nevertheless, he agreed with the friar that "the empire of Constantinople" would soon be recovered, that the churches of the East and West would be reunited and the Church reformed. Charles VIII, of the race of the Carolingians and the Kings of France, was God's appointed instrument for this task, and he would be the last Emperor. As for the Florentines, Angelo said, they were almost alone among the people of Italy in recognizing and preserving the truth, and therefore God had given to them more light and wisdom than He had given to anyone else, for He does not impart His revelations to all nations.

[11] See above, pp. 44-46.

[12] *Frate Angelo peccatore Anachorita del heremo di Vallombrosa exhorta li Magnifici S. et Po. Fiorentino che reiecte le passioni et ogni dubio perseverino nellamicitia del principe di dio Carlo Re di francia* (n.p. or d.); *GW* nos. 1908, 1909. The letter itself is dated "xv kl. Iunias" (May 18) 1496.

Clearly, although he maintained a careful orthodoxy with respect to the Church of Rome, Angelo subscribed to some version of the Second Charlemagne and Last Emperor prophecies and was strongly attracted to the notion that Florence had been elected for a special role in the coming renovation.[13] Even before his reply to the Florentines he had urged them together with the Venetians to support the New Charlemagne, "the Prince of God" who fulfilled the prophecies of the Apocalypse and of Isaiah, and he celebrated the Florentines' "coming felicity and glory."[14] But toward Savonarola himself Angelo rapidly soured. The main reason for his hostility was Savonarola's anti-Romanism. Apparently Angelo soon came to believe what he had earlier dismissed as rumor—that Savonarola prophesied the actual substitution of Jerusalem for Rome and the transference of the Church's capital to the Holy Land. This he connected to what he regarded as Savonarola's damnable notion that the Church should give up its worldly goods, and he charged that such ideas derived from the false prophecies of Joachim of Flora and Saint Bridget of Sweden. Rome, he countered, is the world city; the Pope is the leader of Christendom and occupies a holy office. He who offends the Pope offends Christ. In refusing to submit to examination Savonarola was like Mahomet who preferred to spread his doctrine by means of the sword.[15] He was wrong even in calling Florence the center of Italy.[16]

[13] Although he expressly disavowed the prophecies of Joachim of Flora and the Joachites. According to Schnitzer, *Savonarola*, vol. I, p. 359, the belief that Charles VIII was the instrument of God for world reform was strong among the Vallombrosans. This was maintained by Fra Giorgio Benigno, see below, p. 243.

[14] *Angelo Peccatore Anachorita di Valembrosa, desidera che li Magnifici Signori et Populo florentino conservino inviolata unione et perpetuo amicitia con lo principe di Dio Carolo Re di Francia* (n.p. or d.); and *Angelo peccatore anachorita dello heremo di Valle umbrosa desidera che el serenissimo principe et magnifico dominio Veneto non si opponga alla incommutabile dispositione divina* (n.p. or d.); *GW* nos. 1907, 1910-12. Both letters are dated "kl. Ianuarii" (January 1) 1496. That they are correctly dated 1496, rather than 1497 as in *GW*, is established by Ridolfi, *Vita*, vol. II, p. 161, n. 28.

[15] *Epistola dell' heremita de Valle Ombrosa dello stato della chiesa et reformatione di Roma contro a moderni inscripta a Roma nel mccccIxxxxvi. In essa si pruova, che fra Girolamo non puo esser propheta et narrasi molti suoi errori* (n.p. or d.); *GW* no. 1916. Letter dated "Idibus Octobris" (October 15) 1496.

[16] All the ancient cosmographers and historians, he wrote, placed "el mezo

In the measure that Angelo's attacks failed to affect Savonarola's position in Florence they mounted in fury, although they changed little in substance. After Savonarola was excommunicated in the spring of 1497, Angelo wrote again, this time to the friars of San Marco who had left Florence temporarily in order to escape the plague then raging in the city. He exhorted the friars to abandon this false prophet, enemy of the clergy, of the Roman faith, and of the Church.[17] When they refused, he castigated them for their blindness.[18] A letter in which Angelo tried to persuade the canons of the Florentine cathedral to bar Savonarola from preaching there was equally unavailing,[19] and after this the hermit of Vallombrosa seems to have given up the fight.

Other critics rejected Savonarola's apocalyptic eschatology altogether. The unknown author of the *Epistola responsiva*,[20] for one, denied that Savonarola's references to the *novissimi giorni* in Scripture signified the consummation of time. It was "Jewish blindness" which misinterpreted Isaiah's prophecy—"And in the last days the mountain of the house of the Lord shall be prepared on the top of mountains, and it shall be exalted above the hills, and all nations shall flow into it" (Isaiah 2:2)—since, he said, Isaiah was not referring to the end of the world but to the last days of the Prophets,

---

unbilico et centro di Italia" at "ellacho velino" which is now called "de peluco" and is in "agro interanensi in confinibus sabinorum. . . ." *Ibid.*, p. 11 (unnumbered). Angelo may have misread Pliny the Elder who, after describing the old Sabine territory near the lakes of Velinus (of which one is the modern Piediluco), passes on to the district of Rieti in which are located the lakes of Cutiliae, "said by Marcus Varro to be the umbilicus of Italy." *Natural History* 3. 109. See also A. F. von Pauly, G. Wissowa, et al., *Real-encyclopadie der classichen Altertumswissenschaft*, s.v. "Aquae Cutiliae." I owe this reference to Professors John and Lydia Lenaghan.

[17] *Epistola del Romito di Vallembrosa a frati usciti di Sancto Marcho confortatoria alle persechutione dello excommunicato frate Hyeronimo tanto che si converta* (n.p. or d.); *GW* nos. 1913, 1914. Letter dated July 11, 1497. For the friar's reply, see *GW* no. 1919.

[18] *Risposta duna lettera feciono efrati di Sancto Marco a Romito di Valenbrosa alla risposta de frati di San Marco* (n.p. or d.). Letter dated July 31, 1497. *GW* no. 1918.

[19] In E. Sanesi, *Vicari e canonici fiorentini e il 'caso Savonarola'* (Florence, 1932), pp. 84-90.

[20] See above, n. 6.

when the prophecy whose consummation was Christ was to be fulfilled. Savonarola's was an old error, he claimed; men even more truly inspired than he had been similarly deluded. In the early Church many "saints and apostolic men" had believed that the day of Christ's advent and the end of the world were at hand, as had many of the holiest doctors and learned men of later times. More recently, from the time of Saint Bernardino on, the fable was maintained that the Turks were about to be converted to Christianity and the government of the Church reformed by Christ.[21] This, the *Epistola responsiva* continues, was the common opinion of men who had been preaching the Word of God in Italy these many years.

The most detailed attack upon Savonarolan prophecy was the work of a fellow Dominican, Giovanni Caroli of the Convent of Santa Maria Novella in Florence. Name-calling, ridicule, character defamation and distortion—Giovanni Caroli shrank from none of these; nevertheless his polemic stems from an anti-millenarian and anti-Hermetic position which deserves attention. He was born in the same year as Savonarola, 1452, and was a man of some learning. A bibliophile steeped in both classical and sacred letters, he had been a disciple of both Antoninus, the saintly former Prior of San Marco and Archbishop of Florence, and of Cristoforo Landino, the Florentine Platonic philosopher.[22] The occasion of Caroli's attack was the appearance of Giovanni Nesi's *Oraculum de novo saeculo*, which

[21] On the interest of Saint Bernardino da Siena (I take it this is who is meant) in apocalyptic ideas and his dependence upon Matthew of Sweden's *Expositio super Apocalypsim* which Bernardino copied from a MS in the Brigittine convent of the "Paradiso" in Florence, see D. Pacetti, "L'Expositio super Apocalypsim' di Mattia di Svezia (c. 1281-1350) precipua fonte dottrinale di S. Bernardino da Siena," *Archivum Francescanum Historicum*, 54 (1961), 273-302.

[22] Biographical and bibliographical references to Caroli are to be found in J. Mabillon and M. Germain, *Museum italicum*, 2 vols. (Paris, 1687-89), vol. I, part I, p. 161; Jacques Quetif and J. Echard, *Scriptores Ordinis Praedicatorum*, 2 vols. (Paris, 1719-21), vol. I, pp. 898-900; Angelo Maria Bandini, *Specimen literaturae Florentinae Saeculi XV*, 2 vols. (Florence, 1747-51), vol. I, pp. 189-98; S. Orlandi, *La biblioteca di S. Maria Novella in Firenze dal* sec. XIV al sec. XIX (Florence, 1952), pp. 17-18 et passim. The only discussions I have found of the writings of Caroli are by Professor Garin. See *La cultura filosofica del Rinascimento italiano* (Florence, 1961), pp. 224-25; and "Il centenario del Savonarola," *Giornale critico della filosofia italiana*, 32 (1953), 413-16.

epitomized everything that Caroli despised in the Savonarolan enterprise, and he made the *Oraculum* his prime target.[23]

Caroli's strategy was to rush his enemy's defenses. By what means did Nesi or his prophetic bird, the *picus*, or his "Ferrarese Socrates" prove their "oracular" knowledge? By which authorities? By what good results? What did Nesi, a layman, know of Sacred Scripture, its teaching about prophets and prophecies? If even the pagan Cicero had not presumed to call his man-made dream (*Somnium Scipionis*) an oracle of the gods, how did Nesi, a Christian, pretend that his dream was something more than poetic fiction? The idea of a *reformatio* of the Church implies that it suffers from a *deformatio*, a corruption of form; but since the form of the Church is a work of divine grace, what mere man could pretend to prescribe what the perfection of form might be? Surely not Nesi, a mere layman, ignorant of sacred literature. Surely not Pico della Mirandola, that man so well known for his holy doctrine and pious private life![24] Surely not that demagogue from the swamps of Ferrara who could hardly be said to possess the simplicity and humility which God has always required of His prophets! That a renovation would some day come about Caroli did not deny; but that men should presume to say when it was coming, and indeed to claim that it was coming in the present lifetime, was impious presumption, an offense against God who alone knows the future. In this connection Caroli quoted Saint Paul (somewhat out of context): "Sensual man does not perceive these things which are of the spirit of God; for it is foolishness to him, and he cannot understand what may only be examined spiritually" (I Corinthians 2:14). While Caroli did not dispute the idea of a *renovatio*, he specifically denied Nesi's and Savonarola's millenarian interpretation of it. *Renovatio* must be distinguished from the idea of a *novo saeculo*. Scriptures, he maintained, neither predict nor

---

[23] Caroli's invective is found in manuscript together with his *De comparatione aliarum aetutum ad senectutem* (1498), MS BNF Conventi soppressi C.8.277, fols. 157 recto–193 verso. All the following references are based on this.

[24] No doubt a jibe directed at Pico's escapades of 1486 and perhaps also at the rumor that Pico had kept a concubine to the last, despite his inclination toward the religious life. On the latter point see Ridolfi, *Vita*, vol. II, p. 133, n. 11.

imply such a new era; after every *flagellum* in history the same world, the same people, the same religion remain. The final change (*novissima mutatio*) is entirely unknown to the world and remains hidden in the judgment and the will of God. We may indeed believe that some day the world will come to an end, but the renovation of the Church and the conversion of the infidel are not matters for men to predict. Therefore everything "the Socrates of Ferrara" says in his *Compendium of Revelations* about his visions, about great changes to come, about angels conversing with men, and all the rest, is vain dreaming and fantasy. Again, as to Savonarola's prediction that these things will come about *cito et velociter*, in our own day, this is entirely against our faith and contrary to the Gospel truth. No one ought to pretend to know what God wishes to be kept secret. The *cito* of the Apocalypse (Revelation 11:14, 22:12, 20) is beyond man's understanding, since that which to God is close at hand, to us is of the utmost remoteness. Therefore, Caroli concludes, no man can know when the Mahometans will be converted or when the world will be reduced to a single faith and a single sheepfold. All such oracles are fantastic.

Caroli heaped particular ridicule upon Nesi's efforts to impute to his "rabble-rouser" esoteric wisdom, a knowledge of deep mysteries, astral science, Pythagorean aphorisms, and oracular visions. All of these came in for a share of his scorn. Such wonderful science! How surprising that neither the [Florentine?] Academy, nor the schools of Padua nor those of Bologna have invited him to teach them what he alone knows! We must not believe in dreams, for they remain but dreams. We must not believe that anyone can reveal what the angels in heaven do not know. Nesi's six eagles of philosophy which mix truths with falsities the better to be believed, ought to be avoided just as much as if they were totally false. We ought not seek to know more than is fitting; as the Apostle says, it is enough to be wise unto sobriety (Romans 12:3). Let us leave to divine Providence those superfluous things which are in abundance so that we may not lack what is essential.

Apparently, Caroli's opposition to the Savonarolans also stemmed in part from his political loyalties. He looked back upon the Medicean years as sixty years of felicity for the city, while he regarded this new "government of frati" and of a foreigner at that, as the real tyranny. His criticism of Savonarolan politics derived from a notion of a right order of society in which the possibilities of liberty are decidedly limited. All that talk of Nesi's about being purged in a flowering meadow and a flowing stream and putting on the cap of liberty—what was it but demagoguery and an invitation to license, he scoffed. As the Apostle said, "All things are lawful but not all things are expedient; all things are lawful, but I will not be brought under the power of any of them" (I Corinthians 6:12). According to Caroli, moreover, Savonarola's program for Florence was of a piece with his religious millenarianism, equally false, equally heterodox. The Plato of Nesi's description and Nesi's representation of the Platonic ideas are fictions: Plato dealt with things incorruptible and immortal, with universals, which are everywhere and eternal, not with corruptible things like the politics of real cities. As for the model of the supernal Jerusalem, how closely this fictitious city of the Savonarolans resembles *that*; let the effect speak for itself! Besides, he asked, whoever heard of anyone being sent as a prophet to a particular city or people, to tell them what he has heard from the divine mouth? Whoever heard of anyone being delegated by God as an advocate (*patronus*) for a particular city? Indeed there is a way to reform a city; this is to begin by reforming the lives of the members of a single household, to lay a foundation which will provide a good example and thus spread its influence throughout the city.

Plainly Caroli did not direct his polemic at Savonarola's eschatology alone, but also at the Ficinians' notion of an esoteric wisdom, as well as at their religious syncretism and their efforts to identify Savonarola's apocalyptic millennium with their own dreams of a coming golden age. The bitterness of his hostility to occultism may be partly explained as that of a reformed sinner, for, as he admitted, he himself had once been interested in oracular dreams.[25] Now, however, his chief authority was Scripture, particularly the writings of Saint Paul; of scholastic theology there is even less in Caroli than in Savonarola. Paradoxically, the contemporary writer with whom

[25] Garin, *La cultura filosofica*, p. 225, n. 1; also Caroli's *Liber dierum lucensium* [1461], Book III: "Continet autem praesentum temporum conditionem ad modum Sompni Scipiones," MS BNF Conventi soppressi C.8.279, fol. 42 verso.

Caroli might have had the strongest affinity in other circumstances was Gianfrancesco Pico, to whom Nesi's *Oraculum* was addressed. Gianfrancesco too had attacked the vanity of human learning and the pretensions of man-made oracles in the name of a divinely revealed Biblical wisdom. But where the younger Pico saw in Savonarola the restorer of Gospel faith, Caroli, the Dominican, Medicean sympathizer, and Florentine patriot, saw only the arrogant demagogue mouthing vain and blasphemous millennialist hopes.

Playing upon Florentine chauvinism by complaining that it was shameful to be ruled by a foreigner was a common theme in the anti-Savonarolan tracts. Civic pride, as we have already seen, was an emotion deeply felt among Florentines of every class. Since a foreigner was anyone who came from outside Florentine territory it is not surprising that there were objections to Savonarola as a *forestiero*; but in his case such objections were compounded by his clerical status and his claim to special divine illumination. However inaccurate the taunt that Florence was now governed by friars, it was repeatedly hurled against the Piagnoni, even by other friars. Priests and friars, like women, had their place in the scheme of things, but that place was not in the councils and counsels of state, however many precedents Savonarola might muster. Why, asked Francesco Altoviti, did the Florentines have to find a leader from outside the city? If they needed a religious there were plenty of worthy Florentines who could have served.[26] Giovanni Caroli raised the same question and, indeed, offered a list of eligible alternates, both laymen and religious, from good families and good Florentines all.[27]

The basis of these objections seems to have been the fear that to follow the leadership of a foreigner, not to speak of a rootless friar, was to jeopardize the city's well-being. This was not merely because a foreigner might not have Florence's good at heart, there was the further worry that someone who was not a true Florentine would not be eligible to perform the city's spiritual obligations and thus to insure Florence the continued protection of her patron saints and of divine Providence itself. *La chiesa fiorentina*, words frequently on Savonarola's tongue, were no chance phrase. In celebrating the city as the

---

[26] Altoviti, *Defensione* sig. a fols. 2 verso–3 recto.
[27] Caroli, MS BNF Conventi soppressi C.8.277, fol. 172.

Lord's chosen, the friar had penetrated to the religious core of Florentine civic patriotism, but, ironically, not everyone was ready to accept Savonarola's own credentials for membership in the holy community.[28] Francesco Altoviti charged that Savonarola had suspended the old civic ceremonies and festivals, such as the celebration of the feast of Saint John the Baptist, the city's patron, against the divine will, and that one immediate material result of this was that the city was on the verge of economic disaster, since the civic festivals had provided employment to many workers.[29] In this connection, the obvious counter to Savonarola's claim of prophetic illumination was the argument that he had brought discord and other misfortunes upon the city and therefore whatever special powers he may have had came not from God but from the devil. This was the contention of Marsilio Ficino, as we have seen, and of the humanist poet Ugolino Verino, once an ardent Piagnone, who also publicly turned against Savonarola in 1498.[30] The creation of civic discord was one of the signs of Antichrist, and Fra Leonardo da Fivizzano, the Augustinian preacher in Santo Spirito, believed that Antichrist was alive in the friar of San Marco, who, by promoting civil discord among the Florentine citizens, revealed his secret hatred of their city.[31]

II

I believed and I believe, because his preaching
made Florence a paradise on earth.
                —Bartolomeo Redditi, *Breve compendio*

[28] For some interesting insights into the religious aspects of citizenship in fourteenth-century Italy which would undoubtedly also apply to the period under discussion here see Peter Riesenberg, "Civism and Roman Law in Fourteenth-Century Italian Society," *Explorations in Economic History* VII (1969), 237-54.

[29] Altoviti, *Defensione* (sig. a fols. 4 verso–5 recto). Savonarola had used his influence to bring about the suspension of the Palio, the horse race normally held on the day of Saint John the Baptist, June 24, and he had substituted pious processions in place of the traditional pre-Lenten carnival celebrations.

[30] Alessandro Gherardi has published some of Verino's writings relating to Savonarola in his *Nuovi documenti e studi intorno a Girolamo Savonarola*, 2nd edn. (Florence, 1887), pp. 290-308.

[31] *Epistola di Frate Leonardo da Fivizano*, pp. 235-58. See also above, n. 4.

never was there so much unity or such loving citizens,
each tasting the sweetness of liberty.

—Alessandro Braccesi to Pope Alexander VI

Against the doubting Thomases who questioned Savonarola's
authenticity as a prophet and the Cassandras who wrung their hands
over the new dangers threatening the city, the Piagnoni had certain
distinct advantages: they were able to point to the achievements of
the recent past. The new Cyrus had come, just as the friar had predicted he would; the Medici tyranny had been overthrown and a
governo libero established; the city had been saved from apparent
disaster; a beginning had been made on religious and moral reforms.
True, all was not well in Florence; but this was because of those
very same enemies who questioned the friar's divine mandate and
refused to do the work of repentance and reform which he demanded
of them in God's name. In answer to Angelo the Anchorite the physician Girolamo Cinozzi could reply that one had but to look around
to see that the time of tribulations and persecutions, the time of the
great devil whose name was death, had come just as "our venerable
father" had predicted, and that all those who followed his true
preaching were saints.[32] In reply to the author of the *Epistola responsiva* Domenico Benivieni, brother of Girolamo and a canon of the
Basilica of San Lorenzo, was able to retort that far from prophecy
being impossible in these latter days, Savonarola had proven his
prophetic gift when the *flagellum* had come to pass.[33] In addition to
this, the holiness of the frate's personal life and the effects of his
preaching for the reform of morals in the city were known to all and
were further proof of his divine mission.[34] As to his interference in

---

[32] There are three extant letters by Girolamo Cinozzi: *Epistola di Hieronymo Cinzoi* (sic) *fisicho al venerando P. Abbate & Generale di Valembrosa
contra all'Abate Anachorita* (n.p. or d.), *GW* no. 7044; *Epistola del predecto
Hieron. a tucti i fedeli et amatori della verita*, published together with the
above; *Epistola di Hieronymo phisico in favore della verita predicata dal venerando padre Hier. da Ferrara* (n.p. or d.), *GW* no. 7043.

[33] *Epistola di maestro Domenico Benivieni Fiorentino, canonico di S.
Lorenzo a uno amico responsiva a certe obiectione et calunnie contra a frate
Hieronymo da Ferrara* (n.p. or d.), *GW* no. 3847, sig. a. fol. 4 recto.

[34] *Tractato di Maestro Domenico Benivieni, prete fiorentino in defensione
et probatione della doctrina et prophetie predicate da frate Hieronymo da Fer-*

the government, he did so only to augment the life of the spirit which had been threatened by tyrants, and he had brought about "the compilation of many good laws and statutes for the maintenance of the real liberty of the people and good morals." Bartolomeo Scala, the humanist who had been chancellor under the Medici and now served the new republic,[35] replied to the criticism of a government of frati: there were ample precedents in Florentine history for the involvement of the religious. Besides, the Florentines had been in mortal danger from which their prophet had rescued them with divine help, and he had restored the state to the rule of her best citizens after the removal of the former tyranny.[36] To the charges of the Franciscan, Samuele Cascini, who maintained that Savonarola confused the spreading of divine grace with the spreading of the Florentine empire,[37] no less a personage than Gianfrancesco Pico replied. Scripture itself, he said, gave kings their authority to carry the sword in order that they might promote the cause of good against evil. As to Samuele's complaint that Savonarola ought not to have made promises of material gain to the Florentines, Gianfrancesco Pico replied that he had only sought so much wealth for the city as was necessary, and that he had already brought about an "incredible restitution" of usurious profits.[38]

It would serve little purpose to go through every apology and

---

rara nella citta di Firenze (Florence: Ser Francesco Bonaccorsi, 1496); *GW* no. 3849, sigs. a fol. 8 verso–b fol. 5 verso.

[35] Biographical notices in Demetrio Marzi, *La Cancelleria della Repubblica Fiorentina* (Rocca San Casciano, 1910), pp. 236-39 et passim; see also, Michele di Lupo Gentile, "Bartolommeo Scala e i Medici," *Miscellanea storica della Valdelsa*, XI (1903), 129-38; Nicolai Rubinstein, "Bartolomeo Scala's *Historia Florentinorum,*" *Studi di bibliografia e di storia in onore di Tammaro De Marinis*, vol. IV (Verona, 1964), pp. 49-59.

[36] Bartolomeo Scala, *Apologia contra vituperatores civitatis Florentiae* (Florence, 1496), with an introduction by the Florentine humanist Pietro Crinito; Hain no. 14498, sig. b fol. 5, recto.

[37] Samuele Cascini, *Invectiva in prophetiam fratris Hieronymi* (Milan, 1497); Reichling, fasc. II, p. 140. On Fra Samuele, who seems to have had Lodovico Sforza of Milan as a patron, see Luke Wadding, *Scriptores Ordinis Minorum*, 3rd edn. (Quaracchi, 1906), p. 313.

[38] Gianfrancesco Pico della Mirandola, *Defensio Hieronymi Savonarolae Ferrariensis . . . adversus Samuellem Cassinensem* (n.p., 1615); Reichling, fasc. I, p. 178.

polemical tract written on Savonarola's behalf. Gianfrancesco Pico alone wrote one for practically every Piagnone crisis, including Savonarola's excommunication, his imprisonment, and the first public reports of his confession.[39] As a whole the Piagnone literature reveals a common set of beliefs; despite the variety of men who made up the Piagnone movement there was a generally shared appreciation of both the religious and the political program of Savonarola's preaching. Whether notary (Bartolomeo Redditi) or humanist (Bartolomeo Scala) or theologian (Dominico Benivieni) or physician (Girolamo Cinozzi), the response was remarkably similar. These writers accepted Savonarola's contention that Florentine political and religious reforms were connected with the coming universal reform of the Church, and they were convinced that Florence was divinely elected to lead the way toward the new era. Florence is God's chosen, just as the prophet has announced, wrote Domenico Benivieni;[40] the New Jerusalem will be adorned in splendor, sang Fra Domenico da Pescia.[41] Why did God choose Florence, passing over Venice, Milan, and Rome? asked the Franciscan theologian Giorgio Benigno. He answered: because God knew that Tuscany was the region most dedicated to religion and Florence, the very heart of Italy. Geographically her position was secure and, since her people were the most intelligent as well as the ancient allies of France, she was the most suitable of all cities for the reception of the prophecy of the coming of Charles VIII.[42] Fra Giorgio, who had once been the tutor of Piero de' Medici,[43] wrote that he had come

---

[39] *Ioannis Francisci Pico Mirandulae in libros de iniusta excommunicatione pro Hieronymi Savonarolae innocentia ad illustrissimum virum Herculem Aestensem* (n.p. or d.); Reichling, fasc. I, p. 178. This is the same work published as *Apologia R.P.F. Hieronymi Savonarolae*, in Gianfrancesco's *Vita R. P. Hieronymi Savonarolae*, ed. Jacques Quetif, 2 vols. (Paris, 1674), vol. II, pp. 3-50. *Epistola del Conte Zoanfrancesco da la Mirandula in favore de fra Hieronymo da Ferrara dappoi la sua captura* (Mirandola, 1498). *Argumentum eiusdem obiectione* MS BNF Magl. XXXV 116, fols. 77 verso–79. (At the end, "Operetta dello d.M.S. Jho. Johanfrancesco" is crossed out).

[40] Domenico Benivieni, *Tractato*, sigs. e fol. 8 verso–f fol. 1 recto.

[41] Fra Domenico da Pescia, *Canzone spirituale*, MS BNF Magl. II. II. 437, fol. 8.

[42] Giorgio Benigno, *Prophetica solutiones* (Florence, 1497); *GW* no. 3845.

[43] Benigno has been mentioned earlier, in connection with the Santa Croce riots of 1493. See above, p. 123. Born in Ragusa (Dubrovnik), his family name

to see that Savonarola's prophecy confirmed what he had learned in England about the correct exposition of the eighteenth chapter of the Apocalypse.[44] He himself, he said, had been preaching the same doctrine and he believed that the monks of Vallombrosa held similar views:[45] the time is at hand in which the church of Christ is to be spread throughout the world; the emperor of the Turks will be killed and one sheepfold will be created under a single shepherd; the reign of Christ will last for a thousand years. At first he had been indifferent to the preaching of Savonarola, but he had been persuaded to give it his serious attention by Zanobi Acciaiuoli.[46] Benigno believed that the Church would always be ruled by a successor of St. Peter and that Savonarola's prayer that God might choose Jerusalem and cast down Rome was only to be understood

---

was Dragisic, but he was also known as Dobrotic and as de' Salviati, this last because he had been a tutor in the Salviati household. A protegé of Lorenzo the Magnificent, to whom he had been recommended by Cardinal Bessarion, he tutored both Piero and Giovanni de' Medici and taught in the Studio of Pisa. In 1511 he was elevated to the episcopate, then to an archbishopric. He attended the Fifth Lateran Council and died in 1520. See Parenti, *Storia fiorentina*, MS BNF II. II. 169, fols. 145-46; Luke Wadding, *Annales Minorum seu Trium Ordinum*, 26 vols. (Rome-Quaracchi, 1731-1933); vols. IX, 226; XV, 144, 456, 533; Angelus Fabronius, *Laurentii Medicis Magnifici Vita* (Pisa, 1784), vol. I, p. 159; vol. II, pp. 289-90; Schnitzer, "Die Flugschriftenliteratur," pp. 208-13.

[44] Revelation 18 deals with the vision of the fall of Babylon.

[45] Benigno's earlier interest in questions of prophecy is indicated in his *De natura caelestium spiritum quos angelos vocamus* (Florence, 1489). At that time he was not altogether hostile to astral magic.

[46] Zanobi Acciaiuoli, member of the prominent Florentine family which had been forced into exile during part of the Medici period, was at this time close to Giovanni and Lorenzo di Pierfrancesco de' Medici around whom some opposition had begun to form in 1494. Zanobi became a friar in San Marco under Savonarola, who set him, together with another learned convert, Giorgio Antonio Vespucci, to work at translating the writings of Sextus Empiricus from Greek into Latin, according to Gianfrancesco Pico, *Vita R.P.F. Hieronymi Savonarolae*, p. 8. Although (or perhaps because) he had been a faithful Piagnone, he was called to Rome by Pope Leo X (Giovanni de' Medici) to serve as papal librarian, in 1513. See below, p. 356. Many of Zanobi's writings, poetry, translations, and letters, are unpublished in Florentine libraries. They reveal both his humanist and his religious interests. Miss Paris Legrow is preparing a doctoral dissertation on Zanobi Acciaiuoli under my direction.

in a figurative sense. All the same, he agreed that God had chosen Florence for a special role over Rome as well as over Milan and Venice, because "He knew that the provinces of Etruria and Tuscany are the most dedicated to religion," that Florence especially has always been outstanding in religious leadership and dignity, "wherefore it was fitting to send His religious prophet to the most religious city."

In their praise of Savonarola's political reforms the Piagnoni apologists reconstructed a link with the pre-Medicean Florentine tradition of civic liberty. Bartolomeo della Scala recalled Florence's longstanding abhorrence of a *regnum*, a rule by one man which easily led to tyranny, and he invoked the city's old love of liberty. With the removal of the recent tyranny, he argued, the *patria* had been returned to the hands of its best citizens, many of whom had suffered exile under the previous regime. The republic stood for the resolution of discord and envy and the recovery of the city's honor abroad.[47] Domenico Benivieni and Bartolomeo Redditi argued that the recovery of liberty was a prerequisite for the assumption of the city's spiritual role. The citizens, who had been chosen to do the Lord's work, had to be protected by good laws. Florence was the chosen center for reform, therefore Savonarola, God's prophet, had to preach a suitable and "natural" regime for the city.[48] Tyranny threatened the Christian life of the spirit; Savonarola's reforms, by the passage of good laws, protected liberty as well as they promoted good behavior.[49] The Great Council distributed offices so that the benefits of the city were shared by all.[50] Benivieni's conception of Savonarola's civic leadership even seems to have incorporated Ficino's mystical conception of the mediator:[51] the work of the prophet was an illumination which united God and man; the

---

[47] Scala, *Apologia*, sig. b fols. 1 recto–4 verso.

[48] Benivieni, *Tractato*, sig. a fol. 4 recto. Also Bartolomeo Redditi, *Breve compendio e sommario della verità predicata e profetata dal R.P. fra Girolamo da Ferrara*, ed. Joseph Schnitzer, *Quellen und Forschungen zur Geschichte Savonarolas*, vol. I (Munich, 1902), pp. 37-38.

[49] Benivieni, *Epistola*, sig. a fol. 4 recto; *Tractato*, sig. b fol. 6 recto.

[50] Benivieni, *Tractato*, sig. a fol. 4 recto.

[51] On Ficino's conception of the mediator, see Paul O. Kristeller, *Il pensiero filosofico di Marsilio Ficino* (Florence, 1953), pp. 101-106.

prophet was a bond and mediator between the two spheres, divine and natural, just as man himself was a bond between the various orders of created things. For this reason, he said, Savonarola's preaching, which necessarily included the preaching of the proper mode of government, prepared Florence for her great mission.[52]

None of the Piagnoni apologists claimed that the *governo popolare* was a democracy in the sense of extending participation in the state to all the city's inhabitants. Both Scala and Domenico Benivieni contrasted the liberty of the *governo popolare* with domestic conflict and tyranny. While Scala explicitly stated that the new republic granted power to its "best citizens," Benivieni saw the Great Council as extending the benefits of government to all; but neither admitted the principle that all might share power equally. However, it was that pragmatic politician Francesco Valori who perhaps best summed up the meaning of Florentine liberty as the Frateschi saw it: the rule of law, freedom of action for Florentine citizens, self government, and no outside interference, not even from the Church.[53]

The Piagnoni also eagerly grasped Savonarola's promise of the extension of Florentine hegemony; they saw it as a fulfillment of long-expected, and richly merited, civic goals. Bartolomeo Scala recalled Florence's long history of empire, and saw in the 1494 restoration of the republic the first step in the recovery of her historic dignity. Domenico Benivieni too saw the constitutional reform as the beginning of the extension of the Florentine *imperium* and this, he said, was right, because Florence was God's chosen.

In sum, the Piagnoni apologists responded to Savonarola's prophetic message by emphasizing just those features which related it to the strongest civic traditions in both the religious and the political realms—indeed, as Savonarola had perceived, the two were difficult to separate. The idea of Florentine election to a special religious and political destiny and the idea of Florentine political liberty were both components of the Florentine myth as it had been elaborated over two centuries; they were also the two central components of

---

[52] Benivieni, *Tractato*, sig. a fols. 6 recto–8 verso.

[53] On this last point Antonio Canigiani concurred: "This city has never recognized any superior." These statements were made in a *pratica* on the occasion of Savonarola's excommunication and published in Lupi, ed., "Nuovi documenti," pp. 45-48.

the Savonarolan ideology. This makes it easy to understand the inherent advantage of the Piagnoni over their antagonists. Since they had identified their enterprise with the traditional values and goals of civic patriotism, the Piagnoni were able to put their enemies in the position of seeming to argue against those cherished values and goals as well as against the divine will which, according to the Florentine myth, had always sustained the glorious destiny of their city. Against them their opponents had no clear alternative doctrine or ideology to put forward. They could point out that Savonarola was a foreigner; they could heap scorn upon a government of frati; they could deny that Savonarola was a true prophet, that the new government had brought the blessings of liberty and independence, or that the future would be as glorious as Savonarola had promised. But these were negative, essentially defensive arguments with none of the glamor of the Savonarolan vision. With the persistent difficulties of the new republic and the repeated delays in the fulfillment of the dream, especially with Savonarola's own downfall and subsequent "confession," the imputations of secret malevolence and demonic possession would take on greater force. But not for the present: the Florentines needed Savonarola's vision to sustain them in their difficult time, and the more it reflected their own traditions and their own deeper fantasies, the more firmly did they cling to it. So long as it was possible to believe in it, they believed.

VIII

Savonarola and the Republic of 1494

YOU OF THE ORDER OF SAINT DOMINIC WHO SAY THAT WE OUGHT NOT
TO BUSY OURSELVES WITH THE STATE, YOU HAVE NOT DONE YOUR
READING. GO, READ IN THE CHRONICLES OF THE ORDER OF SAINT
DOMINIC WHAT HE DID IN POLITICS IN LOMBARDY, AND LIKEWISE
WHAT SAINT PETER MARTYR DID HERE IN FLORENCE, HOW HE
INTERVENED TO SETTLE AND PACIFY THIS STATE, EVEN COMPOSING
HIS TREATISE ON DEATH IN THIS CITY. THE CARDINAL MESSER
LATINO OF OUR ORDER WAS THE ONE WHO MADE PEACE BETWEEN
THE GUELFS AND THE GHIBELLINES. SAINT CATHERINE
OF SIENA ARRANGED FOR THE PEACE IN THIS
STATE AT THE TIME OF [THE WAR WITH]
POPE GREGORY. ARCHBISHOP ANTONINUS,
HOW OFTEN DID HE GO TO THE
PALACE TO PREVENT THE
MAKING OF BAD LAWS!

—Savonarola, Sermon of January 20, 1495

SAVONAROLA first intervened in the Florentine political crisis as a peacemaker, urging the reconciliation of all citizens as the essential first step toward a religious reformation. He justified his intervention by appealing to the example of the great Dominican peacemakers of the past. Unlike them, however, he was neither able nor inclined to limit his efforts to peacemaking; the fears of the citizenry, their dependence upon him for consolation and leadership, and his own prophetic temper made this impossible. Soon he began to identify the cause of civic peace with the need for good government and hence for constitutional reform. On December 7, he said that God would help the Florentines "to find a good form for this new government of yours, so that no one can raise himself above it," either as the Venetians did it or in some better way that God would show them.[1] On December 14, he preached his great political sermon, in which he urged reform after the Venetian model and presented a plan whereby the Florentine citizenry might be represented in the reform deliberations.[2] Little more than a week later, on December 22-23, the Councils of the People and of the Commune passed a law establishing a new *Consiglio Maggiore*. This new Great Council, with its broader popular base and its wide powers, was the most important innovation of the new republic. It has been regarded as the hallmark of Florence's imitation of the Venetian constitution (at least until the establishment of the lifetime Gonfaloniere in 1502). On the other hand, its links with Florence's own constitutional practises and traditions have recently received considerable stress. The establishment of the Great Council has also been seen as visible proof of Savonarola's decisive influence upon the formation of the new republic, a view that can be traced back to Savonarola's own claim that he had introduced the new government under divine inspiration.[3] Confronted with this rather awkward, if not mutually contradictory ensemble of interpretations, we shall try to unravel the problem by examining in detail the actual process by which the constitutional reform came about.

Before the generally unsatisfactory *Parlamento* of December 2 took place, Savonarola had limited his political advice to such generalities as urging laws to prevent the recurrence of tyranny and to ease the tax burden upon the people. His intervention in the discussion of a reform of the constitution on December 7, was sudden, and his manner of referring to the Venetian model or to some better way that God might point out suggests that he was alluding to discussions already under way. Moreover, between his political sermon of December 14, when he suggested a procedure for discussing reform proposals, and the actual adoption of a new reform law only

---

[1] *Prediche sopra Aggeo*, ed. Luigi Firpo (Rome, 1965), p. 135.

[2] *Ibid.*, especially pp. 225-28.

[3] The relevant quotations from Savonarola's sermons and writings are given in Nicolai Rubinstein, "Politics and Constitution in Florence at the End of the Fifteenth Century," *Italian Renaissance Studies*, ed. E. F. Jacob (London, 1960), p. 155.

one week elapsed; it seems unlikely that this would have been sufficient time for the city to rally behind a totally new and unfamiliar
plan. We know too that the Venetian constitution had long been
admired in Florence and that the idea of using it as a model for
constitutional reform was particularly in favor among the aristocrats
of the Medicean circle.[4] Parenti tells us that with the mounting
attack on the settlement of December 2, some of the leaders of the
November revolt came to feel that it was necessary to undertake
further constitutional revisions and, finding their colleagues ada-
mant against such a step, they turned to Savonarola "who had
such authority among the people that whatever he said had to be
approved."[5]

The first reason these leaders had for enlisting Savonarola's support, then, was to force the hands of their more obstinate colleagues.
The second reason has to do with the nature of the understanding
arrived at between the friar and these reform-minded leaders. In his
political sermon of December 14, Savonarola made two general proposals for reform. In addition to coming out in favor of a constitutional revision, he called for a general political amnesty as the means
of securing *la pace universale*. Indeed, the amnesty was the first order
of business: "And in the first place, and the first thing you must do,
is to make a general peace with all citizens and see that all past
offenses [*tutte le cose vecchie*] are forgiven and wiped out. I tell you
this and I command you in the name of God. Pardon everyone, I
tell you, and consider that what these people have done anyone
would have done had he been called upon to do so."[6]

This idea of a general reconciliation is such a familiar aspect of
Savonarola's prophetic message that it has generally been taken for
granted as another of his unvarying themes. The fact is, however,

---

[4] Felix Gilbert, "The Venetian Constitution in Florentine Political Thought,"
Florentine Studies: Politics and Society in Renaissance Florence, ed. Nicolai
Rubinstein (London, 1968), especially pp. 475-77.

[5] Piero Parenti, *Storia fiorentina*, ed. Joseph Schnitzer, *Quellen und Forschungen zur Geschichte Savonarolas*, vol. IV, *Savonarola nach der Aufzeichnungen des Florentiners Piero Parenti* (Leipzig, 1910), p. 26; Francesco Guicciardini, *Storie fiorentine*, ed. Roberto Palmarocchi, *Opere*, vol. IV (Bari,
1931), p. 108. See also above, pp. 148-53.

[6] *Prediche sopra Aggeo*, p. 227.

that while Savonarola had been urging the Florentines to behave more tolerantly to each other, the first time he called for a general peace in the form of a political amnesty—and the first time he used the term *la pace universale*, for that matter—was in his sermon of December 14, as part of his proposal for constitutional reform. The inference is that this, as well as the proposal for constitutional change, came from the reforming *ottimati*, who were as anxious for one as for the other.[7] For Savonarola a general amnesty was a concrete expression of his moral ideal of universal reconciliation, but the practical implication of a political amnesty was that it would protect the former Medici collaborators from possible reprisals. It is clear that in the last sentence of the statement just quoted he is referring to this group as those who had done what "anyone would have done." So far reprisals had been limited to a few agents of the Medici who had had the misfortune to be identified with the more publicly odious aspects of "tyranny": Antonio di Bernardo Miniati, *provveditore* of the *Monte* was hanged; Ser Giovanni di Bartolomeo Guidi, an official of the chancery, imprisoned; while Bartolomeo Scala, First Chancellor under Piero and Lorenzo, had been dismissed from his post.[8] These were career officials, men of modest origins, readily sacrificed by the aristocrats to the popular clamor for victims; but the prospect of a more general punishment for Medici collaboration was something else altogether. Even if the leaders of the revolt had been willing to punish the *Bigi*, the die-hard supporters of Piero, in their midst, it would have been very difficult to limit such action to that group alone. Almost all of the present leaders had at some time in the past been involved with the Medici regime, while many of them were related to prominent *Bigi* by family ties.[9] Furthermore, the true anti-Mediceans, many of whom were now returning from

[7] Rubinstein notes this, although he does not suggest that they originated the idea. "Politics and Constitution," p. 164. Parenti, however, notes the close connection between the two proposals. Parenti, *Storia fiorentina*, ed. Schnitzer, p. 27.

[8] Rubinstein, "Politics and Constitution," p. 163.

[9] Rubinstein points out that of the twenty *Accoppiatori* no fewer than fifteen had been included in the electoral lists for Gonfalonier of Justice in 1472; in other words, they had been "both prominent and trustworthy supporters of the Medici regime." *Ibid.*, p. 154.

exile, were disturbed to find former Medici collaborators still in power and they added their voices to the growing chorus of protest against the architects of the new regime.[10] All this makes it easy to understand why the *ottimati* needed Savonarola's help in gaining a general amnesty and why, in the following months, they continued to press for the passage of an amnesty law against heavy opposition. The successful outcome of this campaign, which led to the passage of such a law on March 19, 1495, strengthened their position.[11]

If the *ottimati* were motivated by considerations of survival in working for *la pace universale*, the same motivation probably underlay their conversion to the cause of constitutional reform. In this they were giving in to pressure, but, by proposing that constitutional reform be guided by the Venetian model, they were hoping, so Parenti contended, "to strengthen or consolidate their position."[12] Venice was an aristocratic republic, its *Consiglio Grande* an exclusive, virtually hereditary corporation. It was much admired in the fifteenth century for its stability and continuity, as well as for having successfully maintained its independence. In Florence it was the aristocratic ruling circle around Lorenzo the Magnificent that found the Venetian system attractive,[13] and it is most likely that the proposal to use Venice as a model for reform came from the members of this same group who were now in the forefront of the struggle for power. The conservative implications of using Venice as a model suggest another reason why the *ottimati* were anxious to enlist Savonarola's support. They could not let the discontent of the citizenry go unheeded, perhaps to take a radical and uncontrollable turn; they had to direct this discontent into a safer channel, one that they could safely navigate; but they had to convince the people that their proposals were in the general interest, that a reform on the model of Venice would give the people the liberty they had hoped for from the revolution of November 9. No one but Savonarola could convince the people of this—if he would.

[10] *Ibid.*, p. 163.

[11] *Ibid.*, p. 164. Savonarola intervened in favor of the measure, as did Fra Domenico da Ponzo, who was considered a spokesman for the anti-popular faction. Parenti, *Storia fiorentina*, ed. Schnitzer, p. 40.

[12] *Ibid.*, pp. 26-27.

[13] Gilbert, "Venetian Constitution," pp. 475-76.

That he would, a shrewd observer of the friar's career might have predicted. Savonarola too was concerned that the government "be stable and strong and very durable," and for him too the chief reason for following *la forma del governo de' Veneziani* was that in Venice it had eliminated civic dissension.[14] He was no radical ideologue and he knew how to cooperate with those in power. He was not inflexible. To hear him now excoriating the tyrannical oppressors of the former regime it would have been difficult to recall that this was the same humble friar who had pledged his devotion and obedience to Piero de' Medici little more than a year ago.[15] Indeed, a cynical observer might well have commented that such an astute opportunist as Fra Girolamo would see the advantage of an alliance with the influential leaders of the present regime. The cynic would have been right, but for the wrong reasons. Savonarola's espousal of a program of general amnesty and constitutional reform was probably less a matter of opportunism than another step toward understanding the political realities of his situation. In coming to regard Florence as God's elect city he could not remain indifferent to the political context in which that role would be fulfilled, nor, particularly in the midst of the tensions that were mounting after the *Parlamento* of December 2, could he ignore the full consequences of his claim to be Florence's own prophet whose mission it was to be a father to her people. In Florence, in December 1494, *la pace universale* was no abstract eschatological notion but an immediate concrete necessity; without a workable solution to the social and political problems that divided brother from brother Florence could never be the New Jerusalem of his prophetic vision, nor could Savonarola retain for long the unique position which he had come to hold among this people.

As for Savonarola's espousal of the specific reform plan of the more liberal *ottimati*, a number of observations may be made. With

---

[14] *Prediche sopra Aggeo*, p. 228.

[15] "Such people have neither the grace of God nor His special providence, and they are usually the worst sort of men and without intelligence or faith, . . ." *Ibid.*, p. 224. On January 6, 1495 he said, "Have you ever seen me in the past to praise the *grandi* or to say, 'Magnificent Such-and-such,' or 'Messer So-and-so'?" *Prediche sopra i Salmi*, vol. I, ed. Vincenzo Romano (Rome, 1969), p. 9.

his overriding concern for civic peace he was from the outset less concerned with being the champion of any particular class interest than with working for domestic harmony. Right up to the eve of his entry into the constitutional struggle he persisted in his view that the moral character of the community was more important than its political form, and this was also true of the leaders of the body politic. Thus, on December 7, he had said: "Note, then, Florence, that in your government you ought to raise up good men, those who have the virtue of humility. But proud and wicked men do not deserve to be raised up; the humble and those who fly from power out of humility, those you ought to try to lead to govern...."[16] In the same sermon, a week before his major political sermon of December 14, he observed that "good citizens fly from being placed in offices and magistracies,"[17] and insisted that these were the very ones who had to be made "almost by force" to serve. Moreover, Savonarola's Thomist political philosophy hardly disposed him toward egalitarianism. By applying Thomistic reasoning he arrived at the conclusion that a government of the many was better for Florence than a government of the few or of one, but this fell considerably short of democracy, for, he said, there was a natural hierarchy among men, not as servant to master but as disciple to teacher, and "those who are of greater judgment and superior intellect always direct the others who would not know how to rule themselves."[18] His willingness to accept the Florentine aristocrats as the natural leaders of the political community was entirely consistent with these views, and we can, therefore, understand how he could accept Venice as a satisfactory model for achieving civic harmony and social justice. In his judgment the greatest danger to the republic was domestic discord. He repeatedly warned that the persistence of faction and class strife would surely lead to one-man rule, just as it had led to the Medici tyranny in the past.[19]

If Savonarola does not conform to the image of the anti-aristo-

---

[16] *Prediche sopra Aggeo*, p. 137.   [17] *Ibid.*, p. 138.

[18] *Ibid.*, p. 315. See also his attacks on the institution of *Parlamento*. *Prediche italiane ai Fiorentini*, ed. Roberto Palmarocchi and Francesco Cognasso (Perugia-Venice, 1930-35), vol. II, *Giorni festivi del 1495*, pp. 410, 427; III¹, *Quaresimale del 1496*, p. 220.

[19] *Prediche sopra Aggeo*, p. 257.

cratic, democratic hero which some have fashioned for him, neither was he merely "the authoritative spokesman of more responsible political groups who took cover behind his work of preaching and external reform."[20] The first image ascribes too much originality and initiative to a religious visionary who was essentially a political conservative and only accepted his role as a popular leader with reluctance; the second underestimates the vigor and independence with which he finally grasped that role. It seems clear that the *ottimati* intended to use Savonarola for their own purposes,[21] and that, up to a point, they succeeded in doing so;[22] but the friar was never simply their mouthpiece or compliant tool, a fact they soon realized and deplored.[23] Despite his initial reluctance to involve himself in the political controversy and notwithstanding his inherent conservatism, he was sensitive and sympathetic to popular aspirations, and he understood what the role of popular leader demanded. Moreover, he was freer than the *ottimati* to recognize that the root cause of political instability in Florence was the failure to broaden the base of power and to extend participation in the offices of state. Consequently, once he became the champion of constitutional reform he sought to give it a more democratic stamp than was acceptable to some of his would-be sponsors. What he envisioned, he said in his sermon of December 14, was a new regime in which the artisans would have more representation and therefore more responsibility. This would be achieved by broadening the distribution of offices through a combination of election for the major offices and sortition for the minor ones. He also called for a more equitable distribution of the tax burden, with taxes based on property rather than on the

[20] Renzo Pecchioli, "Il 'mito' di Venezia e la crisi fiorentina intorno al 1500," *Studi storici*, III (1962), 482.

[21] On the importance of Savonarola in keeping the people peaceful by promising to champion their cause, see Parenti, *Storia fiorentina*, ed. Schnitzer, pp. 25-26.

[22] See the interesting letter of Piero Capponi in Volterra to Francesco Valori in Florence, July 7, 1495, in which Capponi advises Valori to have Savonarola write a letter to Charles VIII and also give his attention to the matter of Siena which was leaning toward the Italian League, in G. Aiazzi ed., "Vita di Piero Capponi," *Archivio storico italiano*, IV (1853), 54-55.

[23] Parenti, *Storia fiorentina*, ed. Schnitzer, pp. 28-29.

arbitrary determination of the men in power.[24] The next step was to initiate discussion of specific proposals according to a procedure which would adequately represent the views of the citizens. "You have in your city sixteen standard-bearers (*confalonieri*) of the companies, as you call them, who have under them all the citizens of the whole city. Have the citizens meet together under their standards and let them consult and decide what is the best form for your government. Let each company choose the form that its citizens decide upon, thus there will be sixteen plans. Have the standard-bearers come together and out of all these plans choose the four that seem best and most stable, and bring them before the magnificent Signoria. There, after the mass of the Holy Spirit has been sung in the hall, they will choose one of the four. And know that, without doubt, the one that will be chosen will be from God."[25] To the men in power it must have appeared that Savonarola was now trying to seize the initiative with reform proposals and a plan for the democratic discussion of reform that went beyond their own intentions. Instead of accepting his proposal to solicit plans for constitutional revision from the citizenry at large, they instructed the members of the major magistracies—the Signoria, Sixteen *Gonfalonieri* of the Companies, Twelve Good Men, Ten of Liberty and Peace, etc.—to submit proposals. In other words, the *ottimati* were determined to control the reform discussions and therefore the final shape of the new constitution. Whether this was a setback for proponents of popular reform, however, is difficult to determine, since some of the *ottimati* in the magistracies were also sympathetic to broadening representation. In any case, Savonarola's own views appear to have been represented in the ensuing discussions of constitutional reform.

Several of the reform schemes have been preserved and from them we are able to see that there was a common core of agreement as to the need for two fundamental innovations—the establishment of a Great Council with broad powers and the reform of the system of choosing public officials.[26] Moreover, while these innovations were

---

[24] *Prediche sopra Aggeo*, pp. 223-24.   [25] *Ibid.*, pp. 227-28.

[26] Professor Felix Gilbert kindly made available to me his transcripts of the draft proposals; the originals are in ASF, Carte Strozziane, 2nd ser., 95, fols. 69-78, 233-42. I cite the folio numbers of the originals.

presented as adaptations of the Venetian system, in which a *Consiglio Grande* exercised broad legislative and electoral functions, they were also treated as modifications of traditional Florentine practice. For example, since Florence had no such system of hereditary eligibility for seats in her councils as that on which the Venetian *Consiglio Grande* was based, the Florentines attempted to create a quasi-hereditary system out of their own materials, so to speak: all the surviving drafts propose that membership in the new council should devolve upon those citizens whose names had been drawn for one of the three major magistracies, or whose fathers' or grandfathers' names had been drawn.[27] Similarly, in the matter of selecting public officials, while tending to accept the Venetian principle of granting the power of electing officials to the Great Council, the Florentines called upon their own past experiences of the alternative methods of election and sortition. In his sermon of December 14, Savonarola himself, proposing that the major offices be filled by election and the minor ones by lot, was drawing upon Florentine rather than Venetian practice.

Beyond the general consensus about participation in the new council and selection of office-holders, however, the proposals differed in important details. Domenico Bonsi, one of the leaders of the new regime (a member of the twenty-man commission of *Accoppiatori* empowered by the *Parlamento* of December 2 to hand-pick the Signoria during the succeeding year), submitted a draft which set forth a complex method of establishing eligibility for the *Consiglio Maggiore*.[28] By distinguishing between two types of *beneficiati*, or

---

[27] Citizens whose names had been drawn for one of the offices, but who had been temporarily disqualified from accepting office were *veduti*, or "seen." Those whose names had been drawn and who had actually been invested with the office were *seduti*, or "seated." See Rubinstein, *Government of Florence Under the Medici* (1434-1494) (Oxford, 1965), p. 37 et passim.

[28] "Discorso di Mess. Domenico Bonsi" (the title was added to the draft later), in ASF, Carte Strozziane, 2nd ser., 95, fols. 233-36. Bonsi was to become a strong partisan of the new government, and, as Florentine envoy to the Papal court, made strenuous efforts to persuade Alexander VI to reverse his excommunication of Savonarola. See Ridolfi, *The Life of Girolamo Savonarola*, trans. Cecil Grayson (New York, 1959), pp. 228-29 et passim. Savonarola later mentioned him as one of the citizens upon whom he relied for political leadership. Pasquale Villari, *La storia di Girolamo Savonarola e de' suoi tempi*, 2nd edn.,

citizens eligible for the Council, Bonsi's plan would have given a two-to-one edge in the Council to members of the existing ruling group. Similarly, for the selection of office-holders he proposed that eligibility be restricted to the Council members themselves, to be chosen in the Council by a complex combination of sortition, nomination, and election. Taken together these two proposals would have assured the *ottimati* continued control of the new government under the cover of having given in to the popular demand for constitutional reform. An even more prominent oligarch, Piero Capponi, gave the opinion that Bonsi's plan for establishing eligibility to the Council was overly complicated, although he was just as concerned with preserving the aristocratic character of the new regime. In his own draft, Capponi insisted on the need for a *Consiglio di scelti*, or Select Council, in addition to the *Consiglio Maggiore*. This would be composed of the more important officials, to the number of eighty or a hundred. Such an elite body, argued Capponi, was "most necessary both for holding certain elections of greater importance and for conducting certain deliberations, as is customary in Venice, as well as for serving more frequently as an advisory body (*pratica*) and council of the Signoria. . . ."[29] This is another example of a proposed borrowing from Venice that was equally defensible in terms of Florence's own traditions, for Capponi's Select Council was both the counterpart of the Venetian council of the *Pregadi* and an effort to institutionalize the long-standing Florentine *pratica*, or *consulta*, a practice by which the Signoria convoked bodies of leading citizens for consultation. Whether justified by reference to the Venetian model or to Florentine custom, however, the addition of a Select Council was obviously designed to protect aristocratic initiative in the new regime, since the civic officials of which it would be composed would most likely have been elected from among the *ottimati*.

---

2 vols. (Florence, 1926), vol. II, appendix, p. clvij. Bonsi's is also the second name on the list of over 350 citizens who signed a petition to Alexander VI on Savonarola's behalf in 1497. See P. Villari and E. Casanova, *Scelta di prediche e scritti di fra Girolamo Savonarola* (Florence, 1898), p. 514; and the variant list published by Attilio Portioli, "Nuovi documenti su Girolamo Savonarola," *Archivio storico lombardo*, I (1874), 341.

[29] "Ricordi di Piero Capponi," in ASF, Carte Strozziane, 2nd ser., 95, fols. 241-42.

Of the two remaining drafts, both anonymous, one is a straight-forward endorsement of the *Consiglio Maggiore* and of the principle of selecting all office-holders from among the Council members, with the exception of the Signoria and its Colleges (the Sixteen *Gonfalonieri* and the Twelve Good Men). Office-holders would be chosen by a combination of election, nomination, and sortition: a body of nominators were to be drawn by lot, these would nominate candidates for the offices, and the members of the Council would elect from this list. No mention is made of a Select Council or of Bonsi's distinction between two classes of eligibles for the *Consiglio Maggiore*.[30] The remaining draft, of considerably greater length and interest, is entitled "Unde veniet auxilium mihi? Auxilium meum a Domino, qui fecit coelum et terram."[31] It is likely that this was the draft of the proposal put forward by the Ten of Liberty and Peace, a commission which included among its members Paolantonio Soderini, Lorenzo Lenzi, and some of the other *ottimati* leaders of the reform initiative discussed earlier.[32] The document begins with a brief discourse on Florentine history which was designed to demonstrate that the political instability which had plagued the republic throughout its past was due to its methods of selecting public officials. On one extreme, according to the draft, the city had selected its chief officials by controlled sortition (*tenere le borse di quegli primi magistrati a mano*), a practice that favored a small number of citizens who corrupted the civic officials in order to gain power for themselves. On the other extreme was the method of unrestricted sortition (*il suo contrario, cioè el tenere a sorta*), a practice which stemmed from the Florentines' exaggerated egalitarianism and resulted in the selection of ill-qualified officials. Both extremes, according to the author of this draft, had repeatedly led to dissen-

[30] "Diputisi uno Consigl[i]o, chiamato el Consigl[i]o maggiore, nello infrascripto modo, cioè," in ASF, Carte Strozziane, 2nd ser., 95, fol. 78.

[31] Also in ASF, Carte Strozziane, 2nd ser., 95, fols. 69 verso–73 verso.

[32] The names of the ten citizens elected for six months on December 3: Piero di Bertoldo Corsini, Paolantonio di Tommaso Soderini, Piero di Francesco Vettori, Piero di Jacobo Guicciardini, Lorenzo di Matteo Morelli, Lorenzo di Anofri Lenzi, Jacopo di Giannozzo Pandolfini, Francesco di Luca degli Albizzi, Lorenzo di Michele Benintendi, Piero di Giovanni Pieri. See ASF, Tratte Intrinseci, vol. 83, fol. 115.

sion and ruin in the past. Not that the ancient Florentines had been any less intelligent than those of the present, but that circumstances had again and again prevented them from giving sufficient attention to this problem. Thus the document presents Florentine history as a gloomy tale of repeated conflict—Guelf-Ghibelline dissension, Blacks versus Whites, Cerchi against Donati, the rebellion of the Ciompi who had "almost destroyed *e' buoni popolani*," and—just when the republic had begun to grow great with the conquest of Pisa (1406)— the rise of new strife which brought on the Medici tyranny after 1434. Now, however, the Florentines had turned to "liberty, equality, and steadfastness," and, as God had summoned them by the mouth of him who prophesied the truth to them in other great matters, they must believe that it was now time "to shed their skin." The Florentines had been given extraordinary grace and therefore they should abandon their ordinary way of life, take up a new form, and learn from their Venetian neighbors who had a single powerful state for a thousand years. From them the Florentines should borrow what was suitable for their own needs.

Whoever the actual author of this scheme may have been, its inspiration is unmistakably Savonarolan, from its religious title (derived from Psalm 120) to its style, tone, and reference to the true prophet in their midst. Like Savonarola, the document argued for constitutional reform on three grounds. Political reform is seen as part of the conversion to a new life; divine grace has been extended to the Florentines, challenging them to transform the ordinary into the extraordinary, to take up a new nature. Political reform is also seen as the lesson to be derived from the experience of history, *la quale è maestra delle cose*; the overthrow of Medicean tyranny now offers the wonderful possibility of a civic reconciliation which will wipe out the baneful factionalism of the past. Finally, Venice provides a model for selective imitation.

The substantive proposals of this draft scheme also indicate the blending of Savonarolan interests with those of the more liberal *ottimati*. Although in the main they coincide with the proposals of the other drafts, there are important differences in their details and their omissions. The two major innovations are the establishment of a new Great Council—here called *Consiglio del Popolo et Comune*, after two of the oldest of the Florentine councils—and the reform of the electoral system. With regard to eligibility for the Council, this draft stands between the extremes of Bonsi's proposal and the more liberal anonymous draft already discussed. As in the other schemes, eligibility for the new council was to be based upon a quasi-hereditary principle; but an advantage was given to those who had been seated in one of the three major offices, or whose father or grandfather had been seated, over those who have merely been drawn for a major office without having been seated. In keeping with Savonarola's urgent appeal for civic reconciliation, this draft further advocates that some number of men from the *grandi* families which had been excluded from office in the past now be added to the list of eligibles to the Council, on the grounds that the number of *popolani* families had increased relative to the *grandi* who were therefore no longer to be feared. With respect to the electoral system, this draft makes the same clear-cut distinction between unrestricted sortition for the bulk of public offices and election for the more important offices that Savonarola had made in his sermon of December 14. Elections were to be held in the Council, but—and this is a significant difference from the other schemes—nothing is said about limiting eligibility for office to the members of the Council. In other words, the traditional Florentine principle that all citizens were eligible to hold public office is here defended against the Venetian principle of restricting eligibility to an hereditary group.[33]

The rest of the draft is mostly filled with details of procedure, but one other clause is worth our notice. The framers of the scheme were much concerned with restricting the arbitrary exercise of power by the Signoria and its two colleges. On all important matters, those involving changes in law and those involving decisions to imprison or exile citizens, the draft proposes that the Signoria ought not to act without the approval of the members of the Council in a two-thirds vote. Such a restriction of the Signoria's authority was not to apply to routine matters of "reason and justice"; in other words, this restriction upon the Signoria's authority was meant to apply to

---

[33] But the more exclusive principle was adopted after November 26, 1495, when the old electoral bags were burned. Nicolai Rubinstein, "I primi anni del Consiglio Maggiore di Firenze (1494-99)," *Archivio storico italiano*, CXII (1954), 329-30.

political decisions. As such it would seem to have been linked to the general issue of *la pace universale* and therefore to another of Savonarola's and the *ottimati*'s main concerns. One aspect of this concern had already been formulated in the proposal for a law of political amnesty; the other was soon to be embodied in Savonarola's proposal for a law of appeal according to which anyone whom the Signoria condemned for a political offense might appeal to the Great Council.[34] That the two proposals were so related is indicated by the fact that the law of March 19, 1495, which provided for a political amnesty also established the law of appeal.[35]

From this examination of the surviving draft schemes we can distinguish an oligarchic from a popular tendency in the reform discussions, but these are relative as well as approximate terms. The drafts agree on the need to broaden participation in the state, although none of them, certainly not the one most closely reflecting Savonarola's views, indicate any disposition to experiment with what modern political judgment would regard as a democratic alternative. As the Florentines themselves would have put it, the issue stood between *governo stretto* and *governo largho*, between a somewhat more exclusive and a somewhat more expansive regime, not between oligarchy and democracy in any absolute sense. Moreover, the appeal to the model of Venice was highly ambiguous; the Great Council of Venice was the prototype for the new, broader Florentine *Consiglio Maggiore*, but Venice was also the source of justification for the more restrictive proposals, such as the limitation of office-holders to the quasi-hereditary members of the Council and Capponi's advocacy of a Select Council. This ambiguity of the Venetian model reflected the ambiguity of the reforming enterprise itself: the search for stability, of which Venice was the prime symbol and example, was being conducted under the banner of a restoration of liberty, which was the essence of Florence's own tradition. Between the proposals of the patricians Bonsi and Capponi on one hand and the Savonarola-inspired proposal on the other there were some signifi-

---

[34] Savonarola, however, wanted appeals to be heard by a specially chosen council of eighty or one hundred rather than by the entire Great Council. *Prediche italiane ai Fiorentini*, vol. II, pp. 11-12.

[35] Rubinstein, "Politics and Constitution," p. 164.

cant, if not earth-shaking, differences. Only the Savonarolan draft reflected a concern with restraining the arbitrary exercise of political power which had been one of the chief causes of civic strife in the past, while its principle of eligibility for the Great Council was slightly less restrictive than Bonsi's. Moreover, the Savonarolan draft defended the traditional Florentine principle of making offices available to all citizens against the newer, probably Venetian-inspired, tendency to restrict offices to members of the new Council, and it did not support Capponi's attempt to interpose an oligarchic Select Council between the Signoria and the *Consiglio Maggiore*. In the main, however, the Savonarolan draft was in agreement with the others: no more than they did it propose a democratic regime. Its chief distinction is that it provided the reform enterprise with a legitimacy rooted in Florentine history, in the prophecy of spiritual renewal, and in the successful example of Venice. It viewed the whole Florentine past as leading up to this special moment and the whole glorious Florentine future as radiating out from this point. God had given the Florentines a mandate for renewal; they must not miss the opportunity.

How much of this opportunity did the Florentines grasp? The law of December 22-23 established the *Consiglio Maggiore* (originally called the *Consiglio del Popolo et Comune*)[36] along the lines suggested in the surviving drafts. The quasi-hereditary principle of eligibility for the Council, based on three generations of *seduti* or *veduti* for the three major magistracies, was adopted. None of the special restrictions proposed by Bonsi—or by the Savonarolan draft, for that matter—were accepted; *seduti* and *veduti* were to be equally eligible, so long as they were *netti di specchio*, that is, unencumbered with tax debts. A Council of Eighty was established in the spirit of Capponi's proposal, although it was to be elected in the Great Council rather than co-opted from the major magistracies as Capponi had advocated.[37] For the coming year the members of the Signoria and Colleges would continue to be hand-picked by the twenty *Accoppiatori*; after this the three magistracies would be filled

---

[36] *Ibid.*, p. 156.
[37] *Ibid.*, p. 162.

by election in the Council.[38] The rest of the electoral system was revised according to the distinction between election in the Council for the more important offices and sortition for the minor offices, and, for the time being at least,[39] office-holding was not confined to members of the Council. However, the list of offices subject to election was fairly lengthy, including a number of the important posts outside the city as well as the leading domestic ones.[40] Did this new electoral system favor the *ottimati* or the *popolo*? Piero Parenti believed that the adoption of the method of election for the important offices "rendered the state to the nobility";[41] but the *ottimati* themselves were not so sure that this was the case, and they continued to worry over the issue for some time to come. So long as the old *tratte* purses, filled with the names of the supporters of the former regime, continued to be used it could be expected that sortition would favor the old ruling group, that is, the *ottimati*. On the other hand, the *ottimati* were afraid that election in the new Great Council with its broader membership would favor new men. In short, no one knew how it would work. The new constitution was a patchwork of traditional Florentine institutions and Venetian-inspired innovations, an accommodation between the oligarchic *ottimati* and their reform-minded rivals in a whole that was as yet untried. No one knew, for example, how many citizens would be eligible for the Great Council, although it was certain to be the largest such body in the history of Florentine politics; nor did anyone know how to calculate the effect of Savonarola's great influence upon the workings of the new regime.

Some of these uncertainties were, of course, clarified in the coming months of the new year as the new regime went into effect. Some fears were allayed; others were justified; further modifications were made. It turned out that election in the Council neither guar-

---

[38] This was a defeat for Capponi who wanted to extend the term of the *Accoppiatori* indefinitely until it could be seen how matters were working out. "Ricordi di Piero Capponi," fol. 241 recto.

[39] See above, n. 33.

[40] As in the draft "Unde veniet auxilium mihi?" fol. 70 verso, where a lengthy list of offices subject to election is proposed.

[41] Quoted in Rubinstein, "I primi anni," p. 324.

anteed control of the state to the *ottimati* nor revolutionized it in favor of new men. Election tended to favor men of experience, reputation, and influence, so that a considerable degree of continuity is observable in the formation of policy and the wielding of power. The lists of the Priors of the Signoria and the principal magistracies for these years are still replete with the names of Capponi, Nerli, Bonsi, Corsi, Benci, Soderini, and the other prominent members of the Florentine ruling class.[42] The voices heard in *pratiche* and council debates were still the voices of Piero Capponi, Bernardo Del Nero, Filippo Rinuccini, Piero Guicciardini, Iacopo Pandolfini, and other men of the old regime.[43] In July 1495 it was still possible for Piero Capponi to write that if they put aside their private passions, ambitions, and avarice, twenty-five or thirty leading men (*uomini da bene*) could govern the city by tacit agreement among themselves.[44]

And yet certain facts of Florentine public life had changed. The Great Council made a difference in the political climate of the city by greatly increasing the number of citizens who participated in legislation and in the election of officials. While none of the older civic councils had contained more than 300 members, and most had been considerably smaller, the total number of citizens eligible for the Great Council rose to about 3000.[45] To be sure, the whole body

[42] The names of office-holders are listed in ASF Tratti Intrinseci (1470-1507), vols. 82, 83; and Tratti Estrinseci (1472-1508), vols. 69, 70. Parenti thought that the loss of Sarzana, Pietrasanta, Pisa, and Montepulciano deprived the Florentine citizenry of many lucrative offices and that this, together with the business recession, intensified the desire and the competition for the offices still available. Parenti, *Storia fiorentina*, ed. Schnitzer, p. 291.

[43] For the minutes of the *pratiche* of this period, which usually give the names of the speakers, see ASF Consulte e Pratiche, vols. 61-64. Some of the crucial *pratiche* of 1497-98 have been published by C. Lupi, "Nuovi documenti intorno a Fra Girolamo Savonarola," *Archivio storico italiano*, 3rd ser., T. II, part I (1866), 25-77. See also the fundamental article by Felix Gilbert, "Florentine Political Assumptions in the Period of Savonarola and Soderini," *Journal of the Warburg and Courtauld Institutes*, vol. XII (1957), 187-214, which is based mainly on an analysis of *pratiche*; also his *Machiavelli and Guicciardini: Politics and History in Sixteenth-Century Florence* (Prnceton, 1965), pp. 28-45.

[44] Capponi to Valori, July 28, 1495 in Aiazzi, "Vita di Piero Capponi," p. 59.

[45] Rubinstein, "I primi anni," p. 181. For valuable discussions of the political issues of the period, see Gilbert, *Machiavelli and Guicciardini*, chap. I; and

of *beneficiati* never met together at one time, and a quorum was set at 1000 at first; nevertheless the difference in the extent of participation in government before and after 1495 is impressive.[46] To an extent it justified the growing tendency to refer to the new regime as a *governo popolare*.

This had some important effects. For one thing, there is evidence that the new electoral system did result in a more democratic distribution of at least the minor offices. Sixty-nine per cent of the men who had held some public office in the last six years of Medici rule did not hold another post in the six years following the revolt of November 8. In other words, there was a substantial turnover, even allowing for the customary Florentine limitations on repetitive office-holding, chiefly in the occupancy of the provincial vicariates, castellanies, captaincies, *provisori*, and *regulatori* which made up the bulk of public honors in the Florentine state.[47] It is difficult to tell whether those who now won posts were men of more modest social origins than their predecessors, whether they were the "artisans" whom Savonarola had sought to enfranchise in his sermon of December 14; but to the extent that they were new men who had not played an active role in the Medici period, Savonarola's objective of broadening participation in the state would seem to have been achieved in this way as well as by means of eligibility in the Great Council itself.

Paradoxically, however, the attainment of this objective may have made it more, rather than less, difficult to achieve one of the goals for which it had been sought, that is, the reconciliation of antagonisms within the city. Broadening the base of the republic resolved the immediate crisis of December, but it also increased popular expectations of further reforms, set the supporters of *governo popolare* jealously on guard against any signs of bad faith among the oligarchs, and provided, in the Great Council, an unprecedented

---

Antonio Anzilotti, *La crisi costituzionale della Repubblica Fiorentina* (Florence, 1912).

[46] On the organization and operation of the Great Council and its successive modifications, see Rubinstein, "I primi anni."

[47] This is based upon my study of the lists of all the major and almost all of the minor offices both domestic and foreign in this period, a total sample of over 1,000 names, drawn from ASF Tratti Intrinseci, vols. 82-83; and Tratti Estrinseci, vols. 69-70.

opportunity to exercise a check on the ruling group which still tended to dominate the executive agencies of the state. The Signoria might make policy, but legislation had to be approved in the Council, and the confrontation that resulted from this fact uncovered deep resentments and aspirations that had long been muffled. Under more relaxed conditions the new regime might have been able to work its problems out more satisfactorily for all concerned—but then, of course, there would probably have been no new government at all. The republic of 1494 was a child of crisis, reared in a climate of apprehension, rumor, mutual distrust, and an increasing tendency toward violence climaxed by the torture and execution of Savonarola himself in 1498.

To a large extent Florence's problems in the Savonarolan period were due not to any fundamental disagreement about ends but about means. No single policy was more widely approved than the prosecution of the war to recapture Pisa, and no single commitment was so debilitating of public morale. The war dragged on, draining the city's resources, shaking the Florentines' confidence in their prophet, and undermining their trust in each other. Another constant policy, the alliance with the French, was also almost universally popular. Florence's continued loyalty to Charles VIII may have been based on sound calculation; certainly it was dictated as much by a consideration of material interest as by idealism; but it generated an unnerving hostility and pressure from the other Italian powers without providing any quickly visible benefit, since Charles showed no signs of returning to Italy despite Savonarola's repeated predictions that he would do so.[48]

Economic troubles, little understood and difficult to cope with, made matters worse. The crisis in the fall of 1494 had disrupted the normal routine of work, although to what extent is difficult to determine. Parenti writes of the closing of shops in the city and the interruption of cultivation in the surrounding *contado*, and this situation seems to have persisted into the following year. There is evidence

---

[48] See the statement of Piero Guicciardini: the King had to be made to understand that Florence could not continue to hold out against the combined pressures of the Papacy and the other Italian potentates. ASF Consulte e Pratiche, vol. 61, fol. 99 (November 27, 1495).

that workers' wages dropped in the autumn of 1494 and continued at a depressed level throughout this period. For example, the wages of skilled stonemasons, which between 1490 and 1494 had ranged from thirteen to fourteen *soldi* per day in winter and fifteen to sixteen *soldi* per day in summer, fell to the ranges of ten to eleven and eleven to twelve *soldi* respectively and remained at this lower level until the end of the century. This was a drop of some twenty-five per cent. The wages of unskilled laborers also fell, although less dramatically, from a seasonal variation of eight to nine *soldi* per day to an unvarying eight *soldi*. Moreover, employment in this period seems to have been much less regular, perhaps due to the uncertainties of the business outlook resulting from the war and the loss of the Florentine ports and to the difficulties engendered by Florence's diplomatic isolation.[49]

Closely related to all these issues was the unrelenting struggle over taxes. Among the underlying grievances against the regimes of Lorenzo and Piero had been the steep augmentation of *gabelle*, indirect taxes levied mainly on commodities and hence most deeply resented by the workers and by the merchants and artisans who lived by retail trade. No doubt it was to gain the goodwill of these segments of the population that the leaders proposed the abolishment of the *gabelle* which was carried out by the *Parlamento* of December 2. No doubt too, Savonarola's espousal of such a reform constituted an important bond between him and the populace. Further tax reforms were promised in the reform law of December 22-23, which committed the new government to regularize imposts and to make immovable property the basis of assessment, in order "to pacify and to give security to every citizen. . . ."[50] This promise was honored on February 5, 1495, with the adoption of the *decima*, a tax based on property holdings. But such measures barely scratched the surface of the problem and in some respects made matters worse, for the *decima* was not graduated according to differences in property

[49] This information on wages and working conditions has been kindly supplied to me by Professor Richard Goldthwaite who is engaged in a study of the construction of the Palazzo Strozzi in Florence.

[50] What follows on the problems of taxation is based mainly upon Louis Marks, "La crisi finanziaria a Firenze dal 1494 al 1502," *Archivio storico italiano*, CXII (1954), pp. 40-72.

wealth. Moreover it was totally inadequate to provide the revenues needed for the war and other extraordinary expenses, such as the subvention to Charles VIII.

The inadequacies of the *decima* focused attention on other means of raising revenues, chief among which was the imposition of forced loans, and to these the government resorted with increasing frequency and intensity in order to feed the war's insatiable appetite. In January, almost at the same time as the establishment of the *decima*, the Signoria provided for an *accatto*, a forced loan to be levied on the citizenry. Public reaction was swift and sharp. Luca Landucci, the pharmacist-chronicler, reported that "this frightened the people a great deal and almost everyone stopped working and was discontented. Everyone was saying that they could not go on like this, that the poor who lived only from industry (*di manifatture*) would die of hunger and have to exist on the charity of [The Good Men of] San Martino."[51] These alarms were soon echoed in the Great Council. Among the rank and file there was strong opposition to forced loans as a form of tax which was prejudicial to trade and manufactures. There was also an unshakeable conviction that the *grandi* who sat in the commissions responsible for assessing such loans discriminated against the men of modest means who lacked the power to protect themselves from being saddled with a disproportionate share of the burden. While the initiative for proposing new fiscal measures still lay with the Signoria the Great Council could exercise a veto by rejecting the Signoria's proposals, and this it did with increasing frequency and mounting bitterness on all sides in the months to come. In December 1496, finding its current bill for a loan blocked in Council, the Signoria ordered a certain Francesco di Piero Ambrogini to speak in support of the measure on behalf of the *popolo*.[52] But to everyone's astonishment and great,

[51] Lucca Landucci, *Diario fiorentino del 1450 al 1516 continuato da un anonimo fino al 1542*, ed. Iodoco Del Badia (Florence, 1883), pp. 97-98.

[52] The Tratti records show that Francesco di Piero Ambrogini was first chosen for office in January, 1497 when he was elected to the *Otto di Guardia* (Eight of Watch and Ward). Perhaps he is the same man referred to by Marks as Francesco di Piero Ambrogi who had been forcibly restrained from continuing his attack upon a certain tax in the Great Council on August 1496. Marks, "La crisi finanziaria," p. 45.

although privately expressed, delight,[53] Ambrogini attacked the bill and declared that it had failed to pass because it was "injurious to the people"; that forced loans threatened merchants, artisans, and businessmen (*huomini danarosi*) with ruin; and that, by discouraging trade, they caused great distress among the *plebe*, who could no longer go on "feeding on famine." Moreover, declared Ambrogini, it was not to be borne that in such times this authority be given to men of questionable motives (*ad huomini poco volentieri*) who had already proven their bad faith more than once in the past. Again and again, he charged, the present Signoria and its predecessors had been presented with a variety of schemes for raising revenue and been advised to place them before the people, to let the people choose between them, but again and again the Signori had refused. At one time, according to Ambrogini, the people had been master of the city and the Signori had carried out the people's will, but now they did the bidding of a small group of citizens and this group wanted to impose the new tax. What was urgently required, he concluded, was that taxation be established on a basis of law and not upon the arbitrary will of individuals.[54] Thus the controversy over taxation unearthed in the city deep social antagonisms which, far from being resolved by the constitutional reform, now came to the surface in a political struggle which jeopardized the very existence of the new regime.

By the end of 1496 fiscal matters were at a standstill, the Council refusing to meet the urgent money needs of the state through still another forced loan, the Signoria unable or unwilling to offer an alternative which would meet the demands of the insurgents. The immediate situation was eased somewhat when the new Signoria headed by Francesco Valori as Gonfalonier of Justice entered office in January. No popular hero, Valori, a member of the old guard who had played a leading role in the overthrow of the Medici,[55] now emerged as the leader of the pro-Savonarolan political faction, the

---

[53] On the limitations on debate in the sessions of the Great Council, see Gilbert, *Machiavelli and Guicciardini*, p. 11, n. 10.

[54] Parenti, *Storia fiorentina*, MS BNF Magl. II. II. 130, fol. 74. (This is a sixteenth-century MS copy. The original of this part of Parenti's history is lost.) Partly cited in Marks, "La crisi finanziaria," p. 49.

[55] Parenti, *Storia fiorentina*, ed. Schnitzer, p. 154.

Frateschi. Piero Parenti explained Valori's motive as a combination of personal ambition and concern to save the French alliance from the partisans of the Italian League. Until now he observed, Valori had been "a head without a tail," the *Frateschi* "a tail without a head."[56] Valori must have seen that without more nourishment the creature would die,[57] and that it was therefore absolutely essential to reach some kind of compromise with the popular elements in the Council on the revenue question. Under Valori's leadership the new Signoria proposed a loan which would be administered by a special board of twenty elected in Council, and this measure at last overcame the resistance of the Council.

But the *ventina*, as it was called, was no more a real solution than the *decima* before it. Inadequate from the standpoint of the *popolari* who wanted a fundamental reform of fiscal structure, it was also insufficient to fill the bottomless pit of public spending. Ironically, the wealthy *ottimati* were not much more enthusiastic about public loans than the shopkeepers and tradesmen, for the men with great fortunes claimed that they were being forced to the wall by the repeated demands for new sums. Piero Soderini, widely regarded as one of the most conscientious and disinterested of civic leaders, as well as one of the wealthiest, complained in the fall of 1496 that he had already furnished twelve thousand florins in loans and was unable to provide any more; Iacopo Salviati, whose family owned one of the city's richest banking firms, said the same.[58] There is little reason to challenge the sincerity of these protestations. Soderini and Salviati were making their complaints to their peers in a *pratica*, not in open council; twelve thousand florins was an enormous sum of money, even for so rich a man as Soderini, and the soundness of public credit was increasingly coming into question.[59] Cognizant of this reaction among the *ottimati*, Savonarola could insist, on October 28, that citizens should lend to the state not at "usury . . . but *gratis*," for the common good; but he hastened to add that this did

---

[56] *Ibid.*, p. 155.

[57] ". . . cum bellorum (ut vulgo dicitur nervii) sint pecuniae." ASF Consulte e Pratiche, vol. 61, fol. 148 recto (January 7, 1496).

[58] Marks, "La crisi finanziaria," p. 65.

[59] *Loc. cit.*

not apply to public debts already incurred.[60] The friar was as aware as anyone that public credit must be maintained.

Without questioning the accuracy of the people's suspicions or the justice of their complaints against the inequities of the fiscal system, it seems evident that the intransigence of the members of the patriciate to undertake further reforms was not alone responsible for Florence's plight, since no one else was proposing a workable set of alternatives. Economic difficulties, a dangerous external political situation, a policy of Tuscan supremacy which was almost universally popular, and class suspicions bred of many years of indifference and mutual incomprehension produced a situation of such complexity as to defy the best efforts of Valori as well as Savonarola.

AND so *la pace universale* continued to elude the new republic. What difference, then, did Savonarola make to Florence during the years between the revolt in November 1494 and the burning in May 1498; what impact did he have upon the life of the city? In one respect his impact is manifest in the style of Florentine public life in this period. For three and a half years following the expulsion of the Medici the figure of Savonarola—preaching, exhorting, prophesying—dominated the Florentine scene. The public life of the city was shaped by the friar's initiative and breathed his spirit: public games, like the *palio*, were suspended;[61] old time festivals were transformed into pious processions; hymns celebrating Florence as the New Jerusalem replaced profane *canti carnascialeschi*;[62] laws were passed to suppress immodest dress and conduct; and the youth of the city were mobilized to roam the streets on the lookout for violators.[63]

[60] *Prediche sopra Ruth e Michea*, ed. Vincenzo Romano, 2 vols. (Rome, 1962), vol. II, pp. 324-25 (October 28, 1496); and earlier (March 13), *Prediche italiane ai Fiorentini*, vol. III², pp. 59-60.

[61] "Per ordine di frate Jeronimo el palio di sancto Giovanni et prima (et poi) delli altri non si corsono, ne si reputo inconviente a stanza sua non observare la antica consuetudine et patrio costume: tanto valeva apresso di noi la sua auctorita." Parenti, *Storia fiorentina*, ed. Schnitzer, p. 68.

[62] Ridolfi, *Life*, pp. 151-52, 183-84.

[63] Parenti, *Storia fiorentina*, ed. Schnitzer, pp. 105-106; Cerretani says they were *tutti e fanciulli della nobiltta*, but this is doubtful. Cerretani, *Storia fiorentina*, ed. Joseph Schnitzer, *Quellen und Forschungen zur Geschichte Savonarolas*, vol. III, *Bartolomeo Cerretani* (Munich, 1904), p. 38. For a lively descrip-

Above all the city echoed with the words of preachers, particularly those of Fra Girolamo and his lieutenants, Fra Domenico da Pescia and Fra Sylvestro Maruffi, but also those of his enemies' spokesmen, men like Fra Domenico da Ponzo and Gregorio da Pisa who were engaged to fight fire with fire. In the council halls, in the dispatches of foreign emissaries, in *ricordanze*, chronicles, and letters, in the workshops, and no doubt at the dinner tables of *grandi* and *popolo* alike, the friar's latest sermon was a prime topic of discussion. During those years Savonarola was the conscience of Florence.

But conscience exercises an uncertain sovereignty, its strength varying with mood and circumstance; at times its prompting is clear and irresistible, at times muffled and weak. It may influence action much, little, or not at all. So it was with Savonarola in Florence. Clearly his power extended beyond the domain of the purely spiritual, even beyond the sphere of private morality, into the life of the state itself; yet it is easier to describe that power in metaphor than in concrete terms. We have already seen this in regard to the constitutional reforms. The new constitution has been called Savonarolan with some justification, since at the least Savonarola was its most effective champion; but when we try to define his part in the reform movement more precisely we see that opinions differ not only in our time but also in his own. The chemistry of the interaction between a popular hero, his public, and the political process is not easily reduced to a precise formula.

The same difficulties apply to Savonarola's political role in the new regime. Analogies with the behind-the-scenes lordship of Lorenzo de' Medici are misleading.[64] Lorenzo had gained a large degree of control over the selection of public officials and the composition of councils and commissions, and he had had virtually a free hand in formulating and carrying out foreign policy. Medici power derived from a long record of participation in civic politics, generous and

tion of a Piagnone procession in which the boys played a leading part, see the account of Paolo Somenzi, Lodovico Sforza's envoy in Florence, published in Isidoro Del Lungo ed., "Fra Girolamo Savonarola," *Archivio storico italiano*, new ser., vol. XVIII, part I (1863), 8-9.

[64] E.g., as made by Cantimori in his review of Schnitzer, "Giuseppe Schnitzer: Savonarola," *Annali della R. Scuola Normale Superiore di Pisa. Lettere, Storia e Filosofia*, II (1932), 90-104.

shrewd expenditures from the enormous family fortune, and a following built out of marriage ties, business connections, and patronage. These resources were not available to Savonarola, and therefore he was never in a position to command obedience, even from his own political allies, much less to control elections.[65] He engaged in a certain amount of politicking in the privacy of the cloister; this seems clear. To San Marco came a steady stream of his partisans, some out of simple devotion to the man of God, others, whether pious or not, seeking an indispensable ally in the struggle to protect the new *governo civile* and the French alliance. Parenti said that the political supporters of the frate were of two kinds, those who believed in the truth (of his doctrine) and "those who made a show of believing it"; the latter frequented San Marco "under the pretext of piety" and took part in the religious ceremonies there and political dealing at the same time (*et pratica tenevano*).[66]

The Florentines had an almost superstitious fear of political caucuses, which they regarded as conspiracies with the unholy purpose of organizing opposition to existing governments or of intriguing to interfere with the free exercise of voting. Such caucuses, or *intelligenze*, had repeatedly been forbidden by law, most recently in the reform law of December 2, 1494, and in a law to protect the free functioning of the Great Council, on August 13, 1495.[67] Naturally, San Marco came under suspicion, and more than once Savonarola took the trouble to deny publicly that any *intelligenze* had been held there,[68] going so far as to declare that "in our San Marco there has never been held a conventicle or any meeting whatever."[69] But some remained unconvinced. Afterwards, when Savonarola had been discredited and imprisoned, the Signoria was eager to discover evidence of *intelligenze* in San Marco and interrogated the friar and a score

[65] For Savonarola's comparison of his own position with the positions of Lorenzo and Piero de' Medici, see his deposition in Villari, *Savonarola,* vol. II, appendix, p. clx.

[66] Parenti, *Storia fiorentina,* ed. Schnitzer, p. 136.

[67] Rubinstein, "Politics and Constitution," p. 136.

[68] *Prediche sopra Ruth e Michea,* vol. I, pp. 24-25; II, p. 145 (May 8, and August 21, 1496).

[69] *Prediche sopra Ezechiele,* ed. Roberto Ridolfi, 2 vols. (Rome, 1955), vol. II, p. 360 (May 4, 1497).

of his supporters on this point. In his own statements Savonarola steadily denied that he had mixed into the *particulari* of Florentine politics, partly, he said, because he had had to maintain his "reputation," partly because he knew few of the details of what was going on. On the other hand, he clearly regarded himself as the indispensable statesman of the new regime, and he admitted to a considerable degree of political involvement of a general nature designed to gain and to protect his goals.

Besides using the pulpit to exert political pressure—as he confessed to having done in order to force the *Accoppiatori* to resign before their allotted year had expired[70]—this involvement took several forms. One was to reach agreement with a few prominent political leaders as to general aims. Thus, he said, "realizing that Francesco Valori, Paolantonio Soderini, Gianbattista Ridolfi, and their adherents were prudent men and knew more than I, I left matters to them."[71] This was a weak system, not only because Savonarola had little real control over the political activities of these patricians, but also because they distrusted each other, so that Savonarola was forced to deal with each of them individually, with the result that he was the principal common link between them. He was aware of this, and he even considered the establishment of a lifetime Gonfalonier of Justice, on the model of the Venetian Doge. He rejected the idea because there was no one who seemed suitable for such a dangerous post. Instead, he threw his weight behind a single political chief, selecting as the most able and trustworthy Francesco Valori, who had already come to him to seek his support for just such a move.[72] As we have already seen, Valori was elected Gonfalonier of Justice for January-February 1497, emerging as the political leader of the *Frateschi* who were henceforth more united than they had been before. However, this new consolidation brought Savonarola new problems. Some of his less prominent followers, *mediocri cittadini* like Lionello Boni and Antonio Giraldi, objected to this trend toward the domination of their party by such powerful men, and Savonarola was inclined to share their concern.[73] The danger that the *cittadini maggiori* would settle their differences and create *uno stato fra*

---

[70] Villari, *Savonarola*, vol. II, appendix, p. cliv.
[71] *Ibid.*, pp. clvj-clvij.   [72] *Ibid.*, p. cliv.   [73] *Ibid.*, p. clv.

loro più stretto by manipulating the affairs of the Council to suit themselves and thus ruin the new government was constantly in his mind;[74] but he felt that he had no choice but to entrust Valori with the leadership which he himself was disqualified from exercising.[75]

In addition to his dealings with Valori and other *maggiori* about high level policy matters, Savonarola kept a hand in the direction of affairs through intermediaries. These were mostly men of less exalted stature whom, he said, he sent "here and there," to the Signori, to the Ten (of Liberty and Peace), and to the Eight (of Watch and Ward), exhorting them to stand firm, to live good lives, and to trust in God's aid, but always keeping his resolve not to interfere in *particulari*.[76] "As to having held consultations (*pratiche*) with citizens, I say that in the time I have been in Florence many citizens have talked to me, but with no one have I consulted specifically as to affairs of state in the sense of deliberating how to do this or that, but in general (*universalmente*) it has been my intention to keep them united and in good spirits."[77] Such lofty restraint was not always feasible, however, and Savonarola cautiously admitted to having dropped a word here and there in favor of some good man who was seeking election to one of the magistracies.[78] Moreover Savonarola was aware that while some came to San Marco out of devotion, others came to see and to be seen and thereby to reap some benefit in the form of political support; this he described as *una meza intelligentia*,[79] for the *forza principale di questa cosa* was the fact that his supporters recognized each other by sight and therefore knew whom to vote for in council.[80] For the most part he left such direct political transactions to his trusted disciple, Fra Sylvestro Maruffi: "and if I wanted something specific I would not discuss it

---

[74] *Ibid.*, pp. cliv-v and clxxx-clxxxj. Such suspicions were not groundless; we have only to recall Capponi's letter to Valori, in which he said that twenty-five or thirty *uomini da bene*, if they put aside their private differences and ambitions, could govern the city. See above, p. 264.

[75] Parenti says that Savonarola's fears were realized. *Storia fiorentina*, ed. Schnitzer, pp. 155-56. He also says that the Frateschi increasingly drew people to their "intelligentia" on the promise of securing offices. See also Ridolfi, *Life*, p. 183.

[76] Villari, *Savonarola*, vol. II, appendix, p. clvij.

[77] *Ibid.*, p. clviij.

[78] *Ibid.*, p. clvij.

[79] *Loc. cit.*

[80] *Ibid.*, p. clvj.

with citizens: in order to preserve my reputation I would do it through Fra Sylvestro or some other friar as seemed advisable, as in the matter of offices, although very rarely, because I did not know them [the candidates] and did not understand these matters."[81] Both Sylvestro Maruffi and Fra Domenico da Pescia repeated Savonarola's denial of organized *intelligenze* in San Marco, although the former admitted a certain amount of discussion as to candidates and governmental affairs.[82] In general the testimony of the other friars and laymen who were interrogated supported this version of the case, although Fra Roberto Ubaldini, the chronicler of San Marco, testified that while he had seen no evidence that Fra Girolamo had engaged in secret or dishonorable dealings of any kind, he had noticed that Fra Sylvestro Maruffi was always surrounded by a circle of citizens, that either in his cell or the cloister or garden there was always "an almost innumerable number of *huomini da bene* who remained with him throughout the day, albeit this was displeasing to the other brothers."[83]

While we might have some reservations about the testimony of men who were terrified of incriminating themselves by confessing that they had engaged in illegal activities, these depositions strongly suggest that the *Frateschi* were neither an organized party nor even a coherent faction. The advent of Valori's leadership in 1497 brought a somewhat greater degree of coordination but did not overcome the fundamental limitations of the group. The extent to which they were able to act together by prior agreement on legislative issues or in elections was hampered by the deep Florentine aversion to conspiracy which they themselves shared, by the vagueness of their common political aims, and by mutual distrust arising from personal and class antagonisms. Certain other difficulties derived from the special nature of a political movement that looked to a cleric for leadership. As a religious Savonarola was excluded from participation in the political process and especially vulnerable to charges of

[81] *Ibid.*, pp. clvj-clvij.　　　　[82] *Ibid.*, pp. cxix, ccxxiij, ccxxv.
[83] *Ibid.*, pp. cclxj-ij. Among the thirty-one he mentioned by name were such men of prominent families as Leonardo and Raffaello Strozzi, Francesco Rinuccini, Domenico Mazzinghi, and the poet of the Laurentian circle, Girolamo Benivieni.

interference—thus his constant preoccupation with his "reputation."

But we ought not to follow those historians who exaggerate the special weaknesses of the Frateschi and cite Savonarola's personal failure to create a viable political party, for in this the Savonarola movement was no exception. In describing the various factions in Florence, Piero Parenti refers to all of them as *intelligenze in spirito* which were held together "neither by inscription nor by oath but by a similarity of views and a common consensus and will."[84] In other words, the Frateschi lack of organization was typical of Florentine politics, at least in the post-Medicean era. If anything, Savonarola's ideological leadership provided a greater degree of coherence than the other groups were able to muster, while San Marco provided a convenient cover for the political activities of the friar and his allies.[85]

Strange to say, the weaknesses in Savonarola's position in Florence derived from the same sources that endowed him with such great personal influence—his moral leadership and the people's belief in his prophetic powers—for these were subject to quick shifts of public opinion and mood. In addition, his status as a cleric made him subject to an external authority which had ways of reaching over city walls to claim its own. Thus, in a *pratica* of March 10, 1496, Piero Capponi (who was to lose his own life six months later fighting against the Pisans) admitted that Fra Girolamo's preaching had borne "great fruit" in the city, and he advised his colleagues to do everything they could to see that he continued to preach; but he also advised that they should be ready to reconsider Savonarola's position "in order not to act against the will of the Supreme Pontiff, because one should render to Caesar the things that are Caesar's and to God the things that are God's. At other times [Capponi pointed out] the censures of the Pontiff have done great harm to the city, and Christians especially, in diverse places, have hampered our commerce."[86] This *pratica* took place shortly after Savonarola had

---

[84] Parenti, *Storia fiorentina*, ed. Schnitzer, pp. 136-37.

[85] Rubinstein, "Politics and Constitution," p. 166.

[86] ASF Consulte e Pratiche, vol. 61, fol. 210. This is also cited in Ridolfi, *Life*, p. 159.

broken the first silence imposed upon him by the Pope,[87] and it was a harbinger of things to come.

For the time being, however, the signs were favorable. Savonarola's Lenten preaching rang with all the exciting themes of Florentine glory and the coming reform.[88] Sundays were given over to public processions; the Palm Sunday celebration of 1496 was an especially colorful tribute to his own leadership which Savonarola carefully staged as a prelude to his appeal for the founding of a *Monte di Pietà*,[89] the communal loan fund once so ardently preached by his old rival, Bernardino da Feltre.[90] Even more salutary for the friar's popularity was the arrival in April of ambassadors bearing the news that King Charles VIII was returning to Italy, and Savonarola made the most of it by arranging for the envoys to announce the good tidings in public.[91] The Signoria elected in May was strongly Savonarolan.[92] Even the Pope made overtures of reconciliation toward Savonarola that summer,[93] while events conspired to stage a *reprise* of the drama of 1494.[94] In the autumn Lodovico of Milan and the partisans of the Italian League persuaded the Emperor Maximilian to mount a counter invasion of Italy; an Imperial fleet, supported by Venetian and Genoese galleys, swooped down toward Livorno, Florence's remaining port, while a League army prepared to march; once more it seemed that the Florentines would be overwhelmed by vastly superior forces. In their fear the citizens reached

---

[87] The Papal brief was dated October 16, 1495; the Signoria had ordered Savonarola to preach in the following Lent, having received verbal authority from the Pope. Ridolfi, *Life*, pp. 142, 150-51.

[88] *Prediche italiane ai Fiorentini*, vols. III¹ and III² cover this period.

[89] *Ibid.*, vol. III², p. 366; Landucci, *Diario*, p. 128; Parenti, *Storia fiorentina*, ed. Schnitzer, pp. 112-14.

[90] On Savonarola and the *Monte di Pietà* in Florence, see F. R. Salter, "The Jews in Fifteenth-Century Florence and Savonarola's Establishment of a *Mons Pietatis*," *Cambridge Historical Journal*, V (1936), 193-211.

[91] Parenti, *Storia fiorentina*, ed. Schnitzer, pp. 114, 116.

[92] *Ibid.*, p. 116.   [93] Ridolfi, *Life*, pp. 170-71.

[94] The German envoys argued that Charles the Great, King of France, whose beneficence the Florentines had enjoyed, was a German and therefore that they ought to show their gratitude to the Germans, not to the present Charles who was not the true king of France. Parenti, *Storia fiorentina*, ed. Schnitzer, p. 134. Obviously the envoys were aware of the importance of the Charlemagne legend in Florentine tradition.

out for divine help. A procession was organized to fetch the Madonna of Impruneta, traditional protectress of the city, and the Signoria ordered Savonarola to preach.[95] On October 27, he spoke in the Cathedral, boldly assuring the Florentines that all that heaven had promised them would be fulfilled to the last iota, if only they would renew their repentance and rededicate themselves to the holy cause. ". . . I have told you that the Church will be renewed and so it will be in any case. I have also told you that Florence will have many blessings and a greater empire than she has ever had, and I reaffirm this to you. But you become confused because you see how matters are going today, and because they seem not to be going in such a way as to bring those things about, and you fail to consider that God rules these matters and that this is His way, and God does not enlighten you to know the truth because you are wicked and therefore you are confused."[96] Reminding his listeners of how he had intervened in times past to lead them to liberty by recalling them to prayer and repentance, he commanded them to repeat the remedy: "Let come what may, I have no fear: if you turn back to God, I tell you that you will be liberated no matter what. This is the word I want to give you now."[97]

Perhaps this extraordinary display of confidence was due in part to the simultaneous arrival (on the 27th) of letters from Lyons promising that French help was on the way. According to Parenti the letters greatly encouraged the Florentines who were now generally inclined to believe more than ever both in the miraculous powers of the Lady of Impruneta and Savonarola's doctrine of trust in the Lord.[98] Thereafter the news from Livorno was good: the French arrived in wonderfully fast time; the enemy fleet was battered by storms; on November 27, the Florentines learned that the Emperor was withdrawing his forces. Savonarola now solemnly urged the Florentines to regard their blessings in the light of God's glory rather than as an earthly triumph,[99] but with the wonderful

---

[95] *Ibid.*, p. 144; see also Savonarola's statements that he was preaching "to obey the Magnificent Signoria." *Prediche sopra Ruth e Michea*, vol. II, p. 300, and p. 320.

[96] *Ibid.*, p. 305.   [97] *Ibid.*, p. 326.

[98] Parenti, *Storia fiorentina*, ed. Schnitzer, p. 147.

[99] *Prediche sopra Ruth e Michea*, vol. II, p. 398.

news of the sinking of nine Genoese and Venetian galleys he was unable to conceal his sense of personal triumph against his enemies. "First laughter, now tears; first the wicked are gay, then they are saddened. Only a little while ago they were rejoicing and saying, 'Do you see how we have been deceived?' Now they keep quiet. Messer Lord God plays with us. Well, what do you see now? The noose was in the rope, but it didn't go in. What do you say, you wicked ones, that this was chance, or fortune?"[100] Parenti observed that the news of the sinking of the galleys was taken as a sign from heaven, and that Savonarola rose in repute as a man of God who preached the truth, although he added sourly that the news turned out to be a lie spread by a false report from a Florentine commissioner.[101]

What the Lord gave the Lord could take away. Despite this brief surge of activity at Livorno, Charles VIII continued to postpone the return to Italy so devoutly wished by the Florentines, so confidently prophesied by Savonarola. At the end of February 1497 came the news that the French had been forced to withdraw their occupation troops from Naples and, still worse, that the King had concluded a truce with the King of Spain and the Italian League. With what devastating effect this news fell upon the hopes of the Savonarolans can be read in the awful reproaches the friar now hurled at Charles VIII: "Did I not also tell him that if he did not keep faith he would have many tribulations and that the Kingdom [of Naples] and its people would rebel, and so it was? And he has had many tribulations, his son has died and he will have more [troubles]. If he does not do what he has to do he will be rejected, God will kill him and he will lose his temporal and spiritual realm and God will quickly elect someone else."[102] Parenti (whose own enmity against the friar and his pro-French policy increased every day)[103] wrote that, despite Savonarola's "huge efforts" to keep Florence in the French camp,

---

[100] *Ibid.*, p. 402. This contradicts Ridolfi's assertion that Savonarola did not crow over his triumph but merely gave thanks to God. *Life*, p. 177.

[101] Parenti, *Storia fiorentina*, ed. Schnitzer, p. 149.

[102] *Prediche sopra Ezechiele*, vol. I, p. 286. In fact, Charles died in 1498 at his chateau of Amboise from an accidental blow on the head.

[103] Parenti seems to have turned against the French alliance as early as January 1495. See *Storia fiorentina*, ed. Schnitzer, pp. 89-90.

the city became increasingly divided on the issue as "little by little the greater peril was revealed to us and the outcome was awaited."[104] The growing fissure was also partly due to Valori's assumption of leadership at this time, for, as events were to demonstrate, Valori's greater efficiency in directing the *Frateschi* and his greater ruthlessness in putting down opposition were not unmixed blessings for the friar's cause.

Meanwhile the engine of Roman justice began again to turn. Regretting his earlier decision to set San Marco on a free course, the Pope now ordered the houses of the Congregation of San Marco to join a new Tuscan-Roman congregation, and, as he no doubt expected, they refused.[105] During the spring of 1497 Florence was filled with rumors that the Pope was preparing to excommunicate Savonarola, and at last, on June 18, the Bull reached the city. Vaguely charging Savonarola with spreading pernicious doctrine, with defiance of the papal prohibition against his preaching, and with disobeying the order to join San Marco to the Tuscan-Roman congregation, the Pope excommunicated him and all those who spoke to him, listened to him preach, or gave him any support.[106] The effect of the Pope's anathema was not a sudden paralyzing shock; alone it would probably not have been lethal to the friar or to his cause. His supporters did not desert him *en bloc*, and no one in that violent summer of 1497 could have predicted that in less than twelve months from the publication of the Bull Savonarola would be publicly discredited, tortured, and put to death; his chief followers dead, imprisoned, or cowed into silence; the mass of the people hostile, indifferent, or confused. Rather, the effect of the Bull was as a wasting poison, spreading slowly, implanting new doubts, eating away at old loyalties, weakening the unity and resolve of the body politic already ravaged by other fevers.[107]

The summer of 1497 was grim. Food shortages, unemployment, the plague, and an abortive raid by Piero de' Medici which was checked just outside the city walls heaped up the misery.[108] In May Savonarola's enemies had already turned his Ascension Day sermon

---

[104] *Ibid.*, p. 162.   [105] Ridolfi, *Life*, pp. 178-80.
[106] Published in Villari, *Savonarola*, vol. II, appendix, pp. xxxix-xl.
[107] E.g., the mixed effects described by Ridolfi, *Life*, pp. 200-201.
[108] *Ibid.*, pp. 191ff.

into the scene of a riot.[109] In August a conspiracy to restore Piero de' Medici to power was uncovered and many leading men were incriminated.[110] Five of Florence's most prominent *ottimati* were condemned to death as ringleaders; the others, imprisoned or sent into exile. When the five invoked the appeal law of March 19, 1495, claiming that they were entitled to a final hearing before the Great Council, communal justice confronted the ugly face of communal vengeance. All the hatreds and fears of this terrible time were now heated to a new boil. The people were "universally" determined, according to Parenti, to take revenge upon these proud aristocrats and make them an example for the future. Participants in a *pratica* called by the Signoria argued into the night, but they were deadlocked. Some were for summary execution; others insisted that a fundamental principle was in danger: if the government failed to grant the five an appeal to the Council they would be depriving the people of its sovereign right to judge. At last Francesco Valori turned the tide. Rising to his feet and banging the desk in front of him he demanded that "justice" be meted out to the conspirators, and that very night the five were hurried to their deaths.[111] After this affair, Parenti noted, Valori was more than ever regarded as the ruler of the city as well as of the Frateschi,[112] but this did not free Savonarola from the suspicion of having urged the death of the plotters nor, more justly, from the reproach of having made no effort to invoke the law of appeal for which he had once so ardently fought.[113] In such ways was the lofty idealism of Savonarola's cause compromised

[109] *Ibid.*, pp. 193-95; Landucci, *Diario*, pp. 147-48.

[110] See the depositions of Lamberto della Antella, in Villari, *Savonarola*, vol. II, appendix, pp. iv-xxv. The five condemned ringleaders were: Bernardo Del Nero, Niccolò Ridolfi, Giovanni di Bernardo Cambi, Gianozzo Pucci, and Lorenzo Tornabuoni. Parenti, *Storia fiorentina*, ed. Schnitzer, p. 208.

[111] Parenti, *Storia fiorentina*, ed. Schnitzer, p. 211.

[112] The death of Pierfilippo Pandolfini at this time also removed a potential rival for the leadership of the *Frateschi*. *Ibid.*, p. 213.

[113] Cerretani, *Storia fiorentina*, ed. Joseph Schnitzer, *Quellen und Forschungen zur Geschichte Savonarolas*, vol. III, *Bartolomeo Cerretani* (Munich, 1904), pp. 48-49. In his deposition Savonarola denied any responsibility for the punishments, but admitted that he had been satisfied with the sentences of death and exile. Villari, *Savonarola*, vol. II, appendix, p. clxxxix. See Machiavelli's comments on this in his *Discorsi sopra la prima Deca di Tito Livio* I. 45.

by the political passions of the agonized republic. By the time he arrived at his own hour of trial, he was but one more victim of a blood lust of which he himself was not entirely innocent.

By the winter of 1497-98 events were moving toward that hour. Under the Papal ban Savonarola could not preach, and preaching was his life and the life blood of his movement. Although his supporters did everything they could to persuade the Pope to reverse the friar's condemnation, they were unsuccessful; the Pope's price was Florence's adherence to the League, and this neither Savonarola nor the Florentines were ready to pay.[114] At last Savonarola's concern that his own work "was going to ruin" outweighed his respect for the Pope's authority,[115] and in Lent he took the fatal steps to the Cathedral pulpit. Once more the crowds flocked to hear him, once more the Lenten processions rang with the hymns of the faithful and the streets blazed from the bonfires of vanities. But the crowds were smaller than before, and the processions were attacked by hostile bystanders.[116] Everyone feared the Pope's wrath, which was quick to come.[117] In that same February Alexander VI sent a letter to the Signoria repeating his threat to excommunicate those who attended the friar's sermons and another to the Cathedral Chapter, warning the canons and all parish priests against celebrating mass in the Cathedral when Savonarola preached there. When Savonarola indicated his intention to persist, the canons appealed to the Signoria, complaining that they were in danger of losing their benefices. The Gonfalonier of Justice was then Giuliano Salviati, a Savonarola partisan, who refused to countenance the appeal of the canons;[118] but Savonarola withdrew from the pulpit of the Cathedral to that of his Church of San Marco.[119] In March the Pope decided to seize Florentine goods in the papal territories until Savonarola had been surrendered up to him; and that failing, to confiscate the goods and

---

[114] Ridolfi, *Life*, p. 214.

[115] Villari, *Savonarola*, vol. II, appendix, p. clxiij.

[116] See Savonarola's reference to this in *Prediche sopra l'Esodo*, ed. Pier Giorgio Ricci, 2 vols. (Rome, 1955), vol. I, pp. 111-12 (February 28, 1498).

[117] Ridolfi, *Life*, pp. 217-22.

[118] Parenti, *Storia fiorentina*, ed. Schnitzer, pp. 226-27; Savonarola, *Prediche sopra l'Esodo*, vol. I, p. 146.

[119] *Loc. cit.*

imprison the merchants themselves.[120] Under such threats the Signoria, headed by Piero Popoleschi, an open enemy of Savonarola, held a series of *pratiche* to decide what was to be done. Here, speaking frankly in what they all knew to be a moment of truth, the *primati* voiced their faith and their doubts, their courage and their fears, their devotion to a high cause and to their profits.[121] What is, perhaps, most remarkable is the unshakeable loyalty voiced by so many of them to the friar and to their common cause. To Paolantonio Soderini, Savonarola was to be cherished as a precious jewel; to Lorenzo Lenzi, as a saint who had brought Florence an inestimable treasure; to Filippo Sacchetti, as a servant of God whose prayers had saved the city. These men were ready to defy Pope and League, for, as Lenzi put it, "only by pleasing God rather than man can the city be saved, not to say increased," and Domenico Malegonnelle maintained that if they might lose one Paradise by listening to Savonarola's sermons (which he doubted), they would gain another by the same means. Less remarkable were the waverers who, while praising Savonarola's saintliness and doctrine, argued that this was a time to think of the unity and safety of the fatherland, or who confessed that while they had formerly attended the friar's sermons with regularity, now, since the excommunication, they were afraid to go. An out-and-out enemy, Giuliano de' Gondi, condemned Savonarola for teaching that the Pope was no Pope and therefore ought not to be believed: "he is creating a sect of Fraticelli like the one that once existed in this city, and this is a sect of heresy that you are making in this land." While such opposition seems to have stemmed from passionate disbelief, the coldly calculated words of Guidantonio Vespucci, a proponent of the League, still strike a chill: ". . . considering one and the other, that is, the good and the harm, it seems to them [the Doctors, for whom he was speaking] that it is better to satisfy the Pontiff." The Pope, Vespucci continued, could help the city to recover her possessions, while papal opposition would strengthen the danger from the other potentates of Italy and the interdict would subject their goods to plunder. Vespucci said that

---

[120] Ridolfi, *Vita*, vol. I, p. 349 and nn.
[121] The following excerpts are from the minutes of the *pratiche* in Lupi, "Nuovi documenti," pp. 30-53.

merchants were already refraining from shipping their goods, that safe conducts were being denied, and, in a dictum of self-appraisal which reminds us where Machiavelli learned his candor, that "we in Italy are what we are."

On one point everyone agreed—the safety and well-being of Florence came before everything else—but whether safety was to be found with the Pope or with the prophet was impossible to decide. Nor was the question settled on March 17, when the Signoria voted by a slim margin to try a compromise.[122] Fra Girolamo was to stop preaching, but he was not to be handed over to the Roman authorities nor interfered with in any other way.[123] The following day he preached his farewell sermon, comparing his afflictions to those of the prophet Jeremiah. Jeremiah had also been persecuted, yet he had continued to preach for more than forty years; he himself was but in his eighth year. Jeremiah had said that Nebuchadnezzar would come to destroy Jerusalem, seize the King, the priests, and the chiefs, and carry them into captivity while slaying many sinners; and so it had come to pass.[124] But Nebuchadnezzar did not come again. For a time Savonarola pursued the idea of calling a general council of Christendom and even began to write letters to the Emperor and the princes of Europe, urging them to "expunge the internal enemies of Christ,"[125] and to rid Christendom of this Alexander VI who was neither Pope nor Christian.[126] But from the princes there was silence.

In Florence, however, the din grew louder. Although the Signoria had forced Savonarola out of the pulpit, he continued to say mass and to consult with his followers, while Domenico da Pescia and Sylvestro Maruffi preached in his place. To many this was a scandalous violation of the Papal ban with dangerous consequences for the city, and hostile preachers in the other churches made the most of their fear. In the Great Council and in the streets the young anti-Savonarolans, known as the *Compagnacci* or Bad Companions, grew bolder and more violent.[127] Charges and countercharges were flung back and forth across the city, between San Marco and Santa Croce,

---

[122] Ridolfi, *Life*, p. 234.   [123] Lupi, "Nuovi documenti," pp. 53-54.
[124] *Prediche sopra l'Esodo*, vol. II, p. 303.
[125] *Lettere*, p. 207.   [126] *Ibid.*, p. 206, also pp. 208-11.
[127] Landucci, *Diario*, p. 166; Parenti, *Storia fiorentina*, ed. Schnitzer, pp. 244-46.

between Piagnoni and Arrabbiati, while those who felt themselves caught in the middle looked for some miracle to lead them out of this unbearable situation. Suddenly, a way seemed to open up. On March 25, 1498, the Feast of the Annunciation and Florence's New Year's Day, the Franciscan preacher in Santa Croce, Francesco di Puglia, challenged Savonarola to prove his doctrine by undergoing with him an ordeal by fire. Fra Domenico da Pescia quickly offered to champion Savonarola, and almost before the principals knew what was happening they were swept along by a flood of intense public enthusiasm. Savonarola was not happy about this naïve method of putting his divine mission to the test;[128] neither was Francesco di Puglia;[129] but once each side had taken a step toward the fire it was impossible to draw back without serious damage in the eyes of an intently watching public. The *primati* who were consulted expressed themselves more or less on party lines.[130] On one side, they were exasperated with both parties to this "contest between frati," reluctant even to dignify such matters by discussion in a council hall which was more suitable for discussions "of war and money," and eager to see an end of "friars and non-friars, *arrabbiato* and non-*arrabbiato*," for Florence had become "the laughing stock of the world." On the other, they were relieved to think that at last God would intervene to make a clear judgment. Gianbattista Ridolfi, Lorenzo Lenzi, Paolantonio Soderini, and the other familiar Savonarolan leaders were all eager to see the trial take place, while the others were less opposed than indifferent. It was arranged that the trial by fire be held on April 7. Five propositions were to be tested: that the Church was in need of renewal; that the Church would be scourged and reformed; that Florence would be scourged

---

[128] For an exhaustive treatment of the trial by fire which concludes that it was instigated by a coalition of Savonarola's enemies in the Signoria and the Franciscans, see Joseph Schnitzer, *Savonarola und di Feuerprobe Eine Quellenkritische Untersuchung, Quellen und Forschungen zur Geschichte Savonarolas,* vol. II (Munich, 1904); Ridolfi, however, expresses reservations about this explanation in his *Vita,* vol. II, pp. 210-11, nn. 44-47. On Savonarola's attitude toward the trial, see Ridolfi, "Due documenti savonaroliani sopra la prova del fuoco," *La Bibliofilia,* XXXVIII (1936), 234-42.

[129] Ridolfi, *Life,* pp. 236-37.

[130] References to these discussions in the *pratiche* have been published by Lupi, "Nuovi documenti," pp. 55-65.

but afterwards renewed and would flourish; that all this would come about in those times; that the excommunication of Fra Girolamo was invalid and that he who did not observe it did not sin.[131] Two friars, Domenico da Pescia and Mariano Ughi, were to sustain these propositions on behalf of Savonarola; the challengers from Santa Croce were Francesco di Puglia and Giuliano Rondinelli. All would walk into the fire together. If a man from one side perished, that side would be condemned, its leaders banished forever. If all perished, the cause of Fra Girolamo alone would be condemned. If one of the brothers refused to enter the fire, his side would be the loser and suffer banishment. To this it was added on April 6, that if his champion Fra Domenico were to die in the fire, Savonarola would be given three hours to leave the city.[132]

The next day all Florence crowded into the Piazza della Signoria to see "the miracle" as it was being called.[133] The soldiers were in formation; the friars sang their hymns; the elaborately prepared fire was lit; but hour after hour went by while the friars hesitated, wrangled, laid on new conditions, and, as darkness came, departed. When a sudden storm dropped rain and hail on the waiting fire many cried out that this was a miraculous sign from heaven, although in whose favor it was hard to tell. The crowd, drenched by the same miraculous rain, went away feeling perplexed and cheated, and the next day, Palm Sunday, it was easy for a few agitators to raise a howling mob and lead it to San Marco. One boy in the mob's path was run through with a lance; a workman who appeared before the Convent door was stabbed to death. The laymen surrounding Fra Girolamo inside the Convent fled; Francesco Valori and his wife were murdered in the streets. Part of the mob finally broke into San Marco and were met by the resistance of some of the friars who had seized weapons, while Savonarola continued to pray quietly, first in the choir, then in the Convent library. At last an armed guard arrived from the Signoria which had, in the meantime, declared Savonarola a rebel and ordered his banishment. Fra Girolamo and Fra Domenico da Pescia were taken into custody

---

[131] Ridolfi, *Vita*, vol. I, p. 354 and nn.

[132] Villari, *Savonarola*, vol. II, appendix, pp. xci-xciij.

[133] See the excellent description of these events in Ridolfi, *Life*, pp. 240-50.

and conducted to the tower of the communal Palace, where they were soon joined by the third doomed man, Sylvestro Maruffi. In the *pratica* called the next day no voice was raised in the friars' defense; there was a quick and unanimous decision to "interrogate with diligence," in other words, to put the prisoners to the torture.[134]

As we have already seen, the depositions wrung out of the three prisoners, as well as those extracted from other friars and citizens, reveal very little secret plotting of the kind the examiners were so anxious to discover. But the statement Savonarola signed contains his confession that he had not spoken to God nor God to him "in any special way" and that his prophetic certainty had been a sham.[135] He had undergone two "trials" with many turns of the rope; the bones of his left arm were crushed. If he confessed out of terror and pain it would be understandable; if he confessed because his belief in his own divine mission had deserted him that too would be understandable. On April 20, he faced still a third ordeal from the ecclesiastical commissioners who had arrived from Rome. Yet, while he admitted his culpability in calling for a council, negotiating secretly with other governments, and disobeying the Papal ban, he confounded his tormentors by repudiating his earlier confessions: suddenly dropping to his knees he cried, "If I must suffer, I wish to suffer for the truth; what I have said, I have received from God. God, you are giving me this penance for having denied You. I have denied You, I have denied You, I have denied You out of fear of the torments!"[136] The commissioners' verdict had strangely little relation to the substance of the friars' confessions: Fra Girolamo, Fra Domenico, and Fra Sylvestro were found to be heretics and schismatics and to have preached "new doctrines" (*cose nuove*), and they were consigned into the hands of the secular judge.[137] On May 23, the three friars were hanged and burned on the same spot where, six weeks earlier, the ignominious outcome of the fire trial had sealed their death warrants.

[134] Lupi, "Nuovi documenti," pp. 65-66.

[135] Villari, *Savonarola*, vol. II, appendix, pp. cl-clj.

[136] Ridolfi, *Vita*, vol. I, p. 394 and nn.; also reported by Parenti, *Storia fiorentina*, ed. Schnitzer, p. 282.

[137] Villari, *Savonarola*, vol. II, appendix, p. cxcviij.

IX

Savonarola, Theorist of Republican Liberty

COME, FLORENCE, WHAT WOULD YOU LIKE, WHAT HEAD, WHAT KING
MAY BE GIVEN YOU SO THAT YOU WILL REMAIN AT PEACE? I HAVE
ALREADY TOLD YOU THAT A SINGLE HEAD RULING ALONE IS
NOT BEST FOR EVERY PLACE OR COUNTRY, AND ST. THOMAS SAYS
THAT IN ITALY PRINCES BECOME TYRANTS BECAUSE HERE THERE
IS AN ABUNDANCE OF SPIRIT AND INTELLIGENCE,
WHICH IS NOT THE CASE IN THE
COUNTRIES BEYOND THE
MOUNTAINS.

—Savonarola, Sermon of December 28, 1494

CASTING the ashes of the burned corpses into the Arno, Savonarola's enemies hoped to wash away all traces of the fallen prophet; but his words remained, those graven on the hearts of his followers as well as those already committed to paper and print. Just weeks before his downfall he had published his *Trattato circa el reggimento e governo della città di Firenze.*[1] According to some, this brief tract represents a major legacy to the epoch-making discussions of government which were to take place in Florence in the coming decades. For this reason the name of Savonarola is placed alongside those of Niccolò Machiavelli and Francesco Guicciardini as one of the founders of modern political thought. To others the *Trattato* is but one more product of Savonarola's medieval mind.[2]

---

[1] *Trattato circa el reggimento e governo della città di Firenze*, ed. Luigi Firpo, in *Prediche sopra Aggeo* (Rome, 1965), pp. 435-87. On dating and text, see pp. 519-21. It will be referred to hereinafter as the *Trattato*.

[2] See above, p. 23.

Neither of these extreme views is accurate; both tear the *Trattato* out of context, by ignoring the conditions under which Savonarola wrote it, or by failing to relate it to his earlier political writings, or both. To get a better perspective on Savonarola's political writings, we should begin further back. In the 1480's, probably during his first sojourn in Florence when he was a lecturer in San Marco, Savonarola had compiled a *Compendium totius philosophiae* which contained a book on politics.[3] This he entitled *De Politia et Regno* and, like the rest of his moral philosophy, it was heavily indebted to his master, Thomas Aquinas, particularly to the work known as *De Regimine Principum*, which, although probably completed by Tolomeo da Lucca, was then believed to be wholly the work of the Angelic Doctor.[4] An examination of Savonarola's *De Politia* affords us an insight into his earlier political ideas, and therefore gives us a baseline from which we can measure the distance he traveled to become the theorist of the new Florentine republic.

Savonarola begins his work in good Thomist-Aristotelian fashion. Man is a social animal who can satisfy certain needs only by forming associations with other men. The political community (*civitas*)[5] is the natural combination of many smaller associations (*vicus*), formed in order to secure those good ends which physical, intellec-

---

[3] *Compendium totius philosophiae, tam naturalis quam moralis. Opus de divisione ordine, ac utilitate omnium scientiarum, in poeticen apologeticum. Compendium logices* (Venice, 1542). Hereinafter cited as *Compendium*. The *De Politia et Regno* is the tenth and last book of moral philosophy, pp. 576-97. Eugenio Garin points out that one MS of the *Compendium* bears the date 1484. *La cultura filosofica del Rinascimento italiano* (Florence, 1961), pp. 207-208. Since this is part of one compendium, it is reasonable to suppose that the whole work stems from the same period.

[4] I cite from Saint Thomas Aquinas, *De Regno ad Regem Cypri* [*De Regimine Principum*], *Opuscula Omnia*, ed. Pierre Mandonnet Tomus Primus (Paris, 1927), pp. 312-487. For a brief review of the question of authorship see Charles H. McIlwain, *The Growth of Political Thought in The West* (New York, 1932), p. 325 n. J. H. Whitfield says that in Savonarola's time the book went wholly under the name of Saint Thomas. "Savonarola and the Purpose of the Prince," *Modern Language Review*, XLIV (1949), 245. And, as we shall see, Savonarola seems to have shared the general belief.

[5] That *civitas* ought not to be translated "city" (*urbs*) is clear from the whole context of the discussion. "Political community" or even "state" is preferable. On this problem in interpreting Saint Thomas, see Thomas Gilby, *The Political Thought of Thomas Aquinas* (Chicago, 1958), pp. 261-64.

tual, and moral limitations prevent man from achieving alone or in smaller groups.[6] In coordinating its efforts to secure the common good, the political community moves toward the attainment of the moral virtues and ultimately towards the eternal blessedness which may be realized only in the next life. The ideal economic base of the *civitas* is agriculture: an agrarian community is more self-sufficient than one which lives by trade, and its citizens have more time to spend on community affairs. Moreover, men who frequently travel abroad are more likely to be corrupted by foreign customs, while the venality of business itself already exercises a corrupting influence. Above all, businessmen are poorly suited to be soldiers and they must depend on mercenaries, as do the citizens of Venice and Florence; this is a dangerous practice, because mercenaries have no patriotic ties to the states they serve.[7] Just as a political community is best founded in a region where the climate is not too hot or too cold but moderate,[8] so the best polities are those made up of citizens who are neither very rich nor very poor, but of the "middle" kind.[9]

Savonarola then goes on to discuss the government of the political community. All communities, since they are ordered toward an end, need leaders who will coordinate the activities of the citizenry and thus maintain a true polity (*vera politia*). If the political community can find one man who is normally superior to the rest he should be chosen ruler, for the rule of one man is the best form of government for several reasons: it most closely resembles the order of nature and the divine government of the world; experience shows that it is the most resistant to injustice and the least likely to fall into dissension and therefore into tyranny, which may be of the many as well as of one man; it is the most productive of unity and peace.[10] The community should take care to choose a man against whom there is no suspicion of evil, to limit his powers of doing harm,[11] and to be ready to resist him if he tries to rule tyrannically.[12]

---

[6] *Compendium*, pp. 576-77.
[7] *Ibid.*, pp. 581-82.
[8] *Ibid.*, pp. 580-81; again, 582.
[9] *Ibid.*, pp. 583-84.
[10] *Ibid.*, pp. 586-88.
[11] ". . . secundo debet principatum eius ita temperare, ut non possit faciliter tyrannizare." *Ibid.*, p. 588.
[12] *Loc. cit.*

A king is a ruler who rules well, in the interests of the community, and the blessings of his rule are many: between himself and his subjects there is friendship and they live together in mutual security and abundant wealth.[13] But the rule of an evil man is the worst tyranny of all. The tyrant is the enemy of excellence and unity; he subverts the public good and sows discord among his subjects. Under him nothing is secure since he seeks to appropriate every- thing for himself. No other kind of regime is capable of such great injustice and evil.[14] While Savonarola, following Thomas Aquinas, allows a right, even a duty, of resistance to tyranny,[15] he does not concede this right to private persons, but "to him who represents God," that is to "public authority." Public authority may reside in "the power of the people," or in the power of some higher lord, "if either has the competence to establish and to depose kings; if no one has such authority, the only resort is to Providence. This holds good only if the tyrant is a legitimate ruler, however; if he is an usurper of power he is a public enemy and anyone may kill him, as in a just war against the enemies of the people he who slays the enemy for the liberation of the fatherland is considered a hero."[16]

Still following *De Regimine Principum*, Savonarola attempts to deal with the problem of the influence of regional or national char- acter upon government. Eastern peoples are deficient in spirit (*sanguis*), while northerners abound in spirit but are weaker intellectually.[17] Such people are naturally servile and lack direction; therefore they ought to be governed by a king who has absolute powers. But those regions where people have abundant spirit and intelligence are not submissive and therefore ought to have a "politi- cal," or limited, form of monarchy or an aristocracy.[18] In Italy those

[13] *Ibid.*, p. 590. [14] *Ibid.*, p. 587.
[15] On this, Savonarola cites Thomas' *De Regimine Principum*, Book I, chap. 6. In general, see Gilby, *Political Thought of Aquinas*, pp. 156, 289, 301.
[16] Savonarola, *Compendium*, pp. 588-89.
[17] For the Aristotelian version of this theory, see *Politics*, Book VII, chap. 7. Savonarola cites Saint Thomas, *De Regimine Principum*, Book II, chap. 9; and Book IV, chap. 8.
[18] Provinciae vero quae et sanguine et intellectu abundant confidentes, et in cordis audacia, et in mentis intelligentia debent regi principatu politico, vel potentatu optimorum qui summitti non possunt. . . ." *Compendium*, p. 585.

who have wanted to rule despotically have had to become tyrants in order to overcome the resistance of the people; this has always been true in the insular regions, in Sicily, Sardinia, and Corsica; likewise in Lombardy no one has ever been able to make himself a prince for life except through tyranny, the Doge of Venice excepted.[19]

From the foregoing we can see that Savonarola closely followed what he took to be authentic Thomist political theory. Where the master argued for the theoretical and practical superiority of monarchy, the disciple followed. Where *De Regimine Principum* adapted monarchism to the special character of the Italian people, Savonarola did likewise, unaware that he had been led out of the authentic Thomist orbit by Tolomeo da Lucca or whoever it was who completed Thomas' treatise.[20] To be sure, he was not completely oblivious to the political experience of his countrymen; the few additions he made to the Thomist and pseudo-Thomist political ideas in his own *Compendium* were illustrations drawn from *experientia*, that is, from the examples and histories of the Italian

---

For a discussion of the terms *dominium politicum* and *dominium regale* in St. Thomas and in contemporary usage, see McIlwain, *Political Thought in the West*, pp. 330-32, 357-63.

[19] Savonarola, *Compendium*, p. 585.

[20] Joseph Schnitzer maintained that Savonarola knew that the latter part of *De Regimine Principum* was not by Saint Thomas, and that Savonarola believed Thomas wrote everything through Book III, chap. 6; but he gives no evidence to support either of these contentions. *Savonarola*, trans. Ernesto Rutili, 2 vols. (Milan, 1931), vol. II, p. 334, n. 2. This may have something to do with the curious fact that in his otherwise thorough summary of Savonarola's *De Politia*, Schnitzer omits the section on geographical and racial determinism which is in Book IV, the part which he says Savonarola knew Saint Thomas did not write. *Ibid.*, pp. 319-25. Savonarola cited from all parts of the treatise without giving any indication that he made a distinction between them. The Savonarolan passage cited in n. 18 above was almost a word for word quotation from the following passage of Tolomeo's part of *De Regimine Principum* (Book IV, chap. 8):

"Qui autem virilis animi et in audacia cordis, et in confidentia suae intelligentiae sunt, tales regi non possunt nisi principatu politico, communi nomine extendendo ipsum ad aristocraticum. Tale autem dominium maxime in Italia viget, unde minus subjicibiles fuerunt semper propter dictam causam, quod si velis trahere ad despoticum principatum, hoc esse non potest nisi domini tyrannizent: . . ."

communes.[21] Still, this first political work confirms what we have already learned from his early sermons: in the 1480's—perhaps in 1484, the very year of his first prophetic illumination—Savonarola was little concerned with the political issues of his time and place.

We have already seen how Savonarola became involved in the constitutional crisis and how he became a champion of the free, popular republic. Yet even then Savonarola retained something of his earlier monarchism by proposing that the Florentines take Christ as their King.[22] In every *genus*, he said, there is one thing which must be given primacy (*quod in omni genere est dare unum primum*)[23] to be "the rule and the measure" of all the others. Thus among the colors white is the first; among hot things, fire; while among all virtuous things the greatest is the virtue of God. In the same way, among governments the government of God, which is a unity, is the most perfect, and any government which approximates the unity and goodness of His may be called good and perfect also. But monarchy is not best for every country, as Saint Thomas says; in Italy princes become tyrants because here there is so much spirit and intelligence.[24] Nevertheless, since the Florentines seem to want a head to govern them, they should take Christ as their King, according to the Psalm which says, "But I am appointed King" (Psalms 2:6). God wants the Florentines to take Christ as their King, but whether or not they will do so is up to them, for Christ will be their King if the Florentines live under God's law, if Florence becomes Zion as the same Psalm suggests. To become Zion means to contemplate divine things, uniting in God's love through

---

[21] Thus he gave the examples of Florence and Venice for the dependence of commercial states upon mercenary armies (p. 582), and he elaborated slightly upon Tolomeo's discussion of the political character of the Italian people (p. 585).

[22] For the first time in his sermon of December 28, 1494. *Prediche sopra Aggeo*, pp. 409-28.

[23] *Ibid.*, p. 421; also in *Prediche italiane ai Fiorentini*, ed. Roberto Palmarocchi and Francesco Cognasso (Perugia-Venice, 1930-35), vol. II, *Giorni festivi del 1495*, p. 405; and *Prediche sopra Giobbe*, ed. Roberto Ridolfi, 2 vols. (Rome, 1957), vol. II, p. 71. For the concept of the *primum in aliquo genere* in Marsilio Ficino, see Paul O. Kristeller, *Il pensiero filosofico di Marsilio Ficino* (Florence, 1953), pp. 153-73.

[24] *Prediche sopra Aggeo*, p. 422.

love of one another; in short, accomplishing that universal reconciliation which Savonarola was urging upon the Florentines and thereby becoming the city of reform for Italy and the world.[25] The idea of Christ as King of Florence was an inspired symbol, brilliantly adapted from a traditional theme to Savonarola's civic purpose, not only to arouse patriotic pride and devotion to the cause of reform,[26] but also to bridge the transition from theoretical monarchism to practical republicanism. With Christ reigning in Florence no one else might aspire to that place; thus the city was both monarchy and republic at the same time.[27]

While *De Politia* was the expression of Savonarola's early theoretical monarchism and the theme of Christ's Kingship represents Savonarola's transition from monarchism to republicanism his later *Tratto circa el reggimento e governo della città de Firenze* shows Savonarola as apologist for the new Florentine republic. The *Trattato* was not a purely theoretical work written in a spirit of detachment, but a tract written and published at the express request of the Florentine Signoria—the last Signoria before his downfall that was Piagnone in sympathy.[28] It was in the first instance a description and defence of the new regime; in the second, a defence of Savonarola's own role in the foundation of this government which he had

[25] *Ibid.*, pp. 422-23.

[26] Later, Savonarola said that with the adoption of reform Christ had become King of Florence. Christ was King of all Christendom, but especially of Florence, where His service was especially celebrated. *Prediche italiane ai Fiorentini*, vol. II, p. 405. On the devotional aspects of this theme, see Jean Leclercq, *L'Idée de la royauté du Christ au moyen âge* (Rome, 1959). On the relation of this to a long-standing Italian communal practice of regarding the patron saint as the leader of the commune, see Hans Conrad Peyer, *Stadt und Stadtpatron im mittelalterlichen Italien* (Zurich, 1955).

[27] I find it difficult to agree with Whitfield's way of putting it, that Savonarola was "prepared to rebel against" the theory of the superiority of monarchy. "Savonarola and the Purpose of the Prince," p. 48. The theory was just what he was *not* prepared to rebel against; and since he believed the whole of *De Regimine Principum* was the work of Saint Thomas (see below), he had no need to feel that he was departing from the teachings of Saint Thomas.

[28] "Ma perché le Signorie Vostre mi richiedono, non che io scriva del governo de' regni e città *in generali*, ma che particularmente tratti del nuovo governo della città di Firenze. . . ." *Trattato*, p. 435.

come to see as an integral part of his preaching mission.[29] Finally, it was intended to offer advice as to the way to "establish and to perfect and to preserve the present good government, so that it may become excellent (*ottimo*) in this city of Florence."[30] Keeping these purposes in mind we may hope to maintain the correct perspective not only on the *Trattato* but on Savonarola's political thinking in general.

The *Treatise* is divided into three books, each of which is called a *trattato*. In the first *trattato*, an attempt to show the form of government best for Florence, he recapitulates Saint Thomas' views on the origins and reasons for the founding of political communities. Since this book is more or less a repetition of what we have already reviewed from the *De Politia*, we shall pass over it, except to note that here Savonarola takes more time to distinguish between the three basic types of government, whereas in the earlier work he had concentrated almost exclusively upon monarchy. In founding governments, political communities have taken different directions. Some have sought to promote their common good by founding governments of a single ruler, and this form is called a *regno*. Some have opted for government by a select group of leaders, *principali e migliori e più prudenti della communità*, who, at intervals, distribute among themselves the magistracies, and this is called a *governo delli ottimati*. Still others have decided that government should remain in the hands of all the people, who then distribute the magistracies as they see fit, and this is the form known as *governo civile*.[31] Men institute governments for the preservation of peace and for the protection of those human activities which help them to live well and to promote virtue, in short, for the *bene*

[29] "Perchè, avendo io predicato molti anni per volontà di Dio in questa vostra città, e sempre prosequitate quattro materie: cioè, sforzatomi con ogni mio ingegno di provare la fede essere vera; e di dimostrare la simplicità della vita cristiana essere somma sapienza; e denunziare le cose future, delle quali alcune sono venute e le altre di corto hanno a venire; e, ultimo, di questo nuovo governo della vostra città: e avendo già posto in scritto le tre prime, delle quali però non abbiamo ancora pubblicato il terzo libro, intitolato *Della verità profetica*, resta che noi scriviamo ancora della quarta materia, acciò che tutto el mondo veda che noi predichiamo scienzia sana e concorde alla ragione naturale e alla dottrina della Chiesa." *Ibid.*, p. 436.

[30] *Ibid.*, p. 437.   [31] *Ibid.*, p. 441.

comune. All three types of government can promote the common good but, "speaking absolutely," monarchy does this best, since it has the greatest power to promote unity. This is confirmed in the government of the world, which is a government of a single Lord, and in nature, as in the government of the bees, as well as in the Church, over which Christ placed Peter as sole head.[32] Nevertheless, speaking practically, rather than absolutely, he says, the character of a people determines what type of government is best for it. At this point Savonarola restates the doctrine of geographical and racial influence on political character which he had already included in his Thomistic compendium, singling out the Italians as the example of a people who could not bear absolute rule.

Having thus set the stage, Savonarola comes to the Florentines: "The Florentine people are the most ingenious of all the people of Italy, the wisest in their undertakings, and the most spirited and bold, as experience has shown many times. Although they occupy themselves with commerce and seem to be a quiet people, when they undertake a civil war against a foreign enemy they are very frightening and courageous; the chronicles tell about the wars they have fought against various princes and tyrants to whom they would never surrender, but held out and finally achieved victory. The nature of this people, then, is such as not to tolerate the government of a prince, not even if he be good or perfect, since, as there are always more wicked men than good, he would either be betrayed and killed or he would have to become a tyrant in order to withstand the shrewd daring of those wicked citizens who are especially motivated by ambition."[33] Thus, both because of the nature of her people and because of long-standing tradition, *reggimento civile* or republican government had become the characteristic type of government for Florence. According to Savonarola this was not controverted by the fact that Florence had actually been ruled for many years by tyrants; even the usurpers of recent times were forced to maintain the traditional forms of republican government, astutely ruling through their placement of friends in the magistracies. Nor is the second type of government, that of *ottimati* or *principali cittadini*, a solution for Florence, for such aristocratic governments have

---

[32] *Ibid.*, pp. 442-43.   [33] *Ibid.*, pp. 446-47.

always led to factional divisions which have not ended until one side or the other has been driven into exile and some citizen has made himself a tyrant. In 1494, when the anti-Medicean exiles returned, there would have been discord and civil war, with the ruin of many families and with much bloodshed, which would have resulted in the complete destruction of the city, if God had not intervened to establish the Council and the *governo civile* and preserved the city's liberty. And anyone who has not lost his natural judgment through his sinfulness can see that only by God's government and protection has the city been preserved through all the dangers of the past three years.[34]

The second *trattato* is essentially an essay on tyranny, both in general and as a problem for Florence. As in *De Politia*, Savonarola repeats the Thomistic arguments that the tyranny of a single man is worse than the tyranny of an oligarchy or a democracy, although he elaborates upon them in such a way as to suggest that he is drawing upon the Florentine experience under the Medici. Other bad forms of government tend towards the tyranny of one man, he says, for as their government dissolves into civil strife the people give power to their favorite citizen who thus becomes a tyrant. This form of tyranny is even worse than that of a legitimate lord, for such a tyrant can only come to power by using force against the citizenry. Hence, a regime of *ottimati* or a *governo civile* must be very careful to protect itself against any citizen who has designs of achieving sole power. It must have very severe laws which punish not only those who discuss such a thing but also those who even hint at it, so that everyone may be careful not to think about it. Indeed, the consequences of tyranny are so evil that anyone who is negligent in applying such severe laws himself sins before God.[35] Savonarola then details the evil consequences of tyranny, and again he combines examples from *De Regimine Principum* with some which are clearly inspired by the Florentine experience. The tyrant is a man imbued with pride, sensuality, and avarice, the roots of all evil, and his rule is an unbridled pursuit of self-gratification during which the citizenry is exposed to every form of violence and injury. But even worse, the exercise of tyranny corrupts the citizenry itself,

[34] *Ibid.*, pp. 448-50.   [35] *Ibid.*, pp. 451-55.

for in order to achieve his wicked ends the tyrant keeps the citizens in ignorance of governmental affairs so that they lose their political aptitudes; he sows discord among them, favors the worst sort of men, and endangers the innocence of women and boys, all of whom are defenceless against his lusts. Even religion is vulnerable, for the tyrant makes a pretence of piety by cultivating the superficial aspects of religion, while all the while usurping both the spiritual and the temporal goods of the Church for the advancement of members of his own family.[36]

For no city, he declared, is tyranny so bad as it is for Florence, because here we are especially concerned to be good Christians and as such we must try to establish a government which leads toward that blessedness Christ has promised us.[37] Good government nourishes the *ben vivere* by supporting good religion, not so much by promoting religious ceremony as by promoting truth through good ministers of the Church. Bad priests provoke the wrath of God against the city. Moreover, every good government proceeds from Him; if He removes His hand from the city the graces that flow from good government will not flow to her. In this circular fashion Savonarola connects the problem of government with the problem of Florence's divine election. As good religion and good behavior grow, the government of the city will become perfect through divine favor, drawn by the prayers of the priesthood and the whole community, as well as by the wisdom (*li buoni consigli*) by which governments are preserved and augmented, since good citizens are especially illuminated by God.[38] On the other hand, good government will promote good religion: "there is nothing that the tyrant hates more than the worship of Christ (*il culto di Cristo*) and the good Christian life," and he secretly tries to destroy them, removing good prelates, giving benefices to bad priests and monks (especially to those who fawn upon him), and corrupting the youth of the city. Thus, the problem of the tyrant is especially acute in Christian cities and above all in Florence, since this is a people strongly inclined to Christian piety. Already, Savonarola claimed, the Christian life of the city surpasses that of all others; nowhere is there a greater number of good Christians or a higher perfection of life

---

[36] *Ibid.*, pp. 456-66.   [37] *Ibid.*, p. 466.   [38] *Ibid.*, pp. 467-68.

than in Florence. How much more then, could the word of God grow and become fruitful, if all opposition were removed and a state of internal peace achieved?[39]

In the third and final *trattato*, Savonarola gives his prescription for the foundation and preservation of a *governo civile* in Florence. The first necessity is to prevent a single private citizen from usurping power by gradually gaining control of the distribution of offices and the other dignities in the state. Hence the first need is to see that this is made impossible, and the best way to do so is to provide that the authority for such distribution remains with all the people. Practical considerations require that such authority be delegated to a representative body, however; this should be neither so small as to be easily corrupted by bribery or the collusion of friends and relatives, nor so large as to create confusion, which would result if the common people (*la plebe*) were admitted. Therefore the representative body should include a great number of citizens, but exclude those who would be dangerous or disorderly.[40] This is the Great Council which, since it distributes all the honors, is the *signore* of the city. Three things are necessary for its protection: first, the passage of laws with strong penalties to ensure the proper working of the Council, laws of compulsory attendance and other such measures; second, the adoption of measures which will prevent the Council itself from degenerating into a tyranny through the corruption of wicked or foolish men, mainly by *intelligenzie*; third, the search for ways to prevent the obligation of Council attendance from becoming too heavy a burden upon its members by wasting their time with inefficient procedures and the like.[41]

Not in such measures, however, does the real heart of the problem of good government in Florence lie. Four things, Savonarola

---

[39] *Ibid.*, pp. 469-70.

[40] ". . . bisogna instituire un certo numero di cittadini, che abbino questa autorità da tutto el popolo: ma perchè il piccolo numero poteria essere corrotto con amicizie e parentadi e danari, bisogna constituire uno grande numero di cittadini; e perchè forse ognuno vorria essere di questo numero, e questo poteria generare confusione, perchè forse la plebe vorria ingerirsi al governo, la quale presto partorirebbe qualche disordine, bisogna limitare per tal modo questo numero de' cittadini, che non vi entri chi è pericoloso a disordinare; e ancora, che niuno cittadino si possa lamentare." *Ibid.*, p. 474.

[41] *Ibid.*, pp. 474-76.

writes, are necessary to perfect the new republic: the fear of God, love of the common good, peace or love of the citizens for each other, and the doing of justice.[42] Let every citizen who wishes to be a good member of his city believe that this Council and this republic have been sent by God, not merely in the sense that every good government proceeds from Him, but by special providence, as the history of the past three years clearly shows. The citizen's obligation to work toward perfecting the regime is an obligation to God,[43] and the government that results from such efforts will be "a government of Paradise," with many spiritual as well as temporal blessings.[44] Among such happy consequences will be an extension of Florentine power, for where justice reigns people will congregate voluntarily "and God, for this reason, will extend their empire as He did for the Romans; they too were severe in doing justice and for that reason He gave them the empire of the world, for He wants His people to be ruled justly."[45]

Savonarola ends his treatise with a vivid picture of the blessings which will be enjoyed under this government "more of God than of men," blessings spiritual as well as material, eternal as well as terrestrial: "First, they will be freed from the slavery of the tyrant, . . . and live in true liberty, which is more precious than gold and silver, and everyone will be secure in his city, concerning himself with his family, with honest gain, with his farms, with joy and peace of mind. And if God increases their goods or honors, they will not be afraid that these will be taken from them. They will be able to go to their villas or wherever they wish without asking permission from the tyrant, to marry their daughters and sons as they please and hold wedding celebrations and be gay and have the friends of their choice, to concern themselves with virtue or with the study of the sciences or the arts as they wish, and to do other similar things, all of which will be a real earthly felicity. Then will follow spiritual felicity, because everyone will be able to give himself to good Christian living without being prevented by anybody. Nor

---

[42] *Ibid.*, pp. 477-79. Whether the reader was to attribute any significance to the equation of the number seven with the perfection of government in Florence (three measures to found and protect the new government, four to achieve perfection) is impossible to say.

[43] *Ibid.*, pp. 476-77.   [44] *Ibid.*, p. 480.   [45] *Ibid.*, p. 479.

will anyone be constrained by threats from doing justice when he serves in the magistracies, because everyone will be free; nor will anyone be forced to make wicked contracts because of poverty, since, with good government, the city will abound in riches. . . . And the people will earn, and they will raise up their sons and daughters religiously [*santamente*], because good laws will be made concerning the honor of women and children. And in this way, above all, religion will grow, since God, seeing their good intentions, will send them good pastors. . . . In a short time the city will become so religious as to be a terrestrial Paradise and live in rejoicing (*jubilo*), songs, and psalms; and the children will be like angels, and they will live together nourished in Christian and civil life; wherefore in time there will be so much happiness among the good that they will have a real spiritual felicity in this world. Third, in this way they will not only merit eternal felicity, but even greatly augment their merits, and their crown in heaven will grow, because God gives the greatest reward to those who govern the city well."[46]

Clearly, whatever interest Savonarola may have had in political theory, his primary purpose in writing the *Treatise* was to explain and to defend Florence's new *governo civile* within the context of his own prophetic program. Even the second *trattato* he conceived primarily in terms of Florence's own recent experience with tyranny rather than as a general treatment of the problem, while the third, with its ode to the coming perfect state, is as much concerned with the temporal and spiritual rewards of religious renewal as with the practical or theoretical problems of republics. This presentation of a moral and religious homily under the guise of political theory did not make for clarity of thought. For example, while Savonarola continues to describe monarchy as the best form of government, it is not at all clear from his analysis that there could be any real political community where monarchy would be suitable, since it does not seem to be necessary for communities where men are wise, good, and harmonious, or safe for communities where men are wicked and dissentious. Equally perplexing: we are left in doubt whether it is good religion that creates good government or whether it is first necessary to have good government before there can be

[46] *Ibid.*, pp. 481-83.

good religion in a state. Apparently Savonarola meant that while some degree of good will and virtue was necessary to make government function well, it was only in the well-ordered state that the ultimate spiritual and terrestrial felicity could be achieved. But how this could be managed where bad government had already corrupted its citizens is difficult to see, unless the hand of God intervened to set things right—and this, of course, was just what he believed to have happened in Florence. God was literally the *deus ex machina* who had not only saved Florence from the fate of civil war and ruin, but also saved Savonarola's argument from foundering on the sharp rock of logic. The point, however, is not to find holes in his argument but to show that in Savonarola's *Trattato* as in all his other thinking, theory was subordinate to prophetic inspiration and to his zeal for religious reform. Insofar as Savonarola tried to establish a theoretical base for his discussion of government in Florence his main source was still the *De Regimine Principum*. His discussion of the founding of governments and of the three good and three bad types of regime is Thomistic, and with Saint Thomas he saw government as the instrument for achieving both practical and spiritual human goals. Both for Saint Thomas and for Fra Girolamo the common good takes precedence over individual human wants, and the achievement of the *bene comune* must be the constant aim of government.[47] For both, also, the main ingredients of the common good are peace and unity, the prerequisites for the attainments of man's other social ends,[48] and this concept served as the theoretical point of departure for Savonarola's personal entry into the Florentine political arena as the healer of factional strife.

Nevertheless, while Saint Thomas argued that monarchy was the best form of government because it was the type most likely to produce unity, because it most nearly reflected the government of the world and of nature, and because experience proves it the least likely

---

[47] *De Regimine Principum*, Book I, chap. I. See also Savonarola's notes citing Saint Thomas on the common good, in Pasquale Villari, *La storia di Girolamo Savonarola e de' suoi tempi*, 2 vols. (Florence, 1926), vol. I, appendix, p. xiii.

[48] *De Regimine Principum*, Book I, chap. II. In addition to the *Trattato*, see the lengthy discussion of the *bene commune* in Savonarola's sermon of December 21, 1494. *Prediche sopra Aggeo*, pp. 336-37.

to degenerate into tyranny,[49] Savonarola had become a champion of the *governo civile*, arguing that both tradition and natural character made the Florentines poorly suited for monarchy. Here the point of departure is Thomas' own discussion of the differences in political talent which derive from the differences of character due to climate.[50] Those who live in cold climates do not live *politice* nor do they have an aptitude for ruling other peoples, while those who live in temperate climates preserve their freedom, persevere in "political" (as against despotic) forms of government, and know how to rule other peoples. While Saint Thomas did not pursue this line of thinking very far in his part of *De Regimine Principum*, his continuator did, arguing that in Italy political regimes had always flourished because of the character of the people.[51] There is, then, no question of originality in Savonarola's basing his preference for republican government in Florence upon "empirical" grounds;[52] such grounds were already established in the Thomistic treatise which was his main authority. But at the same time Savonarola extended these arguments much farther than either Saint Thomas or even Tolomeo da Lucca had done. Nothing in *De Regimine Principum* gave Savonarola his warrant for singling out the Florentine people as the most intelligent and the boldest in their undertakings among all the peoples of Italy, nor did he owe the discussion of republican government in his third book entirely to Saint Thomas or Tolomeo. All of this originates elsewhere, partly in

[49] *De Regimine Principum*, Book I, chap. II. Saint Thomas' arguments were not altogether based on reason; he appealed to experience as well.

[50] *De Regimine Principum*, Book II, chap. I, citing Aristotle's *Politics*, Book VII, chap. V (1327b). It is to be noted that this discussion of geographical determinism begins in the authentic part of Thomas' treatise; thus, even if Savonarola knew that the latter part of the work was not authentic, he had authority for the application of this approach in Saint Thomas himself.

[51] *De Regimine Principum*, Book IV, chap. VIII. He also made another argument, that "political" regimes were proper to cities: "ut in partibus Italiae maxime videmus, et olim viguit apud Athenas post mortem Codri, ut Augustinus refert *De civitate Dei*," and "considerandum etiam, quod in omnibus regionibus sive in Germania, sive in Scythia, sive in Gallia, civitates politice vivunt. . . ." *Ibid.*, Book IV, chap. I.

[52] As Whitfield says in his "Savonarola and the Purpose of the Prince," p. 49, although he acknowledges that Savonarola continued to follow *De Regimine Principum* in some particular points (p. 50).

Florentine patriotic traditions and partly in what Savonarola had learned in his newly-acquired role as the champion of the new regime. This gave to Savonarola's political ideas, despite their deep indebtedness to Thomism, a very different spirit and direction.

His treatment of the problem of liberty is a case in point. Whereas Saint Thomas had regarded political liberty as a condition enjoyed by some men and a condition which a just king must therefore ensure to them as part of their rights in society, he did not regard the achievement of liberty as a general end of political communities in the same way that he regarded justice to be. Savonarola had followed this point of view in his *De Politia*, but in the *Trattato* he treated political liberty as one of the chief aims of political life in general, and of the Florentine revolution in particular. Liberty, he now said, was "above all other treasures" and "more precious than gold and silver."[53] While even in the latter, republican, part of *De Regimine Principum* the argument for a "political" regime or republic is made on the grounds that it is the form most likely to achieve the common good, Savonarola argued for republicanism as the best guarantee of liberty as well as the common good. Indeed, he came to regard the practise and enjoyment of liberty as an indispensable component of the common good.[54]

But what did Savonarola mean by liberty? Did he understand it, as Rudolf von Albertini maintains, as the right to participate in the state, rather than as freedom from the state?[55] The distinction is von Albertini's, not Savonarola's. For the friar a fundamental consideration was that men be free from subjection to arbitrary rule; this was the main point of his attack upon tyranny. The tyrant was a ruler who imposed his will upon the people for his private interests and pleasures, and in liberating themselves from tyranny the

---

[53] *Trattato*, pp. 486, 481.

[54] *Ibid.*, pp. 448-50, 481, 486. For his idea that liberty was a major aim of the reform of 1494, see *Prediche sopra Aggeo*, pp. 225-26, 297, 315.

[55] ". . . nicht als Freiheit von Staate verstanden, sondern war das Recht, am Staates beteiligt zu sein, als gewissermassen Teil des Staates zu sein." Rudolf von Albertini, *Das Florentinische Staatsbewusstsein in Übergang von der Republik zum Prinzipat* (Bern, 1955), p. 21. Von Albertini further maintains that this was the traditional Florentine communal view of liberty.

Florentines had freed themselves from servitude.[56] But for the Florentines even a legitimate, non-tyrannical government of one man was not satisfactory, for they were a people *ingegniosissimo* and *sagacissimo nelle sue imprese*, and their *animoso e audace* spirit needed freedom.[57] As we have already seen, he argued that their nature would not tolerate the government of a prince, even if he were "good and perfect," for there would always be more bad than good citizens to cause trouble, with the result that a ruler would either be overthrown and killed or he would maintain himself in power by ruling tyrannically. The same principle, moreover, applied to an aristocratic government; for Florence only a *reggimento civile*, a broad-based republic, would do. This, he said, was confirmed by the city's history, and history or long-standing custom is a second nature; "just as nature is inclined in a determinate direction and cannot be diverted, as a stone is inclined to fall and cannot be made to rise except by force, so custom (*la consuetudine*) is converted into a second nature, and it is very difficult, almost impossible, to change the customs of men and especially whole peoples, even evil [customs], because such customs have become natural to them."[58] For the Florentines, popular government, in which the people retain the power of distributing offices, was not founded upon an abstract conception of right, but upon a necessity of their nature, grounded in their historical experience, inseparable from the problem of preventing the loss of their liberty through tyranny and through their own inclinations toward selfish aggrandizement.

Still, the right to participate in the state was not one which Savonarola was ready to concede to everyone. If, in theory, he defined a *governo civile* as one in which *tutto el popolo* retained the power to distribute offices,[59] in fact, such power must be delegated to a council of citizens who sit there by virtue of their special position in the state, not by popular election. While Savonarola could repeatedly refer to Florence as a *governo popolare*, he did not equate this with direct or mass democracy. Access to the Great Council, he argued, must be limited for practical reasons. First, because it would be difficult to assemble all the people every day; second, because were *la*

---

[56] *Prediche italiane ai Fiorentini*, vol. III¹, *Quaresimale del 1496*, p. 233.
[57] *Trattato*, pp. 446-47.   [58] *Ibid.*, p. 448.   [59] *Ibid.*, pp. 441, 473-74.

plebe to intrude (*ingerirsi*) into the Council this would quickly create disorder. Therefore, while the Council should include a large number of citizens, large enough to prevent control of the government by bribery or by a clique of relatives or friends, it should exclude those who are dangerous or disorderly, and this would seem to eliminate *la plebe*. This Great Council, with its power to distribute all the honors of the city, is the sovereign body—the *signore*.[60] What the principle of selection for the Council should be Savonarola did not say in his *Trattato*, but he was clearly defending the system that he had helped to create, a system which distinguished a quasi-hereditary political class from the mass of the people. Florence, he said in one of his sermons, must protect her liberty by establishing a rule of "the wiser and the more intelligent."[61] For Savonarola liberty was freedom from arbitrary rule protected by a broad, but not an equal, degree of participation in the electoral and legislative processes.

If this analysis is correct, it does not support the notion that Savonarola was the originator of a new and fuller concept of free citizenship, the first theorist of man's rights in the city.[62] The main source of his idea of republican liberty, and he himself insisted on it, was Florentine tradition.[63] Even if there were reasons for instituting another type of government in Florence, he declared, a *reggimento civile* was so impressed in the minds of the Florentines that it would be difficult, almost impossible, to detach them from it. So jealous of their tradition of liberty were the Florentines that even the recent tyrants had been forced to keep up the appearance of a free republic while secretly controlling appointments to civic offices.[64] The concept of liberty as freedom from tyranny was a commonplace of Florentine thought, one of the frequent themes, for example, of the orations delivered by the gonfaloniers of the companies on the

---

[60] *Ibid.*, p. 474.

[61] *Prediche sopra Aggeo*, p. 315.

[62] Ireneo Farneti, *Genesi e formazione del pensiero politico di Girolamo Savonarola* (Ferrara, 1950), p. 4.

[63] Professor Felix Gilbert makes the point that Savonarola's reform was conceived as a return to the *antico vivere popolare*. "Florentine Political Assumptions in the Period of Savonarola and Soderini," *Journal of the Warburg and Courtauld Institutes*, XII (1957), p. 211.

[64] *Trattato*, p. 448.

occasion of the bi-monthly entry into office of a new Signoria, even during Medicean times.[65] Savonarola's new (and non-Thomist) contention that popular government was the best guarantee against tyranny was another such commonplace,[66] while the characterization of the Florentines as an intelligent and high-spirited people who were prone to dissension and factionalism was yet another.[67] Even Savonarola's suggestion that the Florentines look to the Venetian constitution for a model of stable republicanism was something less than a novelty. The "myth of Venice," the admiration of the Venetian constitution as the ideal solution to the problem of reconciling freedom and stability in the state, was, as we have noted earlier, well-established in Florentine ruling circles.[68]

If the myth of Venice was useful as a model of stability and success in that moment of extreme crisis, in the longer run it was the myth of Florence herself which counted with the Florentines, and this too Savonarola understood. Once the Great Council was established, Savonarola emphasized its Florentine rather than its Venetian character, declaring that Florence needed a different type of government from that of Venice—a *governo civile e politico* rather than a government of *ottimati*—and that Florence's reformed republic was a government of the people, of the citizens, while Venice's was a government of *gentiluomini*.[69] In the *Trattato*, where he discussed both the theory and the practice of an optimum government for Florence, he did not mention the Venetian constitution.

[65] Emilio Santini, "La Protestatio De Justitia nella Firenze Medicea del Sec. XV (Nuovi testi in volgare del Quattrocento)," *Rinascimento*, 10 (1959), 33-106, especially pp. 38-39.

[66] Gilbert, "Florentine Political Assumptions," p. 212.

[67] E.g., the anonymous *protestatio* from the time of Cosimo de' Medici (1434-64): "questa tenpestosa e pericolosa citta. . . ." Santini, "La Protestatio," p. 88. For a sketch of the earlier history of popular government in Florence and the attempt to secure impartiality in the distribution of offices, see Marvin Becker, "Some Aspects of Oligarchical, Dictatorial and Popular Signorie in Florence, 1282-1382," *Comparative Studies in Society and History*, II (1960), 421-39; together with a companion piece on Siena by David Hicks (pp. 412-20), and a comment by Hans Baron (pp. 440-51).

[68] In addition to the articles of Felix Gilbert and Renzo Pecchioli already cited, see F. Gaeta, "Alcune considerazioni sul mito di Venezia," *Bibliothèque d'Humanisme et Renaissance*, XXIII (1961), 58-75.

[69] *Prediche italiane ai Fiorentini*, vol. III¹, p. 56; and vol. III², p. 234.

Rather, he declared that with God's help the city had found a form of government which was true to the nature of the Florentine people as this nature was expressed in tradition and practice.

However, for all of Savonarola's debt both to Thomist theory and to Florentine tradition, his view of politics was not merely the sum of those two parts, for he incorporated both of them into an apocalyptic framework which was the product of his own prophetic impulse, and this led him to a view of the state which was neither entirely Thomist nor completely Florentine. Savonarola's approach to politics, as to all else, was determined by his belief in the coming religious renewal. This can be seen, for example, in the way in which he transformed the lesson of Roman success presented by Tolomeo da Lucca in his portion of *De Regimine Principum*, according to which the spread of the Roman Empire was God's reward for the Romans' cultivation of the three virtues of love of country, zeal for justice, and concern for civic harmony.[70] If, said Savonarola, the Florentines behaved as had the Romans, "in a short time the government will become perfect, . . . and they will have made a government of Paradise, and they will have the results of many graces, spiritual as well as temporal."[71]

As we maintained earlier, Savonarola's involvement in Florentine politics caused him to intensify rather than to diminish his search for apocalyptic meaning in events. Upon his entry into the struggle for constitutional reform in December 1494 he had begun to formulate the millenarian vision in which Florence was the center and he the chief spokesman of the New Jerusalem. Having earlier regarded political events chiefly as verifying the imminence of God's scourge and the Last Days, he came to see the revolutionary events of November and December 1494 as the first stage of the great renewal which, beginning in Florence, would spread throughout the world. Whereas earlier he had considered tyranny only as one of those instances of moral corruption which were signs that the *flagello* was at hand, rather than as a concrete evil to be fought and overcome, he came to argue that the elimination and permanent prevention of

---

[70] *De Regimine Principum*, Book III, chaps. IV-VI. This, according to Tolomeo da Lucca, the presumed author, is a summary from a lengthier treatment of the same theme by Saint Augustine (*City of God*, Book V, chap. XII).

[71] *Trattato*, p. 480.

tyranny was necessary in order to provide the proper political and moral setting for the establishment of the New Jerusalem.

Such views had very important implications for the development of his view of the state, of the Florentine state, at any rate. According to Saint Thomas, the temporal power, since it is concerned with the ordering of life toward limited ends, should be subordinate to the priestly power, which is concerned with ordering life to its highest end, the celestial good.[72] For Savonarola, however, the new Florentine state, as a divinely chosen vehicle for religious reform, was by no means limited in its exercise of power to temporal matters, nor should it be subordinate to priestly power. He charged the city government with responsibility not only for promoting virtue among its citizens, but also for removing bad priests and establishing the correct divine cult.[73] The reign of the Spirit was to come in their lifetimes, and the initiative had to come from the Florentine people and their reformed civil government. In their new freedom the Florentines could establish *uno perfettissimo culto* and an *ottimo vivere cristiano*. Florence would return to the early Christians' mode of life and would be as a mirror of religion for all the world.[74] The city would be *uno paradiso terrestre*, living in *giubilo e in canti e salmi*, while her children would be like angels. The combination of a republican and a Christian regime (*vivere cristiano e civile*) would make the government celestial rather than earthly, and the joy of the virtuous would be so great as to give them "spiritual felicity in this world."[75] Savonarola tended toward eliminating the distinction between temporal and spiritual power as toward eliminating the distinction between heavenly and earthly felicity.[76] In

---

[72] "Sed in nova lege est sacerdotium altius, per quod homines traducuntur ad bona coelestia: unde in lege christi reges debent sacerdotibus esse subjecti." *De Regimine Principum*, pp. 343-44.

[73] *Trattato*, pp. 469-70.

[74] *Ibid.*, pp. 466-69. [75] *Ibid.*, pp. 481-87.

[76] Schnitzer recognized the difference between Savonarola and Aquinas with respect to the relation between priestly and temporal powers, and he also noted Savonarola's even more radical anti-clerical tendency: "one almost has the impression that he would have liked to entrust the service of God to hands other than those of priests." *Savonarola*, vol. I, p. 32. But Schnitzer attributed such tendencies to Savonarola's lack of faith in his ecclesiastical superiors, in whose hands he was dubious about entrusting the salvation of souls, whereas

the chosen city of Florence politics and religion reinforced each other and used each other's means to achieve a common end. With the coming of the New Jerusalem all such distinctions would become meaningless. The city would be a church, the world would be spiritualized. Yet, in a sense, the church took on the configurations of the city as well; the spirit would become flesh in the form of the new Florence with its new government and its new empire.

This tendency to envision the great renewal in worldly terms, begun in the winter of 1494, reached its culmination in Savonarola's *Trattato*, where he saw the fulfillment of God's purposes through the concrete agency of the new *vivere civile* which would also be a *vivere cristiano*, in the most exalted sense, and a new Roman empire at the same time. Starting from a position of radical dualism, in which the world had to be destroyed in order to bring about the victory of the spirit, he had come to believe that the agencies of religion and the Florentine state could unite to achieve the victory of the spirit in this life. This in itself was a major departure from his earlier views, but there was a still further step—the identification of that spiritual victory with the apotheosis of Florence, and such an identification he spelled out in the *Trattato*.

With this in mind it is impossible to agree that Savonarola was "in opposition to the almost completed bourgeois revolution" of his time.[77] That he attacked the vices of the city's potentates and the greed of the rich is indisputable, and that he foresaw the establishment of a new moral order is equally so. But—and it is precisely this point that makes Savonarola's career such a fascinating subject of study—the new order that he came to envision reflected, to a remarkable extent, the aspirations of that same Florentine bourgeoisie, both its modest hopes for a stable constitutional system of a middle-class character and its more extravagant fantasies of riches, power, and worldly glory. How the Florentines were to reconcile these riches, power, and glory with the new rule of the Spirit, and what a Florentine hegemony over its neighboring cities had to do with the com-

---

I believe they are more fully explained by reference to his millenarianism, to his vision of the transformation of the relations of clergy and state in the coming new age.

[77] As Carlo Curcio claims. *La politica italiana del '400* (Florence, 1932), pp. 200-201.

ing of the New Jerusalem, Savonarola did not say; but this is a paradox deeply embedded in the civic patriotic tradition. As for Savonarola himself, the statesman was born of the prophet and the reformer, as he himself acknowledged; what was important was to get the Florentines started on the work of religious and constitutional reform; God would see to it that they were richly rewarded.[78] Nowhere in his sermons or in his writings does he concern himself with the details of the new order (an omission, it may be observed, which is characteristic of millenarians of all times).

In pursuit of his new order, Savonarola was likely to try to reconcile irreconcilable means as well as irreconcilable ends. The violent methods he now advocated in defense of the reformed republic seem inconsonant with his exhortations to brotherly love and peace; they also contrast with his earlier preaching, counseling the Florentines to suffer the most grievous oppression.[79] Now he called for strenuous punishment for the tyrant and the would-be tyrant; tyranny was the one sin for which he was unwilling to allow any compassion.[80] Just as Saint Thomas had vested the right of resistance in public authority, Savonarola located this right in the Great Council, while he argued that any effort to subvert the Great Council itself should be regarded as a capital offense equivalent to the assassination of a king or a lord of a city, in other words, a form of attempted usurpation. Every citizen, he said, should defend the Council "with all his strength."[81] One of the greatest dangers to the government of the Great Council he saw in the traditional Florentine popular assembly, or *Parlamento*, and he inveighed against it in his sermons with fury. Signori who tried to summon a *Parlamento* were no Signori at all; they should be torn in pieces

[78] See above, p. 143.

[79] See above, pp. 98-99; in writing the *De Politia*, however, Savonarola had followed the Thomist doctrine of resistance.

[80] *Trattato*, pp. 454-55.

[81] *Prediche italiane ai Fiorentini*, vol. III¹, p. 129. We might note that laws against tyranny had been passed in Florence before. See Marvin Becker, "The Republican City State in Florence: An Inquiry into its Origins and Survival (1280-1434)," *Speculum*, XXV (1960), 45, n. 33; Nicolai Rubinstein, "Florence and the Despots: Some Aspects of Florentine Diplomacy in the Fourteenth Century," *Transactions of the Royal Historical Society*, 5th ser., vol. II (1952), pp. 21-45.

as soon as they set foot on the public platform! If an individual member of the Signoria tried to call a *Parlamento*, let his head be cut off. If the offender were not a member of the Signoria, let him be declared a rebel and his goods confiscated and let his denouncer be rewarded.[82] No doubt this harangue was in part calculated to overcome the *ottimati*'s resistance to abolishing the popular assembly which had ever been an instrument for manipulation in their hands,[83] and if so it was effective. On August 13, 1495, the Great Council gave the final touches to a bill of abolishment presented to it by an unwilling Signoria.[84]

Zeal for the new order brought out a more pragmatic as well as a more violent side of Savonarola's character. In the early days, before he had become a political personality in Florence, he had referred to that famous saying attributed to Cosimo de' Medici that a state is not governed by paternosters as an example of the irreligious cynicism, typical of politicians, which he condemned. In the first days of the great constitutional upheaval he referred to the maxim again, commenting that, on the contrary, a regime is the stronger for being spiritual, and he pictured the ideal governor in strictly moral terms.[85] Before long, however, he had begun to come down from such lofty heights, claiming that the shrewder and more intelligent members of the community are those who naturally rule.[86]

[82] *Prediche italiane ai Fiorentini*, vol. II, pp. 391-92.

[83] As most recently, it will be recalled, on December 2, 1494. On the use of *Parlamento* in the past, see Guido Pampaloni, "Fermenti di riforme democratiche nella Firenze medicea del Quattrocento," *Archivio storico italiano*, CXIX (1961), p. 33.

[84] "A di XIII nel grande consiglio nostro finalmente si dette l'ultima perfectione alla provisione formatisi dalla Signoria, per ricordi et conforti di frate Jeronimo contro a del parlamento. Difficulta fu da prima a tirarvi la Signoria, la quale benche facta dal popolo, la parte popolare non teneva et al favore de grandi inclinava." Piero Parenti, *Storia fiorentina*, ed. Joseph Schnitzer, in *Quellen und Forschungen zur Geschichte Savonarolas*, vol. IV, *Savonarola nach der Aufzeichnungen des Florentiners Piero Parenti* (Leipzig, 1910), p. 71. Parenti's own comment on the *Parlamento* was: "And in truth there was no other way to take the government out of the hands of the people than by means of *Parlamento*." *Ibid.*, p. 72. For the law of abolishment see Villari, *Savonarola*, vol. I, p. 312.

[85] See above, p. 147. *Prediche sopra Aggeo*, pp. 134-35.

[86] *Ibid.*, p. 315.

Sometime later he stated flatly that in a choice between a prudent man and a good man who was not prudent, the prudent man should be selected for office, citing Saint Thomas to the effect that goodness was not enough in affairs of state.[87] Where Saint Thomas said this Savonarola did not reveal. Saint Thomas seems not to have raised the issue of a dichotomy between virtue and prudence in this way;[88] on the contrary (citing Aristotle as *his* authority), he had insisted that "A ruler must have the virtue of a truly upright man."[89] Besides, it was one thing to say that goodness without prudence was insufficient for political effectiveness; it was quite another to make a flat choice in favor of prudence over virtue. Savonarola referred once more to Cosimo's maxim, this time in a discussion of the responsibility of political participation. The dictum that the state is not governed by paternosters is unacceptable, he maintained still. But so is the avoidance of worldly affairs by men who consider themselves above the ordinary level of godliness. One who has divine illumination must not disdain those who have only the light of natural reason, and even if he has revelations from God, he ought not to reject the counsel of prudent men who understand the affairs of the world.[90] While these words were spoken in the emotional context of Savonarola's preaching, they could well have been repeated in the *Trattato* as the fruit of his own reflections on what he had learned in almost four years of constant struggle to remake Florence into the city of his prophetic vision.

---

[87] ". . . ma se gli è uno sciocco, benchè e' sia buono, non lo fare, perchè manca qui l'onore di Dio, manca il ben commune e l'onore e la reputazione della tua città, la quale tu togli eleggendo uno che non sia atto. Se sono dua, un prudente ed un buono e non prudente, debbi eleggere el primo, cioè il prudente. Come dice Santo Tommaso, che non basta la bontà, senza la prudenzia in queste cose e che non sono li uomini come il angeli, che quanto di più bontà sono, hanno tanta più intelligenzia. *Verbi gratia* se tu hai a eleggere commissari in campo, se tu eleggi uno sciocco, benchè sia d'una gran bontà, non sta bene, perchè starà là e dirà: non gli fate male. Però bisogna che in quello luogo sia uomo animoso e prudente, non di manco buono." *Prediche italiane ai Fiorentini*, vol. II, p. 390.

[88] Saint Thomas Aquinas, *Summa contra gentiles*, Book III, chap. 81.

[89] Saint Thomas Aquinas, *Summa theologica*, Prima Secundae 6.

[90] *Prediche sopra Ezechiele*, ed. Roberto Ridolfi, 2 vols. (Rome, 1955), vol. I, pp. 57-58.

To CONCLUDE, Savonarola was not merely the saintly, ascetic prophet of Roberto Ridolfi's biography or the single-minded and deliberate reformer of Joseph Schnitzer's; he was more accommodating than the first would have him and more fanatical and contradictory than the second would allow. He was far more sensitive to the political and social realities of the Florentine situation than either Francesco Ercole or Federico Chabod were willing to grant, yet he was neither the brilliant original theorist of modern liberalism described by Ireneo Farneti nor the opponent of Florentine middle-class values described by Carlo Curcio. Savonarola attached himself to a centuries-old tradition of Florentine popular republicanism and accommodated himself to Florentine ambitions for wealth and power. And it is inaccurate to say, as Ercole did, that Savonarola had no conception of an independent state, when in fact he steadily increased the scope of the state to deal with all phases of life, including a heavy responsibility for supervision of religious and moral matters. It was not that Savonarola denied the state an independent *existence*, but that he denied it an autonomous *value*. Even here he made concessions to the requirements of political realism, as he discovered that the state had need of men of prudence, whether they were men of virtue or not. If this was still far short of Machiavelli's separation of politics from moral and religious norms, it was Machiavelli, in this sense at least, who was the innovator, not Savonarola. Florentine statesmen might well have agreed with Cosimo de' Medici, that the state was not governed by paternosters, but religious and moral considerations nevertheless played an important part in the political deliberations of the period of Savonarola and Soderini.[91]

The contention that Savonarola's approach to politics was "medieval" is as faulty as is the assertion that it was "modern." If Savonarola incorporated certain aspects of scholastic thought into his reform program, these aspects, the ideas of justice, the common good, and the moral ends of the state, were, and are, deeply embedded in the western political tradition; they are medieval in the sense that all of us are medieval. If Savonarola's basic inspiration was Biblical and his impulse apocalyptic, he shared this inspiration and

[91] Gilbert, "Florentine Political Assumptions," pp. 200-11.

this impulse with other revolutionists of his time. If, on the other hand, Savonarola was an innovator, it was in the sense that he believed that his was the time for fulfillment of long-standing aspirations for a great renewal which would embrace both the civil and the moral life.

X

The Millennium in Florence after Savonarola

O PARRICIDE ARNO, YOU STILL RETAIN
THE SPLENDOR OF THE EVIL YOU RECEIVED
AND CONCEAL IT TO COVER YOUR MISTAKE
· · · · ·
O BLIND PEOPLE, YOU WHO HIDE THE GIFT
OF OTHERS IN YOUR MIDST; HIDE YOURSELVES TOO,
FOR TO YOUR OWN HARM YOU HAVE SPURNED THE GOLD.

—Giovanni Nesi, *Poema filosofica et morale*

I

THE attack upon Savonarola as Antichrist expressed a great dis-illusionment. The events of April and May, from the abortive fire trial to Savonarola's imprisonment, recantation, and death, could not but have dimmed the faith of many who had believed in the threefold vision of riches, glory, and power.[1] For them the best explanation was that they had been victimized by a demon deceiver: Savonarola the Antichrist was the mirror image of Savonarola the prophet of God. Perhaps a kind of exorcism may be seen in the Signoria's order for the removal of La Piagnona, the great bell of

---

[1] See, for example, the words of Fra Benedetto da Firenze, one of Savonarola's most ardent disciples, describing his immediate, dazed reaction: ". . . and, as a thrush stunned in the snare, I went off to Viterbo." Quoted by Roberto Ridolfi, *The Life of Girolamo Savonarola*, trans. Cecil Grayson (New York, 1959), p. 290. For Benedetto's recovery, see my article, "A Lost Letter of Fra Girolamo Savonarola," *Renaissance Quarterly*, XXII (1969), 5-6.

San Marco, guilty of having summoned the faithful to defend the cloister on the night of the mob's attack.[2]

Still, after the initial disarray, Piagnonism proved to have retained much of its appeal. Any Florentine could explain the political forces which had led to Savonarola's downfall, while many were sceptical about the validity of his published confessions.[3] Savonarola's downfall itself was taken as confirmation of his prophetic truthfulness— had he not foretold his own martyrdom?[4] Moreover, were not events taking place as he had predicted?[5] It was impossible to believe that Savonarola had recanted, wrote Gianfrancesco Pico, because his prophecies must be self-evident to all people of sense. Anyone who took the trouble to observe the situation in Italy could understand this by the light of natural reason. Florence had been protected by the Queen of Heaven: the city had begun to enjoy her felicity; she had lived more virtuously than ever before. How then could there be any doubt that the conversion of the Infidel would soon take place?[6] In 1500 Bartolomeo Redditi, Doctor in Civil and Canon Law, reaffirmed his faith: "I believed and I do believe, because his preaching made Florence a paradise on earth." Just as God had chosen the people of Israel, when they were in the Pharaoh's servitude, to manifest His providence to the whole world, so, according

[2] Giovanni Cambi, *Istorie*, ed. Ildefonso di San Luigi, *Delizie degli Eruditi Toscani*, vol. XXI (Florence, 1785), p. 134; Roberto Ridolfi, *Vita di Girolamo Savonarola*, 2 vols. (Rome, 1952), vol. II, pp. 29 and 234, n. 15.

[3] See the discussion of Savonarola's alleged confession described in the chronicle of Simone Filipepi, brother of Botticelli, published in P. Villari and E. Casanova eds., *Scelta di prediche e scritti di fra Girolamo Savonarola* (Florence, 1898), pp. 488-89, 505-508.

[4] *Epistola del Conte Zoanfrancesco da la Mirandula in favore de fra Hieronymo da Ferrara dappoi la sua captura* (Mirandola, 1498), BRF Ed. Rari 222, fols. 1 verso–2; and Giovanni Nesi's poem "Che fai Italia?" of May 8, 1498, in Arnaldo Della Torre, *Storia dell' Accademia Platonica di Firenze* (Florence, 1902), p. 692, n. 2.

[5] ". . . e partigiani di frate Jeronymo ancora rinnovavano la memoria sua, allegando le sue predictioni et che questi erano e nuovi barbieri etc., . . ." (July 1499). Piero Parenti, *Storia fiorentina*, ed. Joseph Schnitzer, in *Savonarola nach der Aufzeichnungen des Florentiners Piero Parenti, Quellen und Forschungen zur Geschichte Savonarolas*, vol. IV (Leipzig, 1910), p. 290.

[6] Gianfrancesco Pico, *Argumentum eiusdem obiectione*, MS BNF Magl. XXXV, 116, fols. 77 verso–79 verso.

to Redditi, God had chosen the Florentines and sent His prophet to them. First He had purged them by removing their tyrant and giving them the inestimable gift of liberty, then He had protected them against the tyrant's repeated attempts to return. To Redditi this was proof that Florence was God's elect, and he declared that his faith in the fallen prophet remained unshaken.[7] *Un arra del paradiso*—that was Florence under the leadership of Savonarola, sang the visionary Marietta Rucellai a year after the friar's death.[8] Florence could be exalted more than any city in the world: she was *ingrata* to have rejected her divine blessings, but after she is duly punished,

> Jerusalem will be made to flourish in you
> and you will be glorious in everything.
> Then you will see many people come
> to adore you in this holy place
> And the City of God will be called
> Shining new Jerusalem.[9]

In such ways did Piagnoni continue to voice their disappointment, their resentment, and their persistent faith. Even in death Savonarola was their prophet and their leader, guiding them and helping them from his seat in a martyr's heaven,[10] and despite her treachery

---

[7] Bartolomeo Redditi, *Breve compendio et sommario della verita predicata et profetata dal benedetto padre Fra Girolamo da Ferrara*, ed. Joseph Schnitzer, *Quellen und Forschungen zur Geschichte Savonarolas*, vol. I (Munich, 1902), p. 49 (based on Psalm 115).

[8] This part of the poem is published in Joseph Schnitzer, *Savonarola*, trans. Ernesto Rutili, 2 vols. (Milan, 1931), vol. I, p. 302, n. 141. On Marietta Rucellai, sister of Fra Santi (Pandolfo) Rucellai, of San Marco, see Mario Ferrara, *Contributo allo studio della poesia savonaroliana* (Pisa, 1921), pp. 12-13. She is not to be confused with Camilla Rucellai who prophesied Giovanni Pico's assumption of the Dominican habit at the time of the lilies.

[9] " che tti fara gierusalem fiorire
siche per tutto sarai gloriato
allor vedrai molta gente venire
per adorarti inquesto luogho santo
ella cipta diddio sara chiamato
Yherusalem novella inluminata."

This part of the poem is unpublished. MS BNF Magl. XXXV, 116, fol. 130 verso. The verses bear the date February 1498 (1499 n.s.), fol. 132 recto.

[10] Mario Ferrara, "Antiche poesie in memoria del Savonarola," *Memorie Domenicane*, XLIII (1926), 232-33.

Florence was still their New Jerusalem, where his promises would be fulfilled.

> My Florence, if you do not repent
> your sins and do penance,
> Famine, war and pestilence await you
> And every other cruel and evil scourge,
> Even though you are the City of God.[11]

But Piagnonism was not nourished by apocalyptic faith alone. Political factors played an important part in its survival, just as they had been instrumental in its birth in 1494. The *ottimati* leaders of the opposition to the republic of 1494 had concentrated much of their attack on Savonarola himself, assuming that his downfall would carry the government of the Great Council with it. Expecting that they would be able to reach an accommodation with their fellow aristocrats, they favored mild, even token, punishments for such *Frateschi* leaders as Paolantonio Soderini and Gianbattista Ridolfi, who were consequently let off with the imposition of forced loans.[12] For a time it seemed as though their calculations were correct. By May 1499 such former political enemies as Guidantonio Vespucci and Bernardo Rucellai, on one side, and Paolantonio Soderini and Gianbattista Ridolfi, on the other, were reported to be discussing joining forces behind the leadership of Lorenzo di Pierfrancesco Popolani[13] in order to share the control of the government. They had the backing of Lodovico Sforza, Duke of Milan.[14] Again, however, as in 1494, the movement toward oligarchy was stymied by divisions within the ranks of the aristocrats themselves as well as by popular opposition. One group of *ottimati*—containing both former Savonarolan sympathizers like Piero Guicciardini, and *Arrabbiati*, like Benedetto Nerli and his brothers—opposed this coalition and, says Parenti, calculating themselves to be the weaker side, "took

---

[11] *Ibid.*, pp. 247-48.

[12] Francesco Guicciardini, *Storie fiorentine, Opere*, vol. VI, ed. Roberto Palmarocchi (Bari, 1931), pp. 155-56.

[13] This was Lorenzo di Pierfrancesco de' Medici, who had been prominent in the opposition to his cousin Piero in 1494 and had changed his name at the time of the Medici expulsion.

[14] Parenti, *Storia fiorentina*, ed. Schnitzer, p. 287.

the way of the people"; that is, they made common cause with those who upheld the popular regime. Together they were able to block all the efforts of the oligarchs.

Another mistake that the latter group repeated was to under-estimate the strength of popular republicanism in Florence. According to Guicciardini (himself no friend of the *governo popolare*), support for the government of the Great Council not only enlisted *universalmente tutto el popolo* but even came from the ranks of the *ottimati* themselves and, more surprisingly, from the *Compagnacci*, those aristocratic youths who had resisted Savonarola's efforts to press them into his republic of virtue.[15] Clearly, popular republican-ism was not identical with Piagnonism, no more now than it had been in Savonarola's lifetime. Not everyone who fought for the *reggimento libero* dreamed also of the New Jerusalem. Neverthe-less, as in 1494, apocalyptic fantasy came to the support of republican liberty. Not surprisingly, the rising determination to save the gov-ernment of the Great Council was accompanied by the appearance of new Piagnoni polemical writings. Such was the anonymous treatise in the form of an exposition of the fifth psalm which was published just then. It lamented Florence's treatment of Savonarola and his two comrades, calling them the three pillars that had sus-tained the city with their teachings.[16] The work must have had its effect, since it greatly agitated both the Signori and the Eight who could think of nothing better than to refer the matter to Rome, no doubt because the treatise also contained an attack against the Pope and because it was suspected, probably rightly, that the author was a friar of San Marco.[17] Similar sentiments were expressed by Gio-vanni Nesi in the poetic rebuke which is quoted at the head of this chapter, although, since it was never published, Nesi's protest may have been a private one.[18]

After a short interval San Marco became once more a home for the movement dedicated to popular republicanism, although to

---

[15] Guicciardini, *Storie fiorentine*, pp. 155-56.
[16] Parenti, *Storia fiorentina*, ed. Schnitzer, p. 288.
[17] Ridolfi, *Vita*, vol. II, p. 31 and nn.
[18] Giovanni Nesi, *Poema filosofica et morale*, ms BRF 2750, fol. 20. (In the margin opposite the first line was written, "Monedula" referring perhaps to the proverb, "Non plus aurum tibi quam monedulae committere.")

what extent it functioned as the center of activities is difficult to say. No doubt the Convent was less important in this respect than it had been during Savonarola's lifetime, but there are indications that the continuation of the cult of Savonarola by the brothers of San Marco also had its political side. As they returned to active roles in Florentine politics, former *Frateschi* leaders began to press for the reinstatement of the fourteen friars who had been banished from San Marco and all Florentine territory for their part in the Piagnone movement. After an initial unsuccessful effort, the *Frateschi* were able to gain the return of the friars by order of the Signoria, in June 1500.[19]

These were trying times for Florence. Already debilitated in substance and spirit by the six years' war to capture Pisa, the city was suddenly faced with new dangers from outside and new political repercussions from within. In May 1501 Cesare Borgia descended on Florentine territory from Bologna and, after an unsuccessful siege of Firenzuola, met with Piero de' Medici at Loiano north of Florence. Pistoia rose in revolt. In Florence the partisans of the Medici were suddenly filled with new hope; the Piagnoni and other supporters of the free republic, with the suspicion that this was part of a conspiracy to restore the old tyranny. For a time it was feared that the people would attack the homes of the *grandi*, whom they suspected indiscriminately of complicity with the enemy outside the city.[20] This danger was alleviated when the Florentines bought Cesare off with the promise of a three-year subsidy of 36,000 florins annually, but the city's troubles were not over. The next year Vitellozzo Vitelli at the head of a Borgia army penetrated Tuscany from the south and pushed up the Valdichiana and Valle Tiberina, seizing towns as he approached. Simultaneously Arezzo took advantage of Florence's weakness to revolt as she had done in 1494. In Florence it was generally understood that Vitellozzo's aim was to restore the regime of Piero de' Medici. During these tribulations it was easy to discern God's retribution for the city's rejection of her prophet. One anonymous Piagnone wrote that Savonarola himself had predicted

[19] Parenti, *Storia fiorentina*, ed. Schnitzer, p. 294.

[20] For an account of these events, see Gino Capponi, *Storia della Repubblica di Firenze*, 2 vols. (Florence, 1930), vol. II, pp. 263-69.

that Florence would be attacked by her enemies in the year 1501.[21]

By the same token, however, any improvement in the city's plight was quickly taken as the sign of divine favor and of the imminent fulfillment of her promised glories. From the depths of despair in 1502, the Florentines arose to new hope when Louis XII of France, who had just led an army to Milan, sent four hundred lancers in answer to a Florentine appeal for help in recovering rebellious Arezzo. Vitellozzo took the French intervention as a signal to withdraw, and with that the revolts of Pistoia and Arezzo collapsed.

In the meantime the Florentines had been taking stock of their shaky government. There was a general feeling that the republic, with its unwieldy Great Council and it weak executive magistracy, had failed to provide the decisive, expeditious leadership which the recent crisis demanded of it, and consequently there was mounting pressure for change. A proposal to establish a select body, a Consiglio dei Richiesti on the order of the Venetian Pregadi, which would have a longer tenure and take over most of the powers of both the old Council of Eighty and the Ten, was strongly supported by influential citizens and carefully given shape in a series of *pratiche*. But such strong opposition was brought to bear against this proposal by the leaders of the popular faction, who, according to Guicciardini, were well pleased with the egalitarianism of the existing system,[22] that it failed to pass in the Great Council. With this aristocratic defeat, support began to form behind a proposal for the establishment of a lifetime Gonfalonier of Justice. The popular faction was at first lukewarm to this proposal as well, but when it was pointed out that this would not prejudice the sovereign prerogatives of the Great Council and that, in fact, a strong executive with democratic sympathies could be a distinct asset to popular government, the popular forces began to throw their weight behind the measure. Contributing to this swing toward the lifetime Gonfalonierate were the Piagnoni, who were anxious to avert a more drastic aristocratic revision of the republic of 1494 and who were encouraged to take this step by recalling that Savonarola himself had been thinking of it

[21] MS BNF Magl. VII, 1081, fol. 55 verso.
[22] *Storie fiorentine*, p. 241.

before his downfall.[23] No doubt this is why the old Piagnone Luca Landucci hailed the reform when it came as the work of God.[24] When it was decided to hold elections for the new lifetime executive, the Savonarolans rallied behind the candidacy of Giovachino Guasconi because of his "sincerity and his partiality," according to Parenti, and some three hundred *Frateschi* held a pre-election meeting in the Convent of San Marco.[25] Guasconi was defeated, but the unified effort of the Savonarolans had at least helped to block the candidacy of Antonio Malegonelle, the choice of the rival group of *statuali*, and thus to ensure the election of Piero Soderini, who had the reputation of being a moderate, sympathetic to popular government and to the Great Council.

For the most part, however, the evidence of continuing Piagnone activity is to be found in prophecies and in prophets. One of the charges repeatedly flung at Savonarola was that he was a sectarian seeking to found a new religion. That a new sect was never his aim, despite certain radical-sounding utterances, was easy enough to demonstrate. That he did not inspire sectarianism in others was much more difficult to maintain. A case in point was the rise of the movement of the *Unti*, or Anointed, who appeared in Florence at least as early as 1496. The leader of the *Unti* was an "ugly and illiterate" artisan from the San Lorenzo quarter of Florence, Pietro Bernardo, or Bernardino, who began preaching in the streets and squares of the city when he was about thirty. The name *Unti* itself, as well as the inspiration behind it, he may have taken from Savonarola, who had said "Christian means anointed (*unctus*), that is, anointed with the oil of the Holy Spirit."[26] Bernardino attached him-

---

[23] Pasquale Villari, *La storia di Girolamo Savonarola e de' suoi tempi*, 2 vols. (Florence, 1859-61), vol. II, appendix, p. clv.

[24] Luca Landucci, *Diario fiorentino del 1450 al 1516 continuato da un anonimo fino al 1542*, ed. Iodoco Del Badia (Florence, 1883), p. 250.

[25] Sergio Bertelli, "Petrus Soderinus Patriae Parens," *Bibliothèque d'Humanisme et Renaissance*, XXXI (1969), 94-98. See also Gilbert, "Venetian Constitution in Florentine Political Thought," pp. 482-84. For a most suggestive discussion of the republican symbolism in the *David* of Michelangelo and its relation to the crucial events of this time, see Saul Levine, "*Tal cosa*: Michelangelo's *David*—Its Form, Site and Political Symbolism" (Ph.D. diss., Faculty of Philosophy, Columbia University, 1969).

[26] Savonarola, *Prediche sopra Aggeo*, ed. Luigi Firpo (Rome, 1965), pp. 28,

self to Fra Domenico da Pescia and his organization of Savonarolan youth.[27] On feast days he led processions of boys from one quarter of the city to another, representing the entry into the Ark of Noah as a symbol of the entry into a life of the Spirit. He embraced Savonarola's prophecies eagerly. They were, he said, already coming true, particularly Savonarola's celebration of Florence as the chosen city. Bernardino himself referred to Florence as the "City of the Lord of the virtues, the City of our God." Another Savonarolan to whom he seems to have been close was Domenico Benivieni, the canon of the Church of San Lorenzo, whom he called "our beloved" and with whom he shared his own secret revelations.[28] Benivieni, he claimed, recognized him, Bernardino, as the "Ambassador of Christ" (II Corinthians 5:20) and the "seed of Abraham" (II Corinthians 11:22), which he interpreted as "he who preaches to the people."[29]

Bernardino's preaching seems to have gotten him into trouble very quickly. In the same letter in which he refers to himself as

---

47-48. Some of the figures dealt with in this section, most notably the three prophets Pietro Bernardino, Francesco da Montepulciano, and Francesco da Meleto, have recently been discussed in an excellent article by Cesare Vasoli, "L'attesa della nuova èra in ambienti e gruppi fiorentini del Quattrocento," in *L'attesa dell'età nuova nella spiritualità della fine del medioevo*, Convegni del Centro di Studi sulla Spiritualità Medievale, vol. III, October 16-19, 1970 (Todi, 1962), pp. 370-432. Our two accounts should be useful supplements to each other.

[27] My account of Bernardino's activity is drawn from various sources, including Parenti, *Storia fiorentina*, ed. Schnitzer, pp. 292-93; Cerretani, *Storia fiorentina*, ed. Joseph Schnitzer, *Quellen und Forschungen zur Geschichte Savonarolas*, vol. III, *Bartolomeo Cerretani* (Munich, 1904), pp. 76-77; and Bernardino's own writings. See also, Ludwig von Pastor, *The History of the Popes*, 40 vols. (London, 1938-61), vol. V (trans. F. I. Antrobus), pp. 214-15; and Joseph Schnitzer, "Pietro Bernardo il capo degli 'Unti,'" *Ricerche Religiosi*, VI (1930), no. 4.

[28] *Epistola di Bernardino de' fanciulli della citta di Firenze mandata a epsi fanciulli el di Sancto Bernaba Apostolo a di xi giugnio 1497* (Florence, 1500); *GW* no. 3896. The copy in BNF Magl. L 6 N 22 contains other works by Bernardino as well.

[29] The full passage from Saint Paul suggests that Bernardino did not hesitate to assert a conception of himself as a chosen leader, equal to others (Savonarola?): "Are they Hebrews? So am I. Are they Israelites? So am I. Are they descendants of Abraham? So am I." (Rev. Standard Version)

Ambassador of Christ he also compares himself to Saint Paul in that both of them had been stoned.[30] What Savonarola may have thought about Bernardino is nowhere recorded. Savonarola never mentioned him, neither in his sermons nor in his trial statements, where he named so many other followers and hangers-on.[31] Since the friar must have known Bernardino personally, or at least known of him through Fra Domenico and Domenico Benivieni, one can guess that his silence signifies disapproval; it would have been difficult for Savonarola to accept this uneducated layman, with his private revelations and his uninhibited public preaching, as an authentic disciple, much less as a fellow prophet who also claimed divine inspiration.

With the removal from the scene of Fra Girolamo and Fra Domenico in the spring of 1498, however, Bernardino's radical impulses began to take their own direction. Whereas, says Cerretani, during Savonarola's lifetime he preached in the squares and porticoes of the city—that is, publicly and openly—after Savonarola's death he formed secret conventicles and began to give new precepts to his followers.[32] About this time, it seems, he began the practise of anointing the heads of his followers and, if the chroniclers are to be believed, of declaring that there was no longer any reason to confess because there were no good priests left; the Church must first be reformed, and with the sword. Among Bernardino's followers, Parenti mentioned some men of status, like the Cathedral canon Amerigo de' Medici and the laymen Piero Temperani and Rafaello di Corso della Colomba; but most were artisans and ordinary folk, people of "low condition."[33] The chroniclers freely used the words

---

[30] "Are they the servants of Christ? I am a better one. . . . Three times I have been beaten with rods; once I was stoned." II Corinthians 11: 23-25.

[31] From this fact and from the fact that the Piagnone chronicler Landucci does not mention him, Schnitzer concludes that the "often psychologically abnormal Bernardino was not a legitimate disciple of Savonarola." Cerretani, *Storia fiorentina*, ed. Schnitzer, pp. 76-77, n. 1. The point turns on the word "legitimate." A similar view is expressed by Ridolfi, *Vita*, vol. II, pp. 237-38, n. 42. But Piero Parenti was emphatic about the relationship: "homo fantastico et de discepoli di frate Jeronymo, s'era preservato nella sua divotione et fede." *Storia fiorentina*, ed. Schnitzer, pp. 292-93.

[32] Cerretani, *Storia fiorentina*, ed. Schnitzer, pp. 76-77.

[33] Parenti gives these names as examples of Bernardino's important followers. *Storia fiorentina*, ed. Schnitzer, pp. 292-93. Cerretani also refers to "some

"heresy" and "new religion" of the *Unti* and hinted at dark practises. Parenti says Bernardino came to an understanding with "other groups" of similar aims and together they made *certa secta* and obliged their followers to participate in "certain ceremonies." Cerretani said that the *Unti* lived a sort of common life and that they elected Bernardino their Pope, with almost complete power (the old accusation levelled against the Fraticelli). Bernardino was suspected of practising sodomy with his *fanciulli*, although this was probably a libel, seeing that one of his ardent admirers, Antonio Buonsignori, called upon the Signoria to suppress that vice in the midst of his defense of Bernardino.[34] To many it was probably damning enough that Bernardino held his meetings late at night in the privacy of his home and in rural villages outside Florence and that he enjoined his followers to secrecy: "You who are here, do not say anything outside lest someone be scandalized. Wait for the time when we have permission."[35] Secret nighttime religious conventicles known as *Compagnie di notte*, were not new in Florence, nor was the suspicion that they led to mischief.[36] Savonarola, for one, had opposed them.[37]

---

canons of noble family" without naming them. Piero di Manni Temperani held the office of Regulator of Receipts and Expenditures in 1499 but, for some reason, was removed. MS ASF Tratti Intrinseci, vol. 83, fol. 11 verso. Amerigo de' Medici was named by Savonarola as one of his clerical friends. Villari, *Savonarola*, vol. II, appendix, p. ccxxx. I have found no information on Rafaello di Corso della Colomba, except that he was one of the signers of the letter to Pope Alexander VI on Savonarola's behalf. See Attilio Portioli, "Nuovi documenti su Girolamo Savonarola," *Archivio storico lombardo*, I (1874), 343.

[34] *Antonio Buonsignori desidera alli magnifici et excelsi Signori Fiorentini salute et pace et consolatione dello spirito Sancto et insieme lo augmento temporale della republica* (June 26, 1500). This is a preface to one of Bernardino's sermons which Buonsignori took down *viva voce*. See n. 35 below.

[35] "Non reportate nulla fuori voi che siate qui presenti: perche nessuno ne pigliassi scandalo: aspectate iltempo che habiamo licentia." *Predica di Pietro Bernardo da Firenze inutile servulo di Iesu Christo: et di tutti li fanciulli di buona volunta. Facta nel populo di San Lorenzo in chasa sua dove erano audientia huomini et fanciulli*, sermon of February 15, 1500 (Florence, 1500); *GW* no. 3898.

[36] According to Guicciardini, the *Compagnie di notte* were occasions for holding political caucuses. *Storie fiorentine*, p. 24.

[37] *Prediche sopra Aggeo*, p. 86, where Savonarola admonishes his listeners to communicate and confess in their own parishes and not in *le buche*, that is, in secret meeting places.

Bernardino's sermons give no clue as to what nefarious practises he may have been conducting, but they contained words enough to offend almost everyone. For the anti-Savonarolans there was his continual assertion of the validity of private revelations and his almost word-for-word repetition of Savonarola's prophecies of tribulations, *renovatio*, and Florentine glory, all of which, he said, would be fulfilled to the last iota.[38] For the religious conventuals there was his insistence upon mendicant poverty,[39] while for the upper classes in general there was his revolutionary-sounding criticism of the avaricious "wolves" against whom the people ought to defend themselves even at the risk of bodily harm.[40] Nor could the intellectual elite of Florence, with the exception of sceptics like Gianfrancesco Pico—and he was a significant exception, as we shall see—have taken kindly to his attacks upon secular culture: "Whoever has taken philosophy for his bride, or astrology, or even rhetoric, has entered into self-love," he cried. "These are the spouses who have ruined the Church." Poetry and grammar were also suspect in Bernardino's sight, for none of these human sciences could transcend visible things "to measure things divine," since none of them transcended the senses but only went around in circles.[41] The practitioners of these worldly sciences, the grammarians, philosophers, and astrologers, should make use of the natural light (of reason) with which they were endowed in order to study the workings of the soul through its exterior effects upon human action. But by relying entirely upon their own wisdom rather than upon God's creation, they had failed even to do this much.[42] One wonders whether Bernardino had Girolamo Benivieni, the brother of his friend, or some of the other disciples of Ficino in mind when he said, "There have been some who have studied the *Dialogues* of Plato with great dili-

---

[38] On the first point, see *Predica di Pietro Bernardo da Firenze inutile servulo di Iesu Christo et di tutti li fanciulli di buona volunta. Facta a Spugnolo di Mugello* (March 2, 1500); *GW* no. 3898. On the second, his *Predica . . . Facta . . . di San Lorenzo.*

[39] *Loc. cit.*

[40] *Predica . . . a Spugnolo di Mugello.*

[41] See the two *prediche* just referred to in note 38.

[42] "Et non hanno bene considerato almanco con illumen naturale che le virtue dell'anima per le opere exteriore del homo si possono sapere." *Predica . . . Facta . . . di San Lorenzo.*

gence and expenditure of time, until, in contemplation of the sweetness of the first Truth, they have destroyed all that they had previously done. The love of our final end makes us behave this way; all those other things are full of snares."[43]

Cerretani wrote that although Bernardino was *idiota e sanza lettera alcuna* he knew "sacred letters, especially the Bible, virtually by heart," so that he was able to deliver sermons which amazed everyone.[44] Cerretani attributed this extraordinary knowledge to Bernardino's having paid close attention to Savonarola's preaching and teaching. However, we should probably take the phrase *idiota e sanza lettera alcuna* not as illiteracy but, in the sense in which it was generally meant at the time, as a lack of formal education, particularly in Latin, for Bernardino's sermons reveal a degree of sophistication beyond that of a simple illiterate. His knowledge of the Scriptures is impressive, and his confidence in his own ability to expound them, in a variety of senses, may have been another reason for his having been regarded with suspicion.[45] Scriptural exegesis (as Giovanni Caroli reminded Giovanni Nesi) was solidly the prerogative of the clergy. But the most pervasive of Bernardino's themes was mystical contemplation, which he regarded as closely connected to prophecy. Indeed, for Bernardino, the prophet *was* a contemplative, one who had successfully separated himself from the world and united with God, different in degree rather than in quality from other contemplatives.[46] But the highest objective of the religious life was not prophecy but love of God, and this, he said, was best achieved through contemplative prayer: "And the closer one is to his end the closer he is to perfection. And he who is closer to perfection is the more united with God. And this union is achieved by means of prayer, because the fire of love grows in praying and in meditating, wherefore the Prophet says, 'The fire burns in my meditation. In my contemplation and in my praying the fire of love,

---

[43] *Loc. cit.*

[44] The text is published in Ludwig von Pastor, *Geschichte der Päpste*, 16 vols. (Frieburg in Breisgau, 1901-31), vol. III, pp. 840-42. See also Cerretani, *Storia fiorentina*, ed. Schnitzer, p. 293.

[45] See his discussion of the senses of Scripture in *Predica . . . Facta . . . di San Lorenzo* and in *Epistola . . . a epsi fanciulli.*

[46] *Predica . . . a Spugnolo di Mugello.*

which the serving man makes, burns in my heart.' "[47] Moreover, "the soul of him who [is] in this stage (*grado*) is empowered by such a light that it is often raised above itself, and in seeing the presence of God the body dissolves."[48]

Bernardino's mysticism gave him another link to the Piagnoni. While, strictly speaking, Savonarola cannot be described as a mystic, some of his close disciples, including Girolamo and Domenico Benivieni were mystically inclined. Domenico, described by Bernardino as his confidant and beloved friend, discussed, in his treatise, *The Ladder of the Spiritual Life*, the five grades of perfection which corresponded to the five letters of the name Maria.[49] Just as Maria was the ladder by which Christ had descended, so she must be the way by which we return to Him. The five steps mark the five stages of ascent from earthly limitations to the final grade of perfection which is "the love of perfect charity." Less optimistically and more conventionally than Bernardino, however, Benivieni believed it was impossible to see God in this life, even in the highest grade of human perfection, "because between the atrium and the tabernacle is placed the veil of mortal flesh." Thus, he said, "this felicity [of seeing God] does not inhere in any created good, but only in the contemplation and fruition of God, which cannot take place perfectly in this present life but only in the life to come." Only on the Day of Judgment will those who have been resurrected in the body be able to see God.[50] Another difference between Domenico Benivieni and the leader of the *Unti* underscores still more distinctly the divergence between the trained theologian (Domenico was nicknamed *il Scotino*, the little Scotist) and the self-taught man of the people. Whereas Bernardino, in keeping with his idea that prophecy was an exalted form of contemplation, said that the gift of seeing the future was given to the deserving, that is, to just men, Master

---

[47] *Loc. cit.*

[48] *Loc. cit.* See also his references to Paul's experience of being *raptum ad tertium celum* (II Corinthians 12:1-4) in his *Epistola . . . a epsi fanciulli*. Bernardino had also written a *Compendio di contemplatione* in 1497; *GW* no. 3895.

[49] *Scala della vita spiritiva la sopra el nome Maria* (n.p. or d.); *GW* no. 3848.

[50] *Dialogo della verita della doctrina predicata da frate Hieronymo da Ferrara nella cipta di Firenze* (n.p. or d.); *GW* no. 3846, sig. b fol. 2 recto.

Domenico took the more orthodox view (which he shared with Savonarola himself) that prophecy was entirely a gratuitous gift of grace, given with no regard to the merits of the person.[51]

But a doctrine that stressed individual holiness and personal inspiration exercised a broad popular appeal, and between Savonarola's death in May of 1498 and the spring of 1500 Bernardino's sect seems to have gained a considerable following in Florence, enough to cause public controversy and some commotion. The disturbances caused by the spread of his "damnable heresy" led to Bernardino's being cited by the Eight, the civic magistracy in charge of keeping public order. The summons was quashed, according to Piero Parenti, because the Piagnoni were still influential in the state and believed that prosecution of the *Unti* would lead to their own discredit; besides the city was preoccupied with other matters, that is, with the Pisan war and "other grave problems."[52] This was not the end of Bernardino's troubles, however. If the civil authorities were reluctant to act against the *Unti* out of concern for the old followers of Savonarola, the ecclesiastical authorities had no such compunctions, and they initiated inquisitorial proceedings against Bernardino on suspicion of heresy. Together with some of his followers he fled the city, taking refuge in Mirandola, in the castle of that other stalwart Savonarolan, Gianfrancesco Pico.[53]

---

[51] ". . . essendo data allhuomo non per sua perfectione ma per utilita degli altri; e potendo ancora Dio dare questo tale dono a chi e quando gli piace." Benivieni, *Epistola di maestro Domenico Benivieni, canonico de S. Lorenzo a uno amico responsiva a certe obiectione et calunnie contra a frate Hieronymo da Ferrara* (n.p. or d.); *GW* no. 3847, sig. a fol. 1 verso.

[52] "Onde chome cosa heretica dannandosi questa openione, in vulgo si sparse et dal popolo erano chiamati li uncti et molto beffeggiati. Ando la querela alli Octo della balia di questa cosa et molto per la terra se ne parlava, tanto che li Octo per cedola citorono detto Bernardino. Ma per rispecto che lo stato era ne' Piagnoni et venivasi a diminutione loro el credito perseguitandosi le reliquie del frate, s'annullo detta pratica et obliterossi." Parenti, *Storia fiorentina*, ed. Schnitzer, p. 293 (entry under May, 1500).

[53] I have not seen the inquisitorial records, but Bernardino's reply to the charges is contained in *Petrus Bernardus de florentia inutilis servulus Jesu cristi et homnium puerorum bone voluntatis: venerabilis viro et Egregio decretorum doctori Domino Jacobo Caniceo parmensi* (dated, at the end, "September 30, 1500, on Mt. Olympus"). MS BNF Magl. XXXV, 116 fols. 73-75. Where "Mt. Olympus" was located Bernardino did not say. Perhaps he was already in Mirandola.

To Gianfrancesco, Bernardino was an authentic disciple of Savonarola as well as a truly inspired prophet in his own right, as he vigorously maintained in a letter to Domenico Benivieni. His account of Bernardino's career gives us some interesting details of the link between prophet and disciple which Gianfrancesco probably had from Bernardino himself, since in other respects it corresponds to what Bernardino had written in his letter to his *fanciulli*. While listening to Savonarola preaching, he relates, Bernardino had felt a ray which emanated from Savonarola's mouth warm his head and breast and members so hot that he could hardly touch them with his hands. From that time on, according to Gianfrancesco, Bernardino was more "animated" to divine matters and more profoundly illuminated with an understanding of the senses of the sacred books. Since he now wanted to take part in the reform of the *fanciulli*, he confided his revelations to Fra Domenico da Pescia. He also began to prophesy, but it did not seem to him fitting to set himself up as another leader of God's elect while father Girolamo was still alive and still preaching his "divine science." So it was, explained Gianfrancesco, that Bernardino only began to come into his own after Savonarola's death, but, he maintained, the seed had been sown by Savonarola, and in Bernardino one saw Girolamo "as the teacher in the disciple." Gianfrancesco conceded, however, that some of Bernardino's prophecies differed from Savonarola's in certain particulars. Moreover, about some of Bernardino's revelations, those which he said "are more suspect to us," Gianfrancesco chose to remain silent, although he insisted that they were such as to command belief.[54]

Neither Gianfrancesco's letters nor his fortress in Mirandola were protection enough for Bernardino, however. On August 2, 1502, the castle of Mirandola was captured by troops of Gianfrancesco's

---

[54] *Operecta dello M.S. Johanfrancesco Pico della Mirandola in defensione della opera di pietro bernardo da Firenze servo di Jesu Cristo* (September, 1501), *ibid.*, fols. 104-16. Also published by P. Cherubelli (Florence, 1943). These secret revelations could not have been the familiar ones of the coming of Antichrist and the renovation of the Church, for Gianfrancesco Pico would have had no hesitation in referring to them openly as he had already done in his own writings, including the *Epistola del Conte Zoanfrancesco* and *Argumentum eiusdem obiectione*.

brother, Lodovico Pico, who turned the leader of the *Unti* and his companions over to the ecclesiastical authorities, who threw them into prison. Bernardino was swiftly convicted and burned at the stake, although his followers were released. Heresy and schism seem to have been the crimes for which he was condemned,[55] but this was disputed by Fra Luca Bettini and Fra Zaccaria di Lunigiana in arguments before a church synod in Florence in 1516. They claimed the actual charge had been sodomy.[56] The two friars, both of San Marco, were not so much concerned with Bernardino as with setting the record straight on Savonarola himself, since the papal brief had linked Savonarola and Bernardino in its charges of heresy and schism.[57] It is just this linking that is interesting in our present context. To Leo X, to his cousin Giulio de' Medici, Cardinal Archbishop of Florence, as well as to the members of the Florentine Synod, Bernardino and Savonarola were part of the same stubborn problem—the seemingly irrepressible expectation of the coming *renovatio* with all its subversive implications for both the Medici Pope and the Medici rulers of Florence. It had begun to look as though Savonarola's execution was the beginning rather than the end of a succession of prophets, each promising in the streets and churches of the city that the new time was at hand. Every repression proved to be a martyrdom, and a further confirmation that the time of Antichrist and tribulations, preceding the time of renewal

[55] Heresy and schism were the crimes referred to in Pope Leo X's brief to the Archbishop and Cathedral chapter of Florence, April 17, 1515. See Domenico Moreni, *Memorie storiche dell' Ambros. Imp. Basilica di S. Lorenzo* (Florence, 1804), pp. 511-13.

[56] "Quod etiam falsum esse apparet ex processu et confessione et etiam sententia ejusdem quibus non de heresis ac scismatis, sed de sogdomie crimine damnatus probatur. Habentur autem scripture huius Mirandule apud Comitem, ubi combustus fuit propter tale crimen." A. Giorgetti, "Fra Luca Bettini e la sua difesa del Savonarola," *Archivio storico italiano*, LXXVII (1919), vol. II, p. 222. See also below, pp. 359-60.

[57] ". . . ad breve autem Leonis X dicitur dupliciter primo quidest subreptitium, qui patere ex hoc quia in ipso dicit fratrem Hieronymum quemdam, et quemdam Bernardinum comdemnatos ab ecclesia pro heretis cum tamen nullibi reperiatur illum Bernardinum usquam fuisse condemnatum pro heretico, sed a comite Mirandulano fuit morti traditus proper scelera sua." *Defensio Fratris Zacharie Lunensis qua tuentur Hieronymum Savonarole sociosque ab heresi.* MS BNF Conventi soppressi J. I. 46, fol. 18 verso (unnumbered).

and the speedy coming of a new, happy age, was about to begin, just as Savonarola had prophesied. "Soon the fruit will come out; already the seed has shown itself a little. In writing and in teaching he was full of prophecy, not human but divine."[58] The seed was Savonarola himself, and the fruit would be produced by his faithful followers, the elect who must carry on his work.[59] The tribulations he had prophesied—the scourge and the Turk—must come; but the sun would shine again in all its glory and make the whole world resplendent; the Prophet himself would reappear:

> The Prophet you will see again
> resplendent like the sun;
> he will dazzle everyone
> with his great splendor.[60]

The prophet did appear, many times, in the person of other men who claimed to share in the same divine inspiration which had guided Savonarola. Already at the end of 1500, Martino di Brozzi, *il pazzo*, the madman, as he called himself, had been preaching in the city streets, dishevelled, in rags, crying that God would punish Italy, especially Rome and Florence, for having killed the friar. Since they had refused to put their faith in a wise prophet, God had sent him, a mad prophet, instead, to announce the fulfillment of His will, and this was to be no less than the "extermination" of the Church.[61] For such temerity Martino was repeatedly imprisoned, but neither his nor other prophetic voices could be stilled, no more than could the persistent faith that Savonarola had been martyred because he had spoken the truth.

About this time another Piagnone, Sandro Botticelli, lettered the following inscription in Greek across the top of a painting of the Nativity: "I Sandro painted this picture at the end of the year 1500 in the troubles of Italy in the half time after the time according to the eleventh chapter of Saint John in the second woe of the Apocalypse in the loosing of the devil for three and a half years. Then he

---

[58] "O profeti, o martir' forti" in MS BNF Magl. II. II. 407, fols. 205-207 recto; and Ferrara, "Antiche poesie," pp. 223-25.

[59] *Ibid.*, p. 224.   [60] *Ibid.*, p. 225.

[61] On Martino *il pazzo di Brozzi*, see Pastor, *History of the Popes*, vol. V, pp. 213-14.

will be chained in the twelfth chapter and we shall see him trodden down as in this picture."[62] (See Plate 1.) The end of the year 1500 in the Florentine system of dating would have been early 1501 in our calendar, just the time when Florence was being threatened by the army of Cesare Borgia and by new domestic strife. Botticelli could have been looking back three years to the death of Savonarola and forward to a speedy end to this "second woe." The eleventh chapter of the Book of Revelation speaks of the holy city which would be downtrodden for forty-two months, while the twelfth chapter describes the woman clothed in the sun who would give birth to the future ruler of all nations. Thus Botticelli's *Nativity* becomes an allegory for the tribulations of Italy which had begun with the invasion of Charles VIII and would end with the exaltation of Florence, the holy city, whence would come the fulfillment of the messianic promise. Above the mother and child, angels holding olive branches and crowns dance in a ring. Below, men and angels embrace beside a gentle stream while tiny devils flee from this reconciliation between heaven and earth. When would the three and a half years, the forty-two months, the "time, times, and a half time" of the reign of the dragon be over and the era of bliss begin? Since the "end of the year 1500" was the half time after the time, then the interval of "times" or two years, remained out of the three-and-a-half-year apocalyptic period. This would have put the great moment of the beginning of the new era at the end of 1502, or the beginning of 1503 in our calendar, just after the new reform of the Florentine constitution.

Whether Botticelli meant to be so precise and whether we read him correctly is impossible to say for sure. It is, however, a fact that the next few years were filled with even more prophecies and expectations of imminent fulfillment. Botticelli himself painted

---

[62] Fritz Saxl called this painting "one of the greatest documents of Joachimist thought." "A Spiritual Encyclopaedia of the Later Middle Ages," *Journal of the Warburg and Courtauld Institutes*, V (1942), 84. The painting is in the National Gallery, London. For the full inscription, see Martin Davies, *The Earlier Italian Schools* (London: National Gallery Catalogues, 1951), pp. 79-83; Herbert Horne, *Alessandro Filipepi, Commonly Called Sandro Botticelli* (London, 1908), pp. 294-301; Mario Ferrara, *Savonarola*, 2 vols., 2nd edn. (Florence, 1952), vol. II, pp. 51-54.

another picture whose connection with Savonarolan prophecy is beyond doubt.[63] (See Plate 2.) This is a *Crucifixion*, in which the relation between millennial hopes and the idea of the election of Florence is most explicit. The cross divides the painting into two lateral scenes: on the right, facing the viewer, is a scene of wrath and punishment; on the left, a scene of repentance, redemption, and glory. On the right, burning brands descend from a murky sky, while an angel stands below, whipping a small, bushy-maned animal. On the left, the sky is illuminated by a shining circle of light in the center of which sits a venerable figure holding a book open to the viewer. White shields emblazoned with red crosses descend upon the city bathed in light. Below, a beautiful woman with long, flowing golden hair lies prostrate embracing the cross. A small fierce animal with bared teeth is escaping from the folds of her cloak. There is no inscription, but to the Florentines it would hardly have been necessary, so evocative of the familiar themes of Florentine tradition and Savonarolan prophecy was this painting.[64] The fiery brands showering from the heavens on the left were the instruments of the *flagellum Dei*, so often heralded by Savonarola,[65] while the

[63] The painting is in the Fogg Museum of Art, Harvard University. Horne believed it to be a Botticelli school piece, *Alessandro Filipepi*, p. 301.

[64] The connection of this painting with Savonarola's prophecy, which is generally accepted, is further indicated by the fact that Botticelli, or his pupil, executed a woodcut illustration of a crucifixion with Florence and Rome in the background for Domenico Benivieni's *Tractato di Maestro Domenico Benivieni, prete fiorentino in defensione et probatione della doctrina et prophetia predicate da frate Hieronymo da Ferrara nella citta di Firenze* (Florence: Ser Francesco Bonaccorsi, 1496), fol. 4 verso. I wish to thank the Marchese Filippo Serlupi Crescenzi for showing me a copy of this edition in his private library in Florence. Horne, *Alessandro Filipepi*, p. 301, notes the relation between this painting and Savonarola's famous "Predica della Rinnovazione" of January 13, 1495, but the correspondence is not exact. In the sermon Savonarola envisioned two crosses, a black cross over Babylon (Rome) and "another cross of gold which reaches from heaven to earth over Jerusalem. . . ." *Prediche sopra i Salmi*, vol. I, ed. Vincenzo Romano (Rome, 1969), p. 52. Nor are the other figures in the painting based on this particular sermon. My own view is that the painting represents a conflation of the essential elements of the Savonarolan prophetic cycle, for which see what follows.

[65] Savonarola, *Compendium Revelationum*, in Gianfrancesco Pico della Mirandola, *Vita R. P. Hieronymi Savonarolae*, ed. Jacques Quetif, 2 vols. (Paris, 1674), vol. II, p. 226.

white shields emblazoned with crosses on the right were the stand-ard symbol of Florentine Guelfism. The prostrate woman embrac-ing the cross was not only the repentant Magdalene,[66] but also Flor-ence, the *bella donna* of Florentine poetry, painting, and prophecy, whose repentance was the first condition of the fulfillment of God's promise.[67] The animal being whipped by the angel suggests the Florentine lion, the *marzocco*, or perhaps the fox in the vineyard, symbol of vice (Song of Songs 2:15).[68] The small fierce beast escap-ing from the lovely woman's cloak was probably a wolf, symbol of the persecutors of the Church,[69] although it might also be a fox, civic symbol of Pisa, which had escaped from Florence in 1494. The city on the left, bathed in light, is clearly recognizable as Florence; we are able to make out her Cathedral, Baptistry, Campanile, and other familiar landmarks, while the city on the right, the wrathful side of the picture, although not as plainly identifiable because of the deterioration of the painting, is surely meant to be Rome.[70] The prophetic intent of the painting is expressed by the artist's treatment of time. Florence is represented three times, the three times of Savo-narola's prophetic cycle: once, under the divine scourge; again, repentant at the foot of the cross; a third time, in triumph, bathed in the light of the open book of God's revelation.[71]

[66] Horne, *Alessandro Filipepi*, p. 302.

[67] Wilhelm von Bode, *Sandro Botticelli* (Berlin, 1921), p. 188. On the *bella donna* in Florentine prophecy see, e.g., MS BNF Magl. VII, 40, fol. 19 recto; VII, 1081, fol. 57 verso. On Florence as the "lovely lady" in literature, see War-man Welliver, *L'impero fiorentino* (Florence, 1957), p. 40; and in poetry, see above, p. 52.

[68] Horne, *Alessandro Filipepi*, p. 302.

[69] Ferrara, *Savonarola*, vol. II, p. 56. On Savonarola's own use of animal symbols in connection with his prophecies of the tribulations of the Church, see especially *Prediche nuovamente venute in luce . . . sopra il salmo Quam bonus Israel Deus* (Venice, 1528), fol. XXVI recto.

[70] A good summary of the symbolism and a bibliography of relevant works is given in *L'opera completa del Botticelli*, ed. Gabriele Mandel, Classici dell'arte, vol. 5 (Milan, 1967), p. 109.

[71] Compare Savonarola's discussion of prophetic time in the "Predica della Rinnovazione": "Time is not a unity as eternity is because time is part past, part present, part future. But God, entirely capable of everything, is eternal and embraces all time because to Him everything is present. That which was and is and will be is always present to Him and He always understands and sees everything as present." *Prediche sopra i Salmi*, pp. 37-38.

This *Crucifixion* was very probably painted in 1502, that is, in the year of Florence's deep despair and sudden new hope.[72] Its Piagnone inspiration is beyond question. Piagnone also was the so-called "vision" of Albertus Cartusiensis of Trent, purporting to have originated in 1436 but almost certainly composed in Florence in 1503.[73] This, the most sensational of all the apocalypses of an apocalyptic decade, "foresees" the future as outpourings of the vials of divine wrath. Out of the first vial came the invasion of Charles VIII, the coming of Savonarola to Florence, his preaching and martyrdom, the expedition of Louis XII and downfall of Lodovico *il Moro* of Milan, the Venetian invasion of Florence's Casentino region, Cesare Borgia's invasion of Tuscany, the revolt of Arezzo and the ensuing crisis in Florence, and the death of Pope Alexander VI, the "rapacious wolf" who had invaded the Lord's sheepfold. In short, Albertus recounts the major events of the dozen years between the beginning of Savonarola's preaching mission in Florence and the end of the Borgia papacy, and he sees them from a Florentine standpoint. After "prophesying" the events ending with the death of Pope Alexander (in August, 1503), Albertus becomes a prophet indeed, describing the coming outpouring from the second and third vials of a fantastic mixture of tribulations and joys, disasters and spiritual triumphs for Florence, Italy, and the whole world.

Rome would become accustomed to misfortunes, her rivers would run with blood, her leaders would leave her a widow. Italy would be despised and her leaders would perish on every side. The kings and princes of the world would be justly punished by their people, and much blood would be spilled. The Florentines would also lose their dominion amid the effusion of blood. After a great battle in which Tuscany would be devastated from the river Tiber to the plain of Lucca, there would appear "a man of the poor, the color of hazel-nut, with piercing eyes and long hair, of middle height." He

---

[72] *L'opera completa*, ed. Mandel, p. 109.

[73] The following discussion of the prophecy of Albertus Cartusiensis is based on the text "Dictante ipsomet Frate Alberto Cartusiensis ordinis Die xii^a septembris salutis 1490. Scripsi Paduae," MS BNF Capponi 121, fols. 1–10 verso, and appears in *Studies in Honor of Hans Baron*, ed. Anthony Molho and John A. Tedeschi (Florence, Sansoni, 1970).

would convert the church of God entirely to religion, restore the vestments of the Bride of the lamb and make her worthy of her faithful—but only after much misfortune for faithful and infidel alike. These things would come to pass "in five hundred and two and three and four after four hundred over a thousand ninety," unless peace were first obtained. But before the arrival of the new era the Italians would suffer further tribulations (which the prophet elaborates in detail). Finally the Italians would drive out the barbarians and recover their liberty, although first the Angel would unsheath his sword and send "black and white dogs to devour the adulterous Church," forcing the keys to fall from the adulterous hand which has mocked "the irreprehensible law and the eternal Gospel."[74] Ultimately the Jews would convert to Christianity because of the signs from heaven, and there would be one sheepfold and a single shepherd. Peter would be restored to rebuild his Church. The Venetians and the Florentines would arise against their enemies and augment their empires. In the city of Florence there would be a congregation of almost all the governors of the Church and they would have the new book in which the whole perfect law would be renewed.[75] Praise and glory would be rendered to God alone; the wolves in the edifice would be devoured by lions; men and women, young and old would carry arms spiritual and temporal; the dragon of Italy would hiss and kill the prince with his fire and poison; with his tail he would bind all heresies and drag them with him down to the depths of the earth. The people would have faith in none but God. But still more tribulations were to come. Not even the suckling babes would be without pain or have quiet in their cradles. Let all who hear the words from the mouth of the most high understand. Let them flee to other nations where there will be peace and quiet. Let them rededicate their hearts to the God of heaven and earth and sea and the entire universe. For there will be great tribulation from heaven reaching down to the earth.

At the end of this prophecy we read that the copyist was "Priest Ioanni d'Angelo di Miglio da Cetica." Giovanni di Miglio da

---

[74] "Evangelium eternum." *Ibid.*, fol. 5. A significant usage because of its Joachite connotation.

[75] "Et liber habetur novis in quo renovabitur tota lex inreprehensibilis." *Ibid.*, fol. 9.

Cetica was a secular priest from the Casentino who served for a time as administrator of the monastery of San Gaggio, a mile south of Florence, where he died in 1540.[76] If there was such a person as Albertus Cartusiensis of Trent, he has left no other trace.[77] Was Giovanni di Miglio merely the copyist of this vision, as he apparently wished his readers to believe, or did he himself invent or at least revise it? It is impossible to decide this with certainty, but the prophecy, if not the work of Giovanni di Miglio himself, must have been largely composed in the year 1503 by a Florentine Piagnone.[78] As when we saw Savonarola's millenarian vision take shape amid the fears and hopes of 1494, we feel that we are witnessing the very genesis of prophecy. Events succeed each other swiftly; suffering and terror suddenly give way to joy and exultation; despair, to the faith that God has not forgotten His people, that once more He has thrust His hand into the human turmoil to punish the wicked and to turn men back to the path of repentance and righteousness. Still the vision of the future is blurred, the exact moment of fulfillment uncertain. Will the new age begin in 1505? In 1511? How many more times will the Lord unsheath His sword over his people? But the main outlines and the main source of inspiration are clear. The prophet is steeped in the patriotic apocalyptic traditions native to Florence. For him the life and teaching and death of Savonarola are valid but not unique or novel parts of that tradition; they confirm what had been prophesied earlier and they point toward what will be prophesied again before the time of fulfillment. In other words, Savonarola has become absorbed into the Florentine apocalypse; he is neither the first nor the last of the city's prophets; his doctrine is not the fountain of her revelation but a further enuncia-

---

[76] Some biographical information was given by his brother, Agostino di Miglio, author of *Nuovo dialogo della devozione del Sacro Monte della Verna* (Florence, 1568), pp. 268-69. I am indebted to my friend Signor Ivaldo Baglioni of the BNF for this reference.

[77] The fact that Gianfrancesco Pico later mentioned Albert of Trent as one who, in 1436, prophesied Savonarola's coming (*Vita R. P. Hieronymi Savonarolae*, ed. Jacques Quetif, 2 vols. [Paris, 1674], vol. I, p. 151) does not establish Albert's existence, although it does indicate that the prophecy circulated and was accepted by Gianfrancesco as genuine.

[78] For a discussion of this problem, see my edition of "Dictante ipsomet Frate Alberto Cartusiensis," referred to in n. 73 above.

tion of it, a further confirmation that Florence is the city elected for the disclosure of the perfected law and as the center of the new Christianity.

The millenarianism of the Albert of Trent apocalypse was much more radical, both from a religious and from a social point of view, than Savonarola's. The vision recorded there of the coming of the Angelic Pastor and the destruction of the Roman Church was closer in spirit to the anonymous radical apocalypses which took their inspiration from Fraticelli and other Joachite and pseudo-Joachite prophecies. Like them, this prophet's roots were in the people, whose suffering and fierce resentment of the princes and lords he obviously shared. Significantly, his description of the Angelic Pastor was that of a humble and unkempt man, reminiscent of a "madman" like Martino Brozzi, rather than a cultured prelate or even a friar; he was certainly not an elected pope as the Angelic Pastor was usually portrayed in the *Il papale* and other apocalyptic literature. For the author of the Albert of Trent vision, the new religion would arise among the poor, it seems, and throughout he extols the virtues of poverty, while he regards the rich and powerful as the corrupters of the holy life.

In addition to placing great stress on lower-class upheaval, this visionary was most unSavonarolan in his hostility toward the kings of France. The "monstrous and unfaithful creature" who would dominate most of Italy was obviously Charles VIII, and the second king who would subjugate the Milanese state was Louis XII, who had invaded Italy in the summer of 1499 and by 1500 had put an end to Sforza rule and Milanese independence. In fact, neither a French king nor any other potentate would succeed to the role of the New Charlemagne. Holy Roman Emperor, Gallic King, Italian princes as well as Roman popes—this prophet regarded them all as the instruments of perdition and predicted that all would be destroyed or ruined. Such was the disillusionment of these years that "Albert of Trent" hoped for some entirely new leadership arising from the Italian people themselves and, specifically, from the last two great independent republics, Florence and Venice, in most unlikely harmony.

Giovanni di Miglio recorded that he copied this prophecy on

December 12, 1512, at the climax of still another time of troubles in Florence.[79] In that intervening decade other prophets had appeared, just as his text "predicted," some of them in the years which he marked for their appearance. On May 30, 1505, a year singled out in his text, a certain Fra Sylvestro had reported a vision in which "those Angels in the fire" predicted the conversion of "our leaders," as well as the beginning of a new schism, the rising of the people, and great terror with much bloodshed. "And there will be tumult in the city, tumult outside the city, tumult in the piazza, tumult in the palace, tumult for forty hours, tumult for eleven hours, tumult for twenty-four hours. Evils worse than evils and most evil. . . !"[80] This visionary may have been Fra Sylvestro Marradi, a brother of San Marco who was preaching in the environs of Florence at that time.[81] Fra Sylvestro was engaged in a running battle with the enemies of the Piagnoni, the "Scribes and Pharisees" who attacked the preachers and practitioners of the life of the spirit. He himself, he confessed, had made "prognostications," and had been told by the Virgin of the coming renovation of the Church;[82] but the Lord had indicated to him that his own predictions would bear little fruit.[83] In the meantime, in Florence, a certain Fra Antonio da Cremona, a member of the group of Franciscan reformers who called themselves Amadeites,[84] was called to account for prophesying, in a ser-

---

[79] It is possible that he revised or added to the prophecy at that time, since the predictions for the decade between 1502 and 1512 are a mixture of fantastic events, real events such as the appearance of a prophet in 1505, and important occurrences in 1511 (year of the Conciliabulum of Pisa and the related schism).

[80] *Prophetia viri cuiusdam sancti f. Silvestri*, MS BRF 2053, fol. 107 verso.

[81] To him is attributed the work *Speculum veri et humilis praedicatoris revelatum opusculum*, ed. Jacques Quetif and J. Echard, in *Scriptores Ordinis Praedicatorum*, 2 vols. (Paris, 1719-21), vol. I, p. 895.

[82] Fra Sylvestro da Marradi, *Sermoni e prediche*, MS BNF Magl. XXXV, 242, fol. 151 verso. Most of the sermons in this codex he delivered in Pescia between 1508 and 1519. In the same codex there is a letter by a better known Piagnone, Fra Bartolomeo da Faenza, without a date (fol. 134). He was Prior of San Marco at the time of the revolution against the Medici in 1527 and took a leading part in the affairs of the last republic. See Cecil Roth, *The Last Florentine Republic* (London, 1925), passim.

[83] MS BNF Magl. XXV, 242, fols. 151 verso–152.

[84] After the Franciscan Amedeo Menez de Sylva (1428-82). Born in Granada

mon of December 23, 1508, the coming of great tribulations to the city because she had rejected her holy prophets.[85] "Not without pain, indeed, I see all this gospel extend itself over all of Italy and especially over my city of Florence, to whom God sent so many prophets, so many preachers to call [her], and not only has she not wanted to listen, but she has even persecuted them and driven them out, and some of them she has killed; wherefore Christ is angry. . . . Do not be amazed if I have said that Jerusalem signifies Florence, because as David honored God in her [Jerusalem], so the holy pastor (*pastore santo*) will do many things in the city of Florence in honor of Christ; but first she will be purged by the fire of tribulation. . . . And you, Italy, sewer of every sin, you are abandoned by Christ. The wild beasts have entered the vineyard left unguarded by the watchmen: just so have the barbarians entered Italy abandoned by Christ, and step by step they will bring her to the ground."

We recognize the familiar themes of *flagello*, reform, and Florentine election, but Fra Antonio was not willing to credit these themes to Savonarola. In his sermon he refers to the many prophets whom Florence has rejected, not just one, and in his ensuing conference with the Archbishop he flatly denied that he was the disciple of Fra Girolamo whom he had never seen and of whom, he said, he knew little. His knowledge of the future was his own, he maintained, and he resisted the Archbishop's efforts to reveal just what the source of that knowledge was. If Savonarola had preached the reformation of the Church it could not have been for this that God had allowed him to be put to death, because that reformation was

---

of a noble family, he came to Italy in 1452. He was confessor to Pope Sixtus IV. The same codex which contains the material concerning Fra Antonio da Cremona contains four of the eight ecstasies (*raptus*) which made up Amedeo's *Apocalypsis Nova*, a work that seems to have come to light just in the year 1502. Giampaolo Tognetti, "Un episodio inedito di repressione della predicazione post-Savonaroliana (Firenze, 1509)," *Bibliothèque d'Humanisme et Renaissance*, XXIV (1962), 190. New light will undoubtedly be shed on this timely "recovery" of Amadeite visions when Professor Cesare Vasoli publishes his findings. He has informed me that there are strong indications that the Piagnone Giorgio Benigno forged at least part of the text. On Amedeo's mystical ecstasies, see Luke Wadding, *Annales Minorum seu Trium Ordinum*, 26 vols. (Rome-Quaracchi, 1731-1933), vol. XIII, p. 415.

[85] The sermon is published by Tognetti, "Un episodio," pp. 193-96.

certain to come. Perhaps, he said, it was because Savonarola had claimed the prophecies of others as his own or perhaps because he had secretly sought his own worldly glory?

To Archbishop Cosimo de' Pazzi, however, such prophesying was "in a manner similar to that of Fra Girolamo of Ferrara, who had aroused this whole city, sowed division among the people, and brought scandal and dangerous disorder."[86] In spite of this pressure, Fra Antonio stood his ground and refused to recant, but we have no other sermons from him and no way of knowing how the affair ended. Clearly, the Florentine authorities were sensitive to the continuing danger of unrest fomented by popular preachers; but that same danger made it difficult to undertake repression without risking public reaction. The alarums and excursions that filled the Italian peninsula all had some bearing upon Florence's situation: Pope Julius II's plots and campaigns were near enough to the Florentine borders to cause concern; the city's own effort to reconquer Pisa was now, at last, in the spring of 1509, coming to a successful climax. In 1511, Florence's ally Louis XII of France convoked a semblance of a Church council in that city newly restored to Florence. This *conciliabulum*, as it was quickly dubbed, was little more than a tactical weapon of the French to counter the Pope's efforts at organizing an all-Italian campaign against the "foreign barbarians"; but for a time it rallied those Florentines who saw Church reform and republican liberty as two sides of the same coin.[87] For their part in it Pope Julius laid the Florentines under an interdict; however the *conciliabulum* was moved to Milan on November 12, and early in the following month the Florentines learned that the interdict had been removed, although provisional resumption of the mass seems to have been delayed until March 21.[88] Apparently the Pope intended

---

[86] On the dispute between the Archbishop and the friar, see *ibid.*, pp. 196-99.

[87] Capponi, *Storia della Repubblica*, vol. II, pp. 297-98. On December 13, the Florentine humanist Bartolomeo della Fonte appealed to King Louis XII for leadership to bring about a reform of the Church. *Epistolarum libri III*, ed. Ladislaus Juhasz (Budapest, 1931), pp. 57-58. In June 1509, writing to the Piagnone Fra Simone Cinozzi, della Fonte had discussed the reasons for believing the "signs and prodigies" of the Antichrist. *Epistolarum*, p. 48.

[88] Landucci, *Diario*, pp. 311-12, 315. Landucci also reported that on the night of November 4-5, a lightning bolt struck the communal palace damaging sev-

to use his spiritual weapons to keep the Florentines in line. On July 11, 1512, they received a Papal letter ordering them to dismiss their lifetime Gonfalonier, Piero Soderini. This was high-handed behavior indeed, even for Julius II. The Florentines understood it as part of his effort to overturn the free republic and restore the Medici,[89] who were presumably more amenable to an anti-French effort; but they also regarded it as a foolish repetition of the mistake of an earlier pope (Alexander VI) who had ignored the coming of King Charles with fourteen thousand horse. "And this was the strength of the Florentines," said Giovanni Cambi, "the faith they had in God that he would liberate them from the injustice of the Pastor."[90]

It is not surprising that in this crisis there was in the city a renewed circulation of Savonarolan memoirs and themes, as well as a renewal of anti-Piagnoni sanctions.[91] Hope continued to alternate with fear as the Florentines watched their fortunes wax and wane according to the day-to-day changes on the larger Italian scene. The French victory over the Spaniards at Ravenna in April, 1512, was a high-water mark which quickly receded. Their great commander, Gaston de Foix, was killed, and they were forced to withdraw in the face of the combined opposition of the Swiss, English, and Spaniards. For Florence, history had repeated itself, just as Giovanni Cambi had confidently predicted, but it was a repetition of 1495 rather than of 1494. Once more their French ally had had to withdraw, leaving Florence at the mercy of the Holy League, whose members in council in Mantua decided to make an end of her current government. On the night of July 14, "a lightning bolt, or truly, a special wind or fortune" toppled the campanile of Santa Croce, dashing it onto the roof of the church which it tore open, also causing much damage to the interior. This was taken as a bad sign, "that these princes and lords who were in a position to restore the Church of Christ and enlarge it, were ruining it instead because

---

eral items including three lilies sculpted over a portal. This was understood as a menacing sign for the King of France. Another bolt struck the cupola (of the Cathedral?) which was understood as presaging some evil for the Church. *Ibid.*, p. 312.

[89] *Ibid.*, p. 319.   [90] Quoted in *ibid.*, p. 319, n. 1.

[91] Vasoli, "L'attesa della nuova èra," pp. 404-405.

of their ambition."[92] On August 29, the Florentines were terrified to hear that their town of Prato had been captured by the Spaniards and was being put to the sack that very day; the Florentine militia that had been sent to defend it had been put to flight. On August 31, the Florentines agreed to pay the Spaniards an indemnity of 140,000 ducats and to readmit the Medici into the city, and on that day Gonfalonier Soderini fled. On September 1, 1512, after an exile of eighteen years, the Medici returned to Florence. Giuliano, youngest son of the Magnificent Lorenzo, was the first to enter, followed a few days later by his brother, the Cardinal Giovanni. Under the terms of the agreement the Medici were admitted merely as private citizens, but everyone understood that the experiment in free republicanism was dead. In the succeeding weeks the Medici brothers consolidated their control, using the familiar Florentine devices of *Parlamento*, hand-picked majorities in the civic councils, and *balie*, the special commissions with extraordinary powers. The Florentines were also well aware that a Spanish army stood ready to give their city the same treatment already meted out to Prato should they prove recalcitrant. The Great Council was "reformed" and a Senate, narrow in base and broad in authority, was established. The term of office of the Gonfalonier of Justice was reduced to one year and made elective in the Great Council. While, in terms of constitutional arrangements, there was no return to the status quo before 1494 because the Savonarolan Great Council was retained and the term of the executive Gonfalonierate lengthened over the traditional two months, the changes were enough to assure a joint Medici and aristocratic domination over the state.[93]

II

GIOVANNI DI MIGLIO completed his version of the prophecy of Albert of Trent on December 18, 1512, three months after the Medici restoration and the collapse of the free republic. The vision ends amid great confusion with predictions of further tribulations, but also with a note of hope. "They flee to other nations who have been

[92] Landucci, *Diario*, p. 320.
[93] On the aristocratic aspects of these constitutional changes, see Felix Gilbert, *Machiavelli and Guicciardini* (Princeton, 1965), pp. 76-81.

living without war in peace and quiet. They restore their hearts to the God of heaven and sea and earth. Heavy tribulations will be seen in heaven above and on earth below. Amen."[94] Perhaps Giovanni believed that a saving few would fly from the new oppressors of the city of the lily in order to preserve the cause of freedom and purity in exile. A few did so, but freedom remained a constant specter to the lackluster successors of the Magnificent Lorenzo. After initial moves which suggested that the new rulers would at least respect the forms if not the substance of republican freedom, it quickly became clear, to almost universal displeasure, that they had no such intention. The Great Council, the stronger Gonfalonierate, free elections—all gave way before the revived instruments of Medicean despotism: *Accoppiatori, balie,* Council of Seventy, and controlled sortition. Grumbling against the regime began soon and continued incessantly. In February, Pietro Paolo Boscoli and Agostino Capponi were beheaded as leaders of a conspiracy to assassinate Cardinal Giovanni de' Medici, his brother Giuliano, and cousin Giulio. Niccolò Valori, also implicated in the plot, was imprisoned. Boscoli's republicanism was tinged with a strong admiration for Savonarola, and his last urgent request was to have a San Marco friar as confessor.[95] According to Piero Parenti, Boscoli and Capponi went to their deaths calling for the liberation of the fatherland from tyranny.[96] In the meantime the prophets of divine wrath and tribulation had little trouble gaining a hearing from a populace anxious to hear how their new tyrants would meet their end. In the following June, the Eight imprisoned two friars of Ognissanti and a certain Michele della Badessa for prophesying revolution in the city and elsewhere. They were tortured and then banished, along with

---

[94] MS BNF Capponi 121, fol. 10 verso.

[95] He asked for Zanobi Acciaiuoli, the humanist Piagnone friar. Ironically Acciaiuoli was not in San Marco, having gone to Rome as the librarian of the new Pope Leo X, against whom Boscoli was alleged to have conspired. Instead Boscoli was attended by Fra Cipriano del Pontassieve, also of San Marco, who became Prior of San Domenico of Fiesole in that year. For these details and an account of the whole episode by Boscoli's friend Luca della Robbia, see "Narrazione del caso di Pietro Paolo Boscoli e di Agostino Capponi (1513)," ed. F. Polidori, *Archivio storico italiano*, I (1842), 275-309.

[96] Parenti, MS BNF II. IV. 171, fol. 85.

the doughty Piagnone, Bartolomeo Redditi, who was accused of having talked with them "about the affair of Fra Girolamo." Parenti believed there was no substance to the charges, that the incident was trumped up in order to set an example and strike fear among grumblers, and that this was a successful maneuver. He described the popular mood as one of melancholy and worry about the future rather than rebelliousness.[97]

The anxiety of both rulers and ruled was soon revealed in the affair of Fra Francesco da Montepulciano, the Franciscan who preached the Advent sermon of 1513 in Santa Croce. One of twelve preachers who were resolved to carry their message of tribulation and repentance to all parts of Italy,[98] Fra Francesco attracted huge crowds to his sermons in the Cathedral and the church of Santa Croce. His message was the familiar one of God's impending judgment on a wicked nation and on the city, which might, however, still save itself by repenting. The tribulations to come would be the last before the appearance of Antichrist, Enoch, and Elias. They would be preceded by three signs: the ruin of the King of France, the ruin of Frederick of Aragon,[99] and the beginning of schism in the Church with the installation of an anti-pope by the Emperor. Rome would suffer the worst punishment. Florence could expect no more prophets; the age of prophets had passed; but there would be false prophets, false interpretations of Scripture, and false friars. Francesco's own predictions, which he claimed to be divulging at the peril of his life, were based upon Scripture; but no one could foretell the exact time of fulfillment, only that these things must soon come to pass. He ordered the Florentines to put away their factions and their sects without delay. "Blood will be everywhere.

---

[97] Parenti, *Storia fiorentina*, ed. Schnitzer, p. 301; also Redditi, *Breve compendio*, ed. Schnitzer, pp. 7ff. According to Ridolfi, a number of friars in San Marco now became Mediceans, "corrupted" by offers of honors and offices. *Life*, p. 296.

[98] He was referred to as a Franciscan conventual by some of the chroniclers, but he seems to have been an Amadeite, like Antonio da Cremona. See Vasoli, "L'attesa della nuova èra," p. 406; and Schnitzer, *Savonarola*, vol. II, pp. 441-42. See Machiavelli's reference to him in a letter to Francesco Vettori, December 19, 1513. English trans. in Allan Gilbert, *The Letters of Niccolò Machiavelli: A Selection of His Letters* (New York, 1961), p. 147.

[99] He may have been referring to Frederick, King of Naples, 1496-1501.

There will be blood in the streets, blood in the river; people will sail in boats through blood, lakes of blood, rivers of blood . . . two million devils are loosed from hell . . . because more evil has been committed in the past eighteen years than in the preceding five thousand."[100]

At the end of this terrible sermon, Ser Lorenzo Violi reports, Fra Francesco kneeled and called upon the people to convert. His impact upon the people was so great that many abandoned their daily affairs, expecting some sort of upheaval (*novità*) to take place.[101] The rulers of the city were disturbed and uncertain what to do about this resurgence of popular excitement and finally resolved to notify the Pope (who, since February, had been Giovanni de' Medici). From Rome came back the advice that the vicar of the diocese should summon the friar and find out what was at the bottom of his preaching. The inquiry was duly made and Fra Francesco agreed to give a public explanation, but before he could do so a sudden fever carried him off. His body was laid out in Santa Croce and "the whole people" came to kiss his hands and feet. Afterwards there was much discussion of the affair and a great difference of opinion among the people. Some thought that had the friar lived to give his explanation he would have exposed himself as a fool, but most believed that he had been truly inspired by the Holy Spirit and that the outlook for the city was bad, as he had predicted. This, commented Parenti, suited most Florentines, who hated the new government and were looking for some way to bring about its overthrow.[102]

Once again, as they had eighteen years earlier, fears of attack from abroad combined with active antipathy toward a Medici regime at home had produced that tense atmosphere to which an apocalyptic preacher might provide the explosive spark. Only now the external

---

[100] *Predica di frate Francesco da Montepulciano dell'ordine de frati minori in Santa Croce di Firenze facta adi xxiii di Dicembre 1513 et raccolta per Ser Lorenzo Violi . . .* (Florence, 1590). I used the copy in the British Museum. The recorder of this sermon, Ser Lorenzo Violi, was also Savonarola's faithful amanuensis.

[101] Parenti, *Storia fiorentina,* ed. Schnitzer, p. 302.

[102] *Ibid.,* pp. 302-303; also Landucci, who also attests to the huge crowds he drew and to his profound impact. *Diario,* pp. 343-44.

situation appeared even more discouraging. Not only did the Medici have at their disposal the most fearsome army in Europe—the Spaniards, who in the sack of Prato had already given the city a taste of what she could expect for resistance—but suddenly they were masters of Rome as well as Florence. News of the accession of Giovanni de' Medici to the Papacy as Leo X reached Florence on March 11, 1513, where it was celebrated with *fuochi e festi*. The celebrations continued for several days and became riotous. Soon rooftops and shops were set afire in demonstrations which revealed something more than random rejoicing: the Eight had to intervene to forbid any further threats to the Piagnoni.[103] The political significance was plain. By placing the Florentine lion on the throne of Saint Peter—explicitly symbolized in Cardinal Giovanni's choice of the name Leo—the Medici grip on Florence would be that much tighter. The Florentines could be expected to be dazzled both by patriotic pride in their home-grown pontiff and by the gold which they would heap up from new business opportunities in Rome.[104] Those who refused to be swayed, like the die-hard Piagnoni, could be forced to do so by a government which now had the backing of Rome. And they could expect no support from the French this time, since, as a virtual appanage of the Papacy, Florence could no longer pursue an independent foreign policy. The Medici Pope had little use for the French.

Even Piagnoni might be expected to show enthusiasm for the election of Pope Leo, however. Girolamo Benivieni, who, characteristically, had suffered a terrible fright when the Spanish troops were on the city's doorstep,[105] was stirred by Leo's accession to renewed faith in the old prophecies and wrote his *Frottola for Pope Leo on the Renovation of the Church*.[106] He said that the sheep were tormented by the wolves in the city of Peter. Peter's bark, badly

---

[103] *Ibid.*, p. 336.

[104] Roth, *Last Florentine Republic*, pp. 6-8.

[105] See his letter "Al mio Reverendo Piovano di Cascina" (September 6, 1512), in Caterina Re, *Girolamo Benivieni fiorentino* (Città di Castello, 1906), p. 317.

[106] Girolamo Benivieni, *Opere novissamente rivedute et da molti errori espurgate con una canzone dello amore celeste et divino, col commento dello Ill. Conte Giovanni Pico Mirandolano distinto in libri III* (Venice, 1522), pp. 199-201.

overloaded and poorly guided, had already gone down twice and could not survive a third disaster. But, in answer to the prayers of "a certain servant of His," God had sent a conquering lion from Judah who would soon put the wolves to flight. Benivieni rejoiced that the seed had been sown in Florence. From her the new fruit would come forth, all would be united in a single sheepfold under one shepherd, and he prayed that he would be allowed to live to see God's glory on earth. Benivieni's friendship was carefully cultivated by Cardinal Giulio, the son of his long-dead patron, Giuliano, brother of Lorenzo the Magnificent. As Archbishop of Florence Giulio was the Pope's personal representative in the home city, and he followed a policy of cultivating the support of former Savonarolans by offering them high posts in the archiepiscopal curia and by inviting their advice.[107] With Benivieni Giulio seems now to have entered into a discussion of Savonarola's prophecy. Whether it had been of divine or human origin, wrote Benivieni, they would soon know.[108]

Benivieni's image of the conquering lion from Judah hopefully combined Savonarolan and older themes of civic patriotism. A similar blending was achieved by an unknown poet who addressed the following lines to Leo on his elevation:[109]

> From the most sublime Throne
> descended to earth a divine splendor
> Glorious lion
> O vessel chosen in Heaven, gentle pastor
> O singular champion
> of the lily standard
> Unique among mortals, celestial gift,
> O unique comfort

[107] Vasoli, "L'attesa della nuova èra," p. 409.

[108] *Vita di Girolamo Benivieni*, MS BNF II. I. 91, p. 258.

[109] The MS bears the inscription at the end: "Hic liber est mei Petri Criniti." Crinito, the Florentine humanist, pupil of Poliziano and of Ugolino Verino, was a great admirer of the Medici, particularly of Lorenzo the Magnificent. But Crinito's death is generally placed between 1504 and 1507, while Leo did not become Pope until 1513. For biographical data see the editor's introduction to Crinito's *De honesta disciplina*, ed. Carlo Angeleri (Rome, 1955), pp. 1-55. The verses are in MS BNF Palatina Baldovinetti 230 (formerly 221) fols. 3-63 verso.

O highest joy, o welcome gentleness
Singular phoenix among us
Tower of the beautiful lion, high fortress,
O happy Florence
because of this immense gift brought you by Heaven.
O laureled ensign
Heaven, earth, sun, stars, and sea
Rejoice and give you glory.
O sempiternal frond, dear to the lily,
O longed-for victory,
Today, because of your memory
Florence teaches prudence to the world.

. . . . .

The new crusade
I see arise through him with great celebration
to make all one sheepfold
Every king, every state, today awakes
to the beautiful, gentle pastor.
O lordly branch,
Blessed is he who regards your emblem.

Perhaps it was the same enthusiast who wrote a long poem in praise of Pope Leo tracing the history of the Medici family. The death of Lorenzo the Magnificent, he recalled, had been attended by signs of future misfortunes, for with his sacred loss, the power of "the beautiful age of gold" could not be renewed. His son Piero had disregarded Lorenzo's wise counsels for maintaining his greatness, but now the "glorious time" had come:

> Therefore, so much goodness rises once again to heaven,
> eternal glory for our Florence.
> It pleases you to lead the beautiful bride of Jesus back
> to that path which justice treads.[110]

The same theme of the return of the age of gold with the accession of "the good pastor" Pope Leo, who had brought *la Medica virtu* to Rome, was also celebrated in a poem by a certain Guglielmo de' Nobili. Pope Leo, he wrote, chosen by God to bear the scepter and wear the crown of the sacred realm, would save Italy together with

---

[110] *Ibid.*, fols. 61-63 verso.

the Christian King, launch a crusade against "the Turks, corsairs, and pirates," and bring all the lands even as far as India and Arabia, under the rule of Rome, under one God and one law. Meanwhile Florence would watch in triumph, rejoicing to see the glory to which she had given birth.[111]

For a time Leo himself may have entertained the idea of having himself cast in the role of the Angelic Pastor, the shepherd who would reduce the world to a single sheepfold and bring about the Church's renewal. He could hardly have failed to see the advantages to be gained for his position both in Rome and in Florence, by appropriating the enthusiasm of the millenarians to his cause. In July, 1514, a Carmelite preached a sermon in Florence in which he identified the Angelic Pastor as Pope Leo. Everyone was amazed. The preacher had the Pope's authorization; did he have Leo's blessing as well?[112] If Leo entertained the idea of promoting himself as the Angelic Pastor, however, he soon changed his mind, for such notions were as unsettling to the populace as they were potentially subversive of ecclesiastical authority. Every day, wrote the historian Pitti, there arose nuns, tertiaries,[113] girls, and peasants to prophesy, "and all the seditious spirits listen to them."[114] Under papal pressure the wreck of apocalyptic expectations in Florence was not long in coming, as we see in the affair of Francesco da Meleto, last of the city's important prophets.

Francesco da Meleto, the son of a Florentine merchant and a slave woman called Caterina da Russia,[115] had some classical education

---

[111] *Scripti e Canzoni in Lode di Papa Leone X*. At the end: "Composto per Guglelmo de Nobili." MS BNF Landau Finaly 183, fols. 48-56. Others in similar vein on fols. 3-48, 57-61.

[112] Parenti also said that the Carmelite prophet repeated certain teachings of Fra Girolamo and the Abbot Joachim, namely that the Angelic Pastor would be a poor man, a prisoner, Italian, and of good morals. Parenti, *Storia fiorentina*, ed. Schnitzer, p. 304. Vasoli seems to think Leo did entertain such notions, "L'attesa della nuova èra," pp. 410-11. For a recent discussion of Leo's policies, see Kenneth M. Setton, "Pope Leo X and the Turkish Peril," *Proceedings of the American Philosophical Society*, 113 (1969), 367-424.

[113] *Pinzochere*, from its earlier meaning as "tertiary," seems to have taken on a pejorative connotation as "hypocrite."

[114] Quoted by Vasoli, "L'attesa della nuova èra," p. 408.

[115] Biographical information in S. Bongi, "Francesco da Meleto, un profeta fiorentino a' tempi del Machiavelli," *Archivio storico italiano*, V (1889), 62-70.

and was a friend of the humanists Girolamo Benivieni and Bartolomeo della Fonte. Notoriety as a prophet did not come to him until he was advanced in years, although apparently he had long been interested in apocalyptic speculation. In 1473 he had gone to Constantinople with another Florentine, Benedetto Manetti, and there he had sought out the ideas of learned Jews about the coming of the Messiah and Jewish conversion. Believing he held the key to the mysteries of the future he wrote, shortly before 1513, the *Convivio*,[116] a treatise in which he tried to show the apocalyptic unity of the Old Testament prophets, particularly Isaiah, and the Book of Revelation.[117] Meleto's method was based on an elaborate combination of number and word symbolism by means of which he worked out a prophetic timetable. Another authority for his method, although he never acknowledged it, was the Joachite apocalypse, which seems to have provided him with much of his chronology, particularly his schemes for dividing history into threefold, fourfold and sevenfold periodizations, all intended to show that the world was on the threshold of a millennial age. His view of the "age of the preachers" as having begun with Saints Francis and Dominic and extending to the time of the great renewal was also similar to that of the Joachites. God had already initiated the first of three universal scourges in 1484 by beginning the persecution of the Jews in Spain and Portugal; this was also the beginning of the reduction of the world to a single sheepfold.[118] The Jews would embrace the true faith in 1517. With the conversion of the world to Christianity there would come the final revelation of the mysteries by "one who will be a man of slight learning and even less renown, and he will write a book in which all the mysteries of sacred Scrip-

---

[116] Francesco da Meleto, *Convivio de secreti della scriptura sancta, compilato per modo di dialogo* (n.p. or d.). I used the copy in the BNF. But Meleto and his prophecies must have come to public notice before this. In Part VI of the *Convivio* he mentions having recently written, at the request of "our Magnificent Gonfalonier," an exposition in Latin of the Psalm "Quare fremuerunt gentes" (Psalm 2). He also mentions an exposition of Psalm 101, "Te Domini exaudi orationem meam et clamor meus ad te veniat" (Psalm 101:2).

[117] That he had Ficino's commentary on Plato's *Symposium* in mind he indicates in Part I.

[118] On the importance of the year 1484 for the beginning of the Spanish persecution of the Jews with the adoption of the "Constitutions," see Heinrich Graetz, *History of the Jews*, 6 vols. (Philadelphia, 1891-98), vol. IV, pp. 325-27.

ture and of every event among the Christians, Jews, Mahometans, and all the other infidels will be described. The Most High will choose him from such a low estate the more to demonstrate His magnificence. . . ."

Meleto's *parvulo ydiota* owed little or nothing to Savonarola, but was strikingly similar to the representation of Bernardino, leader of the *Unti*, as an illiterate layman who had a marvelous knowledge of Scripture, while his notion of a perfect book of the Gospel was close to that of Giovanni di Miglio's *liber novus*. While Meleto himself was a member of the Florentine middle class and had some formal education, his work is another instance of the resurgence of a radical strain of popular Florentine prophetism in the decades after Savonarola, a strain which however much its spokesmen honored the memory of the Dominican, derived as much or more from older civic and Joachite traditions as from him.[119] Like Bernardino, Meleto made much of the idea of a popular, lay leadership. God would choose as his revelator "a little youth of low estate," who possessed almost no learning beyond a bit of Latin (*grammatica*), enough to read the Scriptures and to "breathe the Holy Spirit," just as He had chosen humble men in times past—Noah, Moses, David, and many others—although there had always been plenty of learned and famous men as well as priests and princes.[120]

Meleto's *Convivio* caught the attention of reformers at the court of Pope Leo. Shortly after the book was published he was summoned to Rome for an audience with the Pope by Vincenzo Quirini, the Venetian aristocrat and Camaldolese monk who had himself just arrived at the papal court all eager to get the reform of the Church under way.[121] Meleto's expenses for the trip were paid by Antonio

[119] The figure of the *parvulus* derives from one of Meleto's favorite prophets, Isaiah 9:6. It was also an important Joachite theme. On the wisdom of the child leading the way to the Third Age, see Joachim of Flora, *Super Quatuor Evangelia*, ed. Ernesto Buonaiuti, Fonti per la Storia d'Italia, vol. 78 (Rome, 1930), p. 91.

[120] See also his attack on Aristotelian and other philosophical authorities as against the truth of Christ and the prophetic spirit, in *Convivio*, Part VI.

[121] A brief account of his life and writings may be found in Magnoald Ziegelbauer, *Centifolium Camaldulense* (Venice, 1750), pp. 63-65. See also the many notices in Hubert Jedin, *A History of the Council of Trent*, trans. Ernest Graf, 2 vols. (London, 1957-61), vol. I passim.

Zeno, vicar of the Cardinal Protector of Camaldoli, and Francesco Soderini, Bishop of Volterra (and brother of the ex-Gonfalonier of Florence, Piero Soderini). Meleto stayed in Rome for three months, the guest of Pietro Bembo, the Venetian humanist, now an Apostolic Secretary.[122] According to Meleto's later account, he did have his audience with the Pope, but he did not reveal whether it went well or badly. From the account of an unfriendly witness, however, it would seem that Meleto's trip to Rome was bound to go badly because Vincenzo Quirini was unfavorably inclined toward him even before he arrived in Rome. This witness is Quirini's fellow Venetian and bosom companion in religion, Tommaso Giustiniani. Writing a year later from the hermitage of Camaldoli to the Camaldolese monk Paolo Orlandini in Florence, Giustiniani gave the following account. Quirini had read the *Convivio* during his stay in Florence in late 1512[123] and, seeing in it many "perverse teachings," had summoned Meleto for a conference. During the interview which followed (presumably the one in Rome at which Giustiniani himself had been present) Meleto defended himself and even claimed that his doctrine had been verified by miracles—that he had seen a flame shoot out of the side of Christ on a crucifix— and that Christ often spoke to him. According to Giustiniani, Quirini had tried to persuade Meleto that these were diabolical deceptions, but to no avail. Whereupon Quirini, through Fra Zanobi Acciaiuoli, the Pope's librarian, secured a papal injunction against the printing of Meleto's new book, the *Quadrivium*, which he believed to have been diabolically inspired. How the book came to be published despite the papal ban, Giustiniani did not explain, but he urged Orlandini to publish his own book against the "madness" and "detestable dogma" of Meleto, which Orlandini had just sent him.[124]

---

[122] This information is from the exordium to Meleto's *Psalmi XVIII Enucleatio* (fol. iv), addressed to the vicar Antonio Zeno, published together with his *Quadrivium* (see n. 125 below) where he also says he had humbled himself at the feet of Leo X.

[123] On Quirini in Florence, see Joseph Schnitzer, *Peter Delfin General des Camaldulenserordens (1444-1525)* (Munich, 1926), p. 153.

[124] This letter, with the heading "In causu Meleti," is on fols. 199-200 of a MS which was in the possession of the late Father Giuseppe De Luca, the his-

Undaunted by such hostility, Meleto published the *Quadrivium* with an exordium to the Pope.[125] Essentially it was a restatement in Latin of the views he had already expressed in the *Convivio*, with some even more definite predictions. Still holding to his prophecy of Jewish conversion in 1517, he now claimed that the New Age would begin between 1530 and 1540, with the conversion of the Mahometans halfway through that decade, in 1536. The decade of the thirties would see the end of the Fifth State of the Church, and in the beginning of the Sixth State the second trumpet would sound the coming of the Messiah and the universal conversion "in which the whole world will live under a single pastor."

Such a precise and proximate timetable shows a remarkable degree of confidence in his own inspiration. "Who is there who can deny that the work which I published a few days ago (i.e., the *Quadrivium*) is from all powerful God?" For the time being Meleto's assertion went unchallenged, and he seems to have continued to ply his ideas in Florence. It seems the attention of the authorities was taken up with a less respectable prophet than Meleto, whom Parenti called "a man of good morals and educated."[126] The new visionary was a certain Theodore, a monk of Greek extraction and Florentine birth, who appeared in Florence early in 1515 with the usual predictions of *flagello*, war, the ruin of Rome, and the coming of a great renewal which would usher in the New Era.[127] To these he added the special claim that Savonarola had frequently appeared to him and given his approval of Theodore's prophecies, and that he, Theodore, was the Angelic Pastor. Ecclesiastical proceedings were initiated swiftly; there were the usual charges of sexual misconduct and heretical preaching, and Theodore was arrested and interrogated. He confessed, was ordered to make public abjuration, and he did so, on February 11, before a huge crowd in the

---

torian of religion and publisher of Edizioni di Storia e di Letteratura, who kindly let me read it in Rome in 1955.

[125] *Quadrivium temporum prophetarum* (n.p. or d.). The copy I used, BNF Magl. 22 B 6.41, also contains his *Psalmi XVIII Enucleatio* (see above, n. 122).

[126] Parenti, *Storia fiorentina*, ed. Schnitzer, p. 309.

[127] See the letter about Theodore by the Camaldolese General Pietro Delfin, dated March 9, 1515, in Schnitzer, *Delfin*, pp. 364-65; and Parenti, *Storia fiorentina*, ed. Schnitzer, pp. 305-308.

Cathedral. Theodore was sentenced to ten years' confinement in the local monastery of San Miniato. Such was his continuing popularity, however, that a swindler who claimed to be his follower was still able to raise a large sum of money by public subscription on the promise that he would be able to secure Theodore's release. (Perhaps he was helped by the notion, advanced the previous year by the unnamed Carmelite prophet, that the Angelic Pastor would be a humble ex-prisoner.) With the money in his pocket the swindler disappeared. In 1520 Theodore himself escaped to an island in Lake Trasimene, where he continued to preach and call himself the Angelic Pastor.[128]

This dismal episode probably hastened the general campaign against prophecy which now got under way in Florence and Rome. In April the Pope congratulated his cousin, the Cardinal Archbishop of Florence, for his handling of the case of Theodore and in doing so also referred to the earlier prophets Savonarola and Paolo Bernardino "who were condemned by the Apostolic See for the crimes of heresy and schism."[129] The significance of this linking of the cases of Theodore and the earlier prophets is plain: Piagnoni, *Unti*, popular prophets, and learned Scriptural exegetes were all to be tarred with the same brush of heresy and schism. In February the vicar of the Florentine Archdiocese had already issued a prohibition against unlicensed preaching, as well as one against the persistent cultic veneration of Fra Girolamo, but it was impossible to suppress the belief in Savonarola's sanctity, Parenti observed.[130]

Mistakenly or not, the authorities believed that the continuing influence of Savonarola's prophecy was the root cause of the seemingly endless ferment of apocalyptic sects, preachers, and tracts. Within the year the Medici moved to extirpate that poisonous root. During Pope Leo's visit to his native city, between early December 1515 and late February 1516, it was decided to undertake a new investigation of Savonarola's prophetic teaching in a Synod of the

[128] Vasoli, "L'attesa della nuova èra," pp. 425-26.

[129] See the papal brief of April 17, 1515, in which Leo linked Theodore with Savonarola and Pietro Bernardino, in Moreni, *Memorie storiche*.

[130] Parenti, *Storia fiorentina*, ed. Schnitzer, p. 307.

Florentine Province.[131] Apparently the enemies of the Piagnoni believed that a public discussion would prove the falsity of the friar's teaching and that the specter would thus be exorcised once and for all; but they must have been unprepared for the readiness of Piagnoni to come forward in Savonarola's defense. Among those who wrote statements for the Synod were two friars of San Marco, Zaccaria di Lunigiana and Lorenzo Macciagnini,[132] while from Savonarola's native city of Ferrara the priest Francesco Caloro sent his recently published *Defense Against the Adversaries of Fra Giro-lamo Savonarola, Prophet of the Present Calamities and of the Renovation of the Church*.[133]

From Pisa came the treatise of the devoted young Piagnone Luca Bettini, already Prior of Santa Caterina in Pisa at the age of twenty-seven. An assiduous collector and editor of Savonarola's writings,[134] Fra Luca had a close knowledge of the circumstances of his hero's life and death. His *Treatise in Defense of Fra Girolamo Savonarola* went straight to the heart of the issue—Savonarola's prophecy of *renovatio Ecclesiae*. He began by dealing with the argument that it was heresy to teach that the Church would be renewed since this implied (as Giovanni Caroli and so many other antagonists had long since contended) that the present Church, founded by Christ, must be replaced by a new Church; that new doctrines, new prac-tises, new sacraments must replace those instituted by Christ. Fra Luca denied the interpretation and its applicability to Savonarola. True, Fra Girolamo had prophesied that the Church would be

---

[131] A. Giorgetti, "Fra Luca Bettini," pp. 189-90. On Leo's stay in Florence, see Pastor, *History of the Popes*, vol. VII, pp. 130-40.

[132] *Defensio Fratris Zacharie Lunensis qua tuentur Hieronymum Savona-role sociosque ab heresi*, MS BNF Conventi soppressi I. I. 46; *Sermo venera-bilis P. Fr. Laurentii de Macciagninis de Florentia O.P. in defensione R.P. Fr. Hier. Savonarolae ... Instante Concilio sive Synodo Florentino Post falsum Leonis Brevem contra eundem R. Patrem*, MS BRF 2053, fols. 103 verso–106. (Also, a copy of Fra Zacharia's defense, *ibid.*, fols. 50-58.)

[133] Published together with *Prediche devotissime et piene de divini mysterii del Venerando et sacro theologo frate Hieronymo Savonarola da Ferrara* (Fer-rara, 1513).

[134] Ridolfi, *Vita*, vol. II, p. 239, n. 59, where some mistakes in Giorgetti, "Fra Luca Bettini," are corrected.

renewed, but this was no heresy; the Scriptures implied as much, if one knew how to interpret them. Renewal could be understood in two senses, one heretical and one not. The heretical sense, according to which renewal meant a formal change, was not Savonarola's doctrine. His was the orthodox teaching of a reform of discipline and morals. Fra Luca believed that Savonarola could not be accused fairly of schism, since he had never called for the election of a new pope nor separated himself from the Roman obedience. The worst he could be charged with, Bettini maintained, was calling for the assembly of a new Council, but his purpose was to submit to examination the widely believed opinion that Pope Alexander VI was a Marrano. Moreover, Bettini shrewdly let slip that he had heard that Pope Leo himself believed that Alexander was not a Christian. As for Savonarola's alleged confession, it was Bettini's belief that he had contradicted himself under the effects of torture, which had rendered him incapable of knowing what he was saying, and Bettini pointed out that Savonarola had repudiated his own confession before his death.[135]

A weightier and more disinterested statement of the case came from the respected Venetian reformer Gasparo Contarini. His views on Savonarola were solicited for the Synod by Tommaso Giustiniani,[136] who asked him to discuss two issues. The first was a set of questions relating to the excommunication of Savonarola by Pope Alexander VI. The second had to do with the validity of Savonarola's prophecies and teachings about the reform of the Church. On the first issue, Contarini based his reply on the principle that one ought not to obey a law which contradicted charity. This would apply to papal commands as well, he reasoned. Whether Alexander's excommunication of Savonarola fell into this category Giustiniani would not venture to say; but he obviously left the door open to such a possibility, especially since the Pope in question was the

---

[135] *Opusculum in defensionem Fr. Hieronymi Savonarolae Ferrariensis*, MS BRF 2053, fols. 1–21 verso; partly published by Giorgetti, "Fra Luca Bettini," pp. 217-31.

[136] The correct identities of author and addressee have only recently been established, and the full text published, by Felix Gilbert, "Contarini on Savonarola: An Unknown Document of 1516," *Archiv für Reformationsgeschichte*, 59 (1968), 145-50.

notorious Roderigo Borgia. On the issue of Savonarola's prophecy of reform, Contarini took the position that a man of such profound doctrine and such a holy life could not be laughed at, nor could he be easily suspected of fakery or heresy. As for the latter, only God could judge. What man could say that he understood all the senses of Scripture? Contarini himself admitted to believing in the future renovation of the Church, not by prophecy but by both "natural and divine reason." Natural reason told him that human events did not move in an infinite straight line but in an imperfect circle of prosperity and decline. Divine reason told him that at certain times God must regulate His Church, and this all Christians desired most earnestly. Contarini's reasoned and cautious judgment on Savonarola ended by essentially supporting the friar's basic prophetic doctrine—of the coming *renovatio Ecclesiae*. In the face of such an eminent, respected, and, no doubt, embarrassing opinion, Savonarola's enemies found it impossible to proceed with the condemnation they so devoutly wished, and they dropped the case before it reached the Synod.

But the more recent and more radical prophets had no such defenders. Fra Luca Bettini and Fra Zaccaria di Lunigiana explicitly dissociated Savonarola from the alleged sodomite, Bernardino of the *Unti*; Francesco Caloro of Ferrara argued that Savonarola was the only modern prophet; Contarini made the point that the credibility of modern prophets must first be put to the test of the quality of their doctrine and the holiness of their lives. It had been a long time since anyone of stature had raised his voice publicly in support of a latter-day prophet other than Savonarola, as Gianfrancesco Pico had once done for Pietro Bernardino. Who was there who would speak up for the likes of a Theodore, or even a Francesco da Meleto? The strategy of the Medici had been to associate Savonarola with these more recent radical prophets. That strategy had now failed, but at least it had made it difficult for the new prophets to cling to the skirts of Fra Girolamo or to expect help from Savonarola's respectable defenders.[137] When the Florentine Synod met in Janu-

[137] On the other hand, the general condemnation of prophets who fixed a precise time for the coming of tribulations, Antichrist, and Judgment Day in the decree "Supernae majestatis praesidio" of the Fifth Lateran Council

ary of the following year it took no action on the Savonarola case, but it acted quickly to dispose of Francesco da Meleto. His prosecutor in the Synod was an unnamed "venerable old man" who accused Meleto of daring "to overturn the great treasury of the Scriptures and to confuse every meaning of the Catholic interpreters," forming new and unheard of conclusions from the Scriptures on his own authority "despite the fact that he is a layman and almost illiterate (*cum laicus sit et quidem idiota*)."[138] The Synod swiftly condemned Meleto's works to the fire; he was forced to abjure and to write a retraction within two months.[139]

III

ONE MAN in particular had devoted himself to Meleto's destruction: Paolo Orlandini, the Prior of the Camaldolese monastery of Santa Maria degli Angeli in Florence. Very likely this was the "venerable old man" who prosecuted Meleto in the Synod.[140] Orlandini's hostility toward Meleto's doctrines was the climax of a spiritual odyssey which had taken him through many of the way stations of Florentine intellectual and religious life during the previous quarter century, and since this is just the period with which we have been concerned we shall retrace it with him.

After taking his vows in the monastery of Santa Maria degli Angeli on February 10, 1488, Orlandini did not retire into monastic

---

(December 19, 1516) could have been interpreted to include certain Savonarolan prophecies as well. For the text of the decree, see Giovanni Domenico Mansi, *Sacrorum conciliorum . . . collectio*, 53 vols. (Venice-Paris, 1739-1927), vol. XXXII, cols. 944-47. Text and trans. of pertinent passages in H. J. Schroeder, *Disciplinary Decrees of the General Councils* (St. Louis, 1937), pp. 505-506, 645-46.

[138] Mansi, *Sacrorum conciliorum*, vol. XXXV, cols. 269-70.

[139] *Ibid.*, cols. 273-74.

[140] Orlandini composed the treatise against Meleto which Giustiniani acknowledged in his letter of the previous year (see above, n. 124 and below, n. 164). The similarities of the argument with that of the *venerabilis senex* in the Synod suggests that this was Orlandini, who died in 1519. The identification has already been suggested by Giorgetti and by Vasoli, neither of whom, however, deals with Orlandini's treatise. Biographical details on Orlandini are to be found in G. B. Mittarelli and A. Costadoni, *Annales Camaldulenses*, 9 vols. (Venice, 1755-73), vols. VII, VIII passim, and Ziegelbauer, *Centifolium Camaldulense*, pp. 50-52.

seclusion but took an active part in the intellectual life of the Laurentian circle.[141] He was endowed with a humanistic education and had studied philosophy with Marsilio Ficino, whom he called his "father and master" in everything that he knew,[142] while Lorenzo de' Medici seems to have given him help to pursue his studies.[143]

Santa Maria degli Angeli had once been an important intellectual center in Florence. From it, earlier in the fifteenth century, Ambrogio Traversari had launched the great enterprise of employing humanist methods in the study of patristics and theology; but by Orlandini's time the Convent was distinguished neither for Christian piety nor for Christian scholarship. Not only had it shared in the general decline of the Camaldolese Order, but it had encountered special problems of its own. In 1486 Lorenzo de' Medici had imposed as abbot his personal favorite, the Cistercian Guido da Settimo, who then won Lorenzo over to his plan to transfer the house to his own Cistercian Order. This was strenuously opposed by the General of Camaldoli, the Venetian Pietro Delfin, a veteran of many struggles against lay interference. Consequently, when Orlandini took his vows in 1488 the Convent of Santa Maria degli Angeli was already embroiled in a contest which could hardly have been conducive to the peace of the cloister. Where Orlandini stood in this struggle we do not know; but he must have felt caught between gratitude to his patron Lorenzo de' Medici and loyalty to his own Order.

One of the side effects of the revolution of 1494 was the removal of Medici pressure on the monastery and the consequent end to the threat of a Cistercian take-over. Another effect was the quickening of the monks' impulse toward reform. The reform model, how-

---

[141] On Orlandini and Ficino, see Paul O. Kristeller, ed., *Supplementum Ficinianum*, 2 vols. (Florence, 1937), vol. II, pp. 267-68. Other notices are in Eugenio Garin, *La cultura filosofica del Rinascimento italiano* (Florence, 1954), pp. 213-23.

[142] In Orlandini's poem, "Circa le anime separate da' corpi" (July 15, 1500), quoted in Kristeller, *Supplementum Ficinianum*, vol. II, p. 268. See also Orlandini's account of his discussion with Ficino in the cloister of Santa Maria degli Angeli "where he was accustomed to return often to take part in our discussions," in his *Eptathicum seu opus theologicum et morale*, MS BNF II. I. 158, fol. 228 recto.

[143] *Ibid.*, fol. 297 recto.

ever, was no longer the cloistered life of Camaldoli but the more militant piety of Dominican San Marco. Orlandini himself was eager to emulate the Preaching Brothers, but he was quickly squelched by General Delfin, who was unfriendly toward Savonarola and considered Orlandini's new interests out of keeping with the mission of their Order.[144] Obliged to restrict his reforming zeal to his own cloister, Orlandini's response was "to pour his learning and his wisdom into books."[145] Part of his energies he devoted to his first love, ancient philosophy; part, to the study of Sacred Scripture, no doubt under the influence of the same evangelical impulse that was moving Pico, Benivieni, and other Laurentians. One fruit of these labors was a treatise on reconciling apparently inconsistent Biblical passages, a treatise which grew out of a discussion that took place in the Convent on July 12, 1496.[146] During that discussion one of his brother monks reproved Orlandini for his preference for profane letters, especially philosophy, over sacred ones, and Orlandini resolved to write the treatise which we now have.[147] During the same discussion Orlandini was asked to give his opinion of Savonarola, and he apparently did—but the folio page on which he recorded his views has since been cut out of the manuscript![148]

Despite the reproach and the missing page it seems a safe conjecture that Orlandini was a Savonarolan partisan by that time. At any rate, two years after the friar's downfall he paid homage to him in a poem as "Perfect Doctor, O Ferrarese and grand Savonarola, Wise and prudent although by us reviled."[149] He would, he continued,

---

[144] For Savonarola's involvement in the controversies of the Vallombrosan order in Florence, see Bernardo Serra, *Vita di Biagio Milanese*, MS BNF Magl. XXXVII, 325, fols. 178 verso ff. This work was referred to me by Professor E. H. Gombrich, who indicated his intention of publishing it. There is a seventeenth-century copy in BNF II. II. 434. Some excerpts and a discussion of these materials have now been published by Romeo De Maio, *Savonarola e la curia romana* (Rome, 1969).

[145] Mittarelli, *Annales Camaldulenses*, vol. VIII, p. 12.

[146] *Concordatio seu compositio quaedam super quibusdam scripturae sacrae locis, qui prima frontae videntur oppositi. Facta est autem a Paulo Camaldulensi monacho per modum dyalogi Bartolomei* (at the end: September 8, 1496), MS BNF Magl. XL 45. This codex, unknown to Orlandini's bibliographers, was identified for me as an Orlandini work by Professor Paul O. Kristeller. The note on the discussion of July 12 occurs on fol. 29.

[147] *Ibid.*, fol. 2.   [148] *Ibid.*, fols. 28 verso–29.

[149] Others whom he honored in these lines were: Ficino, Giovanni Pico, his

have liked to ask Savonarola "about those things that everyone disputes so uncertainly here on earth; whether you told the truth about
our war and peace when you were prophesying here below in the
world."[150] Another poem, which he called "Somnium de novo
saeculo," bears witness to Orlandini's Piagnonism, although unfortunately, all we have of it is a fragment.[151] In it Orlandini tells of
being visited by his former prior, Bernardino Gadolo, just as he was
rising to say matins. Bernardino led him into the garden of the
Monastery to show him "where this holy house finds itself, and the
city too," and there Orlandini saw:

> . . . a satyr jump up
> and run, so that it stirred up a wind.
> And I saw a dragon fight with a lion.
> There also were the wolf and the panther,
> and other beasts I could describe.
> I stood there at the entrance amazed,
> Proserpina holding up the torch,[152]
> with my Prior who had brought me there,
> And I said: O reverend and learned Father,
> What means this Battle in the Garden
> which is more fitting for a wilderness than here?
> This appears to me as a tiny corral,
> full of wild and cruel beasts.
> A place for bears, not citizens.[153]

---

late, beloved Prior Bernardino Gadolo (d. 1491), and the theologian Oliviero
Arduini. Garin, *La cultura filosofica*, pp. 221-22. For Bernardino Gadolo's
praise of Savonarola, see *Camaldoli*, VI (1952), pp. 64-71. For Arduini's
admiration and later rejection of Savonarola, see Ridolfi, *Life*, pp. 163, 235.
In one of the MSS of Orlandini's poem the passage introducing Savonarola was
later blotted out. MS BNF Conventi soppressi D. 5. 827, fol. 322 verso.

[150] This passage is in MS BNF Conventi soppressi G. 4. 826, fol. 83 recto.

[151] "Incipit somnium de novo saeculo: in quo ostenditur quid sentiendum
[pro(?) frate Hyeronimo Savonarola], simul et de eventu doctrinae ipsius."
MS BNF Conventi soppressi D. 5. 827, fol. 345 verso. The words in (my)
brackets have been heavily lined out.

[152] Proserpina, or Persephone, in her representation as Queen of the Under-
world, held a torch or a pomegranate, symbolizing death and rebirth. *The
New Century Classical Handbook*, ed. Catherine B. Avery (New York, 1962),
p. 853.

[153] Quoted in Garin, *La cultura filosofica*, p. 224.

The poem breaks off here, before we can know what explanation of this struggle Father Bernardino gave to Orlandini, but the symbolism is plain enough: the wolf of avarice, the dragon of the Apocalypse struggling with the Florentine lion, Proserpina's motif of death and rebirth, all strike a familiar note. So does the title, which is reminiscent of, and probably directly borrowed from Giovanni Nesi's *Oraculum de novo saeculo*. (Nesi had sent Orlandini an explanation of the Pythagorean symbolism which he was later to use in his *Oraculum*.)[154]

Nor was Orlandini limiting himself to poetic visions of renewal, for in spite of Delfin's objections he had been preaching. On November 29, 1499, General Delfin ordered him to desist from criticizing the Pope, charging that Orlandini's sermons in the monastery of Sant'Ambrogio had "scandalized certain respected men." Delfin compared him to "another" who had engaged in open obloquy of the Pope and warned Orlandini that he would no longer tolerate such goings on.[155] A hint that Orlandini's Piagnonism persisted for some years, however, can be seen in another poem written in the early 1500's in which he described a trip to Rome, where he felt as though he were "with Daniel among the lions, with Joseph in [Pharaoh's prison], with Jeremiah among the false Pharisees, with Tobias afflicted . . . in the cave of the fierce robbers."[156]

Eventually, however, Orlandini's Piagnonism cooled, and his admiration for Savonarola turned into hostility against all preachers of the coming millennium. A number of issues were involved in this change of heart. There was, first of all, the steady pressure from Delfin, Orlandini's superior. Camaldoli, the site of the original

---

[154] "De symbolo Nesiano," with a dedicatory letter to Orlandini dated January 10, 1489 (1490 n.s.) in Orlandini's *Eptathicum*, fols. 270 verso–280 recto.

[155] Letter in Schnitzer, *Delfin*, p. 364.

[156] Quoted by Garin, *La cultura filosofica*, p. 222. Professor Garin does not suggest a date, but since Orlandini says his trip to Rome had to do with the struggle of his monastery to retain the adherence of the house of San Giovanni di Sasso in Arezzo, a case which was finally settled in favor of the former in 1508 (Mittarelli, *Annales Camaldulenses*, vol. VII, pp. 377, 397), the poem was undoubtedly written about that time. Another indication of pro-Savonarolan sentiment among certain Camaldolensans in Florence, perhaps including Orlandini, is contained in Ugolino Verino's letter to Fra Bartolomeo da Faenza, July 19, 1507. *Ibid.*, pp. 393-95.

hermitage of the Order, was in Florentine territory, and in the city there were several Camaldolese houses. Since his election to the Generalship in 1480, Delfin had spent much time in Florence attending to the delicate task of protecting the interests of the Order, first against Medici interference, then against what he believed to be the designs of Fra Girolamo.[157] In March, 1498 he undertook a formal attack upon Savonarola in the form of a dialogue in three books.[158] Lacking the passionate involvement of a Florentine, Delfin, while uncompromising in his hostility, was willing to give Savonarola his due as a man of pure life and spiritual teaching. His main objections were to the friar's involvement in politics, which he considered unbefitting a religious,[159] his disobedience to ecclesiastical authority, and his defiance of the papal ban.

Orlandini apparently yielded to Delfin's pressure. At some point, just when is unclear, he expressed the wish to retire to the hermitage of Camaldoli, but Delfin saw to it that he remained in the monastery.[160] In 1503 Orlandini was elected to the Priorate of Santa Maria degli Angeli, and he was elected again in 1513. Twice he served as Vice-General of the Order.[161] From these positions of strength, and making common cause with the Venetians Quirini and Giustiniani, who were bringing a new breath of reform into Camaldoli, Orlandini was at last able to help clip the wings of his old antagonist Delfin. On July 4, 1513, Orlandini and his friends secured a Bull of reform from Leo X in which, among other things, the General's power to interfere in the affairs of individual monasteries of the Camaldolese Order was strictly limited.[162]

---

[157] See his letters to Savonarola, December 30, 1494, January 1, 1495, and May 24, 1496, in Schnitzer, *Delfin*, pp. 334-35, 346-47.

[158] *Petri Delphini, nobilis Veneti, Generalis Camaldulensis Dialogus in Hieronymum Ferrariensem*, in *ibid.*, pp. 366-99.

[159] This is ironic, as Schnitzer points out, since Delfin had been spying for Venice in Florence since 1495. *Ibid.*, pp. 274-75.

[160] Mittarelli, *Annales Camaldulenses*, vol. VIII, p. 13.

[161] *Ibid.*, pp. 381, 416.

[162] The Bull is described by Schnitzer, *Delfin*, p. 166; and the Privilege granted by the Pope for the reorganization of the Order, in Mittarelli, *Annales Camaldulenses*, vol. VII, pp. 436-38. Delfin complained bitterly against his three antagonists, Quirini, Giustiniani, and Orlandini, while Orlandini assured Delfin that he had no wish to contend with him. *Ibid.*, pp. 426-30. For Orlan-

In the meantime, perhaps as he became further identified with more conventional reform procedures, perhaps also because he was scandalized by the radical excesses of the popular prophets, Orlandini was rethinking his old enthusiasm for prophecy. Starting in the early years of the sixteenth century he devoted a good deal of his writing to a consideration of the various forms of prognostication, not only prophecy based upon Scripture, but also astrology and the divinatory arts in general.[163] Prophecy itself he continued to regard as divine revelations in Scripture, and the prophet as one who understood what these revelations meant. But he was now much more critical of individuals who claimed to have the gift of that understanding. Even in Scripture, he wrote, God revealed Himself only in part. No one must pretend to know more than the plain words revealed. Above all it was false to pretend to be able to give specific terms and dates to prophetic passages which did not contain them.[164]

But it was the affair of Francesco da Meleto which showed how far Orlandini had reversed himself from the Piagnone enthusiasm of his early days. Orlandini later recalled how, when he had read Meleto's *Convivio* and *Quadrivium*, he had summoned Meleto for a friendly private talk. Meleto came to Orlandini's cell where the monk tried to persuade him "to come to his senses" and adopt a saner interpretation of Holy Scripture. This Meleto refused to do, maintaining that many "respectable men" in the city read his writings with enthusiasm. Whereupon Orlandini warned him that he would attack Meleto in his own writings and would try to free his mind as well as the minds of those whom he had seduced. The

dini's letter of February 6, 1515, to Quirini in Rome, asking for further protection for Santa Maria degli Angeli against Delfin, see ms BLF Conventi soppressi 525, fols. 38-39.

[163] His treatise *Liber satyricus de noticia futurorum contra astrologos*, Book VI of his *Eptathicum*, fols. 201-36, includes sections against the various forms of predictions—dreams, portents, etc. It was written while he was Vicar General of San Michele di Murano in Venice. On it, see Garin, *La cultura filosofica*, pp. 215-17.

[164] *Contro quelli che pongo[n] termini certi alle prophetie* and *Contro eos qui se putant plene nosse prophetarum mentem* in ms BNF Conventi soppressi G. 4. 826, fols. 89 verso-90; also ms BNF Conventi soppressi D. 5. 827, fol. 337 recto–verso.

result was Orlandini's treatise of January 3, 1516, *Against False Prophets*.[165] In the introduction he stated that he had battled the astrologers in Venice and in Florence, the false prophets who usurped the Holy Scriptures by distorting them according to their own arbitary wills. Meleto's false prophesying, he contended, began with that of Girolamo Savonarola who had written and preached many false and inane things about the future. He was burned long ago, but his spirit persisted in Meleto. Orlandini declared equal hostility toward astrologers and prophets because both predicted that the Antichrist would come in the year 1530 and that the Church would be renovated with the extinction of all other religions. Many in Florence claimed that Meleto's doctrine was sound, and they filled the ears of gullible people. For this reason Orlandini now undertook to correct these views by disputing them from a sound interpretation of the Scriptures.

Orlandini's method was to establish the principle that, while according to Saint Thomas there were four senses of Scripture, a sound exegesis must be based on reading the holy books in the same spirit in which they were written, and this made the literal sense basic to the others. All the great theologians affirm that nothing can be proven from the figures, portents, and parables which Meleto used as the basis of his predictions, he claimed. Orlandini then proceeded to show in detail that Meleto's predictions did not pass any of the tests, which included conformity to the "reason and limits of Scripture, conformity to the teachings of the saints, approval by the infallible Church," and so on. Moreover, they had already proven themselves false because none of them had been fulfilled. (But Orlandini was not denying the legitimacy of portents. Marsilio Ficino himself, he said, had explained portents to him, showing him how God uses natural events as signs to warn men of calamities that He has in store for them; but only certain men, well-disposed and moderate, receive such revelations.)[166] In addition to these fail-

---

[165] Opus III of his *Eptathicum*, fols. 122 verso–147 verso. That he had completed it, or an earlier version of it, in the preceding year is indicated by Giustiniani's acknowledgment of its receipt. See above, n. 124.

[166] Elsewhere, however, Orlandini listed portents among the superstitions: "Negligenda esse scilicet a Christicolis, pro rerum futurarum cognitione." *Eptathicum*, Book VI, fol. 214 recto. In his treatise *Contra astrologos*, he said

ures to meet the criteria of correct Biblical interpretation, Meleto's doctrine was, he continued, patently heretical. Meleto's prediction of a new "speculator" who would reveal the mysteries of Scripture, opening up the Book of the Apocalypse so that the truths of the Faith would be revealed "in the blink of an eyelash" and bringing about the conversion of all peoples to Christianity, and his prophecy of the coming of a *puer parvulus* fell into the category of heresy. Orlandini contended that the Church could not be reformed according to Meleto's definition, since it was not deformed. God is in the Church and it cannot grow old. The idea of an Angelic Pope is also heretical, since the Pope is human and therefore cannot be Angelic.

In a series of sweeping propositions Orlandini, the one-time critic of the Papacy and enthusiast of Savonarola's vision of reform, now reaffirmed the unity and supremacy of papal leadership: the Church is one, catholic, with a single head. The Church will abide and only in the Church is there salvation. The Church does not and cannot err in its sanctions; the Pope represents the Church as founded by Christ through Peter. The Roman Church is the fountain and head of all the others. It judges and is not judged. The Pope is the head of the Church; all are subject to his power and he to no one. Finally, the Pope is superior to Councils. Meleto's doctrine was not only heretical but, wrote Orlandini, in his impugning of papal power Meleto was also guilty of *lèse-majesté*, the most serious of crimes.[167] This was not all; Meleto was also guilty of false teachings and presumption. He, a *vir laicus*, usurped the offices of priest and doctor of the Church. No one ought to teach about ecclesiastical matters who was not a cleric. Meleto's assertions of humility were not to be attributed to probity but to ignorance. Moreover, Orlandini charged, he submitted to the authority of the Church by the subterfuge of

---

that when he once asked Ficino about his alleged belief in the influence of the stars upon human life, Ficino had told him to look at what he had written on the matter to Poliziano, and there, in the ninth book of Ficino's letters, he found that Ficino derided the astrologers and that he agreed with Pico's attack upon them. *Ibid.*, fol. 221. The letter Orlandini referred to is probably in Book XII of Marsilio Ficino's *Epistolarum, Opera omnia*, 2 vols. (Basel, 1561), vol. II, p. 958 (August 20, 1494). See also Poliziano's letter to Ficino, *Supplementum Ficinianum*, vol. II, pp. 278-79 (no date).

[167] This statement precedes the foregoing in the text, *Eptathicum, Against False Prophets*, fol. 129 recto.

claiming to have a dull, weak mind and an impediment of speech, but the real test would be whether he submitted to correction.

And so, Orlandini concluded, he had fought his duel against the prophet Meleto with the aid of the scholastic interpretation of Holy Scripture. Still, if called upon he was ready to fight on, because this plague had infected many men in their city from the days of Fra Girolamo down to their own time. Wherefore he had fought repeatedly against the sectarians, showing up their vanities and their lies. It was embarrassing that their city, the city of the present Pope, lord of the world, was addicted to such nonsense as the belief in the false doctrines of the renovation (*renovatio*) and reformation (*reformatio*) of the Church, the Angelic Pastor, and other "funeral songs" of this kind. But this, he declared, was not characteristic of Tuscans, contrary to what some said. Tuscany with its airy rather than heavy climate and its limpid sky had always been a region of illustrious and scholarly men. Nevertheless nightmares and delusions had obsessed this city for as long as she had been ruled by the mob without a proper leader, especially since the time, some years earlier, when Charles, King of the Gauls, had come and everything had been in tumult, almost moribund. In such a state of affairs the people were receptive [to prophecies], for a people always fears most what it does not understand and is always ready to let itself be led into something new. Besides, the mob was uncertain and divided, so that that man [Savonarola] was able to blame everything upon their leaders. However, all who hated revolution rejected such foolishness. On this double note of apology for his native city and less than subtle adulation of her Medici rulers, Orlandini brought his attack on Meleto to a close. A year later he presented similar arguments to the Provincial Synod and achieved Meleto's conviction.

INSOFAR AS THE AIM of the Medici and their supporters was to suppress new prophets like Meleto they were at last successful. After the decrees of the Fifth Lateran Council and the Florentine Synod no new Meletos or Bernardinos came forward to predict that Florence was to be the center of the New Era. But the vision was not dead and Piagnonism did not disappear. In San Marco and wherever the memory of Savonarola was alive, in his books and in the words of his followers, his prophecies continued to inspire men to believe in the coming of the *renovatio Ecclesiae* and the apotheosis of Florence. Exactly a decade after the Synod, Piagnonism burst into the open once more. The terrible events of 1527 seemed to confirm the prophecies all too wonderfully. The barbarians were in the garden of Italy; the streets of Rome were drenched in blood; the tribulations had come in the time of a pope named Clement, just as Savonarola was alleged to have predicted.[168] Once more the Florentines rose against their Medici rulers; once more they looked to San Marco for inspiration and leadership; once more they elected Christ their King.[169]

But not even such a King could save the Republic, however heroically He inspired His subjects to resist.[170] Besieged by a combined force of papal and imperial troops for ten long months, the Florentines finally surrendered on August 12, 1530. San Marco friars again shared the sentences of exile and imprisonment meted out to the defenders of the Republic. Alone the old Piagnone Girolamo Benivieni, in his eighties and no longer timid, spoke out to the Pope, his former patron.[171] In a long letter to Clement VII, Benivieni made

[168] Ridolfi, *Life*, p. 300.

[169] The revival of Piagnonism in the republic of 1527-30 has been dealt with by Roth, *Last Florentine Republic*. See also, Luigi di Piero Guicciardini, *Del Savonarola ovvero dialogo tra Francesco Zati e Pieradovardo Giachinotti il giorno dopo la battaglia di Gavinana*, ed. Bono Simonetta (Florence, 1959); and Edward Lowinsky, "A Newly Discovered Sixteenth Century Motet Manuscript at the Biblioteca Vallicelliana in Rome," *Journal of the American Musicological Society*, II (1950), pp. 184-87.

[170] ". . . there were also those who were of such great ingenuousness or stupidity that, because of the words of the sermons of Fra Girolamo, which they called prophecies, the more their enemies pressed Florence, the more greatly they rejoiced, holding firmly to the belief that when the city had been reduced to such a point that she had no remedy left and could not be defended by any human power in any way, then, at last, and not before then, angels would be sent from heaven to the walls of the city to liberate her with their swords. Not only common and uneducated men believed this, but also noble ones, like Giuliano Capponi, and cultured ones, like Girolamo Benivieni." Benedetto Varchi, *Storia Fiorentina*, 2 vols. (Florence, 1838-41), Book XI, chap. CV.

[171] *Ibid.*, Book XII, chap. XXVII.

two requests: the Pope should grant Florence the kind of worthy government they had talked about together in Florence, and he should consider the strong evidence for the validity of Savonarola's prophecies, for they were coming true in those very days. Already two of the three tribulations the friar had predicted had come about: the French invasion and the recent devastation of Charles V's Spaniards and Lanzknechten. Whether the third tribulation would prove to be the Turks or the Lutherans it was too early to tell; but Rome would yet suffer a more complete destruction than the Sack of 1527. Savonarola's three major prophecies were still to be fulfilled, Benivieni admitted, but two of them—the coming renovation of the Church and the conversion of the Infidel—were believed by all Christians. Time, and the proper state of repentance, would tell whether Savonarola's third prediction was true, and this was the prophecy of the coming felicity of Florence.[172]

Benivieni's effort was in vain. After a generation of bitter experience the Medici knew how deeply Florentine visions of religious renewal were linked to dreams of civic liberty and were not likely to respond. What we have called the myth of Florence was the personification of the free republic, the creature through whom the Florentines would be liberated, rendered justice, granted riches and power—even redeemed. With her death, which came at the hands of these same Medici during the succeeding decades of the sixteenth century, the myth died too, for without republican hopes to nourish it, it lost its vital reason to exist.[173]

---

[172] Girolamo Benivieni, *Lettera mandata à Clemento VII* (1530), MS BRF 2022, fols. 5-9, 12-20. Another old San Marco Piagnone, Fra Santi Pagnini, wrote from Lucca to King Henry VIII for help for Florence (on April 21, 1530), and did not hesitate to deplore the Pope's action: "Quis non defleat illius pulcherrime urbis calamitates. . . . Quis non deploret Pastoris Clementis inclementiam, qui suas oves ita mactat et perdit?" Edited by Cecil Roth in *Rivista storica degli archivi toscani*, I (1929), 38-39.

[173] Piagnonism as the religious cult of Savonarola did not die out, nor did the discussion of the validity of his teaching completely subside. On this see Schnitzer, *Savonarola*, chaps. XXXVII-XL. Moreover, as I indicated in my Introduction, political Piagnonism revived in the nineteenth century in somewhat altered form, as an expression of an Italian nationalism which, somewhat along the lines of the old myth of Florence, saw its task as moral and religious as well as political.

Conclusion

IN studying the relations between Savonarola and Florence I have
followed the stages by which the preacher of repentance and divine
wrath became the prophet of Florentine millennial glory and republican liberty. This was a process of his appropriating the apocalyptic, imperial, and republican themes already present in Florentine
ideology, giving them the stamp of his own powerful, prophetic
personality, and handing them on to future generations. In creating
his vision Savonarola tapped deep resources of the Florentine consciousness, combining all the persistent themes of civic patriotism—
leadership for liberty, power as the center of Italy and as the daughter of Rome, primacy as the most spirited, prudent, and wisest people of Italy, and God's choice as the New Jerusalem. In appropriating these themes Savonarola himself became absorbed into the civic
tradition of prophecy as a martyr whose blood proved the truth of
Florence's historic mission to future prophets. The real drama of the
Prophet and the City is, therefore, not the story of Savonarola's brief
"conversion" of the Florentines, or even of his ascendancy over the
city, but the story of Florence's decisive conquest of Savonarola. In
the milieu of Florentine culture and politics Savonarola became the
spokesman of the Florentine civic myth; his prophecies mirrored
Florentine yearnings for security, riches, and power; his political
program exalted the old Florentine ideals of republic, liberty, and
vita civile.

I have noted that certain themes of Florentine patriotic mythology
as well as some features of Piagnonism were not unique to Florence
or to Savonarola. The idea of Florence as the daughter of Rome
seems to have been related to the traditional medieval theme of the
Second or New Rome, particularly to the use of this theme by the

Italian communes in the later Middle Ages as they sought to provide themselves with an inspiring and authoritative legitimacy. Similarly, the exaltation of the city as the New Jerusalem was based upon an impulse as old as Christianity itself, although more specifically, the political career of the New Jerusalem theme seems to have begun with Charlemagne.[1] The idea of taking Christ as King belonged to an old Italian communal practice of regarding a civic patron saint as leader of the commune.[2] Even Savonarola's initial intervention in Florentine politics as the promoter of *la pace universale* and the related constitutional reform had been anticipated by other peacemaking friars in other Italian cities of the fifteenth century.[3] Finally, the vision of Florence in her glory as the center of the New Era was anticipated, indeed, it partly derived from, the Joachite-inspired Second Charlemagne prophecy, and was thus another example of fourteenth- and fifteenth-century political messianism.

One way to sum this up is to say that, far from being an anachronistic episode or momentary aberration in the life of the first city of the Renaissance, the Savonarola movement reflected some of that city's most important concerns and was symptomatic of certain significant trends which were not limited to Florence or to Italy alone. Savonarola adopted his universalist Christian vision to the aims of a society in which patriotism was being raised to the level of a virtue,[4] and in which civic republicanism had emerged, in ideology as well as fact, as an alternative to the medieval *respublica christiana*.[5] More-

[1] Robert Konrad, "Das himmlische und das irdische Jerusalem im mittelalterlichen Denken. Mystische Vorstellung und geschichtliche Werkung," *Speculum Historiale*, ed. C. Bauer, L. Boehm, M. Muller (Munich, 1965), pp. 528-29.

[2] Hans Conrad Peyer, *Stadt und Stadtpatron im mittelalterlichen Italien* (Zurich, 1955).

[3] Alberto Ghinato, "Apostolato religioso e sociale di S. Giacomo della Marca in Terni," *Archivum Franciscanum Historicum*, 49 (1956), 106-42, 352-90; Angelo Sacchetti Sassetti, "Giacomo della Marca paciere a Rieti," *ibid.*, 50 (1957), 75-82.

[4] E. Delaruelle, "La spiritualité aux XIVe et XVe siècles," *Cahiers d'Histoire Mondiale*, V (1959), 68.

[5] William Bouwsma, *Venice and the Defence of Republican Liberty* (Berkeley, 1968), especially pp. 8-13, but the whole of this important book is relevant

over, in tempering his otherworldly, ascetic spirituality by embracing Florentine aspirations toward riches and power, Savonarola was serving the spiritual needs of a people who longed to be told that worldly wealth and power were not in themselves immoral or unchristian, and that pursuit of such secular goals might even be reconciled with the striving for renewal and redemption. In exchanging his threat that Florence would be a den of robbers for his vision of the Florentines building the New Jerusalem, Savonarola was throwing in his lot with fifteenth-century laymen in search of a more positive religious role within the framework of those social structures which they found important and meaningful.

Nevertheless, for all its connections with the culture and society of late medieval Europe and Renaissance Italy, the Savonarolan episode was no everyday occurrence but a highly original, intense movement, influential to a degree rarely seen before the Reformation, and we must confront the fact that it occurred in Italy rather than in the more traditional north, and in Florence rather than in some more conservative city. Only to a point can the site be explained by adducing the anti-Medicean revolution of 1494, the crisis of the French invasion, or even the presence of such a compelling figure as Savonarola. To imagine the same response in any other city of Italy—in Genoa, Milan, Naples, especially in Venice—is difficult. What was lacking in the others was just that combination of militant, self-conscious republicanism and piety that Savonarola shrewdly perceived as the special genius of the Florentine people. In this connection it is intriguing to notice that while Florence responded to her crisis in the way we have seen, just fifty miles away Pisa was also fighting for her liberty, against Florence herself, apparently without producing any sort of rival religious-political ideology to sustain her in the struggle. Had there been in Pisa the conditions to stimulate and support such an ideology, a prophet might well have come forward, as prophets continued to come forward in

---

to the problems touched upon here. See also the suggestive remark of Delaruelle, "La Spiritualité," p. 66: "Un esprit commun naît de cet accord profond sur l'essence même de la vie religieuse; la religion universelle et liturgique du Moyen-âge se fait ici religion de petit chapelle; la chrétienté éclate en petits groupes."

Florence.[6] My own conclusion is that the Savonarola movement could take place in Florence precisely because of those forces owing to which she has usually been described as the first city of the Renaissance. The extensive development of a bourgeois, mercantile society, a lay culture, and an ardent republicanism stimulated the Florentines to reflect on the meaning of their city's history and destiny, and provided the materials and motives for articulating their civic ideals and myths by humanists, artists, and prophets to a degree and in an intensity that appear to have been unique up to that time.

Finally, this suggests that, while building upon spiritual and ideological currents which were widely deployed in the fourteenth and fifteenth centuries, the embodiment of the Florentine civic myth in the Savonarola movement had as many portents for the future as it had links with the past. This becomes apparent if we avoid the old controversies about Savonarola's doctrinal orthodoxy and his loyalty to the Papacy, and look instead at the whole movement in terms of the sociology of religion. We can then identify in Florence certain tendencies toward sectarianism, lay piety, and political messianism which, after uncertain and dangerous careers in the Catholic Middle Ages, received new impetus from the changing social and spiritual climate of the fourteenth and fifteenth centuries, but really came into their own in the Reformation. In this sense, Savonarolan Florence was, to borrow a concept from Burckhardt, a firstborn, a harbinger of things to come.

[6] The themes of the Pisans as a holy people and of Pisa as successor of Rome appear in the earliest historical works of the city, in the early twelfth century. But these themes do not seem to have been sustained. On early Pisan self-glorification, see Craig B. Fischer, "The Pisan Clergy and an Awakening of Historical Interest in a Medieval Commune," *Studies in Medieval and Renaissance History*, III (1966), 143-219.

Index

THE first reference to modern authors and the titles of their works have been indexed, often in short title form. Short titles have been used in some cases for primary sources as well, although, of course, the complete titles are to be found in footnotes to the text. The name Savonarola has been abbreviated as S, except where it occurs as main entry and in titles of books and articles.